D1717171

CASS GILBERT, LIFE AND WORK

ARCHITECT OF THE PUBLIC DOMAIN

CASS GILBERT, LIFE AND WORK
ARCHITECT OF THE PUBLIC DOMAIN

Edited by Barbara S. Christen and Steven Flanders

Introduction by Robert A. M. Stern

W. W. Norton & Company
New York • London

Copyright © 2001 by Barbara S. Christen and Steven Flanders

All rights reserved
Printed in the United States of America

First Edition

For information about permission to reproduce selections from this book,
write to Permissions, W. W. Norton & Company, Inc., 500 Fifth Avenue, New York, NY 10110

The text of this book is composed in Adobe Garamond
with the display set in Univers
Manufacturing by Edwards Brothers
Book design by Lauren Graessle

Library of Congress Cataloging-in-Publication Data
Cass Gilbert, life and work : architect of the public domain / edited by Barbara S. Christen
and Steven Flanders ; introduction by Robert A. M. Stern
      p.   cm.
  Includes bibliographical references and index.
  ISBN 0-393-73065-4
  1. Gilbert, Cass, 1859–1934—Criticism and interpretation. 2. Public architecture—United States.
I. Christen, Barbara S. II. Flanders, Steven.

NA737.G5 C37   2001
720'.92—dc21
[B]   00-069946

W. W. Norton & Company, Inc., 500 Fifth Avenue, New York, NY 10110
www.wwnorton.com

W. W. Norton & Company Ltd., Castle House, 75/76 Wells St., London W1T 3QT

0 9 8 7 6 5 4 3 2 1

TO OUR FAMILIES

CONTENTS

PREFACE

STEVEN FLANDERS

The architect Cass Gilbert (1859–1934) lived in several worlds, transforming them as they transformed him and themselves. Born in Zanesville, Ohio, just before the Civil War to a military surveyor and his wife, he grew up in St. Paul, Minnesota, as it matured from a staging area for settlement of the northern plains into a confident outpost of the Gilded Age. But even as he produced the Minnesota State Capitol, possibly his masterpiece, as the culmination of his career there, he found himself to be too large a figure to be confined even by the vast expanse of the "Northwest." The New York practice that he gradually established beginning with the Broadway Chambers Building (1899, see Figures P-1 and C-5) at the turn of a confident new century provided the stage for the national scope he sought.

As Robert A. M. Stern suggests in his introduction, the contributions in this volume address as many dimensions of Gilbert's work and influence as has seemed possible. Drawing upon a November 1998 symposium that was the culmination of a year's worth of celebrations of Gilbert in New York, this book presents perspectives illuminating his life and work by practicing architects, historians, art and architectural historians, and judges and others outside the profession. It offers views of the worlds Gilbert lived in, explored, and transformed through his art and through his highly practical determination that every building must serve not only his clients but also its users.

The users were the starting point for the Cass Gilbert programs that energize this volume. The United States courts for the second circuit, through their Committee on History and Commemorative Events, initiated projects in 1997 through 1999 to draw renewed attention to the architect whose buildings have housed them so well: the United States Courthouse at Foley Square and the United States Custom House at Bowling Green, both in New York. Gilbert took a special interest in courts and courthouses; the United States Supreme Court building in Washington is the best-known example. Gilbert's influence has extended across the decades and into the new millennium through the Foley Square courthouse; the new federal courthouse by Kohn Pedersen Fox, completed at Foley Square in 1994, was the product of a design competition for which Gilbert's building was an explicit and necessary frame of reference. Gilbert's architecture became central to a process by which late-twentieth-century architects relearned how to design courthouses that are both appropriate to their functions and settings and pleasing and useful to their multiple publics.

The federal courts developed programs to celebrate Gilbert because his buildings function preeminently well among the vast variety of designs and settings that house the work of the courts. Moreover, Gilbert buildings enlarge the lives of those they touch, a discovery that resulted in the rapid and spontaneous spread of Gilbert programs beyond the courts, throughout New York and on to many other places. Everyone who enters a Gilbert building designed for public use realizes that they have arrived at a significant place. The school groups that visit the Minnesota capitol or Foley Square need no coaching as to the sort of place where they find themselves—large, enlarging, yet not forbidding. Reflecting different contexts and experiences, the owners of Cass Gilbert houses have recently banded together with other owners of Gilbert properties in Minnesota as the core of a Cass Gilbert Society, based in St. Paul. The public buildings, the residences, and the office buildings have been notable since the beginning of Gilbert's career for the warm and yet enlarging human environment they provide.

As a former administrator of a significant portion of the federal courts (I was circuit executive—roughly, regional administrator—of the second circuit federal courts during 1980–97), I developed the conviction that Gilbert consistently contributed significantly toward a solution to one of the central problems faced by any court administrator as a public employer: the federal courts employ many people who work energetically and enthusiastically for much

OPPOSITE
P-1. Broadway, c. 1905, including Broadway Chambers Building, New York City.
(© Collection of the New-York Historical Society, neg. #58803)

less than they could command on the outside. Gilbert makes palpable the message of the judges and supervisors to their employees that they have entered a calling, even if their own role may be relatively modest. A senior lawyer on the second circuit staff has long spoken of the "psychic income" he gains from working where he works. The file clerk, the hotshot young law clerk, and the judges themselves—Gilbert assists them all in finding the answer to any worker's questions: Why am I at work here? What am I doing here? The humdrum realities of quotidian duties, for judges as for file clerks, gain a reified connection to larger purposes of justice in a constitutional democracy.

This perspective extends well beyond unique or even exalted institutions or employers like the federal judiciary. Let us consider the problem of the office building, sometimes described as the most boring building type in architecture. Since around the time Gilbert came to New York, nearly all of his buildings have been essentially office buildings, though we rarely think of them that way. Consider the United States Custom House at Bowling Green, discussed and pictured in chapters 3 and 18, and the site of the symposium on which this book is based. While it seems a poor example because it is uniquely flamboyant, it was indeed an office building. More obviously, its contemporaries, the West Street Building (see Figure 4-3) and the Broadway Chambers Building were simply turn-of-the-century equivalents of the generic office building that today goes up on spec. Their builders had little fixed idea of who or what would occupy them, thereby denying their architect the kind of natural access to a symbolic visual language that is available for the office building/courthouse or custom house. Nonetheless, Gilbert designed masterpieces.

Less obviously and more notably, even the Woolworth Building began life as no more than a generic office building, all appearances to the contrary notwithstanding. As that beauty was constructed, Frank W. Woolworth's empire was to occupy only a fraction of the available office space. It took a special relationship between architect and client to unfold what today would seem intrinsically a very

modest program and extend it as we are privileged to experience it in the company of visitors—still—from all over the world. (Curiously, the federal courts in the 1920s rented several spaces on the lower floors as an addition to Alfred B. Mullet's old Post Office and Courthouse across the street (see Figure 9-8), before it was demolished and succeeded by Gilbert's Foley Square courthouse. Judge Learned Hand had his chambers in the Woolworth Building for several years; one wonders if he noted the connection when he moved to the Gilbert courthouse in 1936.)

Gilbert's courthouses, and state capitols, and other monumental public and private buildings are the paradigm of what the twenty-first century will learn from him, but they do not by any means exhaust the links he extends across the centuries as we rediscover the importance of design, public and private, in creating and sustaining public spaces. With the help of Senator Daniel Patrick Moynihan, Gilbert serves as an essential link in teaching the federal government how to create civic architecture all over again, and how to think about civic architecture through the troubled aesthetic of our time. The altogether satisfactory new courthouse at 500 Pearl Street in New York is the outcome of a competitive process by which Senator Moynihan insisted that our time must listen to Gilbert—the enabling legislation specified that the new Foley Square courthouse must be respectful of the old. Gilbert was the frame of reference for the new, and the relationship continues. That effort opened a process that continues to unfold, one that truly is a renaissance. History will compare the federal architecture of the 1990s (and especially the federal court architecture) with that of the 1940s and 1950s, and will find that there's no comparison.

The Bauhaus and the International style did many wonderful things, but they did at least two very bad things. They caused the twentieth century to lose its moorings entirely as it tried to undertake civic architecture. And they derailed perceptions of Gilbert and interest in him, a fact that led many of us to undertake his rediscovery. There are countless demonstrations that through the 1920s Gilbert's reputation was preeminent. The 1928 Encyclopaedia

Britannica article about architecture, extending thirty-one pages and displaying countless images, offers more space to the Woolworth Building than to any other two or three buildings combined throughout history. Yet only a few years later when the United States Supreme Court and the Foley Square courthouse opened, Gilbert had become an instant anachronism. Both buildings were mostly ignored. When they were noticed, reaction was tepid at best and savage at worst.

I had the opportunity in September 1998 to address an international gathering of architects in Toronto as they considered the future of the courthouse. The displays, slides, and presentations that the American Institute of Architects assembled at that event would dispel any doubt that the architectural profession today knows how to solve the problem of the courthouse as a building type. Most heartening was the exhibition and related publication of a student competition, the DuPont Benedictus Awards, showing inventive and effective design solutions of winners representing schools from Hong Kong to Zurich to Chicago. Rediscovering Gilbert has helped this process, thanks mostly to Senator Moynihan, who was a steadfast champion of architects and architecture throughout his twenty-four years in the Senate—especially as a member and (briefly) chairman of the Committee on Environment and Public Works.

Thirty to seventy years ago, Gilbert seemed laughably historicist. Indeed, his exuberance in trying on connections to diverse and unrelated visual languages is easy to make fun of today. My late wife likened his successive presentations to the directors of the New Haven Railroad to playing with paper dolls. Gilbert had a successful plan for the train station in New Haven—also an office building, by the way: it was to be the railroad's headquarters. But it needed adornment and a theme. Let's try on the Palazzo Pubblico of Siena! But McKim, Mead & White had done that for them already in Waterbury. Or some later Italian Renaissance idiom! Or French Gothic! Or Georgian! (see Figure C-11). In the end the directors went for a stripped-down version for reasons of economy, leaving the minimum that Gilbert always provided: magnificent interior spaces and outstanding functionality, but none of the familiar exuberance we will see in most of the chapters that follow.

Gilbert's historicism is a good deal more than funny or quaint. It is liberating, and I hope it will remain so. For Gilbert and his clients, historicism provided a connection with an adopted past for a new nation, through the present to the future. In less exuberant form, the principle holds true today as we search for new solutions to the difficult problems every architect and client find in seeking meaning and a frame of reference for projects that seem intrinsically boring and without moorings.

Now and in the future we can learn from Gilbert in another way, already suggested but not articulated. Every Gilbert building that I know responds to the client's practical needs in a degree that is unparalleled. In each project, he was interested, not only in an enlarging vision but also in daily use, in the multiple constituencies of every building. A courthouse is a complex and difficult program that fails very often, yet solving its intricacies seems to have come

naturally to Gilbert. After eighteen years at the federal courthouse at Foley Square I can identify only two functional faults of the building design that Gilbert was in a position to anticipate. Both were remediable and have been remedied rather readily. The court of appeals courtroom, too similar to the trial courtrooms whose design and setting it shares, had to be reconfigured significantly to improve traffic flow and reduce the distraction as people move in and out during argument. And certain minor changes have been made to improve security.

To take a less familiar example, the unfolding of the New York County Lawyers' Association build-

PR-2. The New York County Lawyers' Association, Vesey Street, across from St. Paul's Church, the oldest church in Manhattan. The site was selected by William N. Cromwell to be "near, but not too near, the courts," and because of St. Paul's historical associations and the fact that the churchyard protects the building's south exposure. Wurts Brothers Collection. (Museum of the City of New York)

ing in lower Manhattan (Figures PR-2 and PR-3) is a paradigm of what should be done by a sensitive architect working with a committed and passionate (but highly cranky) client. William Nelson Cromwell, president of the association at the time and one of the most distinguished lawyers of his age, was all over the project as it developed toward a ceremonial opening in 1930. The major donor, Cromwell intruded at an astonishing level of detail. Fourteen Vesey Street is a little jewel that realized a large dream as a result.

Considerably more important as the "Home of Law," it is a realization that has always worked as Gilbert intended.

Gilbert's special genius lay in his capacity to identify and embody the dreams of clients, not an easy task in his day and even harder today. As we enter the new century and the new millennium, it often seems that architects and their clients have abandoned this quest altogether for any building that is to be used in a functional way having something to do with earning a living or making the central institutions of our society and economy work. Where are the dreams and dreamers in today's projects? To read the critics, one might imagine that they are to be found only in a single, improbable building type: the art museum. There, and there only, in constructing flights of the architect's fancy that often overwhelm the work to be displayed—and at colossal cost that

PR-3. New York County Lawyers' Association, second-floor lounge. (New York County Lawyers' Association)

could better have gone to other living artists—we find architect and client dreaming great dreams and realizing them. It is all a remarkable caricature of Gilbert's capacity to identify and enlarge the humdrum realities that more often than not were his starting point.

Sometimes it seems that Gilbert's capacity to make everything work in any setting, no matter how unexpected or extended, was little short of superhuman. As the chapters that follow make clear, he was only partially educated as a professional architect and did not even graduate from high school. Certainly he was not an engineer, far less an acoustical engineer. Yet his auditorium for the American Academy of Arts and Letters on Audubon Terrace in upper Manhattan (Figure PR-4) is the favorite recording space for most of New York's recording engineers (I personally own a dozen or more of the hundreds of commercial recordings that have been made there). And such buildings as Woolworth, the tallest building in the world for many years, and the Brooklyn U.S. Army Supply Base, the largest reinforced concrete structure in the world when it was constructed, demonstrate a mastery of novel engineering solutions that might have eluded many trained engineers.

This celebration of Gilbert's capacity to extend the public domain through the thoughtful design of public and private spaces results from the efforts of countless enthusiasts. The various events in 1997–99 were sparked initially by the second circuit's Committee on History and Commemorative Events, led during the relevant periods by Judges Roger J. Miner, José A Cabranes, and Pierre N. Leval. Co-chairs of the Committee on Cass Gilbert Projects were John Haworth of the George Gustav Heye Center of the National Museum of the American Indian/Smithsonian Institution and the late Judge Jeffry H. Gallet, with Judge Dennis Jacobs representing the court of appeals. Barbara S. Christen served as executive director. The Federal Bar Council provided support in many forms: logistical, financial, and intellectual. Curator Gail Galloway of the United States Supreme Court, assisted by Franz Jantzen, put on a distinguished exhibit, as did the New York County Lawyers' Association. Sharon Irish and Gail

Fenske served as curators for exhibitions at the United States Custom House and the Woolworth Building, respectively. A fine walking tour of Gilbert sites in lower Manhattan was organized by the Alliance for Downtown New York. The Graham Foundation for Advanced Studies in the Fine Arts provided indispensable support for the visual aspects of this book. We thank all of these and countless others who made contributions to the rediscovery of Cass Gilbert upon which this volume rests. Finally, all of the above and all of the authors are indebted to Nancy N. Green, who has been described to me more than once as the finest architectural editor working today, and her colleagues at W. W. Norton. They have contributed mightily to our effort to convert a group of disparate presentations into a comprehensive treatment of Gilbert's life and work.

PR-4. Auditorium of the American Academy of Arts and Letters, New York, NY 1929–30. (Cass Gilbert Collection, Archives Center, National Museum of American History)

INTRODUCTION

ROBERT A. M. STERN

For far too long the achievements of American architects, particularly those active in the nineteenth and early twentieth centuries, have been overlooked and undervalued. Some contend that nineteenth-century America was too young and too culturally dependent to have created a distinct and valuable architecture of its own. Our architecture, this argument goes, is too derivative to amount to much more than a footnote to European architectural history. For many naysayers, New York, above all American cities, was the cause of our national architectural backwardness. Why New York? Well, New York, where Cass Gilbert (Figure IN-1), the subject of this book, realized some of his finest buildings, allegedly was too involved with capitalism, too much at the mercy of business and real estate interests, too bottom-line oriented—in a word, too much about making a buck and not enough about making art— to produce architecture worthy of serious consideration. Worst of all, New York was too cosmopolitan, too sensitive to international traditions and trends, especially those of Europe, to produce anything distinctly American. As a result of this near self-hatred, the scholarly investigation of late-nineteenth- and early-twentieth-century American architecture has barely begun. True, some parts of our heritage from that period are well known—those that connect America with the formal inventions of European modernism—but the larger context of American building and achievement remains comparatively unstudied, unknown, and unappreciated.

While the contributions to the history of architecture of our great American experimenters, Louis Sullivan and Frank Lloyd Wright, and others who followed their example, cannot be overestimated, it is time to open our focus to the wider situation of late-nineteenth- and early-twentieth-century architecture. We must look at the inspired professionalism and artistry of such architects as Cass Gilbert, who, among the many exceptionally accomplished architects of one hundred years ago, has been, until recently, more egregiously overlooked than virtually any other. Cass Gilbert was interested in progress—not artistic progress (he preferred the formal languages of the past) but material progress: the improvement of our public realm. Gilbert put his great talent in the service of an ideal combining artistic excellence with social improvement, that of the City Beautiful, in which the forms of classical architecture and the principles of classical urbanism were employed to help counteract the blighting effects of the materialism of late-nineteenth-century buccaneer capitalism. As a leading exemplar of the City Beautiful, Gilbert believed in the benefits that architecture could bestow on the environment and the culture of American life. His goal, like that of Charles McKim and Daniel Burnham, and many others who followed their lead, was nothing short of the social and artistic reform of American urban life. The movement's proponents helped rebuild our cities with gleaming ensembles of classical buildings and public spaces intended to bring order, efficiency, and social benefit to our cities and towns.

But the movement was not just concerned with beautiful buildings and places. Sanitary systems and well-planned housing developments raised the standards of public health. Even commercial buildings, and especially the newly evolved skyscrapers, were made to conform to the enhanced sense of civic responsibility, not only soaring to new heights but also incorporating innumerable public services and sometimes even, as in the Woolworth Building, grand public spaces. The City Beautiful movement gifted America with superb buildings, public facilities, and public places that attest to the power and pride of a democracy that saw itself as the rightful and enlightened inheritor of western civilization. Enhancing the realities of democratic capitalism in all its complexity, it was neither Pollyannaish about current problems nor cynical about the future.

Until his death in 1934 at the age of seventy-five, Gilbert never flagged in his devotion to the

OPPOSITE
IN-1. Cass Gilbert, c. 1915. (Collection of the Mattatuck Museum, Waterbury, Connecticut)

enlightened ideals of the City Beautiful. Each building in his extraordinary succession of projects was seen as a contribution to the collective public good. Perhaps no building more tellingly reflects both Gilbert's contribution and the ongoing reevaluation of his career than the United States Custom House in New York. Today the Custom House is home to a branch of the United States Bankruptcy Court and the George Gustav Heye Center of the National Museum of the American Indian/Smithsonian Institution. As such, and for its own beautiful mass and details, it is widely admired as a great work of architecture and a landmark of the city that it serves. But thirty years ago, when it was about to be abandoned by the Custom Service, Gilbert's masterpiece was physically decrepit and without a particular constituency, not only among civil servants but also among the rank and file of architects and scholars who should have known better. Fortunately, some New Yorkers appreciated the great virtues of the Custom House and saw to it that it received protection as a New York City landmark. Though the building was one of the first to be designated an official landmark under New York City's pioneering law adopted in 1965, it was not possible to protect Gilbert's wonderful rooms and passageways until 1979, six years after the law was amended to allow for the inclusion of publicly accessible interiors.

But even with legally mandated preservation, the fate of the building as a useful public institution was far from certain. With the Custom Service's move to the World Trade Center in 1973, Gilbert's great stone gateway to Manhattan sat sadly empty at the very center of the important business community it had served so long, until concerned individuals and civic groups revived the building and empowered it with a new life. In 1973, the New York Landmarks Conservancy and the Architectural League of New York (Gilbert had helped to form the latter in 1881 as a sketch club for young architects) threw a splashy dinner party in the rotunda of the Custom House, honoring the New York Times's architectural critic Ada Louise Huxtable, then a passionate and powerful advocate for the preservation of historical buildings and sites. The dinner not only served as a public forum for advocating the adaptive reuse of the landmark building but also introduced many influential citizens to its splendid interiors (in New York, if you make people pay a lot of money, get them all dressed up in dinner clothes, and serve them average food at room temperature in a building without a kitchen, they will stop paying attention to one another and to their dinners and will begin to look around at their environment). And what a hundred or so influential New Yorkers saw at that banquet was splendor in an advancing state of decrepitude. When Huxtable stood up to receive her honor and explain to the assembled crowd what it should have known—that the Custom House was a great building that needed to be reimagined for the future—the crowd was ready to take action. The rest, as they say, is history.

PAGE 17
C-1. United States
Supreme Court,
Washington D.C.,
1928–35. (Photograph by Franz Jantzen,
Collection of the
Supreme Court of the
United States)

THIS PAGE
C-2. Minnesota State
Capitol, St. Paul,
1895–1906. (Senate
Media Services,
David J. Oakes, photographer, Minnesota
State Capitol)

C-3. Rotunda,
Minnesota State
Capitol. (Senate
Media Services,
Mark M. Nelson, photographer, Minnesota
State Capitol)

C-4. St. Louis Public
Library: Entrance,
St. Louis, Missouri.
(Alise O'Brien © Architectural Photography)

C-5. Broadway
Chambers Building,
watercolor on paper,
1899, Hughson
Hawley, renderer.
(Museum of the City
of New York)

C-6. Woolworth Build-
ing, 1911, Hughson
Hawley, renderer, *in
New York on the Rise:
Architectural Render-
ings by Hughson
Hawley, 1880–1931*
(London and New
York, 1998), 47, pl.
26. (Published with
permission from the
Venator Group, on
loan to Museum of
the City of New York)

C-7. New York, skyline
view from the Hudson
River, 1913, in *Above
the Clouds & Old New
York,* 1913, final
photograph. (Library
of Congress)

C-8. Gilbert & Taylor, Town and Country Club, St. Paul, Minnesota (1890), view from a period postcard, c. 1908. (Collection of Tom Blanck)

C-9. C.W. Bunn Cottage, White Bear Lake, Minnesota (1895), c. 1978. (Collection of the Dodsall Family)

C-10. Front elevation, United States Custom House, c. 1900, T. R. Johnson, renderer, ink wash, watercolor, gouache, graphite on drawing paper. (© Collection of the New-York Historical Society, neg. #48756)

C-11. New Haven Railroad Station: 1910, Georgian version. (© Collection of the New York Historical Society, neg. #74548T)

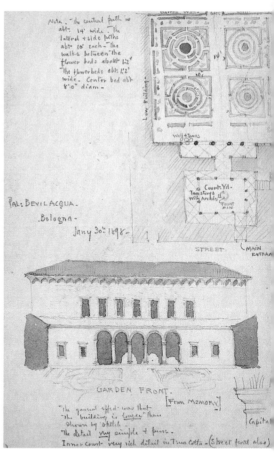

C-12. Interior of St. Mark's Cathedral, Venice, watercolor from Gilbert's Paris sketchbook, February 21, 1880. (Library of Congress)

C-13. Palazzo Bevilacqua, Bologna, garden front from memory, January 30, 1898, watercolor and graphite. (©Collection of the New-York Historical Society, neg. #74426T)

C-14. Proposed Auditorium for Oberlin College (not built), color sketch, 1916. (Allen Memorial Art Museum, Oberlin College, Ohio; lent by Paul F. Walter)

C–15. *Towers from the City Wall,* Nuremberg, 1897. (Smithsonian American Art Museum, bequest of Emily Finch Gilbert through Julia Post Bastedo, executor)

CUNARD

Europe-America

FASTEST OCEAN SERVICE
IN THE WORLD.

C-16. After restoration the quadriga once again appears as it did originally in 1907. Sculptors: Daniel Chester French and Edward Potter, *The Progress of the State.* Quadriga is gold leaf on copper. (Senate Media Services, David J. Oakes, photographer, Minnesota State Capitol)

C-17. Cunard Line poster, c.1914. (Board of Trustees of the National Museums & Galleries on Merseyside: Merseyside Museum, Liverpool)

C-18. Study for an Office Building for Mr. Chase, September 22,1916, Waterbury, Conn. (© Collection of the New-York Historical Society, neg. # 74427T)

PART 1

A NATIONAL PRACTICE BUILT FROM THE "NORTHWEST"

CHAPTER 1

ARCHITECTURAL EDUCATION
AND MINNESOTA CAREER

Patricia Anne Murphy

Cass Gilbert spent much of his early life and began his architectural career in his adopted hometown of St. Paul, Minnesota. Part of the first generation of professionally trained architects in the area, he played a major role in introducing East Coast architectural sophistication and in shaping the development of architecture and the architectural profession. Gilbert practiced architecture in St. Paul for twenty-seven years, from 1883 to 1910. His voluminous personal and business letters and papers from this period reveal his wit and sense of humor, his entrepreneurial and public relations skills, and his pride and faith in his own abilities and accomplishments. He was an astute businessman and prolific designer and writer whose works and papers today are scattered far afield, confounding and enticing present-day researchers. Even after setting his sights on bigger and more prestigious projects in Boston and New York, opening a New York office, and eventually closing his St. Paul practice, Gilbert retained a strong interest in architectural developments in Minnesota. This chapter focuses on Gilbert's nonresidential work during the years he lived and worked in Minnesota; Gilbert's residential work in Minnesota is discussed in chapter 2.[1]

Cass Gilbert (Figure 1-1) was born in 1859 to a well-established family in Zanesville, an agricultural and industrial center located in the rolling hills of southeastern Ohio.[2] He and his family lived first in downtown Zanesville. The brick home where Cass Gilbert was born stood on North Fourth Street near where the Muskingum County Courthouse stands today. The house was demolished in 1952.[3] Within a few years of Gilbert's birth, the family moved to a farm on Frazeysburg Road on the outskirts of town.

Cass Gilbert's father, Samuel Augustus Gilbert (1825–1868), was a topographical engineer for the U.S. Coast Survey and was assigned to projects  along the East Coast, in Alabama, Florida, South Carolina, Texas, and elsewhere. He worked for the government of Colombia on surveying the route of what would become the Panama Canal. He also was a businessman who owned a foundry within a few blocks of the family home in downtown Zanesville. Later, he served in the Civil War.[4] Gilbert's grandfather, Charles Champion Gilbert (1797–1844), was a Connecticut native and Yale graduate who settled in Zanesville, established a law practice, and served as one of the town's first mayors. Cass Gilbert was named after his father's uncle, Lewis Cass (1782–1866), who had been a secretary of state, territorial governor of Michigan, senator, and a Democratic presidential candidate in 1848. Cass Gilbert's grandmother, Eleanor Warden Wheeler, remained in Zanesville until her death on June 5, 1885. She was born in Chambersburg, Pennsylvania on May 12, 1809 and probably played some role in Gilbert's being selected as the architect for a house for a local judge there in the early 1880s.

1-1. Cass Gilbert, July 8, 1880, portrait file. (Minnesota Historical Society)

In 1868, when Gilbert was eight, his family moved to the thriving frontier town of St. Paul, the capital of the new state of Minnesota and well known as the head of steamboat navigation on the Mississippi River. It would soon become a railroading center while neighboring Minneapolis became known for manufacturing and flour milling. An article of 1888 in *The Northwest Magazine* described Minnesota's "excellent climate":

> Comfortable winter weather in St. Paul is from zero to ten below at daybreak, rising to zero or ten above during the day. The air is clear and wonderfully invigorating and the sun shines brightly. The people you meet are in good spirits; every body moves quickly; business goes on with a vim. You are surprised at the amount of work you can do in a day without fatigue. . . . Every time you go out into the pure, cold atmosphere you are braced up anew. It is like the invigoration of champagne without the penalty of subsequent lassitude.[5]

Within one year Gilbert's father died of consumption.[6] After his death Gilbert's mother, Elizabeth Wheeler Gilbert (1832–97), was able to live comfortably in St. Paul. She owned property in St. Paul and in Zanesville. During the last ten years of her life she spent winters with one of her other sons in California. She died at the age of 65 in 1897 at the residence of Cass Gilbert in St Paul.[7]

Cass Gilbert attended public school in St. Paul. He later attended a private Presbyterian boy's school in Minneapolis that became affiliated with what is now known as Macalester College in St. Paul.[8] During the summer of 1876 Gilbert began his architectural career by working as an assistant to a builder/carpenter in Red Wing, Minnesota. Rather than complete his last year of high school, he began a two-year apprenticeship to a long-established, self-taught, Twin Cities architect, Abraham Radcliffe (1827–86).[9] One of Radcliffe's best-known extant buildings is the Dakota County Courthouse in Hastings, Minnesota (1869–70). Radcliffe also designed many large Victorian homes in St. Paul. In this office, Gilbert became well acquainted with the local architectural community and came to the eventual decision that he needed to go elsewhere if he wished to obtain the best architectural education possible. Gilbert also became an avid reader of America's first architectural periodical, the *American Architect and Building News (AABN)*, which began publication in 1876.[10]

After spending the summer working as a surveyor for the Hudson and River Falls Railroad in Wisconsin, in the fall of 1878 Gilbert entered the architecture school at the Massachusetts Institute of Technology (MIT). The school was then under the direction of the country's preeminent architectural educator, William Robert Ware (1832–1915). Another of Gilbert's professors was Eugéne Létang (died 1892), an Ecole des Beaux-Arts graduate who taught using the Ecole's methods and who also did freelance work for Henry Hobson Richardson (1838–86). While at MIT Gilbert greatly enjoyed the company of his fellow students and spent much time traveling and sketching buildings around the Boston area. He was particularly intrigued with the work of Richardson. He also studied the works of contemporary British architects such as William Burgess (1827–81), George Edmond Street (1824–81), and Richard Norman Shaw (1831–1912). Gilbert's official transcript from his year at MIT indicates his performance was less than stellar: Architectural Design—95, A; History—70, C; Ornament—65, P; and Perspective—0, F.[11]

Among Gilbert's classmates and friends were fellow Minnesotans Clarence Johnston (1859–1936), who had also worked in Radcliffe's office in St. Paul, and James Knox Taylor (1857–1927), who later became Gilbert's partner in St. Paul.[12] While at school, Gilbert wrote to Johnston about Taylor that "…when I spoke enthusiastically of a sea, a sky, and a bit of sunlight, he made me think that his artistic soul was thinking of a fat position in a comfortable office, rather than of artistic aspirations and delight."[13] This statement seems ironic given that Gilbert and Taylor shortly thereafter would be on friendly enough terms to form what would become a successful if short-lived architectural partnership.

Gilbert completed only one year of the two-year course at MIT and then worked as a surveyor in New York State in the summer and fall of 1879 in order to save money for a grand tour of Europe.[14] In January 1880 he set off on an eight-month sketching tour of England, France, and Italy. His sketches included buildings ranging from cathedrals to storefronts, architectural details, park benches, general scenery, and people (see Figure C-12). Sketching remained one of Gilbert's lifelong passions. When his friend Johnston was contemplating a European trip of his own, Gilbert recommended that he not prepare himself by reading up on architectural history, but instead encouraged him to read general history and "…become familiar with events. Great epochs are the dates in architecture. Styles place themselves when you are familiar with the history of the country in which you may be."[15] Soon after in a letter home, Gilbert commented on something he observed on his way to Chambord, perhaps indicating a touch of homesickness for Minnesota: "I was on a wide avenue leading straight up to the Chateau. . . . [There was] such an undergrowth as we used to see on the drive from St. Paul to Como and White Bear. In fact, the whole general appearance of this country is remarkably similar to many parts of Minnesota. Where it lacks the natural beauty of our scenery, the deficiency is supplied by a ruined tower, a village church spire, or an old chateau."[16] Gilbert's prolific correspondence and personal papers from his early years as an architecture student and young architect demonstrate his love of aesthetic matters, his strong opinions, and his somewhat temperamental nature.

Gilbert chose not to pursue studies at the Ecole des Beaux-Arts in Paris, even though that was the dream of many young architects of his day. In an autobiographical account written sometime around 1920, he reflected upon this decision: "At this time I was an enthusiastic follower of the Gothic, and looked upon Viollet-le-Duc as its chief exponent. Hence the Ecole des Beaux-Arts did not attract me. Richardson had broken away from the Ecole and was doing great work in America. Street, Gilbert Scott, Pearson, and Burgess were leading the gothic movement in England and Norman Shaw and Alfred Waterhouse were names familiar to the young fellows in America and I eagerly followed the romantic tendency of the time."[17] While in England, Gilbert tried unsuccessfully to get a job working for a London architect. His first choice was George Edmond Street. When no job materialized, he talked briefly of returning to Boston to work for Richardson, but this did not occur either.

Gilbert returned to New York City in the late summer of 1880 and was hired by the new firm founded by Charles Follen McKim (1847–1909), William Rutherford Mead (1846–1928), and Stanford White (1853–1906). As Richard Guy Wilson wrote, contemporaries stressed the partners' differing temperaments and personalities, with: "McKim, the deliberate and persuasive scholar who aspired to the large and grand in both architecture and ideas; Mead, the quiet, unoriginal designer involved in the intricate details of running an office; and Stanford White, the mercurial firebrand of energy and motion, a specialist in the quick effect. The differences might be said to make up an ideal architectural partnership, with the similarities hardly noticed."[18] In working in their large and busy practice Gilbert became acquainted with some of the most talented designers and artists of his day. He later recalled that his first project was assisting with the design of a base for a statue by the noted American sculptor Augustus Saint-Gaudens (1848–1907), possibly the Farragut Memorial: "Naturally I approached the task a bit nervously, and try as I would, I could not seem to make things go at all. When I came to the darkest part of my struggle, [Stanford] White came to my table to see how I was progressing, and I had forebodings of instant dismissal! Luckily, St. Gaudens himself dropped in, and took up the cudgels in my favor, saying that it was a very difficult problem to solve. He took the pencil from me and endeavored to scheme the thing out himself, but he floundered as hopelessly as I did. The thing was eventually solved after considerable experimentation."[19]

Gilbert's work for McKim, Mead & White ranged from supervising construction to completing details in the decorative arts and architectural design. Among the projects underway while Gilbert was working in the firm's New York office were the Villard Houses and Davis House, the Stewart Vault in Greenwood Cemetery in New York City, a yacht for James Gordon Bennett, alterations of a stable for Richard Watson Gilder, decorative arabesques for a project that Augustus Saint-Gaudens designed for Vanderbilt, as well as painting friezes and designing fountains and furniture for various projects. Gilbert also worked on a house for Robert Garrett in Baltimore.[20]

In August 1882 McKim, Mead & White sent Gilbert to Baltimore, where he assisted with the design and supervised construction of the Ross R. Winans House (1881–82) (Figure 1-2). Gilbert's work included designing a fountain for the house, and his correspondence indicates that he was proud of his work and that he had drawn inspiration from Saint-Gaudens's Admiral Farragut Monument in Madison Square Park in New York (1877–81), the base of which had been designed by Stanford White.[21] Gilbert wrote to Johnston from Baltimore that his work in Baltimore was not all that he had hoped for: "I have had no vacation this summer and as it has been confining work, and as I have been fretted to death by the client on one side, the contractor on the other and the office between times, my position is not the 'sinecure' that I thought it would be. At present I am drawing out a lot of furniture—awful stuff—and loaded with ornament."[22] Clearly, Gilbert had other aspirations.

Once Gilbert decided to return to St. Paul, McKim, Mead & White put him to work on several buildings from Minnesota west to Oregon along Henry Villard's Northern Pacific Railway line. They discussed the possibility of Gilbert opening a St. Paul branch office for McKim, Mead & White, but this venture never materialized in part because of the financial collapse of Villard's railroad empire in 1883. During the early 1880s, Gilbert and Clarence Johnston also considered forming a St. Paul partnership, but this also failed to materialize.

St. Paul's population increased dramatically in the second half of the nineteenth century. The city's population was 10,000 in 1860. By 1880, it had reached 41,000. Between 1880 and 1890 St. Paul's

population tripled, increasing from 41,000 to 133,581. The city had become prosperous, in the midst of much real estate speculation and a building boom. Thriving entrepreneurs were beginning to be concerned with replacing the first frontier-era simple wood and brick commercial structures with more substantial and more impressive buildings demonstrating their success and showing the promise of the growing capital city. St. Paul was a land of opportunity and a heady place for an ambitious young architect, even if at times it seemed very provincial compared to the East Coast and Europe.

Harper's New Monthly Magazine reported in 1892 that:

St. Paul in 1881 manufactured $15,466,000 worth of goods with which to trade with the Northwest; in 1890 the sum had grown to $61,270,000, an increase of three hundred percent in nine years. The city is the dairy center of the Northwest. It has made great investments in the manufacture of clothing, boots and shoes, fine furniture, wagons, carriages, farm implements, lager-beer, cigars, fur garments, portable houses for the settlers, dressed stone, boilers, bridges, and the products of large stock yards. To a less yet considerable extent it manufactures crackers, candy, flour, bedding, foundry-work, sashes and blinds, harnesses, brass goods, barrels, brooms, and brushes. Its banks have a capital of $10,000,000; its jobbing trade amounted to $122,000,000 in 1890, it did a business in cattle of every sort to the extent of a million head in the same year. It has fine hotels and opera houses, a typically elaborate Western school system, and is in all respects a healthy, vigorous, well-governed city.[23]

After spending four years on the East Coast and in Europe, Gilbert moved back to St. Paul in January 1883, probably in large part because he wished to live closer to his mother. He later recalled that he left McKim, Mead & White ". . . to go to St. Paul where

1-2. McKim, Mead & White, Ross R. Winans House, Baltimore (1881–82), in *Monograph of the Works of McKim, Mead & White: 1879-1898,* vol. 1 (New York, 1915), pl. 2. (Library of Congress)

family property and home interests demanded my presence."[24] Gilbert began work on the design of a home for his mother even before he left Baltimore for St. Paul, noting that "[i]t has become a little problem to do something which shall be artistic—not fashionable—sensible, genuine and a place I shall not tire of myself."[25] He lived with his mother until 1887, when he married.

During his early years in St. Paul, Gilbert occasionally supplemented his meager architect's wages by selling landscape paintings that he had done. His own lifestyle was hardly opulent at that time, although he did become very much a part of St. Paul society. The medium-sized Shingle-style home that he soon designed for his own family was located on a small lot in a very fashionable neighborhood within footsteps of many of St. Paul's most prominent citizens, many of whom became his clients. Indeed, the residential neighborhoods near Gilbert's mother's home at 471 Ashland Avenue, and near the home Gilbert built for his own family in 1890 at 1 Heather Place (Figure 1-3) at an estimated cost of $6,500, now contain the largest concentration of Gilbert buildings anywhere. Yet Gilbert was just one of many young architects to settle in this rapidly developing neighborhood, which now is a historic district; a resident later recalled there was at least one architect on every block.[27]

Gilbert's mother was well connected in St. Paul society and belonged to the New Century Club of St. Paul and several other women's organizations.[28] She helped her son to enroll in several similarly prestigious social clubs and to develop a reputation as an architect to the local elite.[29] In 1884 he was the only architect among the founding members of the Minne-

1-3. Gilbert & Taylor, dining room of Cass Gilbert Residence, St. Paul, 1891, in *Northwestern Builder, Decorator & Furnisher* 5 (1891). (Minnesota Historical Society)

sota Club, and there he could fraternize with railroad barons such as James J. Hill, fur trade and steamboat magnate Norman Kittson, and lumberman Amherst Wilder, as well as past, present, and future Minnesota governors, mayors, and other local luminaries. An 1888 roster of the club's 245 members includes names of at least 25 (or more than 10 percent) who had been or would become Gilbert's clients.[30] Gilbert also belonged to the Informal Club, the Minnesota Boat Club, and the Nushka Club, among others.[31] Many of his fellow club members were politically influential and socially well established. Many eventually became friends and clients. Gilbert provided some design schemes for alterations to the Minnesota Club building in downtown St. Paul and designed a clubhouse for the Town and Country Club, a golf club at the western edge of St. Paul, in 1890.[32]

By 1886, Gilbert was corresponding frequently with the woman who would become his bride, Julia Tappan Finch, the daughter of Milwaukee attorney Henry M. Finch.[33] Even his love letters reveal his passion for architecture and his desire that his beloved learn to share this interest. When he wrote to Julia on October 31, 1886, he explained, "I am going to send you a copy of last month's 'Atlantic.' There is an article in it by Mr. Henry Van Brunt on H. H. Richardson, which I would like very much to have you read. There is so much in it that exactly coincides with my own ideas that I may be able in that way to explain in a measure by own attitude toward my profession in regard to its higher aim."[34] Cass and Julia were married on November 29, 1887, in Milwaukee. They had four children: Emily Finch, Elizabeth Wheeler (who died of meningitis in 1904 at 14), Julia Swift, and Cass, Jr.

While devoted to building a successful practice, Gilbert also found time for fun. Among the more notable and most elaborate gatherings in St. Paul to celebrate New Year's Eve on December 31, 1889, was a "balmasque" (costume) party given by the Nushka Club at their Summit Avenue clubhouse, reported the local newspaper. Women dressed as French peasant girls, a model choir boy, a sheik, and a student in cap and gown, while men's costumes included an Indian squaw fortune teller, a Russian Hussar, clowns, and Mercury. Gilbert wore a Japanese dress, and one of his clients, W. S. Morton, was a prince.[35]

Chicago architect John Wellborn Root observed "in cases like St. Paul and Minneapolis, every move of either city is watched by the other with keenest interest, and every structure of importance in one city becomes only the standard to be passed in the other."[36] New York architectural critic Montgomery Schuyler noted that "if the physical necessities of the case prescribed ten-story buildings in St. Paul, the moral necessity of not being outdone would prescribe twelve-story buildings in Minneapolis."[37] Both writers noted the intensity of the rivalry between the two cities in the late nineteenth century and suggested the impact this had on architecture and the building trades.

Like most businessmen of the era, Gilbert rarely did work in the neighboring arch-rival city of Minneapolis, but he did follow that city's architectural developments. Gilbert wrote in his diary entry of May 20, 1890, about a visit he made that morning to examine buildings in Minneapolis. Never at a loss for words, especially in aesthetic matters, he spoke with mild enthusiasm of the nearly completed New York Life Insurance Building (1888–90) by Babb, Cook & Willard (since razed) but was less than impressed with Milwaukee architect E. Townsend Mix's nearly complete Guaranty Loan Building (razed): "It is appalling. It has a great effect on the mind from its size, both inside and out, but the design throughout is stupid and in bad taste, either too heavy or too light. . . ."[38] Gilbert gained some recognition in Minneapolis in whatever ways he could, and eventually did design several buildings there. In 1894, for example, he gave a talk to the Art Club in Minneapolis titled "Some Phases of Italian Architecture," an event at which he noted that "his treatment of the Renaissance Period of Rome and Florence was highly appreciated."[39]

While working hard to attract clients in St. Paul and throughout the Midwest, Gilbert did not wish to be forgotten by his East Coast colleagues. He periodically corresponded with various draftsmen, architects, and artists whom he had met during his sojourn in Boston and New York, and he was an avid reader of architectural journals, which in this period were markedly influenced by trends in that region. He followed the debate among many architectural critics of the era on the merits of the uniquely "western" architecture that was said to be emerging in Chicago and elsewhere in the Midwest. Yet clearly he wanted no part of a uniquely western architectural idiom and felt he had an important role in establishing East Coast architectural traditions in St. Paul and elsewhere.

During his Minnesota years, Gilbert submitted numerous drawings, studies for unbuilt works, and commentaries to nationally circulated architectural publications such as *American Architect and Building News (AABN)* and the *Brickbuilder* as well as to local and regional publications such as *Improvement Bulletin* (a contractor's publication that listed building projects throughout the Midwest) and *Northwestern Builder, Decorator and Furnisher* (a St. Paul–based publication that began in 1887 and initially featured photographs of recently built Minnesota houses). For example, a letter from Gilbert was published in the December 15, 1893 issue of *Improvement Bulletin* in which he stated, "Dear Sir—I have found your paper a valuable one and it gives me pleasure to commend it highly as containing accurate and complete reports on business matters relating to buildings in this section." While residing in St. Paul, Gilbert also maintained a nonresident membership in the Architectural League of New York, which he claimed to have helped create during his earlier career in New York, and he submitted examples of his work for the league's annual exhibitions beginning in 1886.

While in St. Paul, Gilbert worked to increase the stature of the architectural profession and to foster architectural sophistication in the Twin Cities. He also helped to nurture the young draftsmen who worked for him. Among those draftsmen in his St. Paul office who went on to distinguished careers of their own were Thomas Holyoke (1876–1925) in Minnesota and Stevens Haskell, Guy Kirkham, Harry J. Carlson, and others who later moved to New York and the East Coast.[40] Once he was well established in the profession, Gilbert also sent several of his talented young draftsmen to study at the Ecole des Beaux-Arts.[41]

Gilbert was among the founders of the St. Paul chapter of the American Institute of Architects (AIA) in 1892, the same year he became a fellow of the AIA. He served as president of the Minnesota Chapter of the AIA for three terms beginning in 1893 and also became a director (board member) that same year. Gilbert continued his tradition of service to the profession throughout his long career. He eventually served as president of many prestigious and influential organizations, including the AIA (1908–09), the Architectural League of New York (1913–14), the American Institute of Arts and Letters, and the Council of Fine Arts. First established by President Theodore Roosevelt in 1909, the latter became the Commission of Fine Arts in 1910. Gilbert continued to serve as a member of the commission during the presidency of William Howard Taft and resigned when Democratic President Woodrow Wilson was elected. Finally, he served as President of the National Academy of Design (1926–34).

1-4. Gilbert & Taylor, Dayton Avenue Presbyterian Church, St. Paul (1886–88), in 1964. (Photograph: Eugene D. Becker, Minnesota Historical Society)

Gilbert's first office was located in the Gilfillan Block in downtown St. Paul where a number of young architects had offices, including Clarence Johnston, James Knox Taylor, and Charles A. Reed (later a partner in Reed & Stem of New York and St. Paul).[42] Gilbert's early 1880s projects prior to forming a partnership with Taylor included several houses, summer homes, a double tenement, and a storefront remodeling.[43] Gilbert and Taylor had known each other for years. Both had grown up in St. Paul. They had been friends at MIT and known each other in

New York, where Taylor worked for Bruce Price while Gilbert worked for McKim, Mead & White.

From 1885 until 1892 Gilbert and Taylor built a successful architectural partnership. Many of their clients became repeat customers. The firm designed numerous houses in the fashionable new neighborhoods of St. Paul and summer homes in nearby lake resort communities; they also undertook numerous projects for larger structures such as row houses, churches, office buildings, commercial buildings, railroad depots, and warehouses. Guy Kirkham, a Gilbert & Taylor draftsman, later wrote that ". . . to have been a draftsman in the office of Gilbert and Taylor was a valuable experience. The men had the advantage of personal and intimate contact with the principals. The professional standards of the firm were high, and Mr. Gilbert's scorn of the petty graft then prevalent among material men, his impatience of amateurishniss, his insistence on definiteness and accuracy, his abhorrence of sloppy workmanship, were impressive."[44]

The Gilbert & Taylor partnership ended during a period of economic depression when Taylor moved to Philadelphia. Taylor eventually became the supervising architect of the U.S. Treasury and was thus responsible for federal buildings constructed throughout the country from 1897 to 1912. In this capacity he oversaw several federal projects designed by Gilbert.

Young Gilbert and Taylor experimented with a variety of styles, and they borrowed details from an eclectic variety of sources including the Richardsonian, Stick, and Shingle styles. Many of Gilbert's early designs for churches, homes, and summer residences are wood-frame structures that are small in scale, picturesque, and playful in layout and detailing; frequently these designs utilize charming, intimate spaces. One often finds such details as leaded glass, wood paneling, and floor patterns that incorporate layered, adjoining, and intersecting geometric architectural forms based upon diamonds, circles, ovals, and squares. By the late 1880s the partners had begun to experiment with Colonial revival and Italian Renaissance elements. In keeping with the influence of neoclassicism in the years after the World's Columbian Exposition of 1893, many of Gilbert's designs became much more formal, imposing, and symmetrical, and typically they were constructed of brick and stone rather than of wood, as many of his first buildings were.

Gilbert's experiences in studying the church designs of Richardson and others on the East Coast and the cathedrals and parish churches in Europe gave him many inspirations to draw from in designing churches in several St. Paul neighborhoods and Minnesota towns. His early church designs ranged from modest but exquisitely detailed Shingle-style chapels to much more imposing masonry buildings for larger congregations.

One of Gilbert & Taylor's first major commissions was the Dayton Avenue Presbyterian Church at Dayton Avenue and Mackubin Street in St. Paul (1886–88; Figure 1-4). Gilbert's mother, who lived nearby, was a member of the congregation and no doubt played a role in having her son selected as the architect, despite his limited experience in church design. Raising the funds to erect the building was indeed a challenge, and church newsletters from 1886 debated the merits of stone versus less expensive building materials.[45] The Dayton Avenue church was built of inexpensive local limestone faced with rusticated Lake Superior red sandstone. It was constructed at an approximate cost of $36,400.[46] Its Romanesque design appears to have been inspired by two Richardson churches in Springfield, Massachusetts (which Gilbert had visited while studying in Boston), and also, as the church newsletter proclaimed in 1886, by "the Romanesque architecture of France in the 12th century."[47] The church was designed to seat approximately 850 people, and its dynamic first minister, Maurice Edwards (a grandson of Jonathan Edwards), cultivated its membership from approximately 30 members in 1878 to nearly 800 in 1918.[48] Gilbert originally planned to include Tiffany windows for the sanctuary, but these were eliminated due to cost considerations.

In 1886 Gilbert and Taylor designed another Presbyterian Church in St. Paul, the Goodrich Avenue Presbyterian Church at 305 West Goodrich Street, one-half block from West Seventh Street. It was built as a mission of the city's well-established House of Hope Presbyterian Church. Among those involved in organizing the church were Taylor's father, H. Knox Taylor, and later Gilbert client W. B. Dean.[49] As originally designed, it was a Shingle-style building with a massive corner entrance tower with a squat spire shaped like a witch's hat. Although it is standing today, it has been altered extensively.

Another early Gilbert & Taylor church is the Virginia Street Church (Church of the New Jerusalem), at the corner of Virginia and Selby Streets in St. Paul (1887, extant; see Figure 2-2), which was built at an estimated cost of $7,000 for the city's only Swedenborgian congregation.[50] In keeping with the desires of the congregation, the building materials of this Shingle-style building were kept as close to their natural state as possible.

The German Bethlehem Presbyterian Church at 311 Ramsey Street, St. Paul (1887, extant; Figure 1-5), was one of Gilbert's favorite designs from his Minnesota years. It is nestled into the base of the Ramsey Street Hill below the mansions of Summit Avenue. The church was intended to serve the German-speaking residents of the nearby West Seventh Street working-class neighborhood, and its minister, Reverend Nicholas Bolt, a Swiss native, made various suggestions to the architect so that the design would recall the architecture of Swiss mountain chapels.[51] The church cost approximately $8,500 and took only three months to construct. Drawings of it were published in the April 4, 1891, issue of *AABN* and were displayed at the World's Columbian Exposition in Chicago in 1893. Gilbert's brothers reportedly teased him about this design and called it "The Church of the Holy Toothpick."[52]

1-5. Gilbert & Taylor, Little Stone Church (German Bethlehem Presbyterian Society), St. Paul (1887), period postcard, c. 1900. (Private collection)

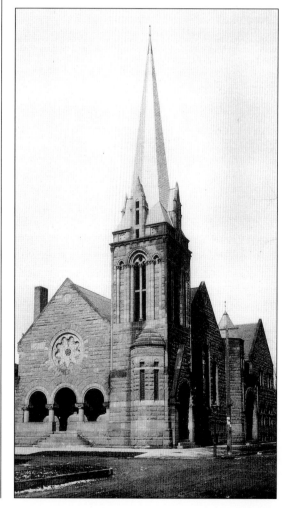

1-6. Gilbert & Taylor, Camp Memorial Chapel, Lake Minnetonka (1887–88), interior in 1983. (Frederick R. Weisman Art Museum, University of Minnesota/ Twin Cities)

1-7. Gilbert & Taylor, First German Methodist Episcopal Church, St. Paul (1892), in *Northwestern Builder, Decorator & Furnisher* 8 (1894). (Minnesota Historical Society)

Camp Memorial Chapel (now St. Martin's by the Lake Episcopal Church) on County Road at Lafayette Bay, Lake Minnetonka Beach (1887–88, extant; Figure 1-6), is a small Shingle-style chapel built for the wedding of the daughter of a Minneapolis lumberman, George A. Camp. It was located along Lake Minnetonka, which at that time was a fashionable summer resort community near Minneapolis. According to local tradition, its design was inspired by a church Camp had visited in Norway. Its unpainted, pine-paneled interior with hammer-beam roof trusses and open-backed pews create an informal, camp meeting atmosphere. Following the wedding, it became an Episcopalian mission chapel on September 2, 1888, and originally was used only for summer services. It was the first of several buildings Gilbert would design for the Episcopal Diocese in Minnesota. Gilbert worked on the project with Episcopalian Bishop Mahlon Norris Gilbert.[53]

First German Methodist Episcopal Church, in downtown St. Paul (1892, since razed; Figure 1-7), by Gilbert & Taylor, was similar in form and plan to the Dayton Avenue Presbyterian Church, but more ornate in detailing and smaller in scale. Its design recalls aspects of Richardson's Brattle Square Church (Boston, 1870–72), which Gilbert had visited. The stonework included some horizontal banding and polychromatic detailing reminiscent of, if less exuberant than, much English High Victorian architecture.

St. Clement's Episcopal Church at 901 Portland Avenue, St. Paul (1894–95, extant; Figure 1-8), clearly demonstrates Gilbert's admiration of English parish church architecture, which he had studied in his travels. *Improvement Bulletin* reported in its August 31, 1894, issue that "Cass Gilbert has plans all prepared for the St. Clemens [*sic*] Episcopal church on Portland Avenue, and the contract has been let. It will be built of solid stone, and fitted up in the most modern style, with slate roof and fine interior fixtures; will be heated with furnaces. Cost, complete, $25,000." *AABN* also reported on this building, which was erected at the expense of Mrs. Theodore Eaton of New York, as memorial to her husband, the late rector of St. Clement's Church.[54]

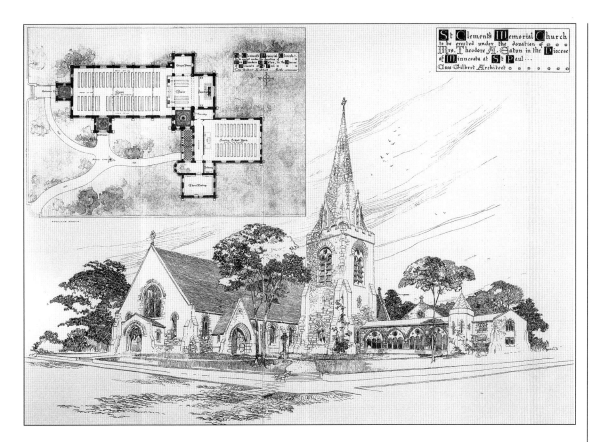

Gilbert received this commission through Bishop Mahlon Gilbert. The intricately detailed, richly colored interior of the church was a marked contrast to the simplicity of the interior of most of Gilbert's other church designs. The plastered walls of the nave were originally painted dark green, while the chancel walls were a deep rose. Various stenciled designs ornamented the arches and reveals of the windows. The floor was originally tiled. Gilbert, Mrs. Eaton, and church officials disagreed about various aspects of the design, especially the windows, and various changes were made from the design as originally proposed. Later, after Gilbert's move to New York City, to Gilbert's dismay Clarence Johnston, rather than Gilbert, was hired to design an addition, as the congregation preferred to award the commission to a local architect.

The Episcopal Mission Church (now St. Paul's Episcopal Church) at 231 South 3rd Street, Virginia, Minnesota (1895, extant) originally was a modest wood-frame church. Described in church records as "of beautiful construction in the Old English style of architecture," it was built as an Episcopalian mission for a town of 3,500 on the Mesabi Iron Range in northern Minnesota. Church records indicate that Archdeacon Appleby brought the drawings from St. Paul to the town of Virginia and he wrote in his journal that:

> . . . we shall build at least two new substantial churches this summer, one in Cloquet [Minnesota], and the other in Virginia, where I hope personally to superintend the work . . . I hope, in order to counteract the baleful influence of forty-two saloons there, to be able to establish a men's club, coffee and reading room . . . Virginia, not withstanding its recent destruction by fire, has a population of 3500 people, and in addition there are twelve mines in the immediate neighborhood. In these mines are several hundred Finns and Cornishmen, among whom our church work will be hailed with delight.[55]

Bishop Mahlon Gilbert was involved in this project also. The church interior was similar to that of the Camp Memorial Chapel and St. John the Divine.

1-8. St. Clement's Espiscopal Church, perspective drawing and first floor plan, in *American Architect and Building News* 48 (June 8, 1895). (Minnesota Historical Society)

A tower and porch were added and later many other alterations were made to the building.

Christ Memorial Episcopal Church was a stone church in the Iron Range community of Hibbing, near Virginia (1896, razed in 1945), built through the influence of Episcopalian Archdeacon Appleby and probably Bishop Mahlon Gilbert. Funds for the construction were provided by a Miss Jane Schmelzel of New York City as a memorial to her father.[56] Its stonework and thin spire recall some of the detailing of the German Bethlehem Presbyterian Church but without the dramatic, picturesque hillside setting and asymmetry. When valuable iron ore was found under the town's streets, an iron company bought the land and in 1919 moved the community one mile south. This church was dismantled, stone by stone, and rebuilt according to Gilbert's design.

St. John the Divine Episcopal Church at 120 8th Street South, Moorhead (1898, extant), was Gilbert's largest and last Shingle-style church design. It has an unpainted pine, cedar, and fir interior that recalls the Camp Memorial Chapel. Its steeply pitched roof almost hugs the ground near its native fieldstone foundation, quarried from the Minnesota lake region, and its design is punctuated by a tall, octagonal shingled tower and spire. The church records note that Gilbert's design fee was a modest $175, probably indicating that he undertook the commission as a charitable project instead of a money-making venture.

Designing these churches sometimes entailed complex negotiations with church boards of directors and ministers and working with congregations with limited budgets and varied opinions. This was valuable business experience for a young architect who would later move on to much larger and more complex public and commercial projects.

1-9. Northern Pacific Railway Building, St. Paul, 1896. (Minnesota Historical Society)

Gilbert welcomed the opportunity to supervise the construction and otherwise assist with the design and building of several major buildings erected in the Twin Cities by East Coast architects. This experience helped to position Gilbert later to secure some of his first commissions in Boston and New York. In 1887, Great Northern Railway "empire builder" James J. Hill (1838–1916) hired Boston architects Peabody, Stearns & Furber to design his Richardsonian mansion on St. Paul's Summit Avenue. Gilbert was given the task of assisting with the adjacent powerhouse, fence, and gates.[57] Gilbert & Taylor were hired by the New York firm of Babb, Cook & Willard to supervise the construction of the New York Life Insurance Building in downtown St. Paul (1887–89, since razed).[58] Gilbert knew the architects from their days together in the McKim, Mead & White offices in New York.

From April 1891 to June 1893 Gilbert worked as the first superintendent of construction for the new federal building on Rice Park in downtown St. Paul that was designed by Willoughby J. Edbrooke, the supervising architect of the U.S. Treasury (1891–1902). This was probably Gilbert's first opportunity to be involved in the construction of a major public building. Gilbert, a Republican, was replaced by another local architect, Edward P. Bassford, a Democrat, when Grover Cleveland's administration came to power in Washington.[59]

Given St. Paul's preeminence as a railroading center in the late nineteenth century, it is not surprising that Gilbert won several commissions for railroad structures.[60] A number of these projects were commissioned by James J. Hill and the various railroads that he controlled. Many of the small depots Gilbert designed show the influence of Richardson, and they combine elements of the Shingle style, Arts and Crafts, and Tudor revival.

Gilbert's early depots include the Great Northern Depot, Anoka (1891, altered), which was a low-lying, one-story brick building that featured a hipped roof with wide, overhanging bracketed eaves and eyelid dormers. The Great Northern Depot, Willmar (1891–92, since razed), was similar in design to the Anoka depot, yet with a central two-story, four-bay, hipped-roof pavilion flanked by one-story, hipped-roof wings, without eyelid dormers. Gilbert also designed the Grand Forks depot on DeMers Avenue in Grand Forks, North Dakota (1892), a rock-faced, two-story stone building with a massive square clock tower with a pyramidal roof. The building survives in altered form.

The Minneapolis and St. Louis Railway Depot, Minneapolis (1891, since razed), was a more ambitious structure. Gilbert's diary notes that he called on Hill at his office on December 24, 1891, to consider plans for this building, which he was working on as conversations began for another Hill project—the St. Paul Seminary.[61] As a one-story, hipped-roof structure, the depot followed the same formula as the Anoka and Willmar depots but on a larger scale. Its brown pressed-brick walls were trimmed with Kettle River sandstone window and door surrounds and quoins.[62]

The Northern Pacific Railway Building, Broadway, between Prince and East 4th Streets, St. Paul (1896, since razed; Figure 1-9), was located at the edge of the Lowertown wholesale and warehouse district adjacent to an earlier Northern Pacific headquarters building that had been designed in 1883 by New York architect Bradford L. Gilbert (who was not related to Cass).[63] Cass Gilbert's massive five-story brick structure had a rusticated stone first-floor base with segmental arched window openings and round-arched Richardsonian doorways. Projecting three-story oriel bays were topped by Renaissance-inspired, rounded arched windows set in pairs within a larger round arch.

The Fargo, North Dakota Northern Pacific Railway Passenger Depot at 701 Main Avenue (1898–1900, extant; Figure 1-10), is a low-lying Richardsonian building with a two-story central pavilion. It is constructed of brown pressed brick with Lake Superior red sandstone trim. The building has been adapted successfully to a new use as a senior citizens' center.

The Little Falls, Minnesota Northern Pacific Railway Depot at 200 First Street Northwest (1899–1900, extant), was built for what was then a major point along its railroad line. Gilbert's steeply pitched roofed, fanciful design combines Shingle-style and

Arts and Crafts influences. The building is now the home of the Little Falls Chamber of Commerce.

Gilbert would later draw on his earlier experiences in designing several railroad depots of various sizes in cities on the East Coast.

After working on several smaller commissions for James Hill, Gilbert became the architect for the St. Paul Seminary (also known as Hill Theological Seminary; now part of the University of St. Thomas; partly extant) at 2115 Summit Avenue. Gilbert designed six seminary buildings that were built between 1892 and 1896 at the end of Summit Avenue over-

looking the Mississippi River (Figures 1-11 and 1-12). An 1895 account described the original buildings at the seminary as being "in the Northern Italian style, simple solid and impressive" and added that they "are all built of red pressed brick, have either plain gable or hipped roofs, and by the solidity of their walls remind one strongly of the monastic edifices of a bygone age."[64]

The complex was made possible by a gift of $500,000 (for both construction and endowment) from Hill, who was not Catholic although his wife was. On May 15, 1892, from Rome, Archbishop John Ireland wrote to Hill that "I enjoyed my last audience with the Pope. He spoke to me at great

1-10. Northern Pacific Railway Passenger Depot, Fargo, North Dakota, 1898–1900. (State Historical Society of North Dakota)

SOUTH DORMITORY

1-11. St. Paul Seminary: aerial view, St. Paul, c. 1921. (Minnesota Historical Society)

1-12. St. Paul Seminary: South Dormitory, St. Paul. (Archives of the St. Paul Seminary)

OPPOSITE
1-13. Gilbert & Taylor, Endicott Building, St. Paul (1888-90), in 1941. (Minnesota Historical Society)

length of his appreciation of your princely generosity in building our Seminary, and of the great honor thereby conferred upon the church in America."[65]

Hill was intimately involved with Gilbert and Archbishop Ireland in working out nearly every aspect of the design and construction of the seminary. Hill was very concerned about stretching every penny, as numerous letters suggested. Several aspects of the project were hotly debated, including the use of sandstone as a foundation stone, the type of brick for the building exteriors, and payment of Gilbert's final bill. For example, on December 12, 1892, Hill reminded Gilbert, ". . . I notice some omissions and changes in the plans. I do not desire any changes to be made without its first being submitted to me. Even if you have made an error in the plan, as submitted, you must, before making changes, resubmit it. Two or three things have already crept in that have apparently increased the cost, and I am not willing that this should occur again under any conditions. . . . I would rather stop the work than have a lot of uncertainty."[66]

Hill's St. Paul Seminary was the first and probably most modest and severe of the several campus plans and school and college building designs that Gilbert completed in his career. Gilbert also did several designs for the Episcopalian Shattuck School for Boys in Faribault, Minnesota, in the mid-1890s. Construction on the armory at Shattuck began in 1894.[67]

Gilbert was approached by Archbishop Ireland about designing the Cathedral in St. Paul. In early 1905, while visiting St. Paul, Gilbert related to his wife, Julia, a visit to the state capitol with Archbishop Ireland the night before: "We had the great building to ourselves except for the attendants. He and I promenaded the corridors alone for an hour then sat in the commissioner's room and talked cathedral. He tried to induce me to enter the cathedral competition. I declined. . . . I have thought of it many times today . . . on the back of this letter is sketched what I think I should do if I had accepted his invitation. . . . It was a romantic evening, last night, and one that I will long remember." Gilbert added that he was convinced Ireland would not forget it either. Gilbert's

sketch that accompanied the letter was labeled "Study for the Cathedral of St. Paul, ["Romanesque"], and includes his French sources: "Clermont Ferrand-Apse, Constances-Towers, and Arles-Porch."[68] Eventually designed by a French-born Ecole des Beaux-Arts–trained architect, Emmanuel Masqueray, the cathedral was constructed in subsequent years (1906–15). The elegantly domed prominently situated Beaux-Arts building provides a visual counterpoint to Gilbert's nearby state capitol. Both landmarks over-

look downtown St. Paul and help to shape the city's rich architectural character.

Gilbert & Taylor's first major office building was commissioned by investors William and Henry Endicott of Boston. The elegant six-story, Italian Renaissance–inspired Endicott Building is located in the heart of downtown St. Paul at 141–143 East 4th Street and 350 Robert Street (1888–90 with later additions; Figure 1-13). Although it appears to be a palazzo-like block, its looks are deceiving, as it encompasses two adjoining structures at right angles, wrapped around the Pioneer Press Building located at 336 Robert Street (Solon S. Beman, architect; 1889). The Endicott enjoys facades on two streets—one with a central atrium and the other with a barrel-vaulted glass shopping arcade.

The building garnered considerable media attention. *Northwest Magazine* reported in July 1890, for example, that "during the day sunlight is mellowed by the colored glass off the roof and at night the rows of electric lamps flood the promenade and . . . the shops and offices with dazzling light."[69] A commemorative publication issued in 1891 recounted every detail of the building's construction and boasted that "[t]he Architects, Gilbert and Taylor, set their hearts upon having everything developed with a nicety which New York architects had never dreamed of, but which was imperatively required by the Italian Renaissance style. . . ."[70]

The building was Gilbert & Taylor's first to command widespread attention from eastern architectural critics. It also was admired by well-known Chicago architect Daniel Burnham.[71] A writer in *Cosmopolitan* stated that the Endicott Building made him "wonder, indeed, if this can be the west."[72] Critic Montgomery Schuyler compared the Endicott Building to the nearby New York Life Insurance Building in St. Paul (Babb, Cook & Willard, 1887–1889) and noted that a ". . . still smaller voice of scholarly protest seems to be emitted by the design of the neighboring Endicott arcade, the voice of one crying, very softly in the wilderness. So ostentatiously discreet is the detail of this building, indeed so minute the scale of it, and so studious the avoidance of anything like stress, and

1-14. Paul H. Gotzian Building, front elevation, St. Paul, 1895. (©Collection of the New-York Historical Society, neg. #56378)

1-15. Chamberlain/ Boston Clothing House Block, St. Paul (1895), c. 1914. (Photograph by C. P. Gibson, Minnesota Historical Society)

the very effort for understatement, that the very quietness of its remonstrance gives it the effect of vociferation."[73] Upon its completion, Gilbert moved his office to this building, where it remained until 1910 when he closed his Minnesota practice. An addition to the building in 1911 extended the arcade to 5th Street. By the time the Endicott Building was completed in the early 1890s, Gilbert had begun making fairly frequent trips to the East Coast, cultivating prospective clients and renewing friendships with those in architecture and the decorative arts.

By the late 1880s and early 1890s, Gilbert was beginning to expand his repertoire to include retail, office, wholesale, and factory buildings. Several of these were built for Boston real estate speculators and a number were in the growing Lowertown wholesaling district of St. Paul, which is now a National Register Historic District. An 1890 article by Condé Hamlin in *New England Magazine* captured the flavor of this area: "The massive structures where lie supplies for the Northwest well nigh shut the sunlight out of the narrow streets on which they stand. With quiet dignity the immense trade goes on, but no casual passer-by would suspect its extent. Near these warehouses are the railroad buildings, the nerve centers for lines that feed thousands of miles of country. . . .The history of St. Paul is so short it is largely connected with business, for necessaries come before luxuries."[74]

Gilbert & Taylor published "Study for a Store Building at St. Paul, Minnesota" in the May 5, 1888, issue of *AABN,* indicating their interest in obtaining this type of commission. Their design (which was probably not realized) was for a narrow, five-story, stone-faced building with a simple first-floor storefront and round arched window openings on the upper floors. Gilbert & Taylor also tried to obtain the commission to design a new Board of Trade Building in Duluth, but a Duluth architect ultimately was awarded the job.

Looking for commissions beyond the Twin Cities also led the firm to design a retail store building in St. Cloud, Minnesota. The three-story, brick and stone C. D. Kerr Store in St. Cloud, Minnesota (ca. 1888), featured Richardsonian Romanesque detailing, such as the round arched window openings and squat engaged columns with simple capitals.

Built at a cost of $65,000, the Conrad Gotzian Shoe Company building at 242 East 5th Street, St. Paul (1892, extant), is a five-story Romanesque-inspired building in St. Paul's Lowertown. It served as the shoe factory of Conrad Gotzian, a German-born manufacturer who settled in St. Paul in the 1850s. In 1883 Gilbert had designed a row house for Gotzian's son-in-law, Theodore L. Schurmeir, who was a vice president for the Gotzian Company, a real estate speculator, and a dry goods merchant.

The Boston Northwest Realty Company Wacouta Street Warehouse, at 413 Wacouta Street (1893–1894, extant), was built for a Boston-based realty and investment firm and located in Lowertown. It features a straightforward treatment of materials with little ornamentation. A civic booster publication of the era described it as "one of the best business structures in St. Paul" and noted its early use as the T. L. Blood Northwestern Paint Works.[75] A photograph of the building appeared in 1897 in the *Brickbuilder,* and a drawing was published the following year. The Boston Northwest Realty Company later commissioned Gilbert to design various other buildings, including a store and office building in Duluth and two warehouses in Minneapolis.

The Paul H. Gotzian Building at 352 Wacouta Street, St. Paul (1894–95; Figure 1-14), is a narrow structure housing a shoe factory, offices, and wholesale stores built for the son of Conrad Gotzian.[76] *Improvement Bulletin* reported on December 14, 1894, that "P. H. Gotzian is having plans prepared by Cass Gilbert for a warehouse which he will have built on Wacouta Street, between 4th and 5th Street. It will be 40 x 100', three stories and basement of pressed brick and stone, and have iron beams, plate glass, gravel roof. Cost $15,000." The completed structure, however, is five stories high. Similar in design to the earlier Wacouta Street Warehouse, the Gotzian warehouse features polychromatic brick and stone trim and a rounded arch window motif. In 1896 Gilbert designed a house for Gotzian's business partner George W. Freeman, and in 1903 Gilbert associate Thomas Holyoke designed a house for Paul Gotzian.

The Gotzian Building provided the sole illustration on the Exhibition of the Boston Architectural Club published in *AABN* in 1899.

The Chamberlain/Boston Clothing House Block, St. Paul (1895, since razed; Figure 1-15), marked the transition in Gilbert's commercial work toward his experimentation with elaborate, glazed white terra cotta. This four-story, steel-frame department store building at 6th and Robert Streets was owned by a St. Paul attorney, E. D. Chamberlain. A book published by the local newspaper in 1897 proclaimed that this structure is ". . . a marvel of architectural skill, beauty and elegance, and a notable feature among the building of the city, is of iron and terra cotta and is of a most attractive and artistic character."[77] The editors were more impressed with the speed of construction (a mere 129 days from demolition of the site's previous building to the date of occupancy) and its terra cotta roundels, figures, and other detailing executed by the American Terra Cotta and Ceramic Company of Chicago, where Johannes Gelert was the sculptor.[78] An elevation drawing of the building was published in 1898 in the *Brickbuilder*.

In February 1893, Gilbert was appointed to serve on the national jury of selection for architecture at the World's Columbian Exposition in Chicago, giving him the opportunity to renew and expand his friendships with the leading East Coast and Chicago architects of the day, including Richard Morris Hunt, Stanford White, Daniel H. Burnham, and Dankmar Adler. He also submitted an unsuccessful entry for the design of the Minnesota Building at the fair. (Minneapolis architect William Channing Whitney won the competition.) Drawings and photographs of three buildings designed by Gilbert were exhibited at the fair: the Endicott Building, the German Bethlehem Presbyterian Society's church, and a cottage on Manitou Island at the resort community of White Bear Lake, north of St. Paul.

1-16. Brazer Building, Boston (1895), in 1983. (Photograph by Sharon Irish)

In the early and mid-1890s Gilbert submitted unsuccessful entries in several other design competitions, including one in 1890 for the American Fine Arts Society Building in New York, another for the Montana capitol (1894), and possibly still another for a courthouse in Baltimore (1894).[79] Gilbert's experience with the Columbian exposition may have served him well in preparing his entry for the Minnesota capitol competition, discussed in chapter 5. Gilbert won the competition in 1895 and construction began the following year. The Minnesota capitol project brought him the national prominence he had long been seeking, and became his ticket to success elsewhere in the country. Edith Seabury Nye, the daughter of Channing Seabury who had overseen the state capitol project as vice president of the Board of State Capitol Commissioners, recalled the fatherly side of Gilbert during this period when she addressed the New Century Club in St. Paul on March 3, 1937, by saying that ". . . to me he was also the simple delightful person who was never too busy to draw pictures for us children."[80]

Even while working on the Minnesota State Capitol, Gilbert in 1895 was devoting considerable attention to the design of an office building in downtown Boston, the eleven-story, Beaux-Arts Brazer Building (Figure 1-16) at the southeast corner of Devonshire and State Streets, which was completed the following year.[81] This structure remains one of Boston's finest examples of architectural terra cotta, and it was the city's third steel-frame skyscraper.[82] Many other commissions on the East Coast followed. Gilbert soon became less interested in Minnesota projects, although he never fully turned his back on the Minnesota architectural scene.

Gilbert opened an office in New York City in March 1899 to work on his first New York City project: the eighteen-story Broadway Chambers Building at the intersection of Broadway and Chambers Street opposite City Hall Park, which had been commissioned by a Boston client. The following year Gilbert and his family moved to New York.[83] Although his focus had shifted to New York, Gilbert could not resist several later projects in Minnesota. Among these were the Mannheimer Fountain at Como Park in St. Paul (1906); a City Beautiful–inspired master plan for the University of Minnesota campus in Minneapolis (see Figure 15-8); his design for the Soldiers and Sailors' Memorial Monument at Daniel H. Burnham's Civic Center/Courthouse Square on 1st Street West between 4th and 6th Avenues West in downtown Duluth (1919–21, sculpted figure by Paul Bartlett), and his design of the Beaux-Arts, colonnaded Federal Reserve Bank (1922) at 73 5th Street South in downtown Minneapolis, his last major work in Minnesota.

Shortly before his death, Gilbert would describe his experience in St. Paul as follows:

> The whole period in the west was exceedingly interesting but very trying and arduous. My spare time was given to writing and illustration but as my practice grew I had to give these up. Some silly newspaper stories have been printed as alleged biographies which give the impression that I had desperate struggles with poverty and came of the usual "poor but honest parents." There is nothing in them—except of course that I was not a good business man, had the usual disregard for money as such and had to learn by experience and under conditions of responsibility to provide means in advance. Temperamentally I detest business. Practically I have had to lick it into shape. I was never a "bohemian" in the usual sense of the word, but just an ordinary young fellow with his mind bent on his art and so intent on it that everything else was second to it. I wanted to fight my own problems and did not want to make myself a burden on the family resources. I had the best of training in the biggest and best of universities—namely the university of the world. It gives no diplomas, confers no degrees.[84]

Gilbert had a profound impact in shaping the architectural character of St. Paul and Minnesota during a crucial period of its development, initially through introducing the latest East Coast architectural styles during St. Paul's residential building boom of the 1880s and early 1890s, and later by designing major buildings that are among Minnesota's most beloved landmarks. During the period from Gilbert's death in 1934 through the heyday of the modernist movement, the great body of Gilbert's Minnesota work (other than the capitol) was largely forgotten and unappreciated both in his adopted home state and among architectural historians generally. As part of a growing appreciation for historic preservation and historic architecture, interest in Gilbert and his architecture has grown since the 1980s. In Minnesota there is a growing appreciation for buildings ranging from modest charming chapels and wood-frame homes to landmark buildings such as the Endicott Building and the capitol. Now, owning a Gilbert-designed building has a certain cachet in St. Paul. A nonprofit organization (the Cass Gilbert Society) has been formed to promote interest in his architecture, researchers are working to discover previously unknown works from his prolific early career, and Minnesotans are quick to claim Gilbert as a native son who did well. Were he alive today, Gilbert would be very pleased that his works of a century and more ago are being widely recognized and appreciated by yet another generation of admirers.

CHAPTER 2

LAUNCHING A CAREER:
RESIDENTIAL AND ECCLESIASTICAL WORK
FROM THE ST. PAUL OFFICE

Thomas R. Blanck and Charles Locks

When Cass Gilbert left McKim, Mead & White in 1882, his intention was to set up an independent architectural practice in St. Paul, Minnesota. He recognized that McKim, Mead & White gained its clients by moving in the same social circles, often designing a client's city residence, summer cottage, and commercial building. Gilbert followed that model when he returned to St. Paul. He joined the Minnesota Club, the Minnesota Boat Club, the Nushka Club, the St. Paul Tennis Club, and the German Club. He belonged to a prominent social circle, and he worked to build his architectural practice through the assiduous cultivation of every professional and personal connection he could identify.

Gilbert did not return to St. Paul without prospects. McKim, Mead & White's parting gift to him was the job to execute for the firm certain Northern Pacific Railway projects in Minnesota and as far west as Montana. What created this opportunity for Gilbert is unclear. William H. Whidden, another employee of the firm, was already designing buildings for the railroad in the West and Midwest. One scenario would be that the office was expecting more railroad work than Whidden could handle. Another possibility is that the western territory was divided between the two men as a favor to Gilbert. In any event, Gilbert carried out the work between Minnesota and Helena, Montana, and Whidden carried out the work between Helena and the West Coast. Gilbert's commissions included hospitals in Brainard, Minnesota, and Missoula, Montana, and depots in Mandan, North Dakota, and Helena.

Henry Villard, whose brother-in-law was married to Charles McKim's sister, was an important McKim, Mead & White client. A European-born journalist who had covered the Pike's Peak gold rush before becoming a financier, Villard, in 1881, gained control of the Northern Pacific Railway.[1] Villard was an avid builder, and in 1883 he was on top of the world. McKim, Mead & White was designing a sumptuous six-unit townhouse project for Villard on Madison Avenue in New York. Also, railroad buildings were being built in the West and Midwest and more were needed.

Renting space in the Gilfillan Block, where his friends and colleagues Clarence Johnston and James Knox Taylor also had offices, Gilbert hired Christopher G. LaFarge, George L. Heins, and a third draftsman identified only as Waterfield and set to work.[2] All the Northern Pacific projects in the contract from McKim, Mead & White were designed and built in 1883. Gilbert was credited with the design work on these projects, although he submitted the plans to McKim, Mead & White for approval. Expectations of more railroad work helped promote considerable correspondence about Gilbert's office becoming McKim, Mead & White's western branch, but even as Villard was heading west from St. Paul to Gold Creek, Montana, in the fall of 1883 to celebrate the Northern Pacific Railway's connection to the Pacific Coast, his fortunes were fading.[3] When Villard lost control of the Northern Pacific Railway early in 1884, plans for further railroad construction faded, along with talk of Gilbert's office becoming the western branch of McKim, Mead & White.

Although Gilbert and McKim, Mead & White never worked together after 1883, Gilbert remained in contact and on friendly terms with the partners of his former firm. William Mead wrote him in 1883 that McKim, Mead & White would uphold him on anything he did.[4] Plans to join forces in 1887 for the New York Life Insurance Building in St. Paul did not come to fruition because Babb, Cook & Willard, another New York-based firm, won the contract, although Gilbert & Taylor did supervise construction of the building. Some years later when Villard was back on top at the Northern Pacific Railway, Mead would contact Gilbert about working together on a hotel project in Winnipeg, Canada, but the project would go to the St. Paul firm of Millard & Joy. Gilbert would continue to correspond with members of his old firm. Stanford White invited Gilbert to his wedding.[5] Despite circumstances that rendered the two firms competitors but never collaborators, in a spiritual sense Gilbert's St. Paul office did become the western outpost of McKim, Mead & White.

In many respects, McKim, Mead & White was the successor to Henry Hobson Richardson. Both McKim and White had worked as Richardson's draftsmen, and McKim, Mead & White practiced the innovative and eclectic architecture promoted by Richardson. At McKim, Mead & White, Gilbert received training in both the business and the art of architecture, and he practiced in that tradition. Always intending to be part of the national architectural community, Gilbert sought important projects around the country and exhibited his designs nationally.

It is apparent that Gilbert made a conscious decision to seek his clientele from the carriage trade, not that any project was too small nor any client too impoverished or too diminished in stature for his services. Because the carriage trade was by its nature conservative, Gilbert's biggest liability was his age.

Gilbert was the sort of man they wanted to do business with, but not just yet. Still, the typical Gilbert client would be a New England Yankee blueblood with a law degree and business interests, men exactly like his own grandfather, a Yale graduate and the first mayor of Zanesville, Ohio, Gilbert's birthplace.

Gilbert was in many respects a Victorian gentleman, but he stopped short of embracing Victorian architecture. His first designs were eclectic but strongly influenced by the Shingle style. Early in his career he borrowed freely from the Richardsonian and Queen Anne styles, but significant for Gilbert was that these architectural styles, especially Queen Anne, made it artistically possible for him to experiment beyond stylistic limitations of the past.

Historically, American architectural "styles" were derived from England. Even the styles that originated in continental Europe were often Anglicized before reaching America. A few architects at various times rebelled against this influence. In the last half of the nineteenth century, one of the most important rebels was Richardson, who believed that Gothic revival—the style predominant in England that would later be usurped by Queen Anne—was too Catholic for the straightforward American sensibility.[6] Indeed many proponents of Gothic revival embraced it with a religious fervor, as if their cathedral-building forebears did have a special relationship with the Deity. Richardson looked instead to the older, simpler Norman architecture, the Romanesque style that had been introduced to England about the time of the Norman invasion. He exhibited a fondness for massive buildings of quarry-cut granite and sandstone with round-arch door and window openings.

In England during the 1860s, Richard Norman Shaw and Eden Nesfield developed a style that they referred to as "free classicism." It quickly became known in England and America as Queen Anne, although it had little to do with that monarch, who had been dead one hundred and fifty years when her name was appropriated. Red brick (crafted into sunflowers, cherubs, and swags in areas of ornamentation), white trim, irregular facades with multi-paned windows in varying patterns of placement, and steep,

complex roofs were the hallmarks of the English Queen Anne style.

The success of the designs inspired by Shaw and Nesfield was in great part due to the wave of nostalgia spreading across England at the time. Their picturesque buildings evoked romantic feelings of a bygone era. Fueled in part by the Centennial Exhibition of 1876, that nostalgia grew in America too. Queen Anne, Shingle, and Colonial revival styles all emerged within a few years of each other, and each of those styles took its inspiration from the past.

The Queen Anne style in America found its greatest success in wood as opposed to brick. The entry porch, corner tower, high brick chimneys, horizontal window bands in gables above the entrance, stucco, and half-timbering were all elements of Queen Anne. One reason for the tremendous popularity of the Queen Anne style was the advent of the machine age and the availability and affordability of materials. Turn-of-the-century builders' catalogs advertised mass-produced Queen Anne windows, doors, trim, and all manner of columns, porch posts, and railings.[7]

From Queen Anne evolved the Shingle style. Shingle-style designs tended to emphasize the horizontal rather than the vertical. Frivolous ornamentation was reduced or removed from exterior walls. Surfaces that were covered by tile or slate in Europe were covered in wood shingles. But an important aspect of Shingle-style buildings was not simply the shingle-clad exterior but the evolution of interior space, especially the transformation of the formal entry hall into the modern living room. This new informality was also promoted in American Queen Anne architecture.

McKim had restored an eighteenth-century house in Newport, Rhode Island in 1872, and his interest in colonial architecture led to a celebrated and well-publicized New England trip in 1877 to explore the roots of Yankee architecture.[8] Mead, White, and William Bigelow (McKim's brother-in-law and White's predecessor in the firm) all accompanied McKim. The ensuing revival developed along two distinct lines. One set of practitioners rediscovered the conservative joy of the precise duplication of the American colonial idiom. Another set of practitioners selected elements from colonial architecture and applied them artistically in a new form. Gilbert initially belonged to the latter group, but as Colonial revival became one of his favorite styles, he expanded his repertoire to include both viewpoints.

Colonial revival was the most enduring of the architectural styles that evolved during the era. It was popular in the Midwest until World War II. Apart from the construction of new "colonial" houses in the early decades of the twentieth century, the exteriors of many Queen Anne and Italianate houses were remodeled using Colonial revival elements. Because of its relative fragility, the porch has often been the first original design element of a house to be lost. Roofs and windows followed. Shingle-style houses, by their very nature, are rural and sprawling and the least suitable for urban housing. Queen Anne style is a curious case. Because of its ubiquity, it is often most associated with "Victorian" architecture and most often deemed old-fashioned. Yet, whether suburban builders are aware of it or not, modern variations of Queen Anne seem to be the dominant style in today's subdivisions all across America.

Between 1883 and 1911, Gilbert's St. Paul office produced approximately 180 designs that took three-dimensional form in stone, brick, and wood. Nearly half of those projects were residences. Important early residential clients in 1883 were his mother, Elizabeth W. Gilbert, Theodore L. Schurmeier, and Dr. William Davis.

Gilbert designed a Shingle-style house at 409 Laurel Avenue for Dr. William Davis, a native of Massachusetts, who became the Gilbert family doctor. The strongly asymmetric composition and the shingled dormer were attempts to create a romantic profile, but the narrowness of the front facade and the corresponding depth of the building reduce the effect. The Davis House was not the largest, smallest, best- or worst-designed of Gilbert's houses, but it is likely Gilbert's connection to the brother-in-law of Davis, Thomas G. Holyoke, who roomed at 409 Laurel Avenue for most of forty years until his death in 1925. Gilbert employed eighteen-year-old Holyoke as a draftsman in 1884, and the two men worked together for nearly twenty years until Holyoke went off to practice on his own in 1904.

The Theodore L. Schurmeier House was originally located at 189 Virginia Avenue.[9] The detailing of the front gable with its courses of shingles, pebbles imbedded in stucco, and half-timbering was current with the work of McKim, Mead & White, and Gilbert would use elements of this design in the front gable of the Goodrich Avenue Presbyterian Church. In 1887, Clarence Johnston would win the contract for the Aberdeen Hotel, which would be built on the site. The house was moved to its present location at 130 Virginia Street, where it was altered somewhat in its reconstruction. Schurmeier was a principal in the dry goods firm of Lindeke, Warner and Schurmeier and a director of First National Bank. He was married to Caroline Gotzian, the daughter of Conrad Gotzian, founder of C. Gotzian and Company, a manufacturer and jobber of shoes and boots, for which Gilbert would design two commercial buildings in downtown St. Paul (see figure 1-14). Gilbert would also design houses for Gotzian's son, the company's secretary and treasurer, and for George Freeman, the company's president.

Another project undertaken in the first year of Gilbert's practice was the Elizabeth W. Gilbert House at 471 Ashland Avenue. The original house was more modest than the building that exists today. Gilbert himself remodeled it at least twice, and when the family sold the property to E. C. Stringer in 1902, it was remodeled again. Still, many features of the design are original, including the Richardsonian porch details and the Queen Anne windows. The attic windows provide important geometric accent to the shingle surfaces. An attractive interior detail of the Elizabeth W. Gilbert House is the design of the fireplace in the front entry. Squares of sky-blue glass cover the fireplace, a design feature Gilbert possibly borrowed from the Ross Winans House (1882; see Figure 1-2), where blue glazed tile on the fireplace provides the only color in the wood-paneled front hall.[10] Then again, Gilbert could have used as his model the fireplace at Richardson's Ames Gate Lodge (1881), which is covered with blue glass designed by The Tiffany Glass Company. Just determining the

2-1. Gilbert & Taylor,
J. Q. Adams House, St.
Paul (1884), in
Picturesque St. Paul,
ed. J.G. Pyle (St. Paul,
1887), pl. 30. (Private
collection)

source of this tiny detail presents overwhelming problems, which exemplifies the difficulty of determining the source of many of Gilbert's design elements.

In 1884, Gilbert designed a house for John Q. Adams, a grain dealer who was reputed to own one of the finest libraries in the Northwest. The Adams House (Figure 2-1) at 2 Crocus Hill was a brilliant design. Photographs of it were published in *Picturesque St. Paul* and in architectural journals of the era.[11] The house features Queen Anne massing with Richardsonian detailing in the stone and arches at grade level. Windows and window trim are in the mode of Colonial revival. The shingled second story was intended to be set off by pebble-imbedded stucco in the third-story gables, but in its construction, shingles replaced the stucco. Gilbert would later design a house for Adams's son on adjacent property. Both houses have been razed.

During the summer of 1883, the first three cottages were built on Manitou Island at White Bear Lake. Just as Easterners had discovered seaside vacations at spots on the Atlantic coast, St. Paul's elite discovered White Bear, a beautiful spring-fed lake ten miles north of St. Paul that in 1882 Mark Twain touted as *the* resort in the Twin Cities.[12] It took several years to develop the island, but by the 1890s, Manitou Island was among the most prestigious summer communities in Minnesota. Today it is among Minnesota's most prestigious year-round communities. Scattered along its wooded shoreline are thirty houses, including four survivors of the ten cottages that Gilbert designed on the island.

An important 1884 cottage that Gilbert designed at 2523 Manitou Island was for Charles P. Noyes. Noyes was in partnership with his brother, D. R. Noyes, and his brother's next-door neighbor on Summit Avenue, E. H. Cutler. Noyes was a Yankee blueblood from Connecticut who came to St. Paul in 1868, the year the Gilberts arrived. He was a director of several banks and businesses and a member of the

Minnesota Boat Club, Town and Country Club, Minnesota Club, and the Informal Club when it was founded in 1894. He was also prominent in the Presbyterian Church. Noyes had previously built the "Red Chalet," a Stick-style cottage (extant) on the western shore of White Bear Lake. The Manitou Island cottage is a modest Shingle-style building. It features a rusticated fieldstone foundation and an arch that is blended and finished with brick, a design Gilbert was using in the Barnum Cottage at the same time and would use later in the stairway of the Virginia Street Church. Surrounding porches on all four facades are fitted with shingled railings. The canted dormer and the ventilator/chimney design are modest elements exploited to the greatest possible effect. The cottage served as a prototype for other summer cottages Gilbert would design. This small project was so important for Gilbert that he presented his client with four watercolor renderings. The Noyes Cottage was razed in 1951.

In 1885, Gilbert and Taylor became partners. It has been long suggested that Gilbert coveted Taylor's social connections. Taylor's father, H. Knox Taylor, was prominent in real estate and in House of Hope Presbyterian Church. He was a trustee of the Baldwin School and treasurer of the St. Paul Library Association and later treasurer of Macalester College. In selecting a partner, Gilbert was certainly looking for as many social connections as he could find; however, Taylor's social connections had provided him only modest success during the previous two years that he had been in independent practice.[13] Also, for Taylor to want to join Gilbert, Taylor must have perceived that Gilbert was bringing something to the new firm. It is logical that by joining forces, each gained the social contacts of the other, and it is likely that their individual talents tended to be complementary. Still, it cannot be overlooked that the two men had become strong friends and would remain so for the rest of their lives. In addition to becoming partners, they roomed together with other friends in downtown St. Paul. It was a Bohemian existence. Their quarters were referred to as "poverty flat," and on other occasions, "the monastery," and the habitués were referred to as "monks."[14]

In 1885, Gilbert & Taylor received commissions for three church projects. Two were for "mission churches" for St. Paul's three established Presbyterian churches. The new buildings were to be constructed for the Dayton Avenue Presbyterian Church and the Goodrich Avenue Presbyterian Church. House of Hope Presbyterian Church likely led the way in the building of these new churches as it had assisted in the establishment of Dayton Avenue Presbyterian Church, going so far as to ask a few families to move from House of Hope to the newly organized church to help it get started. Taylor's father and Gilbert's client, Noyes, no doubt were influential in assisting Gilbert & Taylor to win the projects. Taylor's father was an elder at House of Hope, and Noyes was a trustee and important benefactor.

The Goodrich Avenue Presbyterian Church at 305 Goodrich Avenue is the only Queen Anne-style church that Gilbert & Taylor designed. Horizontal bands of tongue-and-groove wainscot, bevel siding, half-timbering, and cedar shingles are all divided by moldings, details that were used a year earlier on the Schurmeier House. Its Shingle-style tower is notable for its tapered, mitered-square design. Like many of Gilbert & Taylor's churches, it was built without a basement. About 1930, the building was raised four feet, a basement was built, and the building was extensively remodeled, incorporating brick and stucco as major elements of the exterior. A second entrance was added then. All that remains today of the original composition are the nave windows and the lower portion of the tower.

The Dayton Avenue Presbyterian Church at 503 Dayton Avenue is Richardsonian in style (see Figure 1-4). Following the "Akron Plan," the popular plan for Protestant churches, the primary entrance is located in the tower and the sanctuary resembles an auditorium. The floor slopes to the altar, and there is no basement under the sanctuary. It is a large building and was an important accomplishment for Gilbert & Taylor. The Gilbert family would join the Dayton Avenue Presbyterian Church after the building was erected. The stained glass, in mostly abstract patterns, is richly colored. Gilbert tried to contract with The Tiffany Glass Company to build windows for the

2-2. Gilbert & Taylor,
Virginia Street Church,
St. Paul (1886), in
c. 1964. (Minnesota
Historical Society)

project, but the budget was so meager that Tiffany's representative, John DuFais, responded that even if they had no other work, they could not afford to make the windows at the price Gilbert offered.[15] (DuFais would become Gilbert's partner in the winning design for New York's Union Club [1901–03]. Twenty years later, the tables would be turned and it would be Tiffany soliciting Gilbert's business.[16]) In 1903 Gilbert designed a large hall for the building. In 1910 he designed a Sunday school–addition.

The third project was for St. John the Evangelist Episcopal Church at 495 Ashland Avenue. The portion of the existing building generally attributed to Gilbert & Taylor is adjacent to the alley and once housed Barnard School, but the building permit has not been found. The church moved to the site in 1881, and a wood church was constructed. Gilbert & Taylor designed a lean-to addition to the wood church in 1886. Also, documentation shows that Gilbert & Taylor supervised the installation of

plumbing and heating at the site. A letter on Barnard School stationery describes the existing stone building that was built a year earlier to house the school and serve as a guildhall. The wood church was replaced in 1889 with a stone building that was connected to the existing Barnard School building. A fire later destroyed the new building, and it was rebuilt in 1907 and again in 1917 after another fire. The original Barnard School building was damaged but survived the fires. The building was converted to condominiums in the early 1980s after being home to a succession of Christian congregations. The simple Gothic design features a trefoil window in the gable above a bay window and a shorted and relocated flèche.

Lucius P. Ordway's first house in St. Paul was designed by Gilbert & Taylor and built at 257 Summit Place, which was located on the site of St. Paul Technical College. Ordway was a partner in Crane and Ordway Company, a plumbing supplier.

Ordway later took control of 3M Company, and the Ordway family would become one of the most prominent in St. Paul. It certainly didn't hurt Gilbert & Taylor to get the commission, but it is not known whether Ordway had much influence at the time, as he was only twenty-two years old. Gilbert's relationship with Ordway lasted for some years, and they were close friends. During one period when Gilbert's mother was out of town (Gilbert did not cook), he stayed at Ordway's for several days.[17] Ordway, along with Gilbert and other friends, owned an interest in a boat at White Bear. Ordway later bought out his partners.

The church-building business continued in 1886. Gilbert & Taylor designed the Virginia Street Church (Figure 2-2) at 170 Virginia Street for a Swedenborgian congregation. Several of the congregation's members were originally from Boston, where the Church's seminary is still located. A classic Shingle-style design, it is among the more innovative of Gilbert & Taylor's churches. The foundation is constructed of fieldstone. The arches in the porches include Richardsonian details done in wood. The tower and belfry proportions seem quite original in design but may have come from Germany. Hammer beams support the barrel-vaulted ceiling, and the double-hung, leaded-glass windows in the north and south walls are original. The windows have a border of amber-colored bottle-bottom glass. The top sashes carry diamond-shaped panes, and the lower sashes are composed of small square panes. Yellow and blue are the predominant colors. The windows on the west facade have been replaced. Gilbert & Taylor used the Virginia Street Church tower design as a model for two other churches: the South Park Congregational Church in South St. Paul and the Camp Memorial Chapel in Minnetonka Beach.

Many design details employed by Gilbert and Gilbert & Taylor were borrowed from Richardson, including many of those incorporated into the

2-3. Gilbert & Taylor, Lightner-Young House, St. Paul (1886), in *Picturesque St. Paul,* ed. J.G. Pyle (St. Paul, 1887), pl. 68. (Private collection)

Virginia Street Church. Although Richardson's brand of Romanesque gradually lost influence, declining along with the century, its last gasp taken in county courthouses, it is difficult to overestimate his influence on American architecture. Aside from the architectural style named after him, included in his designs are some of America's earliest Shingle-style and Queen Anne–style houses. Just before his death in 1886 at age forty-seven, his peers ranked five of his buildings among the ten best in America.[18] Gilbert and Gilbert & Taylor designed few buildings in the Richardsonian style except for the Dayton Avenue Church, the First German Methodist Church, and two houses for William H. Lightner. It is impossible to know what was going on in Gilbert's mind when

2-4. Gilbert & Taylor, D. W. McCourt House, St. Paul (1887), in 2000. (Photograph by Bill Kelley)

he designed the Lightner-Young House in the year of Richardson's death, but today one likes to think he did it as a tribute to the man Stanford White referred to as the Great Mogul.[19]

The double house at 322–324 Summit Avenue (Figure 2-3) was designed for two law partners, Lightner and George B. Young. The facade is purple Sioux quartzite. While it is decidedly Richardsonian in style, Gilbert & Taylor introduced several of its own details to the building, including a heavily carved gable, diamond-patterned carvings on stone railings, and a massive shingled dormer that carries two of Gilbert's favorite details—a sawtooth edge on the lowest row of shingles and a raised, curvilinear

design that is a canoe-sized version of an eyebrow window. On different facades and different floors, the windows vary in style and design. Some have decorative wood muntins; others are leaded glass. Young was born in Boston, and he attended Harvard College and Harvard Law School. He practiced law, but he was also a partner of Luther Cushing in the St. Paul Land Company.[20] He purchased Noyes's "Red Chalet" on White Bear Lake after Gilbert designed Noyes's Manitou Island cottage. Young was a descendant of Thomas Mayhew, who in 1641 became patentee, proprietor, and governor of Martha's Vineyard, Nantucket, and the Elizabeth Isles. Young was buried in Edgartown, Martha's Vineyard, and Gilbert designed his monument.

Gilbert & Taylor's most exquisite urban Shingle-style design is the Dr. D. W. McCourt House (Figure 2-4) at 161 Cambridge Avenue, built in 1887. Although modest in size, its well-integrated design successfully occupies a site where all of the building's facades are highly visible. The exterior displays a skillful juxtaposition of volumes and voids. Portions of the first story are stucco, and the fireplace is exposed on the exterior for volumetric effect. Porch posts are round and shingled in a rather personal adaptation of the Shingle style. Again, window design provides one of the most individual stylistic themes in Gilbert's residential architecture. In the McCourt House, the device is an interlocking pattern of ovals that could be mistaken for a modern treatment. The stairway window is influenced by the Queen Anne style, and the wood muntins divide a double border of small rectangular panes on the perimeter, while the center is filled with a radial pattern of curving muntins. McCourt was a dentist. He sold his house to George O. Somers and moved a few doors down on Princeton Avenue. The barn was designed for Somers in 1897 by Gilbert, which explains why it fits well with the house. The barn's primary design features are its roofline and the projected gable over the hayloft door.

The building of America's railroads was one of the great undertakings in the nation's history, and it profoundly changed the nature of society and the country. Railroads provided millions of workers with jobs, and the incredible wealth railroads created made thousands of investors millionaires. Not all of the companies were well managed: Northern Pacific Railway received tens of millions of acres of federal land and yet managed to bankrupt itself twice. Still, railroads became the single most important force in unifying the country. For architects like Gilbert and Taylor, the importance of railroads was twofold: it provided the opportunity to design buildings for the railroads, their owners, and their better-paid workers, and railroad travel made it feasible to create truly national architectural practices. Also, local street railway systems hastened the platting of large additions to cities. In St. Paul, the street railway system allowed for the development of Macalester Park where the McCourt House is located.

In an 1887 letter to his fiancée, Gilbert chronicles a day's activities. In the morning, he traveled forty-five miles by train to New Richmond, Wisconsin, where he inspected the construction of the O. W. Mosher House. From New Richmond, he traveled thirty miles by train to Ellsworth, Wisconsin, where he inspected the J. L. Moody House. Later in the day, he traveled another thirty miles, also by train, probably to inspect the house at 459 Eighth Street, Red Wing, Minnesota. He returned to St. Paul at eleven o'clock in the evening.[21]

Just as his tour took him all over the regional map, the buildings he inspected are all over the architectural map. The New Richmond house is conservative and sophisticated. Strongly influenced by the Shingle style, the eclectic design features a three-story Queen Anne bay on the front facade. The front porch was originally supported by Doric columns, adding to the formality of that facade, while the circular wood posts of the rear porch are shingled in the manner of the McCourt House—the only two buildings in which Gilbert is known to have employed this design detail. The building's front porch has been replaced.

The Ellsworth house is eclectic for all the wrong reasons. Either the design was uninspired, or Gilbert was not in control of its execution. A few of the details are excellent. Some are certainly Gilbert's handiwork but are unsuccessful. Others make little sense.

For instance, the eaves are designed differently on three facades. Some rake boards are shingled, some curve at the eaves, and others bear unrelated moldings.

The Red Wing house shows a clever young architect fussing over every creative detail in turning a mid-nineteenth-century farmhouse into an eastern Shingle-style-inspired romance. A remarkable design, it was the least costly and is the most interesting of the three buildings. The exterior was completely re-detailed, and a gambrel roof tops a two-story addition. The porch railing is composed of large up-ended pieces of sponge rock taken from a riverbed, and the ceiling of the porch is constructed of hundreds of carefully mitered wainscot boards.

The New Richmond, Ellsworth, and Red Wing houses are all L-shaped and all have front porches that project beyond the building's mass. Gilbert never used this porch design again, which was typical of how he worked: three times and out, then on to another intriguing detail to explore.

Nearly all of Gilbert & Taylor's early residential work was influenced by the Shingle style. The firm's first major departure was the A. J. Seligman House (1887) at 802 Madison Avenue, Helena, Montana (Figure 2-5). In the Seligman House Gilbert & Taylor employ a clearly stated American colonial element. The colonial wing combines the medieval overhang and diamond-shaped, leaded-glass windows of the seventeenth century with the gable, bay, and siding of the eighteenth century. The balance of the house is a mixture of American colonial and Queen Anne elements. By 1887, Colonial revival was well established on the East Coast, but it had not reached Helena, a city built largely in the Queen Anne vernacular. By designing one half of the house in the accepted Queen Anne

2-5. Gilbert & Taylor, A. J. Seligman House, Helena, Montana (1887), c. 1900. (Collection of Tim Coulter and Samantha Sanchez)

style, Gilbert & Taylor could experiment with the other half.

Noyes was an early and loyal Gilbert client. The C. P. Noyes House (Figure 2-6) at 89 Virginia Street is one of the earliest Colonial revival houses in St. Paul and a most appropriate design for Noyes. The Noyes's ancestral home, the "Old Noyes House" in Newbury, Massachusetts, dates from the 1630s. Newbury was a destination of McKim's field trip in 1877, and McKim, Mead & White is credited with popularizing Colonial revival. One joy of the Colonial revival is its playfulness in exploiting traditional American colonial forms. In the Noyes House, eighteenth-century colonial details combine in a fashion that could only happen at the end of the nineteenth century. Although there are bits of color in the main stairway windows, particularly important is Gilbert & Taylor's use of clear leaded glass. Derived from the austerity of American colonial architecture, this is a feature common to Gilbert & Taylor's houses. The location of the front door is an example of Gilbert & Taylor's whimsy. The porch is centered on the symmetrical front facade, but the door is not.

Gilbert & Taylor was hired to design a bowling alley for the Wabasha Club at 155 N. Western Avenue in 1890. That same year, the firm designed the Town and Country Club at 2279 Marshall Avenue (see Figure C-8). E. W. Peet, for whom Gilbert designed a stable in St. Paul and a cottage at Manitou Island, was chairman of the building committee. Town and Country was the first club designed by Gilbert & Taylor, and Gilbert would remodel it in 1897. Now located in the center of the Twin Cities metropolitan area, it was on the outskirts of St. Paul in 1890. The club's Shingle-style design conveys a distinct rural appeal. The Town and Country Club, the nation's second oldest golf club still operating on its original site, is going strong, but the Gilbert & Taylor clubhouse has been razed.

Gilbert, after being absent from St. Paul for many years, returned in 1930 to work on plans for the Capitol Approach. Apart from the capitol, the buildings he wanted to see were his house at 1 Heather Place and the German Bethlehem Presbyterian Church at 311 Ramsey Street (see Figure 1-5), a building Gilbert & Taylor designed in 1890. Niklaus Bolt, a native of Switzerland, organized the congregation, which met at the Goodrich Avenue Presbyterian Church until its own building could be constructed. House of Hope Presbyterian Church and Noyes were major contributors to the church building. While nominally Shingle style, this building has no precedent, although some of the design inspiration comes from romantic mountain buildings of Germany and Switzerland. Only two of the facades are highly visible, but the success of its design rests on the serious attention Gilbert & Taylor paid to all four facades. The S-shaped stairway and hillside setting are not unlike some of Gilbert's drawings from his days at MIT. The congregation disbanded in 1916—no doubt partly the result of anti-German sentiment fostered by World War I—and the disposition of the church's two-hundred-year-old altar is unknown. The building was taken over by the Gargoyle Club, an extant architects' eating and drinking society that included Edwin Lundie among its founders. An important Minnesota residential architect, Lundie served an apprenticeship with Gilbert and later was a partner of Holyoke. The Gargoyle Club sold the building during the 1960s, and in the years since, it has housed diverse tenants. Niklaus Bolt returned to Switzerland in 1901 and was a minister in Lugano for twenty-three years. He would also gain considerable fame as a writer of children's books.

In 1889, Gilbert & Taylor obtained the commission for the Endicott Building (see Figure 1-13) at 141 E. Fourth Street. It offered Gilbert his first opportunity to employ elements of the Italian Renaissance—his great architectural love—in a large building. Gilbert used this theme in other commercial buildings, most notably the T. L. Blood and Company Warehouse (1893). Gilbert & Taylor moved its

2-6. Gilbert & Taylor, C. P. Noyes House, St. Paul (1889), c. 1965. (Minnesota Historical Society)

office into the Endicott, and the office remained there until it closed for good in 1911. The local architectural firm of Reed & Stem also had an office in the Endicott, as did the Minnesota State Capitol Commission.

The Endicott Building was the largest project the firm designed; critics, fellow architects, and the public applauded it, but its success did not provide enough momentum to sustain the firm in the difficult years that followed. In 1891, Gilbert and Taylor dissolved their partnership. Gilbert moved downstairs into a smaller office on the fifth floor of the Endicott, and Taylor looked for more lucrative business opportunities in the East.

If there were bright moments in 1891, the brightest was certainly the day that James J. Hill became a client of the firm. Although it was too-little-too-late for the partnership, Hill's work kept the office going. Gilbert was hired to finish some details at the Hill House at 240 Summit Avenue after Hill fired his Boston-based architects, Peabody & Stearns. Beyond designing the wall and fence, it is unclear what Gilbert's other duties were at the mansion, the largest house ever built in Minnesota. Gilbert also set about the task of designing Great Northern Railway depots in Grand Forks, North Dakota, and Willmar and Anoka, Minnesota. He also remodeled St. Paul's Union Depot and designed a depot in Minneapolis for the Minneapolis and St. Louis Railway, a railroad under Hill's control.

In 1892, Gilbert was named a director of the American Institute of Architects. A few months later he was elected to the state chapter, a formality that was probably necessary to allow him to qualify for the national post. This unusual sequence suggests that from the beginning of his practice, Gilbert did not consider himself and was not satisfied being a "Minnesota" architect. It points to the fact that he saw himself as part of the national architectural community. He was as interested in what McKim, Mead & White and Bruce Price were doing in the East as in what Clarence Johnston and Reed & Stem were doing close to home. He did not ignore the work of his local contemporaries; he merely placed that work

in the context of what was happening nationally and determined much of it did not meet East Coast standards, his standards.

In 1892, Gilbert's philosophy and ego collided with Hill's during the design and construction of the Hill Theological Seminary on Summit Avenue (now a part of the University of St. Thomas). Hill, not known to have belonged to a specific church but a financial supporter of dozens, financed the seminary for his Roman Catholic wife. The client was ostensibly Archbishop John Ireland, but it was really Hill, and he demanded the final say on every detail. It was more about control than money, although it is likely that Hill, basing his stance on both business and religious principles, was not enthusiastic about Gilbert and Ireland creating more than a bare-bones campus. The two collaborators would come to agreement about various design details, but Hill, upon reviewing the plans, would reject them. He also regularly gave Gilbert a dressing-down if during construction the slightest changes were made without his approval. The resulting design for the six buildings is as utilitarian and lacking in ornamentation as the office buildings of Hill's railroad.

It is likely that squabbling over the Hill Seminary strained the relationship between Hill and Gilbert to the breaking point. Gilbert's last project for Hill was the design of a Triumphal Arch erected on Sixth Street in downtown St. Paul for the ceremony that commemorated the Great Northern Railway's connection to the Pacific Coast in June 1893, ten years after the Northern Pacific Railway had completed its connection. The depression that followed the Panic of 1893 was the worst in the nineteenth century. The Northern Pacific Railway would again go into bankruptcy. Hill's railroad, on the other hand, remained solvent. It is unclear how much of the success of the Great Northern Railway to survive during the depression was due to Hill's stewardship or the deep pockets of his financiers, of whom J. P. Morgan was one.

Business was not booming in 1893, but a few good projects came into the office. One was for William Lightner, the law partner and neighbor of George B. Young and husband of Carrie Drake, daughter of prominent St. Paul businessman E. F. Drake. At the time his new house was being constructed, Lightner served on the Common Council (St. Paul City Council). He later served as vice president and president of the Minnesota Historical Society (as E. F. Drake had). He was a member of the Minnesota and Town and Country clubs, and the St. Paul Tennis Club, and the White Bear Yacht Club. He also belonged to the Minnesota Boat Club, and rowing was one of his passions. Lightner, who had outgrown or grown tired of his house at 322 Summit Avenue, hired Gilbert to design a house next door at 318 Summit Avenue (see Figure 2-3).[22] The design is the most Richardsonian of all Gilbert's residential efforts and one of the most poetic. Its great success is the integration of every element of the facade into the whole. The scale, balance, and surface textures of the composition all contribute to the effect. Here, purple Sioux quartzite is banded with Kettle River sandstone. The detailing—including the brick pattern-work under the eaves, layered masonry and moldings, and bands of windows between columns—is exquisite. Gilbert mixed and matched wood-muntin windows with leaded-glass windows as he had done in the Lightner-Young house. Gilbert also designed a stable for Lightner and an additional stable for Young.

While most of Gilbert's Colonial revival houses were merely gracious, he also sketched a number of grand designs. The William B. Dean Cottage at 2552 Manitou Island was the first grand design that was built. The lakeside elevation is treated as the primary facade and it features a two-story colonnade that is closely related to the river-facing facade of George Washington's home at Mount Vernon. The approach to the Dean Cottage features a two-story, semicircular portico. Gilbert would remodel the building in 1903. The influential Dean and his family became important Gilbert clients. The previous year Gilbert did work for the father of Dean's prospective daughter-in-law, E. W. Winter, at 415 Summit Avenue. The following year, Gilbert would design a house for Dean's son and his new wife. One of Dean's daughters married Dr. Archibald MacLaren, another Gilbert client and friend, and as a member of the

Women's City League, she would work with Gilbert on city-planning issues. Dean, in his official role as state senator, would author and guide legislation that provided for the construction of the Minnesota State Capitol, a project Gilbert would win in 1895.

Of all Gilbert's club memberships, the one that may have most promoted his career was the Informal Club, a neighborhood discussion group of about fifty members.[23] Begun in 1894, the club is still in existence. During the years that Gilbert was active in the group (1894–1900), the club's meetings were held in many neighborhood residences, several of them designed by Gilbert. The Informal Club displayed to St. Paul's elite a continuing three-dimensional, life-size exhibition of Gilbert's work—the living rooms of his clients, including the mahogany interior of the brand-new Lightner House.

Along with clergy, educators, and important men of business, members of the Informal Club included the governor, who was ex-officio president of the State Capitol Commission, the commission's vice president, and the state senator who sponsored the capitol funding legislation. Noyes was a member of the club, as were about a dozen other Gilbert clients, including R. B. C. Bement, for whom Gilbert designed a city residence at 27 Summit Court (1888) and a cottage at 2509 Manitou Island (ca. 1890). Bement was also a member of the building committee at St. John the Evangelist Episcopal Church. Gilbert & Taylor had previously designed a guildhall for the old church (1885–86) at 495 Ashland Avenue, and Gilbert was asked to design another guildhall for the new church (1895) at Portland Avenue and Kent Street. Although the building has Gothic overtones, the style Gilbert selected was half-timbered, which had been reintroduced to America in the eclectic details of the Queen Anne style.

When the guildhall project came along for St. John the Evangelist Episcopal Church, Gilbert was working on St. Clement's Episcopal Church (1894–95) at 901 Portland Avenue, a proper English country church constructed of yellow limestone in the style of Gothic revival. Mrs. Theodore A. Eaton of New York funded the church as a memorial to her late husband, the rector of New York's St. Clement's

Church. The funding provided for twenty-one Tiffany windows, one of which was later donated to St. John the Divine Episcopal Church in Moorhead, designed by Gilbert in 1898–99.[24] Attending the dedication of St. Clement's was J. P. Morgan, who praised Gilbert for his design.[25] The budget of the St. John the Evangelist congregation was more modest. The congregation was unable to raise enough money to erect the church building until 1902, after Gilbert had moved to New York. Clarence Johnston was given the commission for the church, in part because he was a "local" architect.[26]

Like St. John's Guildhall, the half-timbered style of the C. W. Bunn Cottage (1895) at 2550 Manitou Island (see Figure C-9) is in the character of the English cottage of the Jacobean or Tudor periods, yet elements of the design could only have happened in the nineteenth century—specifically, the large Shingle-style porch on the lake facade and the size, number, and style of windows. What is important about this design is not its resemblance to English buildings but its application of European detail to American architectural problems. The Bunn Cottage was razed in 1978. It is the greatest regional loss of Gilbert's residential work.

Gilbert was among the first generation of architects who were to build national practices. Transportation aside, this expansion of operations created another level of complexity in an already difficult profession. Large architectural firms found the need to employ hundreds of workers to keep their many projects staffed. In modern architecture, this has led toward the division of tasks and the necessity of specialization.

Gilbert's method of operation was more suited to the older atelier system of training, where the eager students would cluster around the master to watch his pencil and listen for the words that would direct them toward future success. This system reached its absurd destination at Taliesin. The cult-like atmosphere twisted the aim of the enterprise, so that for many students, leaving Frank Lloyd Wright became an exercise in self-excommunication, instead of embarkation on a great adventure.

Men leaving Gilbert's employ often expressed a keen loyalty toward their former boss. Harry J. Carlson, a former employee who found work first with Richardson and then at McKim, Mead & White before returning to Gilbert to run the Boston office for the Brazer Building project, wrote that he and Stevens Haskell frequently and religiously read Gilbert's instructions on how to proceed in the attainment of their professional goals. Ending his letter, Carlson asked: "May I sign myself as one of your boys?"[27]

Gilbert behaved in a formal manner toward his employees, always referring to them as "mister," but there seems to have been a level of freedom and camaraderie in the office that satisfied both Gilbert and his draftsmen. Three of his key employees, Thomas Holyoke, George Carsley, and Stevens Haskell, at one time or another left Gilbert's employ (often because of lack of work) only to return when he needed them. Thomas Holyoke worked in the St. Paul office almost until it closed. During the last years, he was mostly on his own but would occasionally assist Gilbert. The cornerstone on the Roselawn Cemetery Chapel (1904) names both Holyoke and Gilbert as architects. In 1912, Carsley would take on the Placer Hotel in Helena. Gilbert would assist him in that enterprise.[28] Haskell, after leaving Gilbert's employ for the second time, formed a partnership with John O. Marchand, and they had offices in New York and Montreal. Still, Haskell volunteered to go to Cuba for Gilbert to assist him in obtaining the commission for that country's capitol, though it was inconvenient for Haskell.[29]

When Gilbert sold his mother's house at 471 Ashland Avenue in 1902, the new owner wanted some remodeling work done. Gilbert turned the project over to Holyoke, and told Holyoke they would come to an understanding that would satisfy him.[30] When St. Clement's Church was shopping for an architect to build their guildhall, Gilbert told them that if they didn't want to hire him, they should hire Holyoke, "because he understands how I do things."[31] When Shattuck School was thinking about erecting a new building in 1910, Gilbert told them that they could talk to Carsley, because he and Carsley had come to an understanding that gave Carsley a greater interest in the office's projects.[32]

Gilbert had opened a Boston office for the Brazer Building, and he closed it when the Brazer Building was completed. The Broadway Chambers project provided the necessity of setting up a New York office, which was located in the same block as the office of McKim, Mead & White. Stevens Haskell ran the one-man operation and sent daily reports to Gilbert in St. Paul. When the United States Custom House competition began, Gilbert sent draftsmen from St. Paul. Later, Haskell hired additional draftsmen.

The projects came into the New York office so quickly and continuously that there was never a question of closing it. The United States Custom House, the Union Club, the Essex County Courthouse, the Art Building and Festival Hall for the St. Louis World's Fair are examples of the important projects Gilbert landed around the turn of the century. Almost immediately, Gilbert attained the financial success that had eluded him in St. Paul.

2-7. Cass Gilbert, Crawford Livingston House, St. Paul (1898), in 2000. (Photograph by Bill Kelley).

Always the promoter, Gilbert was quick to exhibit and publish his designs, and as his reputation spread, the demand for his work increased. In 1890, John W. Root had asked Gilbert for photographs to accompany an article on western houses that he was writing for *Scribner's*.[33] By the end of the decade, Gilbert was having logistical problems getting his work to several exhibitions. In 1899 alone, Gilbert exhibited at the St. Louis Architectural Club, T-Square Club in Philadelphia, the Chicago Architectural Club, and the Fourteenth Annual Exhibition of the Architectural League of New York, before the traveling show moved on to Boston.[34] He was also planning for the Paris Exhibition of 1900.[35]

In January 1902, Gilbert wrote to his brother that he still maintained his personal residence in St. Paul, though to all intents and purposes he now hailed from New York.[36] That summer his family stayed at East Hampton instead of White Bear Lake, and that fall they moved into a house in New York City.[37] Before moving into their new house, Gilbert had two fireplace mantels installed that he had salvaged from buildings that were demolished for the United States Custom House. As his New York adventure was beginning, Gilbert designed four more Summit Avenue mansions. The most interesting is the Livingston House.

The front facade of the Crawford Livingston House (1898) at 339 Summit Avenue (Figure 2-7) is inspired by Venetian Renaissance sources. In Venice, the vaporetto would have pulled up to steps rising from the canal to the loggia. Here the loggia is a porch that overlooks Summit Avenue—St. Paul's Grand Canal. Gilbert was in New York ready to sail for Europe when he worked out the design for the front dormer.[38] The detailing of the porch columns came to him while he was on the SS Friesland in the English Channel. He wrote his office that the porch capitals should be strong like those in the chancery arch of St. Clement's Church.[39]

After Holyoke left Gilbert's employ in 1904, Carsley took over the operation of the St. Paul office. Not many projects came into the office, but its existence made it convenient to supervise projects in the West and Midwest. Many of these projects were for the Boston Northwest Real Estate Company, a long-time Gilbert client. During the first decade of the twentieth century, Carsley supervised the remodeling of a hotel and department store in Duluth, Minnesota, a warehouse in Minneapolis, and various projects in Montana. Gilbert may have kept the office open for so long after he moved his headquarters to New York because of his own sentimentality and the fact that he liked to keep up with local news. During his many European trips, Gilbert expected daily reports from his office manager as well as weekly letters from essential employees. Another consideration that made it less burdensome to keep the office open was the cheap rent in the Endicott Building. It is likely that Gilbert started out paying market-rate rent, but this rate was not raised uniformly to keep pace with other rents in the building. It was not until 1910 that the rate more than doubled to $105 per month.[40]

The earliest projects in Montana were for the Northern Pacific Railway and the Boston Northwest Real Estate Company. Most of the Boston Northwest Real Estate Company's projects in Montana were difficult remodeling jobs on rather insignificant buildings, but they afforded Gilbert the opportunity to construct a small business network of influential Montanans. Two important men in Gilbert's Montana network were Seligman, for whom Gilbert had designed a house in 1887, and John S. M. Neill, a schoolmate of Gilbert. Carsley, who supervised the construction of many of the Montana projects, certainly helped to promote his boss in Montana, and Gilbert was able to obtain three important projects: the Montana Club (1903), Butte Savings Bank (1906), and St. Peter's Hospital (1908).

The Montana Club (Figure 2-8) at 24 W. Sixth Street, Helena, provides an interesting contrast to both the Town and Country and Union clubs. The original building burned in 1903. Gilbert retained the strongly Richardsonian design of the existing first floor and added four additional floors. The exterior is a mixture of elements that is a marriage of Italian palazzo and Chicago skyscraper. The basement features a rathskeller with its original furniture. The dining room on the top floor has an English interior with diamond-paned, leaded-glass windows on three walls. The decorative shields in the center of the windows are in stained glass and depict western scenes of cowboys, "Indians," and covered wagons.

After Gilbert moved to New York, he continued his involvement in establishing St. Paul's parks and system of parkways. In a 1904 letter to J. A. Wheelock, editor-in-chief of *The Pioneer Press* (St. Paul) and president of the Board of Park Commissioners, Gilbert acknowledged that he was the "official architect of the Park Board," a position to which he had been appointed the previous year.[42] Gilbert made frequent trips to St. Paul and other cities where he had buildings under construction. He also continued to design buildings in Minnesota even after he

closed his St. Paul office in 1911. Important projects were the Federal Reserve Bank (1922) in Minneapolis and his ongoing involvement in planning the Minnesota State Capitol mall (1903–30).

An artist by nature, Gilbert worked exceedingly hard to master the business side of his profession. F. Scott Fitzgerald, a St. Paulite who followed Gilbert east a generation later, once remarked: "The test of a

first-rate intelligence is the ability to hold two opposed ideas in the mind at the same time, and still retain the ability to function."[43] A greater difficulty than simply retaining the ability to function as an artist and businessman is to excel at both.

2-8. Cass Gilbert, Montana Club, Helena, Montana (1903–5), in 1999. (Photograph by Thomas Blanck)

CHAPTER 3
THE POLITICS OF PUBLIC ARCHITECTURE

Geoffrey Blodgett

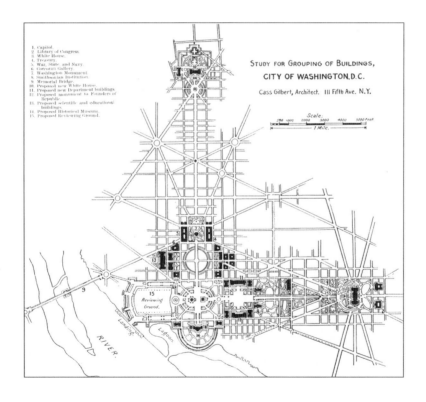

Architecture is a demanding social and political craft. Its practitioners often must use aggressively self-interested tactics to capture potential clients and win juried competitions. Cass Gilbert was very good at meeting these challenges, better than most of his contemporaries. In fact, his special knack for landing big commissions in the public sector led some jealous colleagues to measure their praise for his architectural creations quite sparingly. Even among critics who have judged his work more recently, a clucking note of deprecation or dismay over his aggressive tactics has often seasoned praise for the high caliber of his design solutions.

The lasting distinction of his major solutions in the public sector justifies a close appraisal of the tactics he used to win the chance to design them. There was never any doubt about his ambition. In 1886 at age twenty-six, when he was mostly fashioning homes for his friends and neighbors in St. Paul, he told his fiancée that he wanted to do "great work some day, that will give me the position in the world which will increase my chances of getting [more] great work to do." He added that his ultimate aim was "to stand not only well in, but at the head of my profession." How did he set about trying to gain these lofty goals? One clue is a Ben Franklin adage he wrote into a diary early on: "The sleeping fox catches no poultry."[1]

This chapter focuses on three examples that illustrate Gilbert's lifelong driving search for "great work to do" in the public sector: the Minnesota State Capitol competition of 1894, which brought him national visibility as a young architect on the rise; the New York Custom House competition of 1899, which vaulted his practice from St. Paul to Manhattan; and his climactic political reward, the United States Supreme Court building in Washington, D.C., completed in 1935, the last great commission of his long career.

Like most architects of his generation practicing in the public sector, Cass Gilbert was a Republican in his party politics. No surprise here. Between the Civil War and the New Deal, the administration in Washington was Republican 75 percent of the time, with comparably lopsided statistics for control of the Congress and of the state governments outside the South. The Republican party in the years when Gilbert came of age was the party of Abraham Lincoln, Union victory, whiggish middle-class morality, and government-sponsored economic growth. Meanwhile Democrats were stigmatized not only by the legacy of the Bloody Shirt and opposition to governmental economic activism but also by disruptive class militance among the dirt farmers and immigrant wage workers who joined their ranks.

Gilbert's early Republican preferences became apparent soon after he opened practice in St. Paul in 1882 following his two-year apprenticeship with McKim, Mead & White in New York City. Party pre-

ference deepened into party identity during the decade that stretched from the Haymarket Riot of 1886 to the Bryan campaign of 1896. In their lasting impact, those ten years resembled the depression decade of the 1930s and the youth rebellion of the 1960s, when crisis-forged political loyalties ground into people's minds and remained indelible for years thereafter. In Gilbert's case, the crisis decade from 1886 to 1896 sharpened his mistrust of Populist and Single Tax reformers like Ignatius Donnelly and Henry George, striking labor leaders like Eugene Debs, and Democratic followers of the populistic free-silver inflationist, William Jennings Bryan. To Gilbert and many of his fellow architects, all these people seemed to threaten the broad surge of Republican-sponsored urban growth that crested in the 1880s before coming apart in the 1890s. For architects, urban growth meant a rush of profitable new buildings, and the onset of urban depression could spell quick trouble.[2]

In the fall of 1890 Gilbert, together with his partner James Knox Taylor, felt a sickening slump in their business as the western construction boom began to collapse. Gilbert resorted to his Republican party connections in a desperate search for political patronage to tide him over. He managed to land a party post as construction manager for a big new federal office building in St. Paul (which survives today as that city's recycled downtown Landmark Center). This was Gilbert's first venture into the politics of public architecture, which under the prevailing spoils system of that day required marshalling one's "influence" among politicians of the party currently in power. U.S. Treasury Secretary William Windom, Minnesota's senior Republican politician, gave Gilbert the job after the architect had mustered sufficient support among Minnesota's Republican congressmen and senators. The powerful St. Paul railroader James J. Hill, whose favor Gilbert had cultivated earlier through strategic club memberships, also pitched in his influence. Over the next two years Gilbert drew eight dollars a day from this patronage post, which made a valuable cushion for the sagging business of his firm. The building went up very slowly. The basement was still being excavated when Gilbert gave way to a Democrat after Grover Cleveland returned to the White House in 1893.[3]

THE POLITICS OF PUBLIC ARCHITECTURE

The Wall Street Panic of 1893, which touched off the worst national depression of the nineteenth century, did not spare Gilbert as it rumbled across the country and western banks began to fold. Gilbert was now practicing alone in St. Paul, having dissolved his partnership with Taylor in 1891 for lack of business. Taylor moved east in search of fresh opportunities, and the two friends struggled on separately against hard times.

In the summer of 1893 a bank in Milwaukee holding Gilbert's notes failed, and he spent the rest of the year trying to bring his debts under control. Overdue payments from old clients, combined with fierce competition for suddenly scarce new clients, added to his misery. Meanwhile his two brothers, one in Chicago, the other in southern California, lost their jobs and turned to him for help. He thought of leaving St. Paul himself for the East in search of more stable employment, but all inquiries failed. A leading Boston architectural firm gave him a flat rebuff: "Probably we have no place good enough to offer you. I don't believe we do."[4]

At age thirty-five Gilbert must have wondered some days when and where it would end. A friend wrote to him early in 1894, "I am sorry to hear that you are 'busted.' Hope it will change soon." The birth of his fourth child, Cass Jr., that spring, added an edge of urgency to his search for work. But the architect had long since learned to use adversity to test his own grit.[5]

In mid-March 1894 Gilbert paid a visit to the home of St. Paul wholesale grocer Channing Seabury, a longtime Ashland Avenue neighbor of Gilbert's mother, whose house the architect had designed and lived in during his bachelor years before his marriage to Julia Finch. Seabury had also married a young woman from Milwaukee, and the Gilberts knew the Seaburys well. A gentleman of earnest rectitude, Seabury had recently been elected head of the Board of State Capitol Commissioners charged with creating a new capitol for Minnesota, and the legislature had appropriated two million dollars for the job. Gilbert told Seabury he wanted to come over and have a chat about this project.[6]

He arrived wearing the presidential hat of the Minnesota chapter of the American Institute of Architects (AIA). He had organized the chapter two years earlier in an effort to fortify the status and standards of his profession in the cutthroat competition for choice commissions. In his early conversations with Seabury, and in subsequent meetings with Seabury's board, Gilbert repeatedly made clear not only his interest in the job but also the objections he shared with his AIA colleagues about the terms of the job. They thought the two-million-dollar budget was too small; they wanted close AIA involvement in the competition to select an architect; they wanted the winning architect to control the construction process; and they wanted the architect's fee raised to the standard level demanded by the national AIA. When Seabury failed in his effort to win these concessions from the state, Gilbert organized an effective AIA boycott of the first statehouse competition, and Seabury's board declined to choose among the designs submitted. The legislature then bowed to most of the AIA demands, and a second competition got underway, with Gilbert joining a pack of forty other contestants.[7]

Ever seeking an edge on his competitors, Gilbert included in the commentary on his design the following statement: "I would add that while I would prefer to undertake the whole work on my own responsibility, I am authorized by Messrs McKim, Mead & White of New York to state that I may count upon them as consulting architects should the Board desire." Reminding everyone concerned of his connection with the preeminent architectural firm in the country must have seemed like a persuasive tactic to him. His entry finally won out over four other finalists, but only after Seabury had endured long board meetings heavy with local politics and punctuated by several straw votes favoring other candidates. Finally, Seabury persuaded the board to accept the recommendation of its expert adviser, architect Edmund Wheelwright of Boston, who found Gilbert's design by all odds the best of the lot.[8]

Wheelwright, like Gilbert, had studied architecture at MIT in the late 1870s, and then worked for Peabody & Stearns, the prominent Boston firm whose staff Gilbert knew well. Wheelwright had not rubbed shoulders much with Gilbert in recent years, but by the end of the Minnesota competition they parted on warm terms. When Gilbert sent Wheelwright some photographs of his latest renderings for the capitol, Wheelwright joked that he was going to keep them close by "so that I may refer to them when I build *my* State House" [emphasis added].[9]

Neither Seabury's board nor Minnesota legislators could anticipate that Wheelwright's choice of Gilbert's design for a new statehouse would mark a major advance in the evolving history of this basic American building form. The choice rewarded Gilbert's unquestioned artistic talent, which merged seamlessly with his personal ambition, his professional concern for AIA standards, and his maturing mastery of the classical tradition. He had acquired in his youth a conventional reverence for the "eternal truths" of classical civilization. Decades later he told his wife Julia of his early readings in Greek philosophy: "What led me to read these things when I was a boy is a mystery to me, but I did it—read lots of them—and loved them too. They were my college, all the college I had." His MIT training under architect William R. Ware steeped him in the classical orders and their Renaissance revival. Although his early St. Paul practice registered an eclectic versatility drawn from his apprenticeship with Stanford White, in 1886 he announced the advent of "a second Renaissance" in the artistry of his generation. A little later he put together a lantern slide lecture on the momentous influence of Italian and French Renaissance architecture. His commitment to the neoclassical surge in American public architecture aligned him with the emerging leadership of his profession. It was confirmed not only by his look at the White City of the World's Columbian Exposition in Chicago in the spring of 1893 ("It is a grand, grand sight," he told his wife), but also by the latest work of McKim, Mead & White, including their plans for a new state capitol in Providence, Rhode Island.[10]

By the 1890s the neoclassical tradition had been with Americans for more than a century, although its fortunes rose and fell across that span. The post-Revolutionary work of Thomas Jefferson and Charles Bulfinch made the neoclassical domed temple the most satisfying architectural symbol of the new nation's proud republican aspirations. The Capitol in Washington sustained the republican ideal from its inception in the 1790s, exhibiting in the words of one spokesman "a grandeur of conception, a republican simplicity, and that true elegance of proportion which corresponds to a tempered freedom"—values that prevailed down through the Civil War. But the public architecture of Gilded Age America lost this measured balance. The new state capitols of the postwar era lapsed into an erratic holiday of architectural excess, ranging from the country's largest Gothic revival capitol in Hartford, Connecticut, to the eclectic Romanesque pile in Albany, New York, to the vertically distended, quasi-classical domes of Michigan, Iowa, Colorado, and Texas, to name only the most notorious.[11]

Gilbert was determined to transcend these stylistic aberrations and reassert the purer and more disciplined standards of neoclassicism—"grandeur of conception" and "elegance of proportion," which now ranked at the end of the nineteenth century among the core values of the ascendent Beaux-Arts mood. All this prompted his reach back to the Renaissance monuments of fifteenth-century Italy for the ultimate inspiration guiding his design for the Minnesota capitol.

The most caustic critic of that design turned out to be architect Russell Sturgis, a Ruskinian dissenter from Beaux-Arts doctrine. As the Minnesota capitol neared completion in 1906, Sturgis leveled the awful charge of "copying" against Gilbert's decision to model his marble dome after St. Peter's in Rome.

This charge, echoed in more subtle scholarly language ever since, together with budgetary reservations about the colorful splendor of Gilbert's interior spaces, and rather flatheaded modernist complaints later on over his neglect of functional convenience, never deterred Gilbert from repeated statements that the capitol in St. Paul was the best building he ever created (Figure C-2). The unembarrassed public pride and affection that the capitol continues to inspire among Minnesotans and regional visitors would seem to ratify the architect's considered choice. Even the antique appeal of his didactic mural and sculptural program, executed by the most talented artists he could recruit, including Daniel Chester French, John La Farge, Edwin Blashfield, and Kenyon Cox, still gathers crowds.[12]

Back in October 1895, Gilbert's long campaign to win the statehouse commission left him, in his own words, a "nervous wreck." "When I came through the Capitol competition here . . . ," he told his brother Sam, "I was completely used up for weeks afterwards." But his recovery was swift. His cordial relations with Channing Seabury were enhanced wonderfully by the outcome of the competition and deepened steadily over the next fifteen years as they collaborated to complete their capitol. They even began to hunt ducks together. (Gilbert enjoyed making fun of his colleague's shooting prowess. When Seabury's son sent him snapshots from an outing in the fall of 1903, he replied that he particularly fancied "the patient expression on your father's face where he stands in the blind looking in the wrong direction for ducks.") Despite frequent charges to the contrary in the Minnesota press, never in their long personal interaction from 1894 to 1910 was there any lapse in their circumspect professional conduct toward one another. Still, it is fair to stress that these two proper gentlemen were good friends before Gilbert won the Minnesota job, and good friends afterward, and their gentlemanly friendship never hurt.[13]

More problematic was the role of friendship in Gilbert's victory in the 1899 competition to design the United States Custom House in New York. The Custom House (Figure 3-1) was the first major public building to go up under the terms of the Tarsney Act, an architectural reform measure passed by Congress in 1893 after long years of lobbying by the AIA. Its aim was to improve the quality of federal buildings by allowing architects to be chosen through competition, thus ending the government's habitual reliance on the work of appointed political stalwarts, some of them only marginally qualified as architects. Though the Tarsney Act was applauded widely by the architectural profession, which hoped

that it would somehow institutionalize the cultural glow cast by Chicago's White City of 1893, the law remained unenforced for several years, owing to the refusal of Grover Cleveland's Democratic treasury secretary, John Carlisle, to use it. When Republicans returned to power under President McKinley in 1897, hope rose again that a new era was at last at hand, enhancing integrity in the choice of architects and in the quality of the final results. The Custom House competition would test that hope. Although Cass Gilbert's tactics in winning the competition imperiled the test, the building he created vindicated the hope.[14]

The test got under way when McKinley's treasury secretary, Lyman Gage, with advice from an ad hoc committee of the AIA, chose James Knox Taylor, Gilbert's close friend and former partner, as supervising architect of the Treasury to administer the Tarsney Act.

In December 1898, Gilbert's St. Paul congressman urged him to get in touch with Taylor about the proposed new Custom House, adding what was surely obvious to Gilbert, that Taylor "is in a position to do you a great deal of good." Soon Gilbert was off to Washington to see Taylor and interview Treasury Secretary Gage about possibilities. When Congress finally approved the Custom House project, Taylor wrote to "Dear Cass" asking, "Do you want to be in on it? If so, better file your application from New York City very soon." Gilbert did so the next day, thanking Taylor for the "intimation." Taylor saw to it that Gilbert made the competition's short list of twenty architects—fifteen of them from New York City, two from Boston, two from Chicago, and St. Paul's Gilbert, who had just opened a second office in Manhattan. The other names on the short list were impressive, including Daniel Burnham; Carrère & Hastings; McKim, Mead & White; Peabody & Stearns; and George Post.[15]

The competition jury was less impressive: Jim Taylor in the chair, flanked by Frank Day of Philadelphia, with whom Gilbert had recently served on a national AIA committee, and Thomas Kimball, a thirty-two-year-old practitioner from Omaha who did not belong to the AIA and whom hardly anybody

professed to know. However, both Gilbert and Taylor had met Kimball in the course of their involvement in the Omaha Trans-Mississippi Exposition of 1898. Gilbert suggested Kimball's inclusion on the jury to Taylor. (Taylor passed up Gilbert's other suggestion—Edmund Wheelwright, the expert adviser in the Minnesota capitol competition.)[16]

Meanwhile Gilbert's New York office staff, having taken on a number of talented European-trained assistants for the project, worked feverishly on plans, elevations, and perspectives for his competition entry, determined to render them with "snap and vigor." Gilbert submitted them on September 16, 1899. A cover letter showed his flair for spacious confidence in the mood of imperial nationalism that informed the project: "This building, located upon a conspicuous site, at the beginning of the greatest street in the world, at the entrance of the greatest port of our country, should be given a serious and dignified style. The scale should be large, even grandiose, while not attempting to compete in height with the towering

structures nearby. It should be so impressive by reason of the majesty of its composition, rather than its actual size—it should be truly a monument." Privately he told his wife that his entry was "strong enough to win if they want that sort of thing . . . it is not a copy like so many things now. The whole question now lies 'have I adopted the right type.' If I have, no other of this type will beat it." Two days after his entry was delivered, his brother Sam called on Taylor, who said he hoped that Gilbert would carry the day.[17]

The jury worked with startling speed, taking just four days to reach a strange decision: the entry from Carrère & Hastings and the entry from Cass Gilbert tied for first place. Taylor as chair of the jury had not voted. He called on the tied contestants to meet with the jury in New York immediately. In a letter home to his wife, Gilbert described his rivals with shrill anxiety: "They are moving heaven and earth to get the work. . . . Their prestige is enormous. . . . They are on their own ground, among friends . . . backed by known works of admirable quality. . . . Everything is

3-1. United States Custom House (1899), in 1908, Underhill Collection. (Museum of the City of New York)

THE POLITICS OF PUBLIC ARCHITECTURE

on their side. I stand alone, unadvised, comparatively unknown here, no prestige, perhaps called an 'adventurer.' . . . " [18]

At the meeting in New York, the jury in an odd maneuver proposed that Carrère & Hastings join with Gilbert in patching together a final design solution. Both contestants finally shied from this arrangement, preferring a firm decision one way or the other. Gilbert's report to his wife captures his taut emotions as he waited for the final choice: "I looked in vain into the faces of the jury for the slightest expression of encouragement. And found none! Mr. Day then read the [decision]. It was very brief. I heard my name somewhere in it. Dead silence followed. Then Carrère turned heavily to me and offered congratulations. I put my arm around his shoulder to comfort him. While overcome, not by exultation but by profound sympathy and the sense of deepest responsibility, I thanked the jury and shook hands all around. . . . I couldn't stand the strain, and feeling a sense of almost collapse from the strain, I left the room." [19]

When the announcement went out, it ignited a Manhattan firestorm. New York's Senator Platt was furious at the prospect of losing control of the job patronage for construction of the new three-million-dollar Custom House to a western architect and western contractors. Platt immediately went to the White House to demand presidential intervention against what he called a corrupt decision. Carrère & Hastings in a momentary change of heart fired off a complaint to Treasury Secretary Gage, calling the jury incompetent. Eight other unsuccessful competitors sent their own protest to both President McKinley and Secretary Gage, charging probable collusion between Gilbert, Taylor, and the obscure juror from Omaha, Thomas Kimball. The protesters clearly hoped that McKinley would pressure Gage to use his discretionary authority to overrule the jury. Gilbert hired a lawyer and spent some five thousand dollars in legal fees to combat what he called the libelous charges against him. "I am [up] against the most powerful 'machine' organization and the most wily politicians in the country," he told his wife, "and one can never be safe until the final action is taken." He added in a letter to his brother Charles that "the whole civil ser-

vice merit system of appointment [is] practically on trial." [20]

Gilbert may have stretched things a bit in that last opinion. But in the end it was concern among AIA architects over the viability of the Tarsney Act, which they hoped if used right would introduce merit into the competition for federal commissions, that tipped the final outcome. Forty members of the New York AIA chapter, including Gilbert's main rivals, Carrère and Hastings, met and quietly resolved that it was in the best interests of the architectural profession that the award to Gilbert be accepted. Treasury Secretary Gage made it official the next day. One prominent architect summed it up for the *New York Times* this way: "Had the jury's verdict been set aside it is difficult to see how any architect could have grumbled in the future if the Federal authorities chose to ignore the competitive system altogether." Gilbert himself told the *New York Tribune,* "I am of course pleased at the outcome, both on my own account and because it sustains the Tarsney Act." The Act remained in place for thirteen more years under Taylor's management. [21]

In a letter home to his wife in the fall of 1899, Gilbert inked in at the top of the sheet a sketch celebrating his Custom House victory: a double-masted schooner approaching the Statue of Liberty, with the caption under it, "OUR SHIP'S COME IN. SHE'S IN THE HARBOR NOW!" In his elation he promised his wife a diamond sunburst for Christmas and told her to buy some pretty underwear. As a reward for himself he contemplated "a nice little one-horse coupe with a driver in livery," or maybe even one of the new horseless carriages. The prospect of affluence at last was wonderful to savor. In the end Gilbert's fee from the Custom House came close to a quarter-million dollars. [22]

As the architect intended, the building became a monument not only to the importance of the port of New York but also to the emerging global power of the United States. Its creation coincided fittingly with the climactic events that catalyzed that power. Nine years earlier Captain Alfred Thayer Mahan had published one of the most influential books of that era, *The Influence of Sea Power upon History.* The book inspired many up-and-coming Republican politicians, including young Theodore Roosevelt, to anticipate the entry of the United States on the world's imperial stage through active naval promotion of oceangoing commerce. The end of the great depression of the 1890s, the return of the Republican party to power under McKinley, and then the outcome of the "Splendid Little War" with Spain over Cuba made a chain of events that turned Gilbert's Custom House into a monument for its time. Congressional authorization for the Custom House came just three weeks after Congress ratified the Treaty of Paris, which ended the war by turning Cuba into an American protectorate and forcing Spain to yield the Philippines to the United States. Gilbert's design for the building was chosen within days of Admiral George Dewey's triumphal return to New York City to celebrate his clinching victory at the Battle of Manila Bay. The War turned the Caribbean into an American lake and broke open the Asian rim of the Pacific to American commerce. American power was now not only global but self-conscious and assertive. Of all the memorials to the mood of that war and its momentous consequences, the Custom House can be regarded as the most compelling.

The building's iconography facing Bowling Green was breathtaking. Architectural critic Montgomery Schuyler, writing about the building as it neared completion, confessed doubts about its exterior arrangements, in particular the lack of a sure cadence in the columns along the main entry facade fronting Bowling Green. In this he reckoned without Gilbert's grand program of sculpture to flank the entry—four breathtaking statues emblematic of America, Europe, Asia, and Africa, each rising from its base in front of paired columns in the Bowling Green facade. These figures, the work of Daniel Chester French, and finally installed in 1907, captured contemporary U.S. attitudes toward the four continents with a symbolic candor that can embarrass viewers a century later. Asia is waiting, impassive, and self-contained, seated above a row of skulls; Africa is sound asleep, bare-breasted, obscure in portent; Europe remains secure, established, and commanding; America is young, alert, and supremely

confident about her future. The sculptural program of the building itself mixes nautical allusions with themes of national hierarchy and racial difference, which also dramatized cultural assumptions brought into focus by the war. Seven decades later, critic Brendan Gill praised the Custom House, then an empty relic in need of new functions, for its "look of solemn rectitude and everlastingness." Encrusted with symbolism peculiar to its time, the building receded steadily into the aura of its origins as the new century wore on.[23]

Meanwhile, on the strength of the Custom House, Gilbert's career and reputation ascended decisively. Highly profitable commissions for commercial and institutional buildings began to multiply, and his residential projects dwindled. In 1900 the Gilberts left St. Paul for New York and moved into a West Side Manhattan townhouse. Within another couple of years they migrated to the Upper East Side, and made their way into the city's Social Register. Soon Gilbert was shooting ducks in the Hamptons. A few years after that they acquired a rambling, gray-shingled eighteenth-century country place, the historic Cannonball House in Ridgefield, Connecticut, a cherished retreat for the rest of their lives. Nearly annual journeys to Europe mellowed their summers.

In 1907 Gilbert, at age forty-eight, was elected president of the national AIA, the first of many professional honors awaiting him. He befriended every Republican president from Theodore Roosevelt to Herbert Hoover. William Howard Taft was his personal favorite among them. In 1910 Taft appointed Gilbert to the national Commission of Fine Arts, charged with overseeing the development of the grand design for Capitol Hill and the Mall in Washington, which had been projected by the so-called McMillan Plan of 1902. Gilbert had been actively involved (Figure 3-2) in the inception of this plan. One of its goals was the creation "at no distant day" of a new home for the United States Supreme Court on Capitol Hill. As early as 1899 Gilbert had begun to muse about fulfilling this dream.[24]

Meanwhile the big commissions kept rolling in: New York skyscrapers climaxing in the awesome

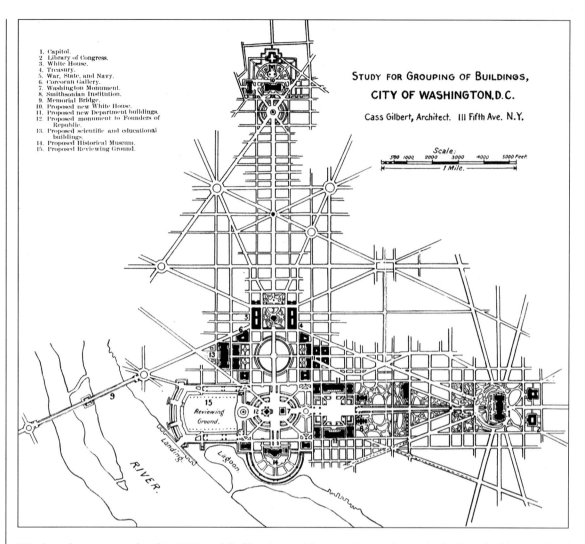

STUDY FOR GROUPING OF BUILDINGS,
CITY OF WASHINGTON, D.C.

Cass Gilbert, Architect. III Fifth Ave. N.Y.

1. Capitol.
2. Library of Congress.
3. White House.
4. Treasury.
5. War, State, and Navy.
6. Corcoran Gallery.
7. Washington Monument.
8. Smithsonian Institution.
9. Memorial Bridge.
10. Proposed new White House.
11. Proposed new Department buildings.
12. Proposed monument to Founders of Republic.
13. Proposed scientific and educational buildings.
14. Proposed Historical Museum.
15. Proposed Reviewing Ground.

3-2. "Study for Grouping of Buildings, City of Washington, D.C.," 1900, from Glenn Brown, comp., *Papers Relating to the Improvement of the City of Washington, District of Columbia* (Washington, DC, 1901), foldout plate. (Library of Congress)

Woolworth tower completed in 1913; public libraries in New Haven, St. Louis, and Detroit; campus buildings in Oberlin and Austin; a notable courthouse in Newark, a train station in New Haven, and city hall in Waterbury; and the last of America's neoclassical state capitols in West Virginia. Good relations with Woodrow Wilson's treasury secretary, William Gibbs McAdoo, brought him commissions to design the U.S. Treasury Annex fronting LaFayette Square in Washington and the remarkably innovative U.S. Army supply warehouse complex in Brooklyn, a commission he landed soon after American entry into World War I.

Across the postwar years, now well into his sixties, Gilbert occasionally acknowledged to his diary that his working pace was slowing down. Plagued now by intermittent sieges of bad health, he felt worn out by the demands of his busy New York office.

Moreover, he was increasingly disturbed by signals of rebellion in his profession against the Beaux-Arts tradition he so greatly admired. This restlessness was symptomatic of a broader postwar alienation from the cultural establishment in which he had prospered since the turn of the century, an establishment now stigmatized as hopelessly ponderous and tradition-bound. He searched for new commissions that might sustain against all the newness the world he had mastered before the war. This was the setting for his final grand reward, long yearned for: the Supreme Court commission in Washington.

In 1921 Warren Harding appointed former President Taft to be chief justice of the Supreme Court. Taft, a large personification of the prewar culture, shared a longstanding Washington dissatisfaction with the cramped quarters in the Capitol where the Court had met since the 1860s. He had started promoting a new building for the Court in 1912. This project gathered momentum when Chief Justice Taft launched a concerted lobbying campaign behind it. He first asked Henry Bacon, architect of the widely celebrated Lincoln Memorial, to come up with a design for the Court's new home. But Bacon died in 1924, just a few months after his temple for Lincoln was completed. Taft next turned to Gilbert for advice, and by 1926 Gilbert was preparing sketches for inspection by the chief and other interested justices. Taft liked what he saw, and beginning in 1928 met regularly with Gilbert, whose seasoned tactical energies were now wonderfully revived in the high arena of Washington network politics. He repeatedly reminded Taft how much he wanted the commission, and kept in touch about his chances with other justices, cabinet members, influential senators, and members of the Fine Arts Commission. He applauded Taft's drive to win congressional authorization for the new building, and supported Taft's moves to prevent the Architect of the Capitol, David Lynn, from interfering with control of the project.[25]

At last in the spring of 1929, Gilbert was officially designated the architect in charge (see chapter 19), and the Fine Arts Commission endorsed his design. Seven months later Congress approved construction bids. "Thus opens a new chapter in my career," Gilbert wrote in his diary, "and at 70 years of age I am now to undertake to carry through the most important and notable work of my life. . . . God grant me strength, courage and intelligence to do it well."[26]

Gilbert's neoclassical design for the building (see Figure C-1) served a number of purposes. Despite its cramped site and proximity to the florid bulk of the Library of Congress, the Court needed to stand with decisive autonomy against the Capitol it faced across the Hill. It must function not only as a symbol-laden monument to justice for the public but also as a secluded workplace for its occupants. And Gilbert was determined that its spatial adequacy as a workplace be lasting. Scholars have cited any number of possible antecedents for the design, ranging from Jefferson's Virginia capitol in Richmond to Theophilus Hansen's parliament in Vienna. In Gilbert's thoughts, the concepts of purity, eternity, and the majesty of

law governed the building's visual impact. His choice of sparkling white Vermont marble for its exterior surfaces reinforced these themes.

Ever more wrenching historical change punctuated the six-year construction process. Taft died and was succeeded by Chief Justice Charles Evans Hughes before the building began to rise. The Wall Street crash of 1929 widened into grim nationwide depression as construction proceeded. President Herbert Hoover, whose reelection Gilbert actively supported, lost massively to Franklin Roosevelt in 1932, and Roosevelt's unprecedented New Deal legislation began to tumble out of Congress the following spring.

The aging Gilbert enjoyed none of this. He mistrusted Roosevelt and feared the New Deal. From what he could tell, Roosevelt had mobilized a headstrong majority that was akin to the militant Democratic and Populist working-class coalitions of his youth, but more dangerous now because Roosevelt promised to service his majority with federal power in ways that seemed to flout longstanding constitutional limits and imperil the economic freedoms of the few. As Gilbert's political anxieties intensified, so did his faith in the constraining authority of the high court whose new home he was preparing. A month after Roosevelt's election, in a talk about the Court to the Bankers Club in New York City, he touched only briefly on the building he had designed, and focused on the function of the Court itself as he now saw it. Above all, he said, "[I]t is a court for the preservation of the rights of the minority—for liberty under law."[27]

Preserving liberty under the law took on urgency in Gilbert's mind as the programs of the New Deal unfolded. When John W. Davis, Democratic candidate for the presidency in 1924 and the most highly regarded constitutional lawyer of the day, attacked New Deal policies as political regimentation destructive of personal liberty, Gilbert lauded his words. "It was time to prick the fantastic bubble which has been developed of wild theories," he told Davis, and concluded at fever pitch, "We are sick of doctrinaires, brain trusts, communists, socialists, and politicians in and out of office." Davis's protest lent authority to Gilbert's insistence that constitutional constraints against the dangers of the New Deal must prevail.[28]

A few months later, in May 1934, seeking his annual respite abroad while his last great work inched toward completion, Gilbert died in Brockenhurst, England, at age seventy-four, his hopes for the Supreme Court—the building and the institution—still intact.

In 1935 the Court marshaled its powers of judicial review to deny the constitutionality of the New Deal's main initiatives, beginning with the National Recovery Administration, whose famous Blue Eagle symbolized its effort to pull the country out of depression. When the justices moved into Gilbert's building in October 1935 to continue their attack, a New York Times columnist noted the obvious linkage between politics and architecture: "The Court did not require a new building to pluck the Blue Eagle's feathers, but the new building does symbolize the power and prestige behind that inexorable depluming." The ongoing judicial assault on major New Deal legislation led directly to the great Supreme Court fight of 1937, which resolved the struggle between the Court and the White House in the New Deal's favor. Right there at the outset of its career, Gilbert's dazzling new citadel on the Hill dramatized the Court's last stand for constitutional conservatism before the New Deal's modern welfare state broke through at last.[29]

The reputation of Gilbert's citadel as architecture fared no better in its early years. A respectful but unenthusiastic silence among architectural colleagues and critics greeted its completion. The only thoroughly positive evaluation of the building to appear in a professional journal came from Cass Gilbert Jr., who nominally took responsibility for finishing the job after his father's death. A few interested observers, including Associate Justices Harlan Fiske Stone and Louis Brandeis, and Gilbert's old friends Frank Bacon and Charles Moore, had earlier expressed private reservations about the building's chilly opulence. Hardly any architectural authority shared Gilbert's faith that the monumental purity of his design would somehow stem the collapse of the beleaguered neoclassical tradition in America. He had written of his temple while it was going up, "I hope it will cause some reaction against the silly mod-

ernistic movement that has had such a hold here for the last few years." As it happened though, exponents of the modernist surge swept past Gilbert's monument with scarcely a passing glance.[30]

It remained for America's most distinguished agent of the architectural newness, Frank Lloyd Wright, to register a few years later his outspoken scorn for the traditions of Renaissance classicism that Gilbert had been trying to assert. Wright chose to put it this way: "When Michelangelo piled the Pantheon upon the Parthenon and called it St. Peters, he, a painter, had committed architectural adultery. . . . It is an imitative anachronism that characterizes our public acts, as illustrated by our capitols, court houses, and town halls. . . . In short, in this present time only the bastard survives even as a temple for the work of the Supreme Court of the United States."[31]

The eclipse of neoclassicism in the shadow of modernism, and the simultaneous decline of Gilbert's standing as a leading classical practitioner, lasted till the 1960s, when the hegemony of the modernists themselves began to lose its grip. A renewed appreciation for Gilbert's historical importance has been spreading ever since. Fresh respect for the integrity and classic beauty of his masterworks, from the Minnesota capitol to the Supreme Court, now makes it all the more important to understand that he was perhaps the most resourceful and successful architectural politician of his age.

CHAPTER 4
THE AESTHETICS OF AN ECLECTIC ARCHITECT

Mary Beth Betts

Cass Gilbert's contemporaries called him a "Master of Style," an epithet that acknowledged his ability to design in diverse historical styles.[1] His repertoire included the neo-Gothic forms of the Woolworth Building, the Renaissance-inspired Minnesota State Capitol, the Georgian-revival New York County Lawyers' Association, and the stripped protomodernism of the Austin, Nichols and Company Warehouse. Gilbert acknowledged his varied tastes: "My friends have sometimes wondered why I do not always work in one style, but my response to this is that I find beauty in so many different things that I like to develop a subject in the style which seems best adapted to the purpose."[2] Gilbert's admiration of historical styles was not limited to Western Europe; he also expressed enthusiasm for Japanese, Byzantine, and American colonial architecture.[3] The statement that he found "beauty in so many different things" became a standard response to a frequently posed question, indicating that even his contemporaries found his eclecticism puzzling. Unlike Gilbert, many American firms at the turn of the century were known and praised for their consistent use of a style. The mature work of McKim, Mead & White was classical; that of Ralph Adams Cram was Gothic. Some firms, such as York & Sawyer or George B. Post & Sons, employed Gothic as well as Renaissance-inspired forms. However, by comparison, Gilbert's breadth of historical references and his facility with diverse styles were unusual.

Today's historians and critics applaud historical references and appreciate the work of McKim, Mead & White, Ralph Adams Cram, and Cass Gilbert. Yet it is difficult to move beyond the identification of historical sources and discussion of context to the aesthetics that shaped their designs. What caused Gilbert to select a certain style for a project? The Gilbert office produced numerous design sketches for every project, studying different configurations, details, and at times, even styles. What, besides the exigencies of budget and client preferences, made the office finally select a certain design? What, for an architect who found "beauty in so many different things," made a design good? The attempt to define Gilbert's aesthetics is complicated by our overall lack of knowledge about the aesthetic standards during this period. With the exception of a few critics, such as Montgomery Schuyler and Royal Cortissoz, there was little critical analysis of American architecture. Articles published about Gilbert's buildings were largely descriptive in nature. The American architectural world of 1900 was not bereft of design discourse; however, it took place on more private levels, in discussions at clubs and dinners as well as lectures at professional meetings. These were rarely published and only exist in the archives of individual firms or organizations. Gilbert was a reluctant lecturer and turned down most offers to publish articles. Fortunately, he was not so reticent in his letters. His correspondence provides a generous opening into his aesthetic sensibility.

Gilbert's correspondence contains reflections about historic buildings, the works of his contemporaries, and his own architectural aesthetics. His sketchbooks and photographs include images of medieval, Roman, and Renaissance buildings. A review of this material provides a fascinating glimpse into Gilbert's likes and dislikes but also creates a basis for establishing the aesthetic standards of this very eclectic architect. This chapter primarily focuses on Gilbert's career from the time of his move to New York City in 1899 up to World War I. After the war, a series of shifts, including changes in his office staff, his own personal taste, and the professional context in which he worked, resulted in a change in Gilbert's architecture.

Thomas R. Johnson, who was the primary designer in the office besides Gilbert, died in 1915; John Rockart, Gilbert's chief administrator of projects, became increasingly inactive during the 1920s. These developments coincided with the arrival of Cass Gilbert Jr. to the office. Gilbert's own taste became increasingly austere, and the Colonial revival or Georgian revival began to predominate as the preferred style in his designs. Gilbert knew and had social contacts with many major American architects from 1900 through the 1910s. By the 1920s, however, he became increasingly out of touch with the new generation of designers that was starting to dominate the profession. Gilbert's career can be divided into three phases: the Minnesota period, New York from 1899 through World War I, and the postwar period to Gilbert's death in 1934.

The breadth of Gilbert's taste did not mean that he was without standards. Very few works rose to the level of masterpiece, in his view. Charles Bulfinch's Massachusetts statehouse was not, Gilbert believed, a masterpiece, nor was Bulfinch a genius. However, he considered the building to be "one of the best things of its time in this country."[4] Included in Gilbert's 1880 European sketchbook are details of Charles Garnier's Paris Opera House. Gilbert admired Garnier and thought that the Opera House was one of the greatest buildings in the world. Yet Gilbert had a very ambivalent attitude toward Ecole des Beaux-Arts–inspired architecture. He encouraged architecture students to study at the Ecole and hired Ecole-trained architects. His design for the United States Custom House at Bowling Green, New York City, is indebted to the Ecole on a number of levels (see Figure C-10). His New York City office manager, Stevens Haskell, had studied at the Ecole and Gilbert imported from France Haskell's former classmate and 1899 Ecole graduate, Ernest Hébrard, to work on the competition drawings, believing that it would give his entry an edge over other competitors. Gilbert felt that the use of Hébrard and Ecole techniques on the Custom House competition was well worth the additional hours and expense. He wrote to Thomas Holyoke, a member of his Minnesota office: "I doubt whether there will be a better set of drawings in the competition."[5] The influence of the Ecole extended beyond the drawings. Gilbert based one of the building's important motifs, the colossal columns of the facade, on Louis Duc's design for the Palace of Justice in Paris. Gilbert, however, warned Haskell not to copy Duc's design, "but simply to use it by way of illustration."[6]

Despite Gilbert's willingness to draw from the Ecole, he was not a totally enthusiastic supporter of the institution and the designs it generated. In 1899 Gilbert wrote in response to Albert Kelsey's inquiry about starting an architectural magazine that an uncritical reliance on the Ecole could cause American architecture to "develop in a wholly artificial and academic way."[7] Instead, Gilbert preferred to work from a broader range of classical forms. In revising the Custom House design, he advised Haskell to make the building "more of the Roman type than expressed in the original drawings—simpler and more severe."[8] As late as 1917, Gilbert was still ambivalent about the Ecole and its influence in the United States. In a letter to William Adams Delano, who also had studied at the Ecole, Gilbert disputed Delano's claim that American architecture's greatest debt was to France, and reminded Delano of the influence that Christopher Wren and his contemporaries had on American colonial churches and early-nineteenth-century architecture, as well as contemporary reliance on Italian Renaissance and classical architecture. Delano was trying to solicit support for France during World War I. While Gilbert argued with Delano's statement about the significance of France, he did agree that France needed support. Later, when he discovered that Ernest Hébrard was a German prisoner of war, Gilbert made several somewhat naïve efforts to have Hébrard released and sent to the United States as a college instructor.[9]

Gilbert's list of great artists in 1903 included Ictinus, Garnier, Michelangelo, Palladio, Brunelleschi, and Bramante.[10] While Gilbert admired the Renaissance, his early sympathies were even more closely attuned to the Gothic (Figure 4-1). In 1898 he was asked to identify the eight great facades of the world.[11] Gilbert expounded on the qualities he believed made a great facade: noble proportions, majestic scale, rich color, and effects of light and shade. This list suggested a picturesque appreciation of architectural form. Gilbert included Notre-Dame in Paris, the Parthenon, Garnier's Opera House, San Marco, St. Peter's, Amiens Cathedral, Cologne Cathedral, and the Farnese Palace as examples of great facades. He added that he would also want to consider the Cathedral at Pisa, Santa Maria Maggiore in Rome, the Colosseum, and the great temple at Paestum. Not surprisingly, many of the buildings were from the medieval era. Gilbert ultimately rejected Sansovino's Libreria Vecchia in Venice because "it produces no great impression on the mind. One has to stop and seek its beauties. . . . It does not draw the prompt response, nor compel the involuntary admiration."[12] Great facades, however, did not have to be perfect. Gilbert described Amiens Cathedral, a building he listed, as "splendid in detail, impressive and romantic, lacks serene majesty, too restless."[13] The early Gilbert preferred the picturesque restlessness of Amiens to the quietude of the Sansovino library.

Gilbert's catholic taste is evident in his sketchbooks. In the winter of 1897–98 Gilbert toured Europe studying classically styled monumental public buildings in order to refine his design of the Minnesota State Capitol. He wrote: "I spent the winter of 1897–98 in Europe studying and examining public buildings with a view to their construction, and mechanical equipment, their planning, proportion, details, and embellishment. . . ."[14] Yet the sketchbooks reveal that Gilbert was equally obsessed with medieval Italian campaniles, a type that would provide the basis for the Broadway Chambers and other buildings. The sketchbooks also provide evidence as to how Gilbert used these diverse historical sources for his own architecture. While Gilbert was known for his beautifully

4-1. Ambert, France, 1880, graphite on drawing paper. (© Collection of the New-York Historical Society, neg. #74449)

rendered watercolor perspectives of European buildings, the majority of his sketches depicted details. A page in his 1880 European sketchbook recorded various examples of metalwork from different buildings in Siena (Figure 4-2); another page was devoted to a single building, San Marco in Venice, but also was composed entirely of details.

By fragmenting his record of historical buildings, Gilbert broke it down into a working vocabulary that he employed for his own designs. Other architects primarily based their designs on a single building; for example, McKim, Mead & White modeled Pennsylvania Station on the Roman Baths of Caracalla. In contrast, Gilbert wove together diverse sources to create his buildings. However, Gilbert's mentor at McKim, Mead & White was Stanford White, who did synthesize diverse motifs in order to create his designs, and it is likely that Gilbert may have absorbed this method of working from White. Of his early buildings the design of the Minnesota State Capitol, St. Paul, comes the closest to relying on a single source: St. Peter's in Rome. However, a close analysis of the building and Gilbert's correspondence about the structure reveal multiple sources: the elevator grilles were based on examples of Spanish metalwork, the color scheme of the main entrance resembled that of the Byzantine Tomb of Galla Placidia in Ravenna, and the Governor's Reception Room (see Figure 5-11) was Venetian in style.[15]

While Gilbert designed in many different styles, he held certain principles about the use of historical references. He believed that the style chosen for a design should be appropriate to the building's pur-

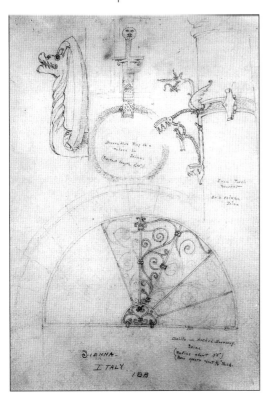

4-2. Sienna [sic]—Italy, 1880, from European sketchbook (1880), graphite on drawing paper. (©Collection of the New-York Historical Society, neg. #74450)

OPPOSITE
4-3. West Street Building, view looking north, photograph, c. 1907. (©Collection of the New-York Historical Society, neg. #74165)

pose. In 1909 Gilbert answered an inquiry about which styles he believed were suitable for churches. Denomination, Gilbert replied, could determine style. The Catholic Church's lengthy history and broad geographic extent enabled an architect to select from a great number of styles including Roman Renaissance, Gothic, and Byzantine. However, an architect should use only the English Gothic for an Episcopal church.[16] Architects, Gilbert believed, should select a style appropriate to the history of the building type and institution. Historical precedent frequently determined Gilbert's selection of style. He designed all three of his state capitols as domed, classical buildings following the precedents of the Massachusetts statehouse, the United States Capitol, and McKim, Mead & White's Rhode Island capitol. Similarly his designs for public buildings such as museums, libraries, and banks employed styles similar to the classical forms first used for these types of buildings in the late eighteenth and early nineteenth centuries. Context could also contribute to the selection of style when the precedent was not clear-cut. Schools had historically adopted any number of styles including Gothic and classical. At Oberlin College, Gilbert used a medieval-inspired style to harmonize with the preexisting buildings, while for the Hotchkiss School he selected a Colonial revival style that was appropriate to the institution's Connecticut setting.

In the case of the skyscraper, a building type that Gilbert found to be largely without direct historical lineage, the architect had more choice (Figure 4-3). In 1911 Gilbert wrote: "I have tried to choose a style in each case which I thought best adapted to the needs. Finding no existing style to the skyscraper problem I had to try to design something or to influence those around me in that direction. So my skyscraper work of recent years has been an attempt at a development along logical lines."[17] When architects had the freedom to choose the style of a building, however, Gilbert stressed that they should choose beauty over originality: "Whichever type or form is adopted it should be executed with a reverent regard for the style and be kept as pure and fine, and above all as beautiful as possible, and again where the designer chooses to work with entire freedom from traditional style to meet modern conditions he should do so but in doing it seek beauty rather than originality for if he achieves beauty originality will take care of itself. . . . I believe that architecture is a matter of development rather than a matter of invention and wherever I can I love to recur to the beautiful old types of the past and study them as closely as possible."[18]

Gilbert was amused by others' fascination with the Woolworth Building's neo-Gothic detailing:

The Woolworth is the outcome of a <u>condition</u> not the result of a <u>theory</u>. It is <u>logical</u> not <u>creative</u> in idea. They get satisfaction out of declaiming for, or against, its so called 'Gothic' detail, and miss the point that any detail would have done just as well if it were in the right scale and handled in the right way. The Woolworth drawings between sketch and contract took about 86 calendar days, and there was no time to try out experiments. I knew the light tenuous liney detail of the 15th century could be used and I used it. The building is a thing of steel and wire and terra cotta all produced by heat and flame and perhaps it is not too much of a stretch of imagination for me to say that it seemed to me that the flamboyant or flame-like form of the ornament bore some relation to the materials and the method by which they were produced.[19]

Gilbert's discussion of style reveals another facet of his aesthetics. He believed that forms should be appropriate to a building's function, setting, and materials. Gilbert's concern with sincerity in the selection of style is probably what led him to use austere, stripped forms for the Austin, Nichols and Company Warehouse and the United States Army Supply Base. The belief that simple, unadorned forms were appropriate for industrial buildings resulted in Gilbert's austere designs for these buildings rather than any conscious interest in modernism. Nothing, Gilbert asserted, was more inappropriate than the tendency to embellish functional buildings with ornate forms. He wrote, "We build in America countless buildings with entablatures, colonnades and pilasters which pretend to be classic or monumental, abasing those great and beautiful forms to ignoble

4-4. Detroit Public Library, front elevation, c. 1915, T. R. Johnson, renderer, ink wash, ink, graphite on board. (©Collection of the New-York Historical Society, neg. #72843)

uses and our work therefore takes on an aspect of insincerity."[20] In discussing the design of libraries, Gilbert stressed that the first factor was choosing an accessible location, and then beauty of design and environment. He explained, "A library should be beautiful, not ornate. Its surroundings should be beautiful. It should invite, not repel."[21] Gilbert designed four public libraries, of which the Detroit Public Library was the most elaborately decorated, with carved reliefs representing the zodiac at the frieze, mosaics on the second floor loggia, extensive murals (see Figures 7-2 and 7-3), and numerous classical details (Figure 4-4).[22] The Detroit library, however, shared with Gilbert's other libraries an open, grassy setting and a distinctly defined entrance reached by a broad set of stairs.

Gilbert's acute sensitivity to site and function sometimes led him to disagree with conventional views about buildings. Gilbert vigorously resisted arguments that he design a dome for the United States Custom House, a conventional sign of civic importance. The setting, floor plans, and functions of the Custom House precluded such a form:

. . . in brief that the building should be disengaged and have ample space around it in order that the dome might be appreciated and its form seen to advantage; that the background of skyscrapers did not admit of a satisfactory dome treatment on the Custom House, that the building was too small to carry a dome, and moreover, that a dome was not a consistent expression of the interior of the building, that there was no

place of assemblage in the building such as is found in cathedral, state and national capitols and other large building for which domes have been designed, and that the dome would have to be larger than the dome of St. Peters at Rome if it were to rise above the office buildings in the neighborhood or such as were likely to be built in the future.[23]

Gilbert prevailed, and no dome interrupts the mansard roof of the Custom House. Only at the rear, where the building reveals the central light court, can visitors see the shallow Guastavino vault of the rotunda.

Gilbert was reluctant to publicly criticize the work of fellow architects; however, his private correspondence is filled with remarks about current work. Gilbert's ambivalence about the Ecole des Beaux-Arts extended to his assessment of American work influenced by the school. In 1909 Gilbert summarized the current state of New York design for his friend, St. Louis architect W. S. Eames: "We hear less of the extreme Beaux Arts talk. . . . The serious men are swinging back to the good old Roman Renaissance or to the Gothic."[24]

In the same letter Gilbert discussed two buildings under construction, Carrère & Hastings's main branch of the New York Public Library and McKim, Mead & White's Pennsylvania Station. While Gilbert admired the development of the library grounds, he was critical of the building, probably finding it an example of the "extreme Beaux Arts." Just after Carrère toured Gilbert through the building, Gilbert

wrote to Eames, "I found some very good color decorations in the large rooms but the exterior does not impress me except for a certain beauty of detail."[25] In a rare outburst of praise, he expressed deep admiration for McKim's Roman-inspired Pennsylvania Station, declaring that it "will have a great influence for it is a most imposing performance."[26]

Gilbert's critiques of contemporary designs often focused on the proportions, correct usage of elements (which he defined as the relation between an exterior element and the interior space), historical accuracy of details, and context. Gilbert reviewed the New Haven Post Office in a 1913 letter to his friend George Dudley Seymour (Figure 4-5). While James Gamble Rogers's building was "a very fine example of good architecture," Gilbert was critical of several aspects. He found the style ill-suited to its context, in that it was "much better suited to a location near the Pennsylvania Railroad Station in New York than on New Haven Green."[27] A more appropriate style, he believed, would have been Renaissance rather than classical. He found the details to be inconsistent, stating that a square arch, instead of the round arch, should have been used for the side doorway, because the round arch made the side appear "to be of one type and the facade of another."[28] His most severe criticism, however, was reserved for Rogers's design of the pediment:

I do not see why architects continue to plaster pediments onto attic stories where the pediment does not in any way represent the slope of the roof. In the Post Office design we have a huge pediment spanning ten columns and absolutely barren of sculpture and yet of the Corinthian order. The fact that the building has a well lighted attic story, as shown by the windows on the side street, makes it obvious that the pediment does not represent anything. It would have been so much finer without the pediment, with a simple attic above the portico. You see the pediment in classic architecture was always the termination of the roof and naturally took the shape and slope of the roof. . . . The pediment is the survival of a traditional form, in this case, quite without meaning.[29]

Gilbert's remarks about the Post Office not only offer a frank analysis of the work of a contemporary but also illuminate Gilbert's designs. Unlike the overly monumental post office, his Ives Memorial Library (1908–11) in New Haven is a Colonial revival building of brick and stone. The style and materials, Gilbert believed, were appropriate to the colonial heritage of the New Haven green (see chapter 12 for further discussion of this issue). Gilbert called attention to the roofline by using a "truthful" stone balustrade rather than a "false" pediment.

4-5. James Gamble Rogers, architect, New Haven Post Office, postcard, c. 1920. (©Collection of the New-York Historical Society, neg. #74382)

THE AESTHETICS OF AN ECLECTIC ARCHITECT

Gilbert was obsessed with proportions and often went to great lengths to study the proportions of various elements of a building. The simple curved concrete cornice of the Austin, Nichols and Company Warehouse in Brooklyn, New York, was subject to the office's intense scrutiny in terms of the relation between the lip of the cornice and the concave portion below, as well as the overall scale of the entire element. When full-size drawings did not provide enough information, Gilbert persuaded the owners to have a full-scale model fabricated and hoisted into place on the building in order to resolve this detail.

If asked, Gilbert sometimes shared his criticisms with fellow architects. In 1914, for example, he wrote Charles Loring that his design for a library in Waltham, Massachusetts, was a "charmingly simple building. Gilbert's critique of Loring's design provides insight into Gilbert's aesthetics and design decisions.

Gilbert was almost effusive in his praise of Theodate Pope Riddle's designs for the girl's school at Westover, Connecticut (Figure 4-8). He described it as a work that was "[b]eautifully designed and planned, [the] best girls school that I know of in the country, the details are very refined and scholarly and the proportions of the architecture are exceedingly well sustained throughout. The building is rather extensive, one forming four sides of a large quadrangle or cloister and is refreshing in its charm and simplicity."[32] Riddle's Westover buildings had all the qualities Gilbert admired: good proportions, historically correct forms, and details studied in terms of the function of the building as well as the relation to other

scheme," with a beautiful porch and a "quiet air of dignity and refinement" (Figure 4-6).[30] However, certain details were not quite right. The facade windows were too large, and the broken pediment over the entrance doorway was too ornate. Gilbert's own recently designed library for Beverly, Massachusetts (Figure 4-7), used simple Colonial revival forms that were the result of his studying "…very closely the old things in Salem and that neighborhood so as to carry out the old tradition of New England."[31] The windows of Beverly Public Library are smaller than those of the Waltham library, and while the entrance is elaborated by pilasters and a half dome, it lacks the ornate, sculptural qualities of Loring's Waltham

elements. The quadrangle or cloister plan, furthermore, was a type that Gilbert favored for school buildings. He used the quadrangle type in his plans for Oberlin College and recommended it as a solution to other architects designing collegiate buildings. When architect Irving Pond ran into difficulties with the trustees with his designs for the Union building at the University of Michigan, Gilbert advised him to start afresh and consider the cloister: "You may find that by a scattered, rambling low structure, each function housed in a separate wing or in a separate section, you could accomplish wonders. Is it not in fact a sort of a brotherhood building? May it not therefore partake of the character of some monastic building

4-6. Leland & Loring, architects, Waltham Public Library, Waltham, Massachusetts, in *AABN* 116 (October 29, 1919): 555, pl. 149. (Library of Congress)

4-7. Beverly Public Library, c. 1911, Birch Burdette Long, renderer, watercolor, graphite, crayon on paper. (©Collection of the New-York Historical Society, neg. #72869)

with its cloister yard, its refectory, its meeting or council hall, its little cells or bedrooms."[33]

Occasionally Gilbert was asked to submit a list of the best recent American buildings. His suggestions were highly selective and yet diverse in style. Included in a 1912 list were Charles McKim's Renaissance-revival Pierpont Morgan Library, New York City; Benjamin Wistar Morris's Morgan Memorial Library and Museum in Hartford, Connecticut (also in the Renaissance-revival style); Cram, Goodhue & Ferguson's neo-Gothic chapel at West Point; Day & Klauder's neo-Gothic Pyne Hall at Princeton University; and Glenn Brown's Colonial revival Commodore Beale House in Washington, D.C.[34] Gilbert found the severely neoclassical Lincoln Memorial by Henry Bacon to be a building that "looks exceedingly well."[35] He also expressed admiration for the work of the British architect Sir Aston Webb. Gilbert wrote that he was particularly impressed by Webb's interiors for the new section of the South Kensington Museum, which he had seen in 1906.[36] Not surprisingly, the obviously modern never registered with Gilbert. In 1915 he was asked to introduce the Belgian Art Nouveau architect Victor Horta to various New York architects. He responded that he would be delighted to help but that he did not know Horta or his work.[37]

From the beginning of his career Gilbert was deeply interested in vernacular architecture, whether it was the colonial buildings of the United States (Figure 4-9) or those of France and Italy. This interest deepened after 1907, owing to Gilbert's purchase of a colonial building for his home in Ridgefield, Connecticut, and his involvement in planning the city of New Haven with its colonial-era green. During the first two decades of the twentieth century, Gilbert could admire both the richness of the Gothic and the simplicity of colonial and Georgian-style buildings. From approximately the time that the Woolworth Building was completed, Gilbert's undated lecture entitled, "Indigenous Architecture," best expressed this duality. About skyscrapers he wrote,

> The symbols of our national genius and unrestraint rise like the crags of a volcanic island still in process of upheaval. The scale is gigantic; the power, irresistible; the daring, licentious; and yet, to those that have eyes to see, there is the germ of the true art. And the Skyscraper is ours.

4-8. Theodate Pope Riddle, architect, Westover School, unidentified photographer, Middlebury, Connecticut. (Westover School)

THE AESTHETICS OF AN ECLECTIC ARCHITECT

It is conceived by business, half in economy of ground, half in extravagance of advertising; it is born of the mechanical ingenuity which evolved the steel frame and the express elevator; and it is sanctioned only by the least paternal of governments. Now because it is ours, because it expresses the most obvious side of our cosmos, because there are no alien conventions to follow, we are evolving, almost unconsciously a new type of interest and even beauty.[38]

But, Gilbert suggested, the skyscraper could be seen with other types, particularly post offices and Carnegie Library buildings, that while not so original, also expressed the aims of the country and through their very simplicity proved that ". . . the general scheme, both in plan and style, has proved itself acceptable from the point of view of use, beauty and association."[39] By the late 1910s, the balance shifted, with Gilbert increasingly favoring adjectives such as "severe," "simple," "refined," and "dignified." Gilbert's enthusiasm for the colonial is evident in a 1916 letter to Professor Roswell P. Angier of Yale:

System, order and formality are not inconsistent with beauty and they are in fact all elements which should be inculcated in the minds of our young people. In saying this I do not mean that cold inhospitable formality which makes certain institutional groups so forbidding, but that graceful formality which makes houses like Washington's home at Mount Vernon, the house of Charles Carrol of Carrolton near Baltimore, White Hall on the western shore of Maryland, the old Independence Hall in Philadelphia, the old Academy at Albany, the original old quadrangle at Yale (now destroyed with the single exception of Connecticut Hall) so very charming and distinguished.[40]

Instead of weaving together details from various buildings, as he did in his early career, Gilbert increasingly based his designs on replicating an older historic design by another architect. The auditorium of the New York County Lawyers' Association (Figure 4-10), for example, reproduced the auditorium in Independence Hall. An early version of the Waterbury Town Hall was directly adapted from Robert Adam's design for the house of Sir Watkin Williams Wynn at 20 St. James Square, London, of ca. 1772 (see Figure 12-12).[41] Even the skyscraper, which according to Gilbert had "no existing style," could be cloaked in Colonial revival forms. Undoubtedly influenced by Philadelphia's colonial origins, several designs for the unbuilt 1919 Atlantic Refining Company building, planned for downtown Philadelphia, were drawn using the Colonial revival style (Figure 4-11). The failure of this project, however, was not due to Gilbert's use of the Colonial revival but rather to the still shaky finances of the immediate post–World War I period.

If Gilbert was oblivious to modernism prior to the 1910s, he became increasingly hostile to modern art and design from the 1910s on. He disagreed with giving the Art Commission of the City of New York, the city agency responsible for reviewing all city-owned art, architecture, and landscape architecture, greater powers, because "[t]he changing membership of the Commission might some day create a personnel that would be less conservative and if extremists, cubists, etc. should by chance be appointed to the Commission and dominate its councils great harm might be done."[42] Gilbert was suspicious of Bertram Goodhue's Art Deco designs

4-9. Sketch of mantel, house on Bridge and State Streets, c. 1881, ink on drawing paper. (©Collection of the New-York Historical Society, neg. #74420)

for the Nebraska capitol: "I know Goodhue very well and admire his work very much indeed, but I do not find myself enthusiastic over this design, as it looks to me more like a crematorium than a public building, though I am bound to say that it has certain artistic qualities, which are characteristic of all Goodhue's work. I have no doubt he will make a very interesting thing of it, though I greatly doubt if the state will ever build that tower or anything like it."[43] Gilbert, in this instance, not only was unsympathetic to Goodhue's design but also was out of tune with the changing taste in architecture. The state did build Goodhue's tower. By the 1920s, Gilbert's use of history had shifted from a flexible vocabulary that could be freely drawn from for specific programmatic and aesthetic needs into a more rigid structure. This stricter, more dogmatic reliance on precedent left him unsympathetic to the work of many of his contemporaries. It also resulted in a more academic quality in the designs produced by his office.

Perhaps the most unsettling result of Gilbert's changing taste was his reevaluation of his own earlier work. While Gilbert continued to list the United States Custom House, Minnesota State Capitol, and Woolworth Building as significant examples of his practice, he was increasingly uneasy about the richness of their forms. In 1921, Gilbert wrote about public buildings, mentioning the Minnesota State Capitol and United States Custom House: "The most monumental buildings are those which are only two or three stories high and practical usage requires many windows, so there is left but little wall surface to give the impression of dignity and serenity which a great structure should convey, so we are tempted to overembellish these buildings with ornament and usually we overdo it. I feel that in my earlier work, like the New York Custom House and the Minnesota Capitol, which were designed twenty years ago, there are many faults in that direction."[44]

In 1920, Ralph Adams Cram wrote Gilbert,

4-10. Auditorium, New York County Lawyers' Association, photograph, c. 1930. (© Collection of the New-York Historical Society, neg. #74383)

THE AESTHETICS OF AN ECLECTIC ARCHITECT

4-11. Atlantic Refining Company, 1919, George P. Koyl, renderer, graphite on trace. (© Collection of the New-York Historical Society, neg. #74410)

requesting information about the Woolworth Building for an article. Cram also wondered if Gilbert could give him a list of the best American buildings constructed between 1900 and 1915. Gilbert replied that the latter question was difficult to answer and the list would be short, but they would discuss that matter when Cram visited the office. About the Woolworth Building, Gilbert wrote, "I sometimes wish that I had never built the Woolworth Building because I fear it may be regarded as my only work and you and I both know that whatever it may be in dimension and in certain lines it is after all only a skyscraper. For that reason if my work is to be illustrated I should like to have it include something else as, for example, the Detroit Public Library, the Minnesota Capitol, the New York Custom House, the Army Base in Brooklyn."[45] In 1914 Gilbert described the tall office building as a "great modern type of building which exists only in America." By 1920 it was "only a skyscraper." This shift signaled a larger change in Gilbert's practice. With the exception of the New York Life Insurance Company building, the third and final installment of Gilbert's neo-Gothic skyscrapers, Gilbert from 1920 to his death left the skyscrapers to the younger generation and turned increasingly to the study of colonial and Georgian architecture and to the conservative commissions for law buildings, state capitols, and universities.

The Cass Gilbert holdings at the Library of Congress, the Minnesota Historical Society, the National Museum of American History, and the New-York Historical Society are so vast that scholars will be able to supplement and probably contradict points in this discussion for years to come. The Library of Congress and the National Museum of American History have Gilbert's sketchbooks, and the Library of Congress has his private correspondence with family and friends. These two resources can be used to reconstruct and study Gilbert's European travels in great detail. I had the honor of spending nine years with the Cass Gilbert Collection at the New-York Historical Society and still have not examined every letter or drawing contained within that collection. Rather than being the final word on Gilbert's aesthetics I hope this chapter encourages other scholars to explore this rich topic.

I started to look at Gilbert's work with the eyes and aesthetics of a historian of modern architecture. Similar to the first encounters with foreign cultures, Gilbert's work was initially beautiful, exotic, and impossible to comprehend. Modernist design and criticism caused a rupture with the historical revival styles of the nineteenth and early twentieth centuries that we are only now beginning to understand. Some of the rupture is permanent. I do not believe that architects today will ever be able to design in a manner similar to Gilbert's. Even if it is possible to assemble the vocabulary of historic details that Gilbert used with such apparent ease and fluidity, the cost of the labor, craft, and materials of such details is beyond the budget of most clients.

Yet if it is neither wise nor reasonable to replicate the past, we can, at least, better understand how Gilbert worked. Aesthetic standards, as Gilbert's architecture reveals, do not reside in the adherence to a uniform set of forms. Rather, they reside in the proportions, consistency of details, and accounting for use and context. Gilbert's success should not be accounted for by how many of his buildings appear in surveys of western or American architecture. Instead, Gilbert's success is better measured by the extraordinary number of buildings designed by his office that still stand and are lovingly cared for and used by their tenants and owners.

PART 2

A DEFINING MOMENT IN AMERICAN CIVIC ARCHITECTURE

CHAPTER 5

THE MINNESOTA STATE CAPITOL: THINKING INTERNATIONALLY, DESIGNING LOCALLY

Thomas O'Sullivan

BIRDS-EYE VIEW, ST. PAUL, MINN.

In the opening years of the twentieth century, Minnesotans watched a new statehouse take form on a rise of ground in St. Paul. Photographs and postcards of the day show the Minnesota State Capitol's broad facade of white marble rising above what Mark Twain had dryly called "a wonderful town. It is put together in solid blocks of honest brick and stone, and has the air of intending to stay" (Figure 5-1).[1] The new structure bore its symbolic duties as seriously as its governmental functions. It was to be an assertion of the state's legitimacy in the national and world arenas, as a Duluth politician observed: "Such a state and such a people deserve a capitol they may be proud to exhibit to a stranger."[2] The new capitol was Minnesota's first major landmark in the Beaux-Arts idiom, a building in which St. Paul architect Cass Gilbert marshaled rich materials, fine craftsmanship, and the collaborative energies of some of the nation's leading artists to fulfill a proudly traditional concept.

As a political entity, Minnesota was young enough for its citizens to need such boosting. The territory's name was coined in 1849 to denote the area created from Wisconsin's western flank. It entered the Union as the thirty-second state in 1858. Forty years later, on July 27, Minnesota's first territorial governor was still vigorous enough to wield a ceremonial trowel at the laying of the capitol cornerstone. Minnesota had weathered its early reputation as the "American Siberia" to become a presence in international markets for lumber, wheat, flour, and iron ore. Far from the eastern states in a region still often referred to as "the West" at the turn of the century, Minnesota had established itself as a hub for transcontinental rail-

little-known builder, N. C. Prentiss.[4] Its modest dome and Doric columns lent a dignified air to the territory's capital city. In the 1870s the building was enlarged twice and restyled in the Italianate mode by Abraham Radcliffe, but a fire in 1881 destroyed it completely. Two years later the second capitol was completed on the same site. Its eclectic design by Minneapolis architect Leroy Buffington featured a two-hundred-foot tower and elaborate interior woodwork, but overcrowding and poor ventilation led to a legislative recommendation for a new capitol in 1893. Two million dollars was budgeted for the building. The architect was to be chosen by competition, as had been done for the second capitol. Minnesota's third statehouse was to be built on a new site to the north of downtown St. Paul, where a slight elevation afforded a view above the business district to the Mississippi River valley.[5]

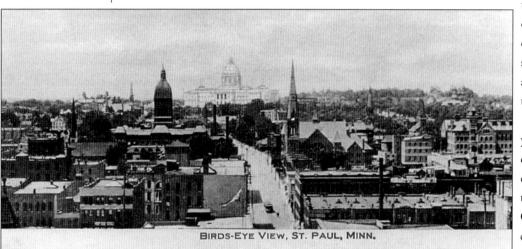

BIRDS-EYE VIEW, ST. PAUL, MINN.

5-1. View of the capitol from downtown St. Paul. Gilbert's marble capitol is prominent on the horizon of this postcard, c. 1910. The tower to the left is the second capitol, built to the designs of Leroy Buffington in 1883 and razed in the late 1930s. (Minnesota Historical Society)

ways and for the Great Lakes shipping trade. The Twin Cities of Minneapolis and St. Paul, with a combined population of 365,000 in 1900, had grown in substance and style, with an impressive array of buildings designed by resident architects as well as national firms.

Gilbert was a rising figure in the young state's design profession, and he had aims to lift himself from local note to national prominence.[3] The announcement of a competition for a new Minnesota capitol in 1893 afforded him the opportunity to exercise his skills in design, diplomacy, and politics in his first major civic building.

This new capitol would be Minnesota's third statehouse. The first had been a two-story brick building, completed in 1853 at Tenth and Cedar Streets in St. Paul's business district following the design of a

In the following two years, the selection of the new capitol's architect required two competitions administered by the Board of State Capitol Commissioners. This body of citizens was appointed by the governor to carry out the building project. Gilbert played a key role in each competition: first as a spokesman for his profession, and in the second competition, as the successful entrant. The first competition in 1894 was open to any qualified architect. Fifty-six firms submitted drawings, but few Minnesotans chose to participate. Competition advisors Edmund M. Wheelwright of Boston and Henry Ives Cobb of Chicago chose five entries, but they recommended against the use of imported or expensive materials for designs that they considered mediocre. Wheelwright further recommended holding a second, invitational competition to attract stronger designs. The board accordingly rejected the results of the first competition and established a new competition, which drew forty-one entrants.

Gilbert and his fellow members of the AIA had lobbied the board and legislature before and during

the competitions, seeking changes that would have notable effects on the new capitol and on Gilbert's career. Pressing the board to recognize an architect's professional status, they sought a substantial increase in the winning architect's fee. They also sought his appointment as superintendent of construction, thus ensuring architectural control over the project. Both proposals succeeded. While the other AIA proposals—that architects design the competition and that architects sit on the board's selection committee—were not adopted, the efforts of the group under Gilbert's presidency had a major impact on the process of selecting the winning design and carrying it through to completion.

The second competition drew higher praise from consultant Wheelwright than had the first. He selected five finalists: George R. Mann of St. Louis; Wendell & Humphreys of Denver; Bassford, Traphagen & Fitzpatrick of St. Paul and Duluth; Clarence H. Johnston of St. Paul; and Cass Gilbert of St. Paul.

The Board of State Capitol Commissioners made the final selection in late 1895, awarding the commission to Gilbert. The board's strong guiding hand, a civic-minded wholesale grocer named Channing Seabury, who was vice president of the board, would prove to be a political and aesthetic ally to Gilbert over the coming decade of design and construction.[6]

Gilbert's design presented a broad symmetrical facade of three stories on a raised basement (Figure 5-2). A flight of stairs led to a projecting central pavilion in which three great arches were topped by a loggia of Corinthian columns, above which a gilded quadriga crowned a flat attic. Behind this rose a dome of white marble. Borrowing closely from classical Roman, Renaissance, and nineteenth-century revival-style predecessors, Gilbert's scheme was not intended to be original in its concept or elements. Indeed, his clients—not only the board members but also the larger taxpaying public—expected an elegant

5-2. Gilbert's design for the Minnesota State Capitol. This 1898 drawing shows minor changes from the winning design of 1895, as well as features (such as the statues on the corners and steps) that are absent from the capitol as built. (Minnesota Historical Society)

but reassuring familiarity. Architectural historian Alan K. Lathrop described the mindset that led Minnesotans to choose Beaux-Arts styles for their public buildings, in preference to the Prairie style that was rooted in the region, but rarely adopted for civic structures: "Sharing the ambitions and prospects of the new western regions of the United States at the turn of the century, Minnesotans were most concerned that their architecture reflect, even reproduce the achievements of older American communities in the east and their even earlier antecedents in Europe. They wanted their buildings to be traditional representatives of the prosperity, dignity, and culture they felt their hard work had recreated along the upper Mississippi."[7]

Gilbert spelled out the goals of his design in a rather disingenuous introduction to his competition

5-3. The capitol seen from the southeast in 1905, shortly after legislators and state offices first occupied it. Daniel Chester French's six statues are in place above the main entrance, but his quadriga was not yet completed at this time. (Photo by Sweet, Minnesota Historical Society)

entry: "The first elements considered in making this design have been the practical ones of *economy* and *good construction.* Next after this, and hardly less important have been the questions of a suitable and convenient arrangement of the interior of the building giving ample light and ventilation to all its parts, and convenient access between those parts of the structure most requiring it. And, finally, that it shall express in all its parts and as a whole the nature of the building and the dignity of its purpose."[8] This latter aspect, though less tangible than matters of cost and construction, helped carry the day for Gilbert's design. The "dignity of its purpose" recalled venerable buildings, and did so with a restraint that was most notable by comparison to the busy facades and pro-

fusion of pediments, domes, and towers that his competitors offered.[9] An editorial in the *St. Paul Pioneer Press,* for example, praised "the symmetry of its proportions and the subordination of all ideas of ornamental detail to the general effect of the mass."[10]

Gilbert's plan sets the main spaces for the dramas of civic life on the second floor: the Senate chamber to the west of the central rotunda, the House of Representatives to the north, and the Supreme Court to the east. Each has its own skylight beneath low copper-framed domes. A suite of offices for the governor occupies the southwest corner of the first floor. Mechanical systems were to take advantage of turn-of-the-century technologies, including electric lighting, telephones, fireproof construction, and a steam power plant safely located in a separate building—important considerations to those who recalled the fire that destroyed the first capitol in the previous decade. Despite its technological timeliness, however, it is the monumental classical presence of Gilbert's design that won the day. For this he drew on the examples of American capitols and landmark European buildings alike. Among the many states with domed, pedimented capitols were Iowa (completed 1886), Indiana (1878), and Michigan (1878), all of which the board members had visited before the first competition was announced.[11] The federal Capitol (completed 1863) was a model that the board found exemplary. One commissioner noted at the laying of the cornerstone in St. Paul that "public sentiment educated by familiarity with the great Capitol building in Washington, required that this should be a domed building, with impressive approaches and an extensive rotunda."[12]

The most telling example of such a structure, however, was a statehouse exactly contemporaneous with Minnesota's. McKim, Mead & White's Rhode Island capitol (1892) was familiar to Gilbert, as it would have been to any architect keeping abreast of major American architectural projects.[13] During his employment with that firm in the 1880s, however, Gilbert developed contacts with whom he corresponded during his work on the Minnesota capitol. Gilbert's design shares with that of McKim, Mead & White a similar composition for the facade, with a flat attic (rather than the more typical pediment) above a tripartite entry pavilion. But where McKim, Mead & White took Sir Christopher Wren's late-seventeenth-century St. Paul's Cathedral in London as its model for the many-ribbed dome and single tall columns, Gilbert's design had earlier Renaissance roots. He closely modeled the Minnesota dome on the mid-sixteenth-century marble dome that Michelangelo had designed for the basilica of St. Peter in Rome. Sitting atop a drum that features pedimented windows between pairs of Corinthian columns, Gilbert's dome rises to a columned stone lantern. Several features mark its Minnesota location and secular identity: one dozen distinctly American eagles are perched on the paired columns, five-pointed stars (representing the state motto, "L'Etoile du Nord") are carved in high relief just above the drum, and a simple gilded sphere (rather than a cross) stands at the top. The dome became an instant landmark in St. Paul. It attracted extravagant praise from such commentators as Kenyon Cox, the muralist and spokesman for classicism in the arts of the new century: "This great dome is a vast piece of sculpture upon which the light falls as caressingly as upon the white breast of the Venus of Milo, while, seen at a distance, it seems of the colors and almost of the very substance of the sky, into which it melts like a snow-peak on the horizon."[14]

The use of marble, the stone of choice for important civic buildings during many centuries, was a mere hope in Gilbert's first presentation of his design. He wrote, "The bell of the dome would be of white marble if contract estimates will allow of such expense otherwise of heavy cast iron either gilded or painted white, as in many of the notable domes of the world."[15] Emboldened by his success in the competition, Gilbert pressed for white marble to avoid crowning Wabasha Hill, as the site was then called, with a gloomy, fortress-like pile. These efforts drew Gilbert, Seabury, and the board into a sharp and highly public debate that mixed aesthetics, economics, and politics. The stone Gilbert had hoped to use was Georgia marble, known for its brilliant white color and rich veins of black and silver-gray. This was

not just an expensive, out-of-state material, but stone from a state that many Minnesotans recalled from their younger days as the scene of Civil War fighting. This choice of a "foreign" material would deprive Minnesota's quarry owners and stonecutters not only of prestige but also of lucrative contracts. Gilbert suggested the compromise of using Minnesota granite and sandstone for the steps, terraces, and ground-floor walls and Georgia marble for the upper walls and dome. The board approved this compromise after lengthy debate and heated newspaper attacks. The combination of types of stone proved to be less expensive than using only a kind of Minnesota granite, and the Georgia stone was shipped in raw blocks so that local stonecutters could work it. In this early controversy and its resolution, Gilbert enhanced his skills in negotiation as well as in design.[16]

Gilbert streamlined the building's silhouette slightly, even as he planned the decorative scheme for the capitol's interior while ground was broken, foundations were prepared, and construction started in the later 1890s (Figure 5-3). Presentation drawings and tracings depict a building adorned with numerous sculptures. Of these, the half-dozen monumental figures at the corners of the central bays on three sides were omitted from the final design. The centerpiece of the entire composition remained: a gilded quadriga group, consisting of a heroic figure erect in a chariot drawn by four horses and guided by two women (Figure 5-4). The conceit of Roman triumph had been imported to America in the form of a massive quadriga group at the World's Colum-bian Exposition, with figures by Daniel Chester French and horses by Edward C. Potter. There the sculpture honored Christopher Columbus himself. In adapting the group for Minnesota at Gilbert's request, French suggested a draped male charioteer, thrusting high a staff with a banner

5-4. Model for Daniel Chester French and Edward C. Potter's *The Progress of the State*, 1907 photograph. The full-size group, in gilded copper, is commonly known as the quadriga. (Photo by A. B. Bogart, Minnesota Historical Society)

reading "Prosperity." French articulated his intention in a letter to Gilbert: "As the two figures leading the horses are female figures, I think the figure in the chariot should be a male figure. I think that it should represent 'Minnesota,' if you think that a male figure can personify a state."[17] Executed in hammered copper with a gilded finish, the group was christened *The Progress of the State.* French also supplied a series of single figures, executed in marble and placed immediately below the quadriga. "These figures represent the six virtues that support and assist the progress of the state," wrote Julie C. Gauthier in a guidebook that was endorsed by Gilbert and Seabury.[18] In their dress and accessories, the representations of wisdom, prudence, courage, bounty, truth, and integrity evoke classical ideals, and they enliven the attic story that had borne only a carved inscription in the competition drawings. Like the building stone, the statues were carved on site, from French's plaster models.

As the new century approached, with construction progressing to the dome level, Gilbert's ambitions for the capitol had quickly outgrown his budget. Increased construction costs had made the legislature's two-million-dollar appropriation inadequate for the fine materials and extensive decorations Gilbert and his allies on the board envisioned. A speaker at the cornerstone ceremony of 1898 had anticipated such a problem:

> The interior of such a building ought to be finished with the most beautiful of native and foreign stone, and made an object of art, educative of the taste of our people and inspiring their pride; but as it is necessary to expend practically all of the appropriation in securing a building of proper size and convenient arrangement, the commission, strictly adhering to the terms of the law under which they are acting, may be obliged to use ordinary wood work for interior finish and leave plain walls, unless the state in its wisdom shall make other provisions.[19]

The board's report of 1901 detailed the consequences of misdirected thrift in some fourteen paragraphs, warning of such inadequacies as the "cheapest possible" work rather than fireproof construction and tile roofing, wood floors rather than stone or terrazzo, and a plain plaster rotunda and chamber walls rather than marble columns, stone facings, and decorative painting.[20] This dreary list, during the next biennium, laid the groundwork for a successful campaign to increase the appropriation by one million dollars. Gilbert set to work developing his interior designs in earnest.

Inside the capitol, Gilbert orchestrated spaces, materials, and the talents of some of the nation's leading artists. Gauthier's guidebook quoted his observations on the versatility in design skills that his role demanded: "We live in an age that has the fad to credit men with 'specialties,' and a 'specialist' seems to be considered in every walk of life. In art there should be no 'specialists,' or at least the lines of subdivision should be very slight. In the old days the architect, painter and sculptor were frequently one and the same man. There is no reason why this should not be so now."[21] While he made no claim to proficiency as painter or sculptor, Gilbert prided himself in handling colors, materials, and spaces and in directing the work of decorators and designers, to create the aesthetic unity he envisioned. This adherence to a Renaissance model of the architect as presiding genius had taken firm hold at the Chicago World's Columbian Exposition and found apt expression in the writings of muralist Edwin H. Blashfield, who wrote, "[T]he sculptor and painter must believe in the architect as commander in chief, leader, designer and creator of a whole, which they enhance as a whole by their art."[22]

Gilbert's adoption of varied stone types and colors inside the capitol established a sumptuous effect overall. His plan proved to be as politically deft as it was visually effective. He selected for the rotunda and stair halls a type of limestone from southern Minnesota quarries known as Kasota stone (Figure 5-5). Gilbert discovered that the stone, previously used only in rough form and in unseen parts of a building, could be honed to a satin finish that set off marble and paintings to great effect. Described as "dull buff limestone with a pinkish tinge," the Kasota stone provided a warm, subtle backdrop for Gilbert's chosen palette. As Elmer Garnsey noted in the *Western Architect,* "Upon this foundation the architect has developed, in logical sequence, richer values of stone and marble, through Istrian and Hauteville, into the superb marbles of Skyros, breche-violette and fleur-de-peche, brilliant and variegated, with highly polished surfaces sufficiently splendid for a king's palace, none too magnificent for the Capitol of a sovereign American State."[23]

As a Minnesota product, the Kasota stone boosted a local industry, and its selection helped offset the memory of the earlier controversy over Gilbert's choice of so-called foreign exterior marble. Contractor William Butler emphasized this point to a St. Paul reporter:

> If any one doubts the fine qualities of Kasota stone in a polished state, he ought to stand in the capitol rotunda and look up at a point just below the lower balustrade. Then I could point out to him a band of Kasota stone and, directly above it, a band of the high-priced, imported marble that the French call Hauteville. He would admit that both of them are very handsome stones, and that the Hauteville marble was well worth sending for across the ocean. But I'd be willing to bet him a new hat that he couldn't distinguish the French marble from the Minnesota limestone.[24]

Other local materials and motifs were utilized in the building for their colors and textures as much as their acceptability to the taxpayers. Eight columns of Minnesota granite, polished to a high gloss, stand prominently in the rotunda. A band of red quartzite from the state's southwestern prairies sets off the murals and dome overhead from the Kasota stone walls below. The incorporation of local motifs into the fabric of a decidedly Beaux-Arts whole also characterized Gilbert's design. A star shape in stone, brass, and glass evokes the motto "L'Etoile du Nord" in the center of the rotunda floor. Additional state symbols appear as details in unexpected, even playful, settings: life-sized gophers rear up in cast iron on the rotunda balustrades, and the many Corinthian capitals feature larger-than-life renditions of the lady's slipper, a tiny wild orchid found in northern forests (Figure 5-6).

In composing the rich palette of colors and materials that marks the major interior spaces, Gilbert worked closely with Elmer E. Garnsey as

5-5. The rotunda, second floor, c. 1910, with two of the four panels of Edward E. Simmons' mural cycle *The Civilization of the Northwest.* (Photo by C. P. Gibson, Minnesota Historical Society)

5-6. View looking west through the stair halls and rotunda, second floor, 1940s photograph. (Photo by Graphic Arts Studios, Minnesota Historical Society)

5-7. House of
Representatives cham-
ber, second floor,
c. 1905 photograph.
The open gallery above
the Speaker's chair fea-
tured allegorical figures
of "History" (at the left
side of the arch) and
"Records," since lost
when the gallery was
walled off in 1938.
(Minnesota Historical
Society)

chief decorator. Garnsey had worked in this capacity at the Library of Congress (John L. Smithmeyer and Paul J. Pelz, 1886–97). Working on site in St. Paul to supervise a crew of decorative painters, he proved to be an effective spokesman as well as a resourceful designer. His explication of the capitol's education mission appeared in a Minneapolis newspaper: "I believe that the capitol will furnish to both young and those who are 'children of a larger growth' lessons in both patriotism and art, once it is complete; for many men and many minds have been busy for several years past in planning, building and decorating it, with the idea always kept in mind that this is to be a building in which shall be made manifest 'the state,' the visible casket in which may be enshrined our ideals of living and accomplishment, honoring the past, and hoping for the future."[25]

Garnsey's hand is evident in the extensive decorative painting along the walls, on the ceilings, and filling arches and spandrels with naturalistic motifs.

Wildflowers and vines line the ceiling arches, while heaps of produce comprise still lifes in third-floor arches. Garnsey also designed figural compositions, which were executed in the halls and chambers by Arthur R. Willett and W. A. Mackay. Twelve monumental figures in the stair halls represent the state's resources and industries, depicted in both allegorical and realistic modes (see Figures 6-8 and 6-9). Classical figures in the Senate and House chambers represent such themes as integrity and history. The culmination of his decorative schemes is found in the House chamber, whose ceiling is an intricate horseshoe-shaped pattern that combines flowers, faces, and texts on a gold background (Figure 5-7). He credited Gilbert freely for the "ability to clothe the whole in as much beauty as the limitations of money and ability would permit" in his published account of the capitol, and wrote to the architect, "Sometimes I have a notion that with your design, I can make a pretty good bluff at decorative painting; but, perhaps the less said about that the better."[26] Gilbert, for his part, found it important to assert his own role in Garnsey's decorations. "I do not want to assume an undue share of credit myself in this matter," he wrote privately to commissioner Seabury,

> but I think it proper that you at least should know that I have personally directed Mr. Garnsey along certain definite lines of color, particularly in the rotunda, stairways and main corridors, and in the House Retiring Room. I do not say this to in any way belittle his own services, which are very great, but simply that I think history should be correctly written, in the statement that I have exercised a general direction of the color scheme as applied to the architecture in its main features, and exercised a critical function as to details, and that where I have not given instructions he and I have advised together.[27]

In 1903, Gilbert summarized "the modern requirements of a first-class building" in a report to the state legislature. He urged, "Nothing will give the building greater distinction or lend more to its educational value and to the evidence of the advancement of civilization and intelligence of the State than the recognition of the arts as represented by the great painters and sculptors of the present day, and I unhesitatingly and strongly recommend that ample provision be made to decorate the building with mural painting and sculpture, and call especial attention to examples which may be found in the new Library of Congress, in the additions to the Boston State House, Boston Public Library, the new Court House at Baltimore, Maryland, and other important buildings in various parts of the United States where this subject has been given serious consideration."[28] Once more a list of practical needs, including furniture, light fixtures, and elevators, was appended to an appeal for artworks commensurate with the building's noble exterior. And once more, the legislature supported the board and its architect (despite challenges in the press and an investigation of its finances), approving one and a half million dollars in additional funds to finish the capitol as a worthy structure to add to the list of prestigious public buildings that Gilbert had evoked.[29]

"If the outside of the building may be considered as a great piece of sculpture, of which the Quadriga will be the most important single detail," wrote Kenyon Cox when the capitol first opened its doors, "the inside may, in like manner, be thought of as a great piece of painting, culminating in the lunettes of Blashfield and La Farge."[30] Gilbert consulted with the Mural Artists Society and his contacts at McKim, Mead & White to estimate a figure of fifty dollars per square foot for mural decorations.[31] He then enlisted several of the leading muralists of the day: not just John La Farge, Blashfield, and Cox but also Edward E. Simmons and Henry Oliver Walker. All had distinguished records in American mural art and, indeed, required some convincing that this new building was deserving of their talents. Seabury urged Gilbert to enlist his chief decorator in this effort: "Mr. Garnsey has been with us, and met five of the seven members of our Board, and has also familiarized himself with the building and its surroundings, so that he can certainly help you to explain to the other gentlemen that this is not the 'wild and woolly West' that many people think it to be, but that our undertaking offers a splendid field for these noted artists, (whose names are, by no means, unknown out here) to help us to make it all that we hope to make it, namely—, one of the few notable buildings of the United States, and one with which it will be an honor to them to have their names connected."[32] Ever diplomatic, Gilbert proposed that French, La Farge, Blashfield, Simmons, and Garnsey join him to form an advisory board for aesthetic matters. This action relieved the capitol commissioners of artistic decisions and also "served as an assurance to the artists that their work would not be marred by non-professional interference, and served to unite them in effort toward a harmonious result."[33]

Their murals were meant to embellish the capitol's primary spaces with decorations that would, as Gauthier's guidebook pointed out, "appropriately represent the growth and progress of the Northwest in the direction of manufactures, commerce and agriculture from pioneer days to the present time. The artists were advised that although the subjects would probably have to be treated allegorically, care must be

5-8. Supreme Court chamber, second floor, c. 1913 photograph. John La Farge's mural *The Moral and the Divine Law,* one of four lunettes on the theme of the development of law, is above the bench. (Photo by C. W. Jerome, Minnesota Historical Society)

5-9. Senate chamber, second floor, c. 1907 photograph. At right is a portion of Edwin H. Blashfield's mural *The Discoverers and Civilizers Led to the Source of the Mississippi,* 1904; the figure of "Equality" in the spandrel is one of four allegorial figures designed by Elmer E. Garnsey and painted by Arthur R. Willett, Kenyon Cox, "The New State Capitol in Minnesota," in *Architectural Record* (August 1905): 106. (Library of Congress)

taken not to fill the building with Greek gods and goddesses, as these were considered inappropriate for a building devoted to the transaction of business."[34] The decorations of the capitol's central spaces nonetheless have a decidedly classical cast of characters.

Gilbert also designed meeting rooms for the Senate, House, and Supreme Court (Figures 5-8 and 5-9) out of the public eye . The Retiring Rooms of the Senate and House all have the air of a gentleman's club (which they were, in effect, until decades into the twentieth century). He worked closely with Garnsey to create spaces derived from French chateaux, with dark wainscoting, elaborate ceilings, and carved wood and marble mantels. The Justices' Consultation Room looks to a different historical model. Gilbert based the white-painted paneled room on the courtroom of Philadelphia's Independence Hall, in an institutional expression of the Colonial revival modes which had earlier shaped several of his St. Paul houses (Figure 5-10).[35] In all these chambers, as in the hallways and offices, Gilbert devoted as much attention to the small details of furnishings as to the artworks and embellishment of walls and domes. His concern for properly outfitting the capitol extended to designing and selecting chairs and tables, choosing pitchers and spittoons, and plating electrical switches to match walls. Gilbert's letters contain marginal drawings of furniture, sometimes made in response to such critiques as that of a judge who found a sofa to be "stately but inadequate for my too too solid frame."[36]

When Gilbert had called for a sophisticated decorative scheme in 1903, he had outlined a simple treatment for the governor's suite: "The executive rooms should be finished in perfectly plain color and without elaborate decoration of any kind."[37] During the following two years, this evolved into what the guidebook calls "the most ornate in the building; in fact it is sumptuous in its every appointment" (Figure 5-11)."[38] Calls for paintings honoring Minnesota's past and, in particular, its role in the Civil War contributed as much to this change as Gilbert's own confidence in directing the decorations elsewhere in the capitol. A Civil War officer who had become president of the state's historical society demanded a change in the tenor of the mural program when he wrote, "I think that I fairly voice the sentiment of the people of our state when I say that we want no Greek or Roman antiques, however classic, no dancing nymphs or goddesses on the walls of the Capitol. The desire is to have our own local history illustrated, our own battles, our own heroes, our own barbarians, our own lakes and rivers."[39] The preferred local history subject was the Treaty of Traverse des Sioux, an 1851 meeting of Dakota Indian bands with a U.S. delegation headed by Minnesota's territorial governor, Alexander Ramsey—an event likened to William Penn's purchase of the site of Philadelphia two centuries earlier. Gilbert considered the subject for the west stair hall lunette but instead designed a place for it in the governor's suite. Receiving suggestions for other historical paintings, Gilbert redesigned the Governor's Reception Room to accommodate them within a spacious room that Cox characterized as "conceived on the lines of a Venetian council chamber, with heavy, gilded moldings intended to frame historical pictures."[40]

Gilbert articulated his approach in a letter to Seabury. "I personally believe in historic paintings for such a room and I think they should be treated from the pictorial standpoint rather than the decorative standpoint," he wrote, and added, "[T]hey should really be pictures of the events as nearly as they can be transcribed."[41] This distinction between mural paintings conceived as integral components of their architectural whole, and pictorial narratives telling historical tales, informed his treatment of the paintings as if they were windows within the walls of carved, gilded oak through which past events may be seen. In addition to the treaty painting, they depict Hennepin's first sighting of the Falls of St. Anthony in present-day Minneapolis and four Civil War actions in which Minnesota troops played prominent roles. Two additional war paintings hang in gilded frames in an anteroom. Gilbert chose leading painters for these specialized commissions: Francis D. Millet and Douglas Volk for the local scenes; Blashfield, Millet, Volk, Rufus F. Zogbaum, Stanley M. Arthurs, and Howard Pyle for the war pictures. All took pains to capture the scenes accurately, interviewing battle survivors and consulting such historical sources as books

and photographs. As he did with the allegories in the halls, Gilbert offered his critiques to the painters. He suggested certain accessories to Volk for his Hennepin painting, for example. The artist, who as the founding director of the Minneapolis School of Art in 1886 was the only capitol artist with prior

Minnesota connections, adopted Gilbert's ideas despite some reservations. He wrote in response to Gilbert's recommendation for the costume of one of the figures, "There is nothing more picturesque, perhaps, than fur, and I would enjoy painting a fur cap on [French explorer] Picard du Gay, as you suggest, but how about it in July? It would be all right here tonight, for it is cold enough for an overcoat, but if you think a coon skin will go, I will be glad to put one on the Picard. I have found just the type for this personage."[42]

5-10. Justices' Consultation Room, second floor, in a 1910 photograph. Gilbert designed the room, which is behind the Supreme Court chamber, after an eighteenth-century courtroom in Independence Hall, Philadelphia. (Photo by C. W. Jerome, Minnesota Historical Society)

In the course of planning the Governor's Reception Room, Gilbert articulated a concern that was part of his earliest efforts in 1895 regarding the capitol. He had lobbied for the designation of the architect as supervisor of construction as well; ten years later he worried about guarding the capitol from politically motivated interference in aesthetic matters. He wrote to Seabury about the Reception Room, "It seems to me that if the Board does not cover the vacant spaces that somebody will get in their deadly political work later on and make that room a chamber of horrors in the name of patriotism."[43] The Reception Room was completed to his orders, but

5-11. Governor's Reception Room, first floor, c. 1907 photograph. One of the capitol's most elaborately decorated spaces, the Reception Room features mural-sized paintings of state history and Civil War scenes including *The Second Minnesota Regiment at Missionary Ridge* and Douglas Volk's *Father Hennepin Discovering the Falls of St. Anthony.* (Minnesota Historical Society)

Gilbert's fears came true shortly afterward when a larger-than-life statue of a Civil War general was commissioned for the rotunda. He refused to approve or even critique the model, and was quick to defend his stance: "What I think they want, is my 'for nothing advice,' and to say to the public that they acted only under my advice, and make me responsible for a damned bad statue, which they have not the nerve, nor the sense to accept or reject by themselves. . . . They shall not mar that building with my concurrence."[44] The statue and three other bronzes were installed nonetheless. Until the disbanding of the

board in 1907, Gilbert and Seabury continued to press for a nonpartisan overseer for the capitol, but seventy years would pass before the state took that step.

The Minnesota legislature first assembled in the new capitol on January 4, 1905, and the building stayed open late that night to accommodate thousands of curious citizens. Ten years and four and a half million dollars had been spent since Gilbert's selection for the project. Although he had moved his primary office to New York City to oversee the construction of the first of his federal commissions, the United States Custom House (1899–1907), Gilbert kept an office and an ongoing interest in St. Paul. There were unfinished components of the capitol to monitor: French's quadriga group and a number of murals were in the works but not yet completed or installed. Gilbert had also expressed concerns for the capitol's larger setting as early as 1895, and made public proposals for a grand setting as early as 1902. These concerns had a far wider scope than plantings or statuary (though his letters revealed minute attention to those as well). The capitol, he felt, should become the focus and impetus for a comprehensive plan that would apply the principles of the City Beautiful movement to St. Paul. In 1906, Gilbert articulated his concepts in a volume illustrated with plates of long axial avenues affording views from the capitol, through downtown St. Paul, to the Mississippi River bluffs and beyond.[45] Drawings of stately monuments and genteel facades tempted readers to imagine the sophistication of Washington, if not Paris, replacing the workaday street plan of St. Paul. This published plan and his talks to the city's commercial and cultural groups suggest a strategy similar to the approach Gilbert had taken in building and decorating the capitol itself: create a farseeing plan, hold to the highest standards and aims, and execute the plan as economic, political, and artistic circumstances permitted. The plan for the city did not materialize, but half a century after Gilbert's death, the vision he set forth was the starting point for a rethinking of the capitol grounds and neighborhood that has brought a measure of decorum to both.[46]

The capitol building, like Gilbert's reputation, has attracted praise and gathered criticism from its earliest days, as Gilbert expected. He lamented to Seabury in a letter of 1904: "We must not look for immediate praise in Minnesota, and we must not be disappointed if some criticism is made, but when they have time to consider I have no doubt that they will approve."[47] Amid the general enthusiasm for the building as it opened to the public, there were complaints that the "beauty pile" was too crowded or too inconvenient. In one of the more extreme attacks on its classical conceits, a local poet took umbrage at French's quadriga as an insult to the state. He demanded in the press that Minnesotans "[t]ake a sledge hammer and smash 'them' Roman bronchos [sic] and that chariot! Clean 'em out and put a grand heroic statue of Alexander Ramsey in their stead."[48] The sculpture remained in place. More subtle but serious dangers came over time with shifts of taste and use. A history of local architecture published in 1958 noted that "within a few years of Gilbert's death in 1934, a new generation trained in a new tradition was to label his work—along with that of both his eclectic admirers and his academic critics—as pretentious and false."[49] By 1976, a survey mustered grudging praise for an architect and a building that were yet to enjoy a reappraisal: "Gilbert's version of this [sixteenth-century Renaissance] scheme added nothing really new, but his building was a success because of the quality of his design, his finesse in handling the proportions of the basic forms, and the relationship proportionately between the volumes below and the drum and the dome. If we look at other state capitol buildings of the late nineteenth and early twentieth centuries, we can sense how considerable Gilbert's talent was."[50] The critics and historians of the 1990s, however, have looked with fresh eyes on the capitol and buildings of its ilk, as Gilbert himself has also been reappraised. Introducing the first book-length monograph on Gilbert, Robert A. M. Stern declared him "[a]n inventor but not an innovator. . . . Gilbert's work is second to none in its command of composition and vividness of detail."[51] And a survey in 1994 of the arts of turn-of-the-century Minnesota pronounced the Minnesota capitol "one of the finest 'American Renaissance' buildings in the country."[52]

Cass Gilbert stepped from his Minnesota capitol to a career of national scope and recognized the building's enduring importance. The capitol appears in Gilbert's 1915 drawing of his proudest achievements to that date, such as the Woolworth Building and the United States Custom House—along with the Pantheon, Notre Dame, and the pyramids of Egypt. Gilbert's list of civic and commercial buildings is such that work on two other state capitols is but a minor aspect of his accomplishments. He helped to complete the Arkansas capitol in 1917, a long-drawn-out project that had begun with the designs of George R. Mann, a finalist on the Minnesota capitol.[53] At the end of his career, Gilbert designed a capitol building for West Virginia. Both fit the general pattern of the domed statehouse, but neither rivaled the adroit handling of composition and materials that marked Gilbert's capitol in St. Paul. That first state commission had illustrated how well he understood the magnitude of the public architect's task: to create a dignified, even elite setting for the frequently contentious and small-minded process of government by the people. He strove for a working building that would express the citizenry's highest ideals in lasting form. At the end of his life, Gilbert looked back triumphantly on the monument he had created for his home state. He told an audience at the National Academy of Design in 1934, "The State Capitol of Minnesota, like a pioneer in the West erecting a standard in a far country, gave new opportunity in a new field. . . . The idea that civilization, culture and the love of beauty stopped short in Hoboken was ill-founded."[54]

CHAPTER 6

THE CIVILIZATION OF THE WEST

Sally Webster

When the Minnesota capitol officially opened in 1905, the state was less than fifty years old and St. Paul still had a "raw utilitarianism." It had "grown too fast" and its citizens were "too much occupied with industry and trade and the creation of wealth to have leisure for the cultivation of art."[1] This prosperity came from lumber hauled to Duluth and shipped to Buffalo, the Erie Canal, and New York City; wood transported to New York came back as furniture. Iron ore from the Mesabi Range and grain from the southern plains were sent all over the world and returned as cash. If Minnesotans did not have time to cultivate refinement, they could buy it; a new state capitol with a well-mannered face would ameliorate their Wild West image.[2] To design such a structure, they hired a fellow Minnesotan, Cass Gilbert, whose ambitions matched their own. Gilbert, an able architect, was an even better administrator and cultural guide. Along with securing approval of his plans and supervising the myriad details of construction, he gave the Board of State Capitol Commissioners lessons in refinement. The result was a dignified, beautifully appointed statehouse. With artworks by the best-known muralists and sculptors of the era, Minnesota's capitol became the pride of the state and the talk of the nation.

In the late nineteenth century, the Midwest was a cultural wilderness. There were few universities, few art museums, no major libraries, no buildings of artistic significance, and few paved streets or public amenities. The exception was Chicago, where modern commercial architecture reached its finest expression. This same standard of functional design, however, was not extended to the city's public buildings, which were criticized as being "monuments not only of civic corruption, and barbaric extravagance, but of a total eclipse of art."[3]

Conditions were about to change, and while it is foolhardy to credit a single event, Chicago's 1893 World's Columbian Exposition brought civilization to the Great Lakes. Here on the shores of Lake Michigan, the canals of Venice, the Baths of Caracalla, and the palaces of Rome were magically transplanted. Responsible for its creation were local businessmen who became partners with the best-known architects of the era to fashion an enchanted vision. Both the alliances and the European-inspired architecture set a precedent for new cities and state capitals and the lessons of the World's Columbian Exposition were not long in coming to St. Paul. For the decoration of its capitol, Gilbert was authorized to hire the finest muralists of the day, John La Farge, Edwin Blashfield, and Edward Simmons, and the equally renowned sculptor Daniel Chester French, all of whom, with the exception of La Farge, participated in the Chicago Exposition. If the World's Columbian Exposition introduced Beaux-Arts classicism to the Midwest, the Minnesota State Capitol made it a permanent resident. Alluding to earlier, and by implication less civilized, forms of government by Native Americans (who only recently had been relocated to the Dakotas), an unidentified commentator noted that "[h]owever short a time the commonwealth of Minnesota has been in making, it is none too soon to bid good-bye to the tomahawk, to see the pow-wow give place to the caucus, the wigwam to the capitol."[4]

One hundred years earlier, similar sentiments were expressed along the shores of the Potomac, at a location even more of a wilderness than St. Paul in the late nineteenth century. The new nation needed a legislative hall and construction on the United States Capitol was underway. Few options existed at this time for public buildings, other than the classical style. This precedent was furthered by President Thomas Jefferson's firsthand knowledge of ancient European buildings and the advice of the British-born architect Benjamin Latrobe. It was Latrobe who hired the Capitol's first decorative sculptors. Italian-born, these artisans created the earliest national symbols: liberty, agriculture, art, science, and commerce. After the War of 1812, when British power no longer seemed a threat, nationhood was secure, and the Capitol Rotunda became an important site for decoration and paintings that commemorated the country's new history and heroes. Here were placed four mural-size paintings by John Trumbull that commemorated celebrated incidents from the American

Revolution.[5] These were supplemented in the 1840s by other historical narratives by four different artists—Robert Weir, John Chapman, John Vanderlyn, and William Powell.[6] At mid-century, Italian painter Constantin Brumidi was hired to embellish hallways and committee rooms with decorative frescoes completed in an elaborate Victorian/ Italianate manner. Nor should the efforts of Emanuel Leutze, of *Washington Crossing the Delaware* fame, be ignored. The theme of westward expansion found in his fresco *Westward the Course of Empire Takes Its Way* (1862) (Figure 6-1), installed in the west stairway of the House of Representatives wing, was later expanded in the rotunda of the Minnesota State Capitol with four panels by Edward Simmons titled *The Civilization of*

6-1. Emanuel Leutze, *Westward the Course of Empire Takes its Way,* 1862, fresco, 20 x 30 feet, United States Capitol, House Wing, west stairway. (Architect of the Capitol, Collection of the United States Capitol)

the Northwest (Figure 6-2). Sculpture by American artists for the nation's Capitol included Thomas Crawford's pediment, *Progress of Civilization* (1863), for the House wing and the colossal finial, *Statue of Freedom,* for the Capitol dome.

These artworks expressed two broad themes: American history and heroes, and the discovery, exploration, and settlement of the United States. Only Crawford's pediment decoration, with its symbolic references, reflected the European allegorical tradition. While not particularly complex, these symbols created for the United States Capitol became enduring icons. Most important, they laid the groundwork for a democratic iconography, the construction of a symbolic program that did not contain allusions to the crown (the king) or the cross (the church) but communicated instead the ideals, virtues, and ambitions of a republican state. During the course of the century, the Capitol would become an architectural model for many statehouses.[7] However, the development of a national iconography did not expand beyond Washington until after the Civil War.

While a home-grown classicism inspired the style of the nation's Capitol, a new sophistication entered America's architecture in the 1870s as architects returned home after training at the Ecole des Beaux-Arts in Paris.[8] Beaux-Arts training in architecture was broadly based and did not promote the exclusive use of classical style. Instead, it instilled principles of overall design or composition, a consideration that many critics felt lacking in public

6-2. Edward Simmons, *The Civilization of the Northwest* (1906), four panels, Rotunda, Minnesota State Capitol, in 1950 (Photo by *Minneapolis Star-Journal Tribune,* Minnesota Historical Society)

architecture in the United States: "*Composition* was the French academic system's term for what it considered the essential act of architectural design. What *composition* signified was not so much the design of ornament or of facades but of whole buildings, conceived as three-dimensional entities and seen together in plan, section and elevation."[9] These new initiatives, however, did not take place in Washington, where the wounds of division had not healed and further attempts to create national symbols had to be postponed. Instead they appeared in state capitols, city libraries, and local courthouses.

The first public building to incorporate this new architectural thinking with a sophisticated civic iconography was the Albany statehouse. Designed by Henry Hobson Richardson, who had trained at the Ecole, and the German-born Leopold Eidlitz, the Albany capitol was the first building in the United States to be inspired by modern European principles of design that incorporated painting, sculpture, and architecture. Although the two murals painted by the Boston artist William Morris Hunt were covered only ten years after they had been unveiled, their memory lived on in reproductions and critical acclaim, which acknowledged Hunt's success in creating a sophisticated response to the European humanistic tradition. Not specific to New York State, these murals symbolized a providential construct that America was the new dispensation, that is, a new beginning for western civilization.[10] This is rendered through Hunt's two murals, which faced each other across the forty-foot width of the Assembly Chamber. *The Discoverer* (Figure 6-3), with Columbus positioned at the center, represents the dawn of a new day following the dark night of barbarism that is represented by the Near Eastern goddess, Anahita, who is seated on an airborne chariot seen in the painting on the opposite wall, *The Flight of Night.*

More than ten years would elapse before further attempts were made to create, in Schuyler's words, "a national monumental art." This occurred in the 1890s with the full embrace of Beaux-Arts design for eminent public buildings. Led by the firm of McKim, Mead & White, their contribution was first evident in the design of the Boston Public Library and in the

appearance of the contemporaneous World's Columbian Exposition (1893). Gilbert, while not one of the participating architects, as the leading practitioner in St. Paul attended the Fair as a jury member of the Board of Architecture. According to Henry-Russell Hitchcock, the World's Columbian Exposition had a direct influence on Gilbert's Minnesota State Capitol,[11] one of the most beautifully integrated of all American Beaux-Arts buildings.

All of the artists commissioned for the Minnesota State Capitol had participated in earlier decorative projects of the 1890s, including McKim, Mead & White's Walker Art Building at Bowdoin College, Brunswick, Maine (1891–95); the World's Columbian Exposition; the Library of Congress; and the Appellate Division Courthouse, New York City. Of these projects, George B. Post's Manufactures and Liberal Arts Building (which contained murals by four of the Minnesota artists: Simmons, Blashfield, Kenyon Cox, and Francis Millet) at the World's

Columbian Exposition was credited with inaugurating national interest in mural painting. Post hired these artists to create allegorical frescoes for the interior of the pendentive domes and lunettes of the building's corner pavilions and entryways, all of which were related to manufactured goods—ceramics, metalwork, textiles, and furniture—that were displayed inside the building. Simmons's decoration for the interiors of the pendentive dome contained representations of stone cutting, wood carving, forging, and mechanics. Similarly, Cox's decorations were personifications of metal work, building, ceramics, and spinning. Millet, who was director of decorations for the fair, contributed two tympanum paintings, *The Return of Ulysses* and *Penelope at Her Loom*, which alluded to the art of weaving and its ancient history. Blashfield's contribution (Figure 6-4), a slightly more elaborate mural for another dome's interior surface, contained images titled "The Armourer's Craft," "The Iron Worker," "The Brass-Founder," and "The

6-3. William Morris Hunt, *The Discoverer,* photograph of finished mural taken from scaffolding, New York State Capitol, Albany, NY, December 1878. (Prints & Drawings Collection, The Octagon, The Museum of the American Architectural Foundation, Washington, D.C.)

THE CIVILIZATION OF THE WEST

Art of the Goldsmith." While these images of commerce and industry were as temporary as the building, the project's significance lay in the opportunity it provided for a new generation of painters to explore the potential of mural painting and to introduce a large public to its aesthetic promise.

The most important decorative project to emerge from the World's Columbian Exposition was the Library of Congress, whose mural paintings were better integrated, permanent, and more representative of national purpose. Collectively its many murals and sculptures, dedicated to the dissemination of knowledge, updated the idea of the advancement of civilization in the New World. The architect who promoted a decorated interior for the library was Edward Pearce Casey, the son of Brigadier General Thomas Lincoln Casey, chief of the Army Corps of Engineers and supervisor of the building's construction. The younger Casey had recently returned from three years' study in Paris in the architectural program of the Ecole and thus had firsthand knowledge of monumental design and decoration. Casey's first initiative was to establish an advisory board of sculptors—John Quincy Adams Ward, Saint-Gaudens, and Olin Warner—in January 1894 to consult with him on the sculpture needed for the library's interior. The decision to hire painters came later, and in April 1895 the final list was announced. Altogether fifty sculptors and painters were hired to decorate the library, and their nationality as Americans was hailed publicly. (In contrast to the need to hire several Europeans to decorate the United States Capitol, by the end of the century the country could boast a plethora of qualified artists, most of whom, ironically, had been trained in Europe.) Of those employed at the Library

6-4. Edwin H. Blashfield. Dome of the Manufactures and Liberal Arts Building, 1893, in Royal Cortissoz, "Color in the Court of Honor at the Fair," *Century Magazine* 46 (July 1893): 327. (Library of Congress)

of Congress, French, Blashfield, Cox, Garnsey, Simmons, and H. O. Walker were hired to work at the Minnesota State Capitol.

Not surprisingly, the building's decorative program reflects the library's function: the transmission of knowledge in all its forms. Yet this was also a library with a national purpose similar to that of the great European ones: the Bibliothèque Nationale in Paris, the Library of the British Museum in London, and the National Library of Vienna. Largely due to newly enacted copyright laws, the Library of Congress, almost overnight, became one of the largest in the world.

The murals generally relate to broad categories of humanistic learning, as seen in Simmons's north corridor lunettes (which depict the nine muses) or Cox's two tympanum decorations for the southwest gallery entitled *The Sciences* and *The Arts.* The keystone of the interior decorative program was widely acknowledged as Blashfield's *Evolution of Civilization,* a circular mural designed for the collar of the dome of the Library's Reading Room. In this work, twelve figures represent twelve different civilizations or epochs, "which have contributed most to the development of present-day civilization," seated on marble benches holding attributes of the arts, sciences, manufacturing, and literature, and so on.[14] Beginning with the personification of Egypt (and its association with the "written record"), Blashfield's mural ends with America and its contribution to science. While placing the United States contribution on a par with other countries might strike some as unpatriotic, the nation's stature is elevated by association. Blashfield's iconography was wholly appropriate for a national library of a new country that only recently had achieved status as an international power. Among the projects that helped further this national iconography was the Minnesota State Capitol.

Gilbert's winning design of 1895 for the Capitol building in St. Paul did not include plans for mural paintings, and little was suggested in the way of sculptural decoration. This lack of architectural embellishment did not mean that Gilbert was unaware of the initiatives of the newly formed Mural Painters society (later called the Society of Mural Painters) in New York.[15] Early in February 1896, when Charles Lamb, the corresponding secretary of the Mural Painters, wrote to Gilbert to congratulate him on his commission, Lamb outlined the society's philosophy and urged him to include murals in the building's interior: "The purpose of the society is to stimulate the question of the enrichment of the interiors of our public, civic and religious buildings, and to do so in collaboration with the architects and the Building Committees, so that the best artistic results will be secured. The monumental effect, so essential to such buildings, has been heretofore much neglected, and it is the purpose of our society . . . to further in every way, the development of the decorative element in architectural composition."[16]

The Mural Painters society was one of several associations—some professional, some civic—established in the 1890s to further the ideals of civic beautification. In New York these associations included, among others, the Municipal Art Society and the National Sculpture Society.[17] This combined activity, which again was an outgrowth of the Chicago fair, contributed to the City Beautiful movement.[18]

Gilbert responded positively to Lamb's letter and forwarded his inquiry to Channing Seabury, the vice president of the Board of State Capitol Commissioners and Gilbert's most enthusiastic supporter. Seabury wrote Lamb to express his general support of the society's efforts but indicated that since ground had not been broken, it was too early to consider mural decoration.[19] After this flurry of interest, Gilbert kept his own counsel regarding the addition of mural paintings and focused instead on the more mundane but essential matters of the procurement of materials and the overseeing of construction. However, Gilbert was committed to having sculpture on the building's exterior, and that same year, 1896, he wrote sculptors Daniel Chester French and Augustus Saint-Gaudens, asking them to submit estimates. French replied by sending a budget for a quadriga, twelve eagles, four lions, eight "groups," four caryatids, and two coats of arms. Saint-Gaudens had been asked to submit a proposal for sculpture for the north (not the south or main) entrance. The sculptor wrote Gilbert from Paris in May 1898 apologizing for

the delay and submitted a large sketch. For reasons that remain unclear, Saint-Gaudens's submission was never approved.

At the time only six "outer figures," which had been proposed by French, were purchased. These more than life-size figures (four female and two male) were completed in 1900 and appear on the central entablature. Titled "Bounty," "Courage," "Integrity," "Prudence," "Truth," and "Wisdom," these personifications were reminiscent of the early decorative sculpture for the United States Capitol. As the ideal attributes of a well-functioning government, they were the underpinnings, literally and figuratively, of French's quadriga, *The Progress of the State* (see Figure C-16), placed on top of the entablature at a later date.

During the next few years Gilbert "educated" the board of commissioners and in 1901 received authorization "to discuss this subject [of decorative work] with the artists and obtain, if possible, preliminary sketches for work."[20] He also organized a trip for the board in March 1902 to several eastern cities, to better acquaint them with the latest developments in Beaux-Arts architecture and to whet their appetites to compete with other cities.

The trip began, appropriately, in Albany. Although William Morris Hunt's murals were no longer visible, New York's statehouse was one of the most admired in the nation. The group then traveled to New York City where they visited James Renwick's St. Patrick's Cathedral (1878–88) and his Grace Church (1845), Charles McKim's Low Library of Columbia University (1897), Napoleon LeBrun's Metropolitan Life Insurance building (1893), and several buildings under construction. These included Gilbert's Custom House and Heins & La Farge's Cathedral Church of St. John the Divine. The group then went on to Providence to see McKim, Mead & White's newly opened Rhode Island capitol. Frank Harrison, who wrote a description of the trip, noted pridefully that "the building is much smaller than ours and [has a] very plain exterior." He also remarked that aside from the governor's room, "the interior was not impressive." From Providence they traveled to Boston, where they visited the new public library. No comment was made regarding its murals, only a note that they went to see "the use of soft stone." The next stop was Philadelphia. Here they visited colonial Independence Hall (1731) and John McArthur's newly built City Hall (1873–90), the latter of which contained more than 250 sculptures that mostly had been executed by Alexander Milne Calder. The City Hall building itself, however, was not admired by the Minnesota delegation.

Traveling south, the committee journeyed to Baltimore where they visited Wyatt and Nolting's courthouse, still under construction and awaiting murals by Charles Yardley Turner, Blashfield, and La Farge that eventually were installed between 1902 and 1907. From Baltimore it was an easy trip to Washington, their last stop. Here they visited the United States Capitol, Renwick's Corcoran Gallery (1859), and Smithmeyer and Pelz's newly completed Library of Congress (1885–97).[21] It was fitting that the final building on their tour was the Library of Congress. With architectural decoration by fifty sculptors and painters, the library's interior was the most lavish in the country. In an ecstatic response to the library's grandeur, commissioner Ebenezer Corliss said he was "going back to Fergus Falls and tell my friends in Otter Tail county that we ought to have another appropriation of two million dollars. And if I had my way we'd spend it all for mural decorations."[22]

Corliss was not the only enthusiast. When they returned to St. Paul, the board of commissioners asked Gilbert to prepare new estimates for murals and more sculpture. In response, Gilbert sent Seabury "an epitomized estimate of the amount necessary to complete the State Capitol in an absolutely first class manner." Gilbert continued to say, perhaps disingenuously, "[Y]ou will recall the many times . . . I have urged on the Board the consideration of inexpensive interior finish" but assented to create a new budget "since it seems to be practically a unanimous sentiment in Minnesota that the building must be of the best in every respect, and to compare favorably with the best public buildings." In estimating the cost of painting and sculpture, Gilbert referred to the new Pennsylvania state capitol in Harrisburg (which had a budget of $500,000 for such work). Gilbert thought this amount was sufficient "to get the services of La Farge, Blashfield, Simmons, Elihu Vedder, St. Gaudens, French and others who decorated the Library of Congress."[23]

Gilbert wanted the same high level of artistic and intellectual content in Minnesota as found in the Library of Congress, and to that end invited Blashfield, Cox, Simmons, Garnsey, and La Farge to meet with him in his New York office in late December 1902 to discuss the Minnesota project in detail. Having met with each artist separately, he now asked them "to take their chances" with him, to submit "preliminary sketches," and to trust that funds will be "provided to carry forward the work." After agreeing to participate, the artists each chose a major room. La Farge took the Supreme Court; Blashfield, the Senate Chamber; Simmons, the decoration of the main staircases; and Garnsey was asked "to undertake the general architectural color decoration of the corridors and such rooms as might be assigned to him." Gilbert mentioned other artists who might be invited to participate: Herman Schladermundt, George Maynard, John Singer Sargent, Vedder, Will Low, Douglas Volk, Bert Harwood, and George de Forest Brush. In deference to their professional standing, Sargent and Vedder were singled out. Sargent at the time was deeply involved in a complex decorative project for the Boston Public Library (*Triumph of Religion*, 1890–1919) and Vedder was esteemed for his mural *Rome* (1894) for McKim, Mead & White's Walker Art Building, and a mosaic, *Minerva* (1896–97) and five lunettes illustrating *Government* (1895–97) for the Library of Congress. Both Sargent and Vedder were living in Europe and declined to participate.

Gilbert also discussed several topics that he thought appropriate for mural paintings for Minnesota's capitol. He had firsthand knowledge of the state's history and its national role—information that would have been known only vaguely to the East Coast, European-trained artists. Gilbert mentioned such subjects as French exploration, early settlement of the state, and Minnesota's proud participation in the Civil War. Even though Minnesota had been a part of the Union for only three years, it was the first to volunteer a regiment to President Lincoln. Gilbert

also noted the state's "great industries," which included "agriculture, mining, lumber, manufacturing," and reminded those present that Minnesota was famous for being at "the head of the great chain of lakes" and "the source of the Mississippi."[24] He presented an exciting prospect to the artists whom he invited; he encouraged them to consider the expansion of a national iconography to include the history and contribution of the Upper Mississippi Valley.

Gilbert needed to secure legislative support for more money and decided to organize an exhibition in St. Paul of the proposed decorative work along with examples of decorative work from other contemporary buildings, such as "the Library of Congress, Baltimore Court House, Appellate Court House, Boston State House, etc."[25] The legislature was so impressed with the exhibition and Gilbert's ideas that they immediately proposed an appropriation of $1.5 million.

With this assurance, Gilbert proceeded to negotiate prices, conditions, and delivery dates with the artists. He first dealt with French, with whom he had already discussed the redesign of French's quadriga at the World's Columbian Exposition. As the central element in Charles Atwood's Peristyle located at the eastern end of the fair's Court of Honor, it was a direct link between the Beaux-Arts

ideals expressed at the exposition and Minnesota's decorative program. Assisted by the animal sculptor Edward Potter, French transformed a chariot for Columbus into a ship of state for Minnesota. Eventually known as *The Progress of the State* (see Figure C-16), French's gilded chariot driven by a male personification of Minnesota and pulled by four horses led by two women, embodied the dual themes of the building's iconography: westward expansion and civilization.

Blashfield, too, was interested in these themes and wrote Gilbert a four-page, handwritten description of his ideas for two fourteen- by thirty-one-foot lunettes, *The Discoverers and Civilizers Led to the Source of the Mississippi* (see Figure 5-9), and *Minnesota, The Granary of the World* (Figure 6-5).[26] As he explained, the central figure of *The Discoverers and Civilizers* is the Great Spirit or Manitou, Father of the Waters, who sits on a rock throne placed in what looks like a fall of rapids, a symbol of Minnesota being "at the head waters of the navigation of the American continent"—the Great Lakes and the Mississippi.[27] The figures on the right were "a group of the discoverers (La Salle & others), navigators, explorers, trappers, etc. of the seventeenth century." To the left, he noted, was a group of "the civilizers, the settlers, men, women and children in furs and

6-5. Edwin Blashfield, *Minnesota, The Granary of the World,* 1904, lunette, 14 x 31 feet, Senate Chamber, Minnesota State Capitol, in Blashfield, *The Works of Edwin Howland Blashfield* (New York, 1937), pl. 1.

woolens, with their guns, axes and dogs. This left-hand group headed by a priest holding out a crucifix and Bible to an Indian squaw who at the feet of Manitou leans forward to look at the crucifix. At the feet of Manitou on his other side a young Indian is seen as starting forward to oppose the advance of the Discoverers. These two figures of Indians, squaw and brave, connected the two side groups with the figure of the Manitou."[28]

It is probable that these "figures of Indians," including the Manitou, were drawn from Henry Wadsworth Longfellow's poem "Hiawatha" (1855), which was set in Minnesota. According to Native American legend, Hiawatha was a mythical Iroquois chief whom Longfellow reincarnated as a member of the Plains Indian tribe, the Ojibway. In both legend and in the nineteenth-century poem, Hiawatha, through the example of his heroic adventures and personal trials, introduced the "benefits" of human progress and civilization. These "benefits" included agriculture, navigation, husbandry, medicine, family, literacy, and faith, which in Longfellow's poem was Christianity.

In the second panel, *Minnesota, The Granary of the World,* Blashfield creates a civic allegory alluding to the state's history and its contribution to present-day America. Above and in the center sits a female figure, symbol of the state of Minnesota. She is surrounded on either side by two winged spirits who represent civilization and progress. Directly below this central image are a pair of oxen, flanked on each side and in front by other symbolic figures, furthering the idea of Minnesota as a wealthy, fecund state. On the far right and left are gatherings of modern-day and allegorical personages whom Blashfield described as follows: "The right hand group suggests the epoch extending from Minnesota's entrance into the union up to the Civil War or a little later, and shows Minnesotan soldiers of the first regiment offered to President Lincoln—also there are representatives of the Sanitary Corps (nurses, doctors). The left hand group symbolizes the *present,* and the main industries of Minnesota (above all agriculture and the lumber industry)."[29]

While Blashfield's mural, more than any of the others, was the most responsive to Gilbert's instruc-

tions, the artist had created a similar scheme in 1895 for George B. Post's Bank of Pittsburgh. This nine-by-nineteen-foot lunette mural (which was destroyed with the building), *Pittsburgh Offering Its Steel and Iron to the Commerce and Manufacturers of the World,* had a strikingly similar composition to Blashfield's Minnesota panel. Both depict female allegorical figures centrally placed: one represented the city and all its wealth, and the other the state and its expanding importance.

Mention also should be made of another contemporaneous project, for the Baltimore Court House that occupied Blashfield and La Farge. For his two murals, *Washington Laying Down His Command at the Feet of Columbia* (1902) and *The Edict of Toleration of Lord Baltimore* (1904), Blashfield chose incidents from the colonial history that had constitutional implications and were thus appropriate for a courthouse. John La Farge, in contrast, for his six spandrels in the courthouse's vestibule, created complex allegories illustrating the history or evolution of the law and directly connected, pictorially and conceptually, to those he did at the same time for Minnesota. Collectively entitled "The Great Lawgivers of History" (1903–1907), the triangular spaces contain images of Confucius, Justinian, Lycurgus, Mohammed, Moses, and Numa Pompilius. Two of these figures also appeared in his St. Paul program. As he proposed for Baltimore, La Farge's four lunettes (1904) for Minnesota's Supreme Court trace, in a similar fashion, the evolution of the law through different periods and countries: biblical times, ancient Greece, China, and the middle ages.[30]

The first mural of La Farge's series, *The Moral and the Divine Law* (see Figure 5-8), is located above the justices' bench. Moses is shown receiving the law on Mt. Sinai, and according to the artist, this episode represents the point at which human conscience and divine law are all that stands between civilization and savagery. La Farge's second panel, *The Relation of the Individual to the State* (Figure 6-6), depicts Socrates and his companions discussing Plato's *Republic.* The third panel shows *The Recording of Precedents,* as represented by Confucius and his followers, who are shown collating and transcribing documents, thus

Copyright, 1904, by John La Farge

emphasizing, in La Farge's words, "the importance of the past and of precedent." The final panel offers a scene from medieval Europe, entitled *The Adjustment of Conflicting Interests,* in which Count Raymond of Toulouse, an eleventh-century crusader, seeks to balance the interests of the citizen, the church, and the state. Overall these murals by La Farge illustrate the law's significance for the individual and society. More importantly, they remind the viewer of the critical role played by the law in a constitutional democracy.

Precedent is also found for La Farge's legal iconography in the exterior decoration of James Brown Lord's Appellate Division Courthouse, completed in 1900. Standing on the roof's balustrade are life-size sculptures of historical figures prominent in the history of the law—including Moses and Confucius as well as Zoroaster, Alfred the Great, Lycurgus, Solon, Louis IX, and Justinian. Inside the elaborately decorated courtroom, a group of murals echo on smaller scale the grandeur of the Library of Congress. These murals, including three along the east wall, were completed in 1900. The central panel is H. O. Walker's *The Wisdom of the Law,* flanked on the left by Edward Simmons's *The Justice of the Law* and on the right by Blashfield's *The Power of the Law.*

Working in collaboration with the Mural Painters society, Lord provided an early opportunity for a new generation of artists to gain experience and expertise in the new American art of mural painting.[31]

It was, however, Simmons's lunette decorations for the rotunda (Figure 6-7 and see Figure 5-5) that Gilbert called "the finest things of the kind in this country."[32] Designed for placement under the collar of the dome, Simmons's four lunette panels are called collectively *The Civilization of the Northwest* (see Figure 6-2). As Gilbert detailed, "[T]he subject in general may be said to typify the development and progress of the West, in which landscape forms a very important part, being used as a background in each painting, and in each picture there are four to six figures of heroic scale."[33]

Each lunette panel is twenty-nine feet long and thirteen feet high. The entire sequence looms ninety feet above the floor. The first panel, subtitled "A Youth, or the Brave American Spirit Leaves Home [the East], in the Company of Hope and Wisdom," is a highly charged scene in which a beautifully proportioned seminude male figure gestures to two female personifications who float slightly above the ground to the right. These beneficent figures accom-

6-6. John La Farge, *The Relation of the Individual to the State,* 1905, Supreme Court, Minnesota State Capitol, in Elizabeth Luther Cary, "John LaFarge's Decorations at St. Paul," *The Scrip* (February 1906): following p. 104. (Library of Congress)

THE CIVILIZATION OF THE WEST

pany the protagonist in every panel. Next in the series is "Cleansing the Soil of Bad Elements," in which, Julie Gauthier, the author of an early guide to the Capitol, explained, "the Young Man Scourges the West of its non-civilizing features: the bear (representing savagery); the cougar (cowardice), a woman who bears deadly nightshade is sin; and a man bearing a sprig of stramonium, another poisonous plant, is dubbed stupidity."[34] The third panel is subtitled, "Breaking the Soil" wherein, as described by Gauthier, "man Rips Stone from the Soil and Releases Wealth and Fertility: a young girl bearing maize emerges from the ground along with crystal and gold."[35] In the fourth lunette, the panel is titled "The Young Man is crowned and sends the four winds to the Four quarters of the globe bearing the gifts of Minnesota: wheat, minerals, fine arts and knowledge"; it is a crowded scene set in a classical arcade. The four winds, Hope, and Wisdom swirl around the hero, now the personification of the state, in celebration of his success.

While this grandiose allegory with its European-inspired figures and inflated visual rhetoric is easy to dismiss, it does encapsulate the building's entire iconographic program. Simmons not only refers to westward expansion but also narrates its consequences through the purging of uncivilized elements, settlement, and the establishment of the state. It also updates and expands upon Leutze's mural, *Westward Ho!*, completed forty years earlier for the United States Capitol. Simmons, however, expanded the story to include the period after the Civil War when, with the establishment of state governments, stability and civilization arrived in the Great Plains.

While Gilbert and the Board were pleased with the work done by the well-established eastern painters, other Minnesotans felt that local history and artists had been neglected. In late June 1903, General James H. Baker, writing on behalf of the Minnesota Historical Society, asked that one of the murals be devoted to the subject of "the great Treaty of Traverse des Sioux."[36] When notified of this appeal Gilbert was unperturbed, saying that perhaps Garnsey or another painter could create such a work, and suggested to the board that he redesign the Governor's Reception Room to accommodate framed easel paintings. The following year Francis Millet was hired to paint *The Treaty of Traverse des Sioux* and Volk (who had been the director of the Art School in Minneapolis) to depict *Father Hennepin Discovering the Falls of St. Anthony.*[37] The latter subject had been requested by Archbishop John Ireland to ensure that the contribution of French Catholics to the state would not be forgotten.[38]

A few months later, another Minnesota group made a demand that local artists be hired to participate in the Capitol's decoration. A local painter's union protested that the decoration of the building was in the hands of an eastern cabal or "gang." Their complaint was not amicably resolved and precipitated a lawsuit. Judge Kelly, who was appointed to settle the dispute, quickly dismissed the union's claim. His decision is important in that it reflected the new sophistication well-educated Minnesotans had acquired regarding the aesthetic difference between murals and painted walls.

Kelly began his decision by expressing his pride and faith in "the magnificent marble structure," favorably comparing its decorations to Michelangelo's *Last Judgment* for the Sistine Chapel. He then articulated what for him was the heart of the legal case: was Garnsey an artist or an artisan? This was an important distinction, and Kelly ruled that Garnsey was an artist.

After inspecting the pleadings and carefully reading all the affidavits, I am clearly of the opinion that the work in its general scope, considered as a whole is artistic, as distinguished from the work of the artisan. Some of it—whether much or little, I cannot say—no doubt might be performed by highly-skilled artisans, but the general plan which the court must consider requires the directing mind and hand of one artist. This artist could not, and would not, if he valued his reputation, permit that his assistants or subordinates . . . be selected by others.[39]

Kelly's decision put an end to local complaints, and Gilbert, with the advice of Garnsey, hired two other professional artists, Henry O. Walker and Kenyon Cox, to paint lunettes above the two doorways at the tops of the western and eastern staircases.

OPPOSITE
6-7. West Stair hall with view of Henry O. Walker's *Yesterday, Today, and Tomorrow,* 1904, lunette. Painted figures in staircase lunettes are by Elmer Garnsey and Arthur Willett and represent Minnesota agriculture and industries (1904), in 1971, Minnesota State Capitol. (Minnesota Historical Society)

Walker's contribution, entitled *Yesterday, Today, and Tomorrow* (Figure 6-7), is at the top of the western staircase, while Cox's *The Contemplative Spirit of the East* (Figure 6-8) is on the eastern stairway leading to the Supreme Court. Both are similar in design and conception to Simmons's academically inspired lunettes in the rotunda. The three allegorical figures in Walker's mural supplement one of the building's iconographic themes, the transmission of knowledge through the ages. In the Cox mural, three female figures hold or are surrounded by emblems of the law: an open book, a bridle and staff (symbols of restraint), and a stone tablet, all of which echo elements employed by La Farge in his Supreme Court murals.

As promised by Gilbert and the board of commissioners, the new capitol was ready for occupancy January 1905. In place were murals by Blashfield, Cox, Walker, Garnsey, and Arthur Willet, and one painting by La Farge *(The Moral and the Divine Law, or Moses Receiving the Law on Mt. Sinai)*. During the year the remaining paintings by La Farge and those by Simmons were installed. The first group of paintings for the Governor's Reception Room by Millet, Volk, Howard Pyle, and Rufus Zogbaum were hung during the next two years. The importance of Gilbert's accomplishment was such that it received extensive illustrated reviews in such national publications as *Architectural Record, International Studio, The Craftsman,* and *Appleton's.* The building's design was admired widely, and the building's murals and sculptures were illustrated abundantly.

Broadly speaking the iconographic program of the Minnesota capitol embraces two related themes: westward expansion and settlement (i.e., civilization), aspects of which were first rendered in the United States Capitol and furthered by projects elsewhere in the country. These themes are found immediately upon entering the building's rotunda, where Simmons's four-part painting *The Civilization of the Northwest* is placed. In the first panel, Simmons renders the civilizing impulse in the form of the "brave American spirit" newly arrived from the East Coast. After purging the region of "savagery," "cowardice," and "sin," he oversees the cultivation of the land and the state's natural resources. Ultimately the state's

"gifts"—"wheat, minerals, fine arts and knowledge"—enable Minnesota to assume its rightful place in the country's transformation at the turn of the century. Simmons's efforts are elaborated further in Blashfield's allegory of Minnesota, which elucidates the state's contribution to the settlement of the Midwest and to the development of the nation, and its role as the breadbasket of the world. La Farge's Supreme Court murals offer a culminating statement. Local references are not included since the laws of a civilized state maintain continuity with ancient precedents.

The pioneers who settled Minnesota repeated an age-old story—westward migration, subjugation of the native inhabitants, settlement, and importation of high culture and the law. This familiar nineteenth-century American story is embedded in the conception and decoration of Minnesota's capitol. The building's complex iconographic program was communicated through allegory and personification and gave local history relevance to Minnesotans (through the easel paintings in the Governor's Reception Room).

Sadly, few art lovers visit the capitol, which is set apart from downtown St. Paul by an interstate high-

way. More accessible and appealing for a modern audience are the Walker Art Center, the Minneapolis Museum of Art, and Frank Gehry's Frederick R. Weisman Museum at the University of Minnesota. The values and aspirations expressed in the capitol's sculpture and paintings are far removed from current urbane taste and sophistication. Yet Minnesota's great prosperity and cultural eminence are in reality an extension of these earlier aspirations. With a large international airport, glittering postmodern architecture, and a celebrated state university, the Twin Cities are the fulfillment of civilization's dream.

6-8. East Stair hall with view of Kenyon Cox's *The Contemplative Spirit of the East* (1904), in 1971. Lunette, Minnesota State Capitol. (Minnesota Historical Society)

CHAPTER 7

HIGH CULTURE BY THE SQUARE FOOT

Bailey Van Hook

A divide existed between the idealistic motivations for Beaux-Arts murals and the actual negotiations, constant supervision, and personnel problems that marked the architect's role in their commissioning and execution. Cass Gilbert, one of the architects who most consistently advocated mural decoration for his public buildings, was also one of the most suited to negotiate that distance. His Minnesota State Capitol in St. Paul (see Figure C-2) and the Essex County Courthouse in Newark, New Jersey (Figure 7-1), were decorated by more than a dozen of the best-known and admired artists of the period. In all matters relating to these murals, Gilbert successfully tempered his high-minded idealism with a practical and hard-headed business acumen. This chapter focuses on the latter qualities, as they unfolded from his initial advocacy through the proud unveiling of the murals.

The Beaux-Arts mural movement had its beginnings in 1876 when architect Henry Hobson Richardson hired artist John La Farge to decorate the interior of his neo-Romanesque Trinity Church, Boston (1873–77). The movement was fueled by the artists, sculptors, and architects who, lured by the superior training offered in Paris, had studied at the Ecole des Beaux-Arts and in various independent ateliers in the years after the Civil War. I refer to American mural painting throughout this chapter as "Beaux-Arts" because it reflected the strong training in figure painting that the Ecole and other institutions afforded them as well as their emulation and identification with such past masters of the genre. By

7-1. Essex County Courthouse, Newark, New Jersey, 1904–8. (Courtesy of the Newark Public Library)

the late 1870s and early 1880s these artists and architects had begun to return to the United States from their training abroad. They inaugurated what they identified as an "American Renaissance," an effort by the three branches of the visual arts to remake American architecture in the collaborative spirit of the Italian Renaissance. Mural painting, the art of Michelangelo and Titian, was considered an essential ingredient in this mix.

The American Renaissance (and mural painting) was at first mostly confined to such private settings as Fifth Avenue mansions and such semipublic sites as New York hotels. The iconography of early murals

was generally light and festive. Music, dance, the times of day, and the seasons were considered appropriate subjects for domestic and hotel sites. For example, in 1887–88 La Farge painted two panels, *Music* and *Dance* (in which young women participated in those activities), for Whitelaw Reid's drawing room in the Villard Houses. In 1892, Thomas Dewing painted *Dawn* (or *Night, Day, and Dawn*) for the ceiling of the café in the Imperial Hotel in New York, designed by Stanford White. Dewing's was a more symbolic representation than La Farge's since the three women in the mural represented those times of day, but the scene was similarly graceful and elegant.

The more public phase of the movement began in 1893 when Charles McKim hired Edwin Austin Abbey, John Singer Sargent, and the French artist Puvis de Chavannes to decorate the Boston Public Library (1887–95), making it the first major public building in the United States for which murals were planned. It was years, however, before these murals were completed. Instead, credit for the first large-scale mural project is usually given to the World's Columbian Exposition of 1893 in Chicago, with its panoply of decorations, both pictorial and sculptural. There, architect George B. Post employed artists to paint lunettes and decorate the sail domes in his Manufactures and Liberal Arts Building. Most of the artists whom Post hired were relatively inexperienced in mural decoration, and they worked under the pressure of a tight schedule. They painted rather traditional symbolic figures embodying the materials and products of the exhibitions in the halls below. For example, Edward Simmons painted four male figures representing stone, iron, hemp, and wood, and Edwin Blashfield, two females, *The Arts of Metal-Working* and *The Armourer's Craft,* and two males, *The Brass-founder* and *The Iron-worker.*

Most scholars agree that the Exposition exemplified the collaborative spirit of the American Renaissance but redirected it toward more public and often government-funded projects in what became loosely known as the City Beautiful movement.[1] The depression of the mid-1890s, however, slowed the growth of the movement, and there were fewer examples from the remaining years of the century than the enthusiasm generated by the exposition might suggest. The Library of Congress, completed in 1896, was an exuberant but singular example of an extensive program of large-scale mural decoration during that decade. (The only other large public commission was James Brown Lord's Appellate Division Courthouse in New York.) By 1900, however, and until about 1917, a substantial number of the new public buildings constructed—libraries, courthouses, statehouses, city halls, and federal buildings—as well as hotels, theaters, and banks, were decorated with murals.

The aims of the Beaux-Arts mural movement coincided with the larger goals of the City Beautiful movement: to plan public spaces along classical lines and to coordinate carefully each of its constituent architectural, sculptural, and decorative parts. The resulting harmonious and ennobling design was expected both to educate the public's aesthetic taste and to inspire democratic ideals. Such a harmonious civic design was thought therefore to produce an enlightened body politic. In keeping with this elevated and idealistic spirit, most of the subjects of the early Beaux-Arts public murals were still allegorical or symbolic but depicted subjects thought more appropriate for public spaces. Rather than the light, festive subjects that graced New York hotels, the language of these murals was weighty and rhetorical. Edwin Blashfield's *Evolution of Civilization* at the Library of Congress, La Farge's *Athens* for the Walker Art Building at Bowdoin College, and Simmons's *Justice of the Law* for the Appellate Division Courthouse in New York were typical of the efforts of the first generation of public murals.

In most cases, the architect in these early years was responsible for commissioning the mural decorations and overseeing their execution, conferring with the artists on issues of iconography, scale, and integration with the architectural design. Charles McKim and Stanford White of McKim, Mead & White, George B. Post, and Gilbert were among the most influential architects of the period, and their enthusiasm for mural decoration went a long way to guarantee the growth and viability of the movement. For their part, the muralists were usually immensely grateful to be chosen. Artists, who had always occupied an ambivalent and largely unappreciated position in American society, now had the opportunity to attach themselves to men like Post and Gilbert, who held far more powerful positions within American society, since their profession bridged aesthetics and commerce, art and engineering, and tradition and progress.

Gilbert's enthusiasm for mural paintings was not surprising. Although he did not train abroad, he traveled to Europe and most of his professional experience was with men who had studied there and were familiar with the great mural decorations of the past. Gilbert's early work for McKim, Mead & White may have influenced his later advocacy of mural projects. Although most of their joint work as a firm postdated his employment in their office (1880–82), by the mid-1890s Gilbert must have been aware that his former employer, by then the most famous architectural firm in the country, was commissioning murals not only for the Boston Public Library but also for the Church of the Ascension, Imperial Hotel, and University Club in New York, the Walker Art Building at Bowdoin College, and the State Savings Bank in Detroit, as well as numerous private homes.

Gilbert was himself an enthusiastic and accomplished watercolorist, and his letters attest to his belief that there was a particular artistic temperament and that he understood it. In one example he wrote Channing Seabury, the chairman of the Board of State Capitol Commissioners for the Minnesota capitol, "I realize more keenly perhaps than you how long a time it takes to perfect a really great picture, and we want nothing less than the best."[2]

The two major sites for mural decoration buildings by Gilbert were the Minnesota State Capitol, where murals were finished by 1906, and the Essex County Courthouse, where murals were completed by 1907. Beaux-Arts decorations were planned for the Custom House in New York but most were never commissioned. (When Reginald Marsh finally painted murals for the site in the 1937, a very different style of mural decoration had emerged, one that combined the influence of European modernism with a

7-2. Gari Melchers, left to right: *The Landing of Cadillac's Wife, The Conspiracy of Pontiac, The Spirit of the Northwest,* Book Delivery Room, Detroit Public Library. (Archives, Belmont Collection, The Gari Melchers Estate and Memorial Gallery)

particularized American iconography.) The lobby in the Woolworth Building was lavishly decorated, but in the main not in the figural style recognized as representing the mural movement and its ideals. However, two small figural murals depicted commerce and labor among the wealth of painted decoration, stained glass, and mosaics. These were completed by the relatively unknown artist Paul Jenewein.

Gilbert won the commission for designing the main branch of the Detroit Public Library in 1915; murals by Gari Melchers (Figure 7-2) and Blashfield (Figure 7-3) were installed in 1921, the year the building was completed. Information about the Minnesota capitol, however, is the most extensive and provides a fine opportunity to concentrate on the situation surrounding that commission. Gilbert himself called the Minnesota capitol the best work he had done.[3]

It is not known exactly what precipitated Gilbert's decision to lobby for murals in the Minnesota

State Capitol. It is important to note, however, that the Mural Painters (later the National Society of Mural Painters), the first professional organization of mural painters in the United States, was formed in 1893, two years before Gilbert received the capitol commission. Charles Lamb, corresponding secretary of the Mural Painters, wrote Gilbert in 1896 as part of a public relations campaign to advance the cause of murals in the United States. The architect wrote back sympathetically but conveyed his belief that any plan to use mural decoration was as much a matter of policy regarding public expenditure and state approval as it was his decision.[4]

More than five years later, Gilbert argued that murals for Minnesota's statehouse were necessary and used idealistic language characteristic of the City Beautiful movement. Writing to the Board of State Capitol Commissioners in St. Paul in 1902, he asserted that "nothing will give the building greater distinction or lend more to its educational value and to the evidence of the advancement of civilization and intelligence of the State than the recognition of the arts as represented by the great painters and sculptors of the present day."[5]

Gilbert's contention was phrased in the typical language advanced by advocates of murals in the popular press, who spoke in terms of its specific benefits. Blashfield, for example, one of the most articulate champions of mural decoration, wrote in 1899 "A Word for Municipal Art," in which he argued for both its educational value and its potential to uplift artistic taste through beauty. In other speeches and published papers written during the next fifteen years, Blashfield continued to trumpet this idea, calling public art a "public and municipal educator," and the decorated public building "that great teacher of history, patriotism, morals, aesthetics." Blashfield also cannily remarked that "down from this high mission of art to a lower plane, we find that municipal art has swelled the revenues of cities." He cited such Renaissance towns as Assisi, whose main tourist industry was its art.[6]

Gilbert's chauvinistic reference to the state's cultural reputation was also a key issue for a Midwestern state only recently advanced from territorial status. In fact, many of the great mural projects of the early twentieth century were implemented in such Midwestern locales as Wisconsin and South Dakota, the latter less than twenty years as a state, and in need of the legitimacy and status brought by the employment of the grand, ceremonial language of classicism and the City Beautiful movement.

Although he was a tireless defender of the muralists' right to choose their own subject, Gilbert preferred to hire artists who could supply ideal subjects, either allegories or symbolic enactments of a historical evolution, rather than more straightforward, realistic depictions of historical events that were gaining popularity elsewhere. In 1900 the Massachusetts state legislature had allocated the funds for mural decorations in the expansion of the state capitol and had mandated subjects from Massachusetts history. In doing so, they had taken over the role that architects had previously held in initiating or approving mural subjects. In the Minnesota state capitol, the grand

ceremonial space under the rotunda as well as the lunettes for the Supreme Court and Senate were sites of the first murals commissioned for the capitol, and by Gilbert's own reasoning, the most significant spaces. Therefore they were reserved for what were designated as "ideal subjects." They were given to artists who had a proven track record in producing ideal subjects at the Library of Congress or elsewhere: Simmons, La Farge, Blashfield, as well as Kenyon Cox and Henry O. Walker.

Grand subjects and elevated language masked the realities of the situations Gilbert had to deal with and the terms the muralists had to follow. One of the tenets of both the American Renaissance in the arts and the later more public City Beautiful movement was the supremacy of the architect in the triad of architect, painter, and sculptor. During this period, the mural aesthetic then in vogue (popularized by Puvis de Chavannes) demanded that the murals harmonize with the architecture, reinforce its structural elements, carry the eye across its surfaces, and create a decorative whole. Murals were supposed to be "decorative" and not move the viewer's eyes too far back into space but echo the building's surfaces and enhance its flat walls. Architecture always came first and decoration second. The latter usually depended not only on the size and the scale of the space allowed for it but also on the cost of the entire project and the money put aside for decoration, relative to other needs such as furnishings, railings, doors, and other hardware.

Considering decorative harmony not aesthetically but in terms of who was in charge of ensuring it

7-3. Edwin H. Blashfield, *The Graphic Arts,* stairway, Detroit Public Library. (Courtesy of the Burton Historical Collection, Detroit Public Library)

moves it from the rarefied realm of aesthetics to the world of politics and economics. The architect supervised the artists and sculptors just as he supervised the building contractors. In essence, the muralists were subcontractors to the architect. The architect oversaw their work and could veto decisions if he thought the mural's compositional or color schemes would negatively affect his architectural design. This was an enormous and time-consuming responsibility.

In 1903, amid negotiations over the St. Paul murals, Gilbert asked architect George B. Post whether the "ordinary charge of the [architect's] profession of the 5% commission on both sculpture and decorative painting" was just. Post defended the policy, citing the large amount of decorative work done in his practice and the amount of time it took. He wrote, "I can only say that there is no part of the work connected with building that has required as large an expenditure of my personal time as Architect to secure a proper result as in the work of sculpture and mural decoration." About the subject of mural painting, in particular, Post was most emphatic: "If the architect does not give the matter constant and unremitting attention during the whole progress of the work from the making of the original sketches to the completion of the paintings on the walls the result as a whole is inevitably disastrous, the work does not hang together and it is entirely unsatisfactory."

The exact details of the selection process of the muralists for the Minnesota commission are not known. Samuel Isham, an artist and surveyor of American painting, claimed that architects usually directed the choice of whether or not to have decoration and who to hire, and that seems to have been the case early on.[8] The more famous the architect, the more choice he was given on the question of who was commissioned to do mural work. Richardson at Trinity Church, McKim at the Boston Public Library, Arnold Brunner at the Federal Building in Cleveland, and Post at the Wisconsin capitol in Madison and elsewhere seem to have had their choices rubberstamped by whatever committee was nominally in charge. In St. Paul, although deferential to the Board of State Capitol Commissioners, Gilbert made his

preferences plain, and although sometimes challenged, they were approved.[9]

Gilbert had viewed the major sites for mural paintings in the United States and indeed took the Minnesota commissioners on a tour of them (see chapter 6). Gilbert alluded to appointments with artists in his letters, but how the meetings came about is not known. The architect was based in New York by this time, as were all the major muralists, so it would have been easy to arrange meetings. These meetings likely were the result of private conversations and recommendations in men's clubs, a significant manifestation of the old boy's network. Artistic reputations were often ignored in comments like "so and so is a good man," which was a way of saying that he had the requisite class, professional, and social affiliations.

By January 1903, Gilbert met with the muralists who would be assigned the lion's share of the mural work in the Minnesota capitol: La Farge, Blashfield, and Simmons and with Elmer E. Garnsey, who was to coordinate the color decoration of the whole interior.[10] La Farge was a natural choice, given his long participation in the movement and his employment on several McKim, Mead & White projects. Although John Singer Sargent had been Gilbert's first choice for the decorations in the rotunda, Sargent declined, citing his ongoing work for the Boston Public Library.[10] Simmons, the artist who was then commissioned to do the rotunda murals, and Blashfield, who was to decorate the Senate chamber, had emerged as leading figures out of the larger pack who had been employed at the World's Columbian Exposition. They both had been hired for major commissions at the Library of Congress in 1896 and the Appellate Division Courthouse in Manhattan in 1898.

Despite his exalted position vis-à-vis the muralists, Gilbert was highly sympathetic and did everything to ensure that both their high ideals and their professional integrity were preserved. At one point he wrote to Chairman Seabury, "I am moved to say that I do not think you fully appreciate how valuable this interest is on their [the muralists'] part. If they are to take hold of such important paintings they want to arrange their programme for the future, as they are all being consulted about other important decorative projects and cannot allow themselves to become involved in engagements which would clash." He continued, "I am aware that I may seem too eager on this matter, but I realized more keenly perhaps than you how long a time it takes to perfect a really great picture, and we want nothing less than the best."[11]

Gilbert was adamant about giving the artists enough leeway in choosing their subject and design. About Simmons he wrote,

> I have stated to him that he shall have a free hand to develop his conception to the fullest extent, without interference on the part of the Board as to the nature of the subject, considering that in point of subject he will have to meet my views as the Architect. In explanation of this, which may not be perfectly clear to you at first reading, I find that the artists are occasionally seriously embarrassed by change of views and by subjects that are insisted upon by various members of committees after a start has already been made, and I have promised him 'the opportunity to do an ideal thing in an ideal way' and this is the feature that makes the project attractive to him. I have therefore guaranteed him this condition.[12]

Yet, Gilbert had a hands-on approach. For example, he offered suggestions to Cox about the design of his lunette mural, *The Contemplative Spirit of the East,* when the artist submitted a sketch to him. Gilbert didn't like the wings on the central figures and suggested drapery instead. Cox took some of Gilbert's suggestions and passed on others. But it is interesting that the architect did not push his advantage, writing to Seabury, "I feel that if I press my criticism much further that he will lose interest in the work and, after all, the artist must be allowed to have a certain freedom in carrying out his own composition or we cannot hope to get the best work from him." Gilbert thus argued for compromise.[13]

Gilbert was even more involved in the production of the secondary decoration. He made it plain to Seabury that although he did not want to "assume an undue share of credit," he had personally directed Garnsey.[14]

When working out the details of the mural decoration, Gilbert solicited and received infor-

mation about the cost of decorating some of the major sites of the City Beautiful movement, including the Boston Public Library and Library of Congress. In his research Gilbert had found that decorative paintings by top artists cost $40 to $60 per square foot and ascertained that the artists he had in mind would work for $50 per square foot. He asked for the sum of $225,000 for St. Paul, which he then divided among the three principal muralists who first received commissions, Simmons, La Farge, and Blashfield, with the remainder going to Garnsey. Gilbert calculated their compensation down to the square foot, using decimals: La Farge would get $48,206 for 964.12 square feet for the decoration in the Supreme Court and Simmons, $46,560 for 931.20 square feet for the pendentives under the dome. Gilbert told Seabury that "this will assure the State ten great works of mural painting which should equal the best which have been produced in this country." He eventually had to slightly lower the payments based on a set amount divided proportionally so the eventual payments were slightly less.[15]

Twenty years later, when capitol commissioners solicited Gilbert's opinion about hiring artists to decorate Tracy & Swartwout's Missouri capitol, Gilbert advised them to avoid haggling with the artists. He urged them to treat the artists as well as possible, saying that he was convinced that

> the more a man is an artist the more sensitive he is to impressions and that in order to get the very best results from an artist he should be impressed with the idea that he is being very generously treated and that his work is not considered from a *commercial* standpoint and especially that there should be no 'trading' with him on the matter of price. . . . I have always tried to make the budget as liberal as possible so that we would really get the very best work of which the artist was capable and pay him if necessary a little more rather than a little less than he might ask.[16]

In Missouri as in Minnesota, there was, however, a distinct class and status difference between those artists and the other decorators employed. Those who had studied painting in Parisian schools and ateliers, with their strong training in drawing the figure, were seen as fine artists and were given the choicest commissions. Since the major murals were oil paintings later attached to the walls, the artists could do their work in studios located far from the site, and then only appear in the building to supervise the hanging of their work. The murals were often exhibited in advance in such locations as the Architectural League or the National Academy of Design in New York, which certified their high art status.

Sometimes another figure painter was put in charge of the secondary decoration. Garnsey served that role at the state capitol in St. Paul as well as at the Library of Congress and many other sites. In some locations professional firms of decorators were hired to provide decorative work like garlands that were stenciled into place—the kind of decoration that would be done in mosaic in the Woolworth Building.

There was an enormous difference in cost between the two kinds of decoration, figural and nonfigural. As at St. Paul, muralists who did figural compositions in lunettes or pendentives could receive upwards of $50,000 for their work. The terms for the journeymen artisans who decorated the areas other than the major mural locations were considerably less, and they were paid by the day, with union regulations specifying the terms of employment. One letter from 1903 illustrates the disparity. It was sent from the Association of Interior Decorators & Cabinet Makers of the City of New York and the New York District Council of the Brotherhood of Painters, Decorators and Paper Hangers of America to the press and forwarded by Gilbert to Seabury for his information. It thus may have been used as a guideline for the capitol project, with its stipulated terms of employment and notations about the following wages: decorators and gilders, $4.00 a day; painters, $3.50; and varnishers, $3.25 a day.[17]

The major muralists, in contrast to these journeymen, had individual contracts. Gilbert, aware that he had not only pushed for the decoration but also supplied the names of those chosen, was careful to protect the state's interests. The Minnesota contracts specified that the artist had two years to complete the work and that the payments were as follows: 15 percent for preliminary sketches of all four lunettes, 25 percent when cartoons were made; 50 percent when the paintings were placed, and 10 percent when final approval was given. The artist retained possession of sketches and all other preparatory materials unless he died, in which case "an artist or artists of recognized ability" would complete the work. The architect was responsible for certifying to the board that work had been completed. The work was guaranteed in form of a bond or bill of sale, dependent on the artist's wishes. Gilbert in turn protected the artists from the state officials, setting up an advisory board of decorative design, made up of the muralists, sculptor Daniel Chester French, and the architect himself, to deal with any questions that arose. Although the group never met formally, its very existence was an important sign of Gilbert's respect for the artists.[18]

The first round of completed murals varied widely in style but the murals were uniformly ideal stylistically and decorative, or relatively flat, compositionally. Under the dome, Edward Simmons's *The Civilization of the Northwest* (see Figure 6-2) was an allegorical narrative showing a young man, the "American Spirit," who in the course of the four panels left home, scoured the west of savage forces, cultivated the land, and finally sent the products of Minnesota all over the world. Simmons's style reflected his long time abroad. The panels were similar to many contemporary French murals, influenced by the Beaux-Arts tradition both in their elegant compositions and figural style as well as their fluid execution.

In the Supreme Court chamber, La Farge painted four scenes from the history of lawgiving, showing historical figures like Moses and Socrates, with weighty titles like *The Moral and the Divine Law: Moses, Aaron, and Joshua on Mount Sinai* (see Figure 5-8), *A Political Discussion by Socrates and His Friends,* and *The Relation of the Individual to the State.*[19] La Farge was both more universal in his breadth of allusion and symbolism and at the same time more naturalistic in his depiction of figures and landscape than the other artists at St. Paul.

In the two lunettes allocated for mural decoration in the Senate chamber, Blashfield opted for his particular blend of history and allegory that he had painted most recently for the federal courthouse in Baltimore. Blashfield represented a central symbolic figure in both *Minnesota, The Granary of the World* (see Figure 6-5) and *The Discoverers and Civilizers Led to the Source of the Mississippi.*

Other ideal subjects at St. Paul included two slightly later commissions. Cox and Walker were given lunettes over stairways that mirrored each other across the rotunda. Cox's (*The Contemplative Spirit of the East*—see Figure 6-9) was the most academic composition.[20] Walker's *Yesterday, Today, and Tomorrow* (each of which was personified by a female figure) was by comparison light and elegant and completed in the modern French style Simmons had also chosen, rather than a classical mode favored by Cox.

As any researcher on Gilbert's architecture will attest, voluminous written material exists for each project. Gilbert dictated hundreds of letters, some concentrating on the smallest of details. The murals were no exception, and comments about their progress often appear side by side with discussions of retaining walls, candelabra, and so on. During the period between 1902 and 1906 he corresponded weekly with Channing Seabury over small details of the commissions.

When the names of the muralists were published, some local sources complained that local talent had not been sought and even sued the commissioners. Gilbert had little patience with such provincialism. At one point, writing to Seabury, his pugnacious streak came through: "I hate to have a fight, and the older and more experienced I get the more I hate it. At the same time I hate to be bulldozed by a political clique." For his buildings Gilbert said he simply wanted the best that could be hired, which for him were the most recognized experts in large-scale, ideal figural decoration, whose talent and experience had prepared them for his momentous commission. He suggested to Seabury that the attorney general should agree that the board "has authority to employ 'experts,' and that in making a contract with an 'expert' they are fully within their legal authority."[21] When Elmer Garnsey was commissioned to oversee the secondary decoration (Figure 7-4), some of the

criticism was muted when a local firm was hired to do much of the actual painting and decorating of the halls and the areas around the murals.

In the course of awarding contracts there were also rumblings about the New York residency of so many of the muralists. Seabury wrote to Gilbert, "Up to this time, we are justly chargeable with 'playing into the hands of a New York ring,' which has been already asserted. Not all the artistic ability in the U.S. is centered in New York City, although I am free to admit that a good share of it is. We have now employed [sculptor Daniel Chester] French, Garnsey, La Farge, Blashfield, Simmons, Millet and Volk, on our artistic work,—7 men—, every one of them a resident of New York City. We must not keep this up forever." In terse fashion, Gilbert also annotated the letter: "I don't know of a 'ring' never heard there was one and don't believe there is." He must have taken Seabury's point, however, for in a subsequent letter two weeks later, he said that Will H. Low, Charles Yardley Turner, and George Maynard were possibilities for additional decorations, but noted that all are "New York men."[22]

Numerous personnel problems also arose. La Farge, who was considered the dean of American mural painting, by then was old and cantankerous and acted like a prima donna. He quibbled endlessly about money and deadlines. Simmons was also a constant frustration to Gilbert, made more so by the fact he was in Paris and could not be spoken to directly. Simmons desperately argued for an advance and offered numerous excuses for the late delivery of his four mural panels. These excuses included boils on his hands, legal hassles with his ex-wife, constant financial problems, and incorrect measurements sent by the architect's office.

7-4. Elmer E. Garnsey (supervisor), hallway decoration, Minnesota State Capitol, 1905. (Minnesota Historical Society)

In an effort to hurry Simmons along, Gilbert even suggested he move from Paris to St. Paul and use the rotunda as his studio. Impatient with delays, he wrote to the artist in Paris in 1904: "You must bear in mind that this is State work, and that their procedure must be governed by considerations that might not weigh if they were acting for themselves individually." Gilbert felt forced to lay down the law, writing that "your long absence has seriously embarrassed me personally and officially in connection with this work, and I would be less than frank if I did not tell you plainly that I think you should have given me better treatment, under the circumstances." He called the capitol "this noble scheme, to which I have devoted so many years of my life" and hoped that it would not be marred by Simmons's failure.[23]

7-5. Edwin H. Blashfield, *Wisdom, Knowledge, Mercy, and Power.* Rotunda, Essex County Courthouse, Newark, New Jersey, in *Essex County Courthouse, Newark, New Jersey* (Newark, NJ, 1908), n.p.

If the less-than-professional conduct of the two artists was not enough, Gilbert had to contend with special interests of representatives of the state who wanted certain subjects painted. Some Minnesota citizens did not understand the desirability of having the ideal and universalizing themes that Gilbert preferred. There were citizens who offered paintings of historical subjects that were too big for their homes. Gilbert received letters from the state historical society asking that a place be designated for a depiction of the Treaty of the Traverse de Sioux, the 1851 treaty that had opened much of the territory of Minnesota to white settlement. Archbishop John Ireland lobbied for the discovery of the Falls of St. Anthony by Father Hennepin.[24] Each of Minnesota's civil war regiments wanted their heroics represented. Gilbert compromised, putting aside the Governor's Reception Room to satisfy those interests (see Figure 5-11). He wrote ominously to Seabury that "if the Board does not cover the vacant spaces that somebody will get in their deadly political work later on and make that room a chamber of horrors in the name of patriotism. I personally believe in historic pictures for such a room and I think they should be treated from the pictorial standpoint rather than from the decorative standpoint, that is to say, that they should really be pictures of the events as nearly as they can be transcribed."[25]

The architect was, however, effectively segregating history into a relatively modest space, away from the grand public entrance and the halls of the legislative and judicial bodies. The Governor's Reception Room served as the receiving area where the people's representative, the governor, would greet his constituents. As Gilbert implied, a very different style would predominate. The historical paintings were painted in a more realistic, illusionist style and were framed and set apart from the wall. Although the historical paintings there were called murals, their relatively small size (ten feet long), as well as their enclosure in heavy frames, made them more like traditional easel paintings and less like the other murals in the building.

In contrast to the painters of the grand public spaces, the artistic counterparts for these spaces were assigned their subjects. To satisfy the Catholic Church, Douglas Volk was commissioned to paint *Father Louis Hennepin Discovering the Falls of St. Anthony in 1680* and Frank Millet, *The Treaty of the Traverse de Sioux.* In addition, battle scenes depicting the glory days of Minnesota's regiments of Union troops that participated in the Civil War were included. These included Millet *(The Fourth Minnesota Regiment Entering Vicksburg),* Blashfield *(Fifth Minnesota),* Howard Pyle *(Battle of Nashville),* Stanley Arthurs *(Third Minnesota),* Rufus Zogbaum *(Battle of Gettysburg),* and Douglas Volk *(Second Minnesota Regiment at Mission Ridge).* It is noteworthy that battle paintings had never been common in American art, and with few exceptions, the most important examples dated from the early nineteenth century, so Gilbert's commission was itself a mini-revival of the genre. In addition, the Civil War was a rare subject for any of the civic buildings of this era. Although historical subjects had become increasingly important after the turn of the century, most localities (perhaps in a desire to put the conflict behind them) chose subjects more safely positioned in the past, especially in the colonial era. It may have been the state's short history that argued for subjects from the more recent past.

Of all the St. Paul murals, La Farge's received the most critical acclaim and even helped the artist acquire an additional commission for the Baltimore Courthouse. Gilbert, however, evidently had had enough of La Farge's temperamental nature. Like a director who never again works with a difficult star, Gilbert never again commissioned some muralists he had worked with at St. Paul. Simmons and La Farge were conspicuously absent when the architect hired

Cox's *The Beneficence of the Law* (Figure 7-6), Low's *Diogenes in Search of an Honest Man*, Maynard's *The State Supported by Liberty and Justice,* and Walker's *Justice* were almost matched in number by Turner and Howard Pyle's paintings (Figure 7-7) about seventeenth-century colonial history and Millet's depiction of an early protest against Britain in the eighteenth century. The contracts for the Essex County Courthouse were also slightly different: a greater percentage of the total payments, 40 percent (as opposed to 25 percent in Minnesota) was given for the cartoons, perhaps to speed the initial work along.[27]

Nearly a decade later, Gilbert won a competition to design the Detroit Public Library, which was to form part of an arts center located on Woodward Avenue. His high ambitions for the library again

muralists for his next major project, the Essex County Courthouse in Newark, New Jersey (1906). For that site, since Gilbert was personally close to many of the leading muralists, he used his influence to appeal to them to reduce their initially high estimates for decorating the courthouse. (They had estimated they would need $130,000 whereas Gilbert insisted only $80,000 was available.)[26] Reliable and capable, Blashfield received the most important commission, for four massive female figures that graced the pendentives of the grand dome, representing wisdom, knowledge, mercy, and power (Figure 7-5). In the courtrooms, both allegorical and historical subjects were painted but New Jersey history was a close second, reflecting the increased popularity of history to local building commissions. Ideal subjects such as

reflected City Beautiful ideals. He wrote that a library "should create an environment of scholarship and refinement; it fails of its purpose as an educative factor if it is other than a beautiful building."[28] In accord with these ideals, in 1921 he hired Blashfield and Gari Melchers to paint the staircase, landing, and book delivery room. Like Blashfield, Melchers was an alumnus of both the World's Columbian Exposition and the Library of Congress, but unlike him, he had not specialized in murals. Melchers and Gilbert knew each other from their mutual membership in the Century Association in New York.[29]

In the Book-Receiving Room Melchers painted three murals that mix the allegorical and historical (see Figure 7-2). In the center, over the door, he painted *The Spirit of the Northwest*, which included

7-6. Photograph of Kenyon Cox's mural, *The Beneficence of the Law* (1906), for the Supreme Court of the Essex County Courthouse, Newark, New Jersey. (Photograph by DeW. C. Ward, New York. Gift of Allyn Cox, 1959–69–80. Cooper-Hewitt, National Design Museum, Smithsonian Institution/Art Resource, NY

7-7. Howard Pyle, *The Landing of Carteret,* Board of Freeholders' Room, Essex County Courthouse, Newark, New Jersey, in *Essex County Courthouse, Newark, New Jersey* (Newark, NJ, 1908), n.p.

Saint Claire in the center, with a pathfinder and trader on either side. As usual, Gilbert was closely involved, sending the artist two photographs of a painting of Saint Claire that he had once seen in a church in Assisi. On either side of this panel were two more strictly historical scenes, *The Landing of Cadillac's Wife* [1703] and *The Conspiracy of Pontiac* [1763]. Blashfield painted a lunette of *Detroit at the Meeting of the Land and Water Ways,* as well as larger lunettes of *Music* and *The Graphic Arts* (see Figure 7-3) and *Prose Writers* and *Poets and Musicians.* In Blashfield's late works, compositional clarity was sacrificed for an encyclopedic comprehension, which included dozens of illustrious figures from western art and literature.[30]

7-8. House of Delegates, West Virginia State Capitol, Charleston, West Virginia, 1924–32. (Photograph by Bailey Van Hook)

Given Gilbert's enthusiasm for murals, one wonders why more were not installed in his numerous public buildings. In the decades after 1910, he followed a trend of using fewer murals as taste gradually shifted from the ambitious and some would say bombastic themes of the earlier decade. He did continue, however, to employ Garnsey for smaller-scale secondary decoration. According to an invaluable, although error-ridden list of murals published in 1922, Garnsey was responsible for the decoration at the Custom House in New York and the Art Museum (originally the Palace of Fine Arts at the Louisiana Purchase Exposition) and the public library in St.

Louis.[31] Gilbert employed Ernest Tyler at the Woolworth Building in New York and the Union Central Life Insurance Company Building in Cincinnati. But except for the Detroit Public Library, he moved away from the large-scale figural decoration that is one of the glories of the City Beautiful movement.

Although City Beautiful projects continued to be built into the 1920s, by World War I its aspirations were both economically and philosophically diminished. Monumental classically inspired buildings were erected but decorated infrequently. Gilbert's West Virginia capitol in Charleston (1924–32) was a curious example of a Beaux-Arts building in the tradition of the Minnesota State Capitol but reflecting a new aesthetic. It is nearly devoid of decorative detail, creating an eerie and strange sight to someone accustomed to finding murals in such a building, as though it were waiting for the painter-decorators to show up (Figure 7-8). Although works were sporadically commissioned, in reality there was a definite hiatus in mural projects in the 1920s. In the decade of the depression, a new generation of artists including Thomas Hart Benton and others (again funded by the government) would inaugurate a mural movement different in style, subject, and mindset from their Beaux-Arts predecessors.

But during the heyday of the Beaux-Arts mural movement, Gilbert was uniquely suited to the demanding task of architect, supervisor, creative arbitrator, overseer, and if need be, nag. He was the rare individual who seemed to handle the details of an immense project single-handedly. His attitude toward and treatment of the muralists revealed that the many-sided architect had no problem balancing the high ideals and the petty details of the architectural commissions of the City Beautiful movement. He assumed naturally the dominant role given the architect during the American Renaissance, taking on the responsibility of advocating the cultural, spiritual, and aesthetic benefits of mural painting while also assuming its more mundane and frustrating details.

CHAPTER 8

THE RESTORATION AND PRESERVATION OF MINNESOTA'S SHOWPLACE

Carolyn Kompelien

On January 3, 1905, on the grand floor of the newly occupied Minnesota State Capitol in St. Paul, 182 legislators opened the thirty-fourth legislative session in the chambers of the Senate and House of Representatives. Later, on the first Tuesday of April, oral arguments were heard by five justices in the Supreme Court in their first term of the year.[1] The monumental capitol that Cass Gilbert had designed now housed Minnesota's state government; it included space for six constitutional officers, seventeen state agencies, twenty-six small legislative hearing rooms, grand public corridors, and a restaurant.

In 1893, the Minnesota legislature had appropriated two million dollars to build Minnesota's third capitol in St. Paul. This initial appropriation ended decades of political maneuvering to move the capitol away from St. Paul. The state constitution mandated that the seat of state government would be determined by a vote of the people. However, as William Dean, author of an early history of the building wrote, this appropriation and not the vote of the people "forever sealed the tripartite action of the territorial legislature of 1851 fixing the university at Minneapolis, the state prison at Stillwater, and the capitol at St. Paul."[2]

This new capitol put Minnesota on the map, as noted in previous chapters. As a symbol to the rest of the nation of the state's economic and cultural progress since becoming a territory in 1849 and a state in 1858, it was a strong source of pride for Minnesota citizens. Likewise, winning this commission in 1895 at the age of thirty-six, Gilbert was thrust into national prominence as an architect. Thirty years later, Gilbert said of his design, "[T]he Capitol was my first important public work and I gave to its design and construction the best that was in me in the hope that a standard might be established for future public works in the State and that the building would be one in which the State would have just pride."[3]

Gilbert reported directly to the seven-member Board of State Capitol Commissioners. Appointed by the governor to represent Minnesota's seven congressional districts, the commissioners' reports were a matter of public record. Intense citizen interest in the project prompted close scrutiny by newspapers throughout the state. Three years after Gilbert won the design competition, he moved to the East Coast

8-1. Citizens filled the capitol's ground floor corridor where the Motor Vehicle License Bureau was located for almost forty years, c. 1941. (Photo by *St. Paul Dispatch–Pioneer Press*, Minnesota Historical Society)

and from there supervised most of the construction. All these factors combined to produce the extensive documentation that illuminates the history of the capitol's construction.

In 1988, the state of Minnesota decided that renovations were needed and should be done in a manner that would return the capitol to its original appearance in 1905, as well as maintain it as a "modern and functional setting for the business of state government."[4] When researchers began the search for the original design of the spaces under renovation, the immense value of the documentation of the construction became evident. The Department of Administration's Division of State Building Construction has managed the restoration work in contract with Miller Dunwiddie Architects and in cooperation with the Capitol Area Architectural and Planning Board and the Minnesota Historical Society. Their use of historical documentation to create accurate restorations of Gilbert's 1905 design constitutes the subject of this chapter.

As times changed, demands on Minnesota's proud capitol changed as well. With the growth of state government, Gilbert's interior spaces could no longer accommodate the needs for office space as they had in 1905. Within three decades after the capitol first opened, rooms were filled to capacity and personnel had to be assigned to open spaces never envisioned for offices. From the 1930s through the 1950s, this dire need for additional office space was temporarily solved by the construction of plywood partitions in the grand public corridors.[5] For example, a photograph from 1941 (Figure 8-1) shows citizens purchasing car licenses at the Motor Vehicle License Bureau in the middle of one of the main capitol corridors. Originally in what was intended as a temporary location, this bureau occupied a hallway for almost forty years. It was only when additional buildings were erected near the capitol mall to accommodate state agencies that the space problems began to be ameliorated. Even today, however, one major corridor remains closed to the public because of its use as government offices.

One major flaw of Gilbert's interior design by

today's standards was the lack of legislative office space. Part-time citizen legislators met for only ninety days every other year, and they handled government bills and correspondence at their desks on the floor of the Senate or House chamber with the help of staff from a secretarial pool. It was not until 1972, when legislators moved into space in the nearby State Office Building and also in the capitol, that this work was done in private offices.

During the course of several years, alterations were made to the public spaces to update them according to the styles, needs, and political climates of the time. By the 1970s new furniture, draperies, floor coverings, lighting, and altered decorative designs had obscured most of Gilbert's architectural intent, not to mention the work of Elmer E. Garnsey, chief color decorator of the capitol (see chapters 5, 6, and 7). The color schemes achieved by these two talented colorists had been lost not only within individual public spaces but also between the public spaces, where originally color relationships were quite apparent. Wall and ceiling decorations in the restaurant and nearby ground-floor corridor were painted over. Most of the remaining motifs were repainted, resulting in altered designs and colors that did not match the original ones.

When the capitol was placed on the National Register of Historic Places in 1972, preservationists began to recognize the historical significance of Gilbert's work. A growing consciousness became evident in Minnesota of the significance of this architectural masterpiece. In 1984, a major initiative by Governor Rudy Perpich established the goal of "remodeling of the State Capitol to restore, inasmuch as possible, the original Cass Gilbert design."[6] By 1988, Miller Dunwiddie Architects completed the "Comprehensive Preservation Plan and Implementation Strategy for the Minnesota State Capitol" for the Capitol Area Architectural and Planning Board. This plan became the blueprint for all of the restoration projects that followed.

A state statute placed responsibility on the Minnesota Historical Society (MHS) for the approval of alterations to works of art and advice about preservation issues in the capitol's public and ceremonial spaces. With this directive in mind, staff at the Society's Capitol Historic Site in 1985 responded to the governor's initiative with a major project to research the capitol's original furniture, which the same statute had designated as works of art.[7] The Governor's Reception Room—designed by Gilbert in a manner befitting the state's highest elected official with gold-leaf ceiling, historical paintings, crystal chandeliers, and dark oak wall panels—was furnished at that time with one piece of furniture known to be original to the space. Most other pieces were traditional living-room furniture collected over the years with no apparent attention to the grand scale of this elegant room. This space became the starting point for the society to begin its research, with the long-term goal of returning the 1905 furniture to the Governor's Reception Room and other public and ceremonial spaces throughout the capitol.

Before preservation efforts could begin, documentation was needed to define the collection of furniture that dated from 1905. Gilbert's specifications for cabinet work, furniture, and furnishings of the capitol provided detailed information for beginning the research.[8] These plans included both standard furniture designs that were available commercially at the turn of the century and special furniture that he designed for public and ceremonial spaces throughout the building. The research goals (to identify, to locate, and to document both of these classifications of furniture) were achieved and resulted in a collection of "approximately 800 pieces of 1905 furniture in fifty-four styles, or roughly one-half the original [purchase] order."[9] Less than half of those located were in use in the capitol, with the remaining half found in fifteen other state buildings in St. Paul.

The loss of original furniture during many decades of use is illustrated by the decision by the House of Representatives to buy new chairs for its members during a 1960s remodeling effort. Legislators were allowed to purchase their old chairs as souvenirs (the original members' chairs) from the contractor who furnished the replacement chairs and was apparently responsible for disposing of the old chairs.[10] However, the ornately carved speaker's chair

(Figure 8-2), one of the specialized designs by Gilbert, was in demand. It therefore was kept and displayed in the House Retiring Room until restoration in 1989 of the House chamber, when the chair was repaired, reupholstered, and restored for use by the Speaker of the House.

Clearly, Gilbert did not anticipate all the furniture needs of the building's original occupants. Associate Justice E. A. Jaggard wrote to Gilbert in January 1905, indicating that Gilbert's order for furniture to Herter Brothers in New York would not be sufficient. Jaggard referred to the much-debated problem among the state Supreme Court justices regarding a chaise lounge. He wanted a "moderately comfortable plain one; not as hard as a rock and not such a one as the Secretary of State has. That is stately but inadequate for my too too solid and ample frame. It does well to set on but is ill adapted for balmy sleep. I would rather have it without a back and certainly do not want a double ender."[11] Responding to this request, Gilbert sent the justice a sketch (Figure 8-3) of a chaise that would meet the needs of the court. Of the five chaise lounges that were ordered, only one is extant today and it is identical to Gilbert's sketch.

The furniture research project culminated in 1989 in the publication of the inventory booklet *Attention to Detail*. Both contemporary and historical line drawings from Gilbert's 1903 specifications identify each piece's style, maker, measurements, description, history, amount ordered, number now extant, and current location. When the booklet was made available to Plant Management (the division responsible for the capitol's management), state movers identified and rescued more than one-dozen pieces of furniture from loading docks, where the pieces were waiting to be sent to state surplus storage facilities. Disseminating information about furniture styles also enabled House staff to identify three chairs from 1905, never found during the research, in a representative's office.

8-2. Speaker's chair designed by Gilbert, as displayed in House Retiring Room, 1970–89. Manufactured by Herter Brothers, New York, NY. (Photo by Tom Olmscheid, Minnesota House of Representatives, 2001)

Whereas before 1986 the furniture was treated as routine office furnishings for use and disposal by state offices, now the eight hundred pieces of original capitol furniture are tracked by MHS staff in an annual inventory of seventeen state agencies where they are located. Personnel changes, which are routine in the offices of elected political officials where the furniture is used, result in frequent movement of the pieces. The inventory provides an opportunity not only to verify locations and condition but also to educate staff about the furniture. This process has increased appreciation among its users. Accession numbers, assigned by MHS Museum Collections staff, are used to identify each style and piece of furniture. The MHS Central Registrar enters results into the capitol furniture database, which has been invaluable in servicing inquiries about the furniture and planning for the preservation of the collection.

Documentation has yielded an increasing awareness of the furniture's importance to the appearance of the capitol. Many historic items original to the Governor's Reception Room and other locations have been returned, and once again there is an appropriateness of proportion, scale, and design between the furniture and the public and ceremonial space in which they are used. Visitors and officials alike can enjoy the furniture as Gilbert intended; it is integrated with related sculpture, artwork, and architecture in his Renaissance-inspired design for the capitol.

Since 1988, carpets now installed in the chambers of the Senate, House of Representatives, and Supreme Court have been remanufactured according to the designs from 1905. Using historic photographs and the specifications from 1905, it was determined in 1998 that the Senate's two-color red carpet in a pattern of rosette motifs nearly matched the original carpet in both color and design. It was the only one of these chamber's carpets that still matched the original carpet.

Further research indicated that the tradition to preserve the Senate chamber carpet had begun with the replacement of the original in 1939. At that time, Secretary of the Senate G. H. Spaeth sent samples of both the original and the new carpet to the University of Minnesota and authorized an analysis to compare them. Assistant Professor of Textiles and Clothing Ethel Phelps reported that "the new carpet measures up to the claims made for it, and would seem to be a worthy successor to the original carpet used in the Senate Chamber."[12]

In 1989, the two-color red carpet in the House of Representatives was not in harmony with the chamber's highly decorative dome, since the latter displayed original gold and green decorative motifs. Curiously, when a small sample of the original House carpet was found, its green color did not find instant acceptance from House members who had been appointed to a standing committee to oversee the restoration of their chamber.[13] Investigating other statehouses, they found that the color red was traditionally used in Senate chambers, not in chambers for the House. Even with this information and available historical documentation, the committee did not fully support the choice of the original green color. Only when the Speaker of the House cast his vote and broke a tie did the issue get decided in favor of reproducing the carpet to match the sample that had been discovered.

With increasing public awareness of the ongoing restoration of the capitol, an interesting development occurred. A few years after this restoration was completed, a citizen came forward with further information. In his late great-aunt's diary, this citizen had found her description of a somewhat clandestine tour of the capitol in late 1904. Sewn into her diary was a small souvenir piece of the original House carpet that she had spirited away.[14] It was the same design as the sample for the reproduction carpet and differed only slightly in color.

The Society's Capitol Historic Site began a second major research effort in 1993 in cooperation with MHS Museum Collections, which produced the "Furnishings Plan" for the public and ceremonial spaces.[15] This report fully documents the original furniture, carpets, window treatments, and lighting that had been used in these spaces as well as that which exists there now. Whereas research on the furnishings for the Senate and House chambers was done during the restoration of those rooms, this "Furnishings Plan" had been completed in 1995—prior to the partial restoration of the Supreme Court. The royal blue carpet of a 1960s renovation had made the courtroom dramatically different from its original appearance. Fortunately, research had produced a design recommendation for the Court Chamber and Retiring Room that would rectify this historical inaccuracy.[16]

As with all capitol carpet specifications, identification was by type and by number, with color to be selected by the architect.[17] It was unclear how many colors were used in the court's carpets, and no design renderings were found in the course of extended research. Black-and-white period photographs provided the only documentation available to determine the design. They showed portions of the carpets, but

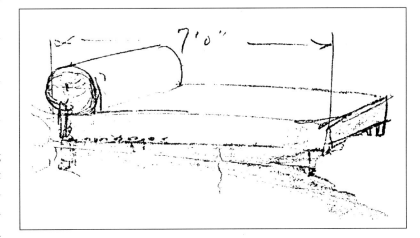

the images were not clear. Photo enlargements focused on the designs, which proved to utilize a pomegranate-artichoke style motif in the chamber and a floral medallion with scroll in the Consultation Room (Figure 8-4). From these details scale drawings were made. An early guidebook to the capitol was useful in identifying the original deep-red color of the carpet.[18] The original color of the court's portieres (heavy curtains that are hung across a doorway) was known from a sample of red velour fabric that had been found in the specifications. The "Furnishings Plan" thus recommended that this sample be used as a guide to select the custom red colors for the carpet.[19]

Elegant red portieres were prominent furnishings for both the Supreme Court and the Governor's Reception Room. Original specifications for portieres

8-3. Gilbert sketched this chaise lounge for Justice E. A. Jaggard in 1905. Manufactured by Herter Brothers, New York, NY. (Minnesota Historical Society)

and draperies in these two spaces were described as "cotton velour curtains, color Empire Red 545, as manufactured by the J. H. Thorp Co."[20] The floor-to-ceiling portieres, which formerly had hung behind the five white Vermont marble columns and defined a corridor behind the Supreme Court justices' bench, had been replaced by three-tiered bookcases. As part of the 1997 restoration, the portieres were reproduced in accord with those shown in period photographs, and their fabric was modeled on the red velour sample. The deep, rich colors of the furnishings and the walls brought about a stunning transformation of the court. Once again, the historic colors of the furnishings complement the four murals above by John La Farge and the dark mahogany furniture, as Gilbert intended.

If a sense of reflection and restfulness was achieved in the court with a return to its historic colors, so was a more vibrant atmosphere returned to the Governor's Reception Room in 1987 with the reproduction of the window draperies. Constructing the elegant panels in the red velour fabric as originally specified was only the first step in this project. The completed drapery panels were delivered to Minneapolis Regina High School where students enrolled in Project Regina, a nonprofit organization to aid Twin City Hmong and Laotian refugees, began the intricate work of decorating the drapery panels. Five Hmong immigrants, four women and one man who were skilled in needlework, labored for four months to cut, interface, lay out, and hand-stitch one thousand gold lamé oak leaves onto the panels to recreate the designs shown in period photographs. Contrary to the treatment of countless nameless immigrants who labored to build the capitol, the names of these new immigrants have been duly recorded.[21] Research done for the "Furnishings Plan" furthered knowledge about the leaf design on

8-4. Photo enlargement of Supreme Court Consultation Room photograph provided design detail needed for reproduction. (Photo by Edmund A. Brush, Minnesota Historical Society)

the portieres to indicate that delicate embroidery (Figure 8-5) was used in addition to appliqué. Perhaps when the original double-sided portieres are restored to the entry between the reception room and the anteroom, where a door is now necessary, this embroidery can be included.

Gilbert's first drawing for the Minnesota State Capitol included the monumental quadriga sculpture instead of a pediment above the main entrance. Inspired by Daniel Chester French's quadriga centered on top of the Peristyle at the World's Columbian Exposition of 1893, Gilbert selected French for the Minnesota commission.[22] Skilled equestrian sculptor Edward C. Potter worked with French to create Minnesota's eight-piece quadriga from copper sheeting hammered over steel framing.

By 1900, this gilded quadriga seemed to suit the expectations of its citizens for a grand capitol building. The quadriga symbolized the state's accomplishments in agriculture and industry, which were allegorically represented by two women. These figures lead four horses that represent the forces of nature—earth, wind, fire, and water. Driving the chariot (and therefore the state) forward toward ever greater accomplishments is the male figure, Prosperity, the name agreed upon by Gilbert and French to replace Columbus who had been the charioteer of French's 1893 fair sculpture.[23] Affectionately dubbed "the horses" by one and all, the quadriga is appropriately titled *The Progress of the State*.

In 1990, the gold leaf was deteriorating at a rapid pace, and splitting seams on the copper figures prompted an investigation into the existing conditions and past repairs of the sculptural group. Only a few documents were unearthed. From 1949, photos and newspaper accounts reported that the sculpture had been regilded (Figure 8-6). From 1979 a mere half page of general specifications from a repair and another regilding was discovered. No documentation was found to indicate any repair of the structural elements of the infrastructure. When an art conservator investigated the condition of the sculpture, it was determined that 5 to 10 percent of the structural supports (Figure 8-7) were unsound.[24]

This investigation also unearthed an unexpected condition of the copper pedestal roof. When the seams of the copper roof were opened, it became apparent that another copper pedestal base was still in place. Again using period photographs, it was identified as the original base, and the decision was made to restore it. Installation of a second copper pedestal base—which the conservator determined to have been added about 1958—contributed to the deterioration of the sculptures because it trapped water between the layers of copper and inside the sculptures.[25] The MHS provided oversight for correcting this problem, and state agencies provided leadership for the roof replacement project, which included restoration of the quadriga.[26]

Further research conducted in conjunction with the restoration of the quadriga found that Gilbert instructed that the initial gilding be done soon after it was installed in late 1906. Almost immediately, complaints began to surface that the gold was too bright, even though shading had been done of the "sunken parts to bring out the highlights," as indicated in the gilder's contract.[27] French suggested to Gilbert that the brilliance of the gold could be removed by applying wax dissolved in turpentine.[28] Before the quadriga's installation Gilbert was also concerned that the copper base might stain the exterior white marble a green color. Thus, he recommended that the copper base be painted white.[29] Both these problems were addressed during restoration, and Gilbert's original instructions were the guide, causing a marked change from the sculpture's pre-restoration appearance. The copper base, which had been green for decades, was painted white. With the application of colored wax to dull the brilliant gold leaf, the sculptural details are clearly visible (see Figure C-16).

In 1995, two public events celebrated the return of the quadriga to its prominent location on top of the capitol. The crane lift-up to reinstall the quadriga on the roof and the grand reopening of the quadriga terrace to the public each attracted more than one thousand visitors, evidence of the high regard that citizens have for this monumental sculpture on top of their statehouse.[30]

8-5. Both delicate embroidery and appliqué decorated the original portieres and draperies in the Governor's Reception Room, c 1919. (Photo by *Minneapolis Journal*, Minnesota Historical Society)

8-6. Workers regilding quadriga, ca. 1949. (Photo by *St. Paul Dispatch–Pioneer Press*, Minnesota Historical Society)

8-7. Five to ten percent of the quadriga's structural support had failed by 1994. (Minnesota Historical Society)

8-8. Interior of the Minnesota State Capitol café This photograph c. 1913 provided the most valuable documentation available for the restoration of the rathskeller. (Photo by Charles. W. Jerome, Minnesota Historical Society)

Whereas the quadriga has been appreciated as an important work of art in Minnesota for nearly a century, the rathskeller design of the restaurant has been long forgotten. The German tradition of a restaurant located in a city hall (*rathaus*) in the basement (*keller*), which in America became more popularly known as a rathskeller, was utilized in the original design of the basement area of the capitol building.

Research in the mid-1980s unveiled an intriguing history about the public restaurant. At that time, white walls and a white asbestos ceiling greeted visitors; contemporary round tables occupied half of the space, and a serving line and kitchen occupied the remaining half. However, a single period photograph from c. 1913 (Figure 8-8) depicts abundant decorative details on the walls and ceiling, and tables covered with white cloths placed along the entire length of the restaurant. This photograph held out the hope that decorative secrets might be recovered beneath the layers of paint.

Newspaper documentation from 1917 and later, in fact, gave support to this hope. It indicated that Governor J. A. A. Burnquist had ordered the rathskeller designs painted over because of anti-German sentiment during World War I. In 1930, Governor Theodore Christianson ordered that the original designs be restored to the restaurant. He agreed, as one of his last acts as governor, to alter three of the original mottoes in response to statewide criticism from the press that drinking wine and beer should not be encouraged during Prohibition. Thus, the 1905 motto "Better be tipsy than feverish" was transformed to "Temperance is a virtue of men."[31]

A conservator's initial investigation in 1985 of the rathskeller designs made this hope of uncovering the original designs a reality. The investigation was limited to scraping off paint layers to uncover the existence of a squirrel motif. In anticipation that funding to restore the cafeteria would be appropriated soon, a more detailed investigation of the room was undertaken a few years later. This more expansive investigation successfully recovered a variety of decorative designs. It was not until nine years later, however, that the Minnesota legislature appropriated the funding to completely restore the cafeteria and add a new kitchen and serving area, a project that is now complete.

As restoration of the restaurant began, the period photograph became the most important documentation available. High-quality enlargements (such as that of Figure 8-9), indicated the location and detail of many decorative designs.[32] Following the removal of asbestos from the ceiling and the study of photographic and paint evidence, an art conservator began a successful six-month investigation to recover the designs.[33] These designs were documented with photographs, drawn on mylar, and made into stencils before commencing the exacting process of transferring them onto new plaster.[34]

Nearly a year of intricate and painstaking work was necessary to transfer the original designs onto the new plaster of the walls and ceiling. Seven such designs were selected to remain on the original plaster, which is now recessed one-quarter inch below the new plaster. This original material was not changed except that the missing areas were painted a semitone lighter than the surrounding areas; they were then varnished.[35] Viewers can compare the differences between the two solutions to restoration: the replication of designs on new plaster and the preservation of original designs on the old plaster. No matter what their preference, they can appreciate a restoration that was made possible by the survival of designs under twenty-two layers of paint after being hidden for nearly a century.

Since none of the original furnishings were extant, reproduction chairs, tables, and chandeliers now supplement the historically restored space. Details of the chairs and the chandeliers were again determined from enlargements of the valuable single photograph. To make this restored space function again as a restaurant, the area beneath the north steps of the capitol was excavated to build a new kitchen and serving area.

The year 2000 marked the first time since 1917, at which time it had only been open for twelve years, that the rathskeller dining area greeted visitors with its unique ambiance. As new generations appreciate this German tradition, they may well ponder the impact of politics on this decorative artwork and appreciate the historical significance of returning this gathering place in the capitol to its original appearance.[36]

Extensive documentation about Gilbert's involvement in the capitol, from the time the building was occupied to the end of his life in 1934, suggests his tremendous attention to the building and its details.[37] In 1907, for example, Gilbert and Minnesota citizens paid close attention to the works of art to be placed in the capitol. Gilbert recommended certain sculptors and identified a second-floor location for the installation of a full-size statue of Civil War hero Colonel William Colvill, who had led the 1st Minnesota Regiment in the Battle of Gettysburg.[38] The architect also provided drawings for three dedication plaques that are located by the main entrance and for one plaque that is installed over the fireplace in the Senate Retiring Room.[39] Some years later, when the Senate was planning to install the bust of former Senator Henry Rice in their chamber, Gilbert responded to their request for advice about what type of pedestal to use with a sketch of his "simple almost severe design of a classical type and suited to both the location and to the bust."[40] Today, busts of both Rice and another Minnesota statesman, Knute Nelson, are still displayed in the two front niches on top of pedestals built according to the architect's sketch.

Even though Channing Seabury, chair of the Board of State Capitol Commissioners, and Gilbert were depicted in a detail of Blashfield's mural *Minnesota, the Granary of the World,* Gilbert in 1926 offered to donate another image of himself. This portrait bust (Figure 8-10) and pedestal of the architect's own design were offered for permanent display.[41] His

8-9. Enlargement from a glass plate negative shows detail of decorative motifs. Elmer Garnsey, 1904, stencil and free-hand; oil on painted plaster. (Photo by Charles W. Jerome, Minnesota Historical Society)

concern for details was still evident in the accompanying prioritized list of four locations where the object might be displayed. In addition, he sent a brass pipe with specific instructions about how to anchor the pedestal to the floor with cement so as to give stability and some degree of permanence.

A few months before his death in 1934, Gilbert contacted Governor Floyd B. Olson about the ongoing plan for a capitol approach. Gilbert had been concerned with this idea since 1902 (see Figure 12-1) and by this point in time conceived it as part of a Works Progress Administration project for the state. Unsurprisingly, he recommended his own firm for the work.[42] Gilbert also mentioned that his advice had been sought previously regarding the location of the State Office Building, which was constructed next to the capitol in 1932.[43]

After more than a decade of work to restore the public and ceremonial spaces to their 1905 appearance, Gilbert's capitol building is slowly being recovered. The mechanical and electrical systems necessary for a modern working seat of state government are being upgraded. The restoration of the roof is complete and work continues on the restoration of terraces surrounding the structure of the capitol. Four major interior spaces (the Senate, House of Representatives, rathskeller restaurant, and porte cochere) have been entirely restored, and three other major spaces—the Supreme Court, Governor's Reception Room, and ground-floor corridors—have been partially restored. Major projects need to be addressed in the future, such as restoring the entire east wing of the capitol and returning the public corridors with all their decorative details to their original colors and designs. Furnishings, works of art, and lighting proj-

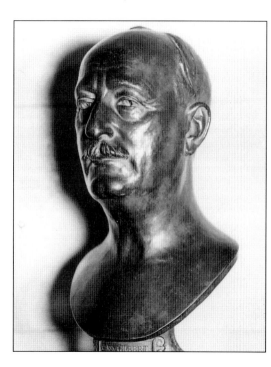

8-10. Gilbert's bust in a prominent niche on the first floor of the Minnesota State Capitol. Edmund Quinn, bronze, 1926. (Photo by Graphic Arts Society, Minnesota Historical Society)

ects also are planned, to enhance the appearance and function of the capitol.

Gilbert and Garnsey's original color palette is becoming evident to visitors. Colors and decorative designs that are clearly related to one another can be noted by even the casual observer who ambles from space to space. The deep olive gray of the rathskeller, for example, relates to the color scheme of the wall panels in the court; the ribbon motifs on the first floor reappear even more boldly as scrolls on which the German rathskeller mottoes were originally inscribed; and a prominent American eagle design in the rathskeller is rendered in translucent stained glass in the skylight over the spiral stairs and in three dimensions in bronze torchieres. Even the appliqué oak leaves in the Governor's Reception Room bear a strong similarity to the grape leaf vines in the ceilings of the grand staircase and rathskeller, and the deep red colors of chambers at opposite ends of the building are connected by Pompeian red wall panels in the vast corridors between them. The color harmony between the spaces, and the vividness and boldness of the colors and designs, will both surprise and delight those who walk into this masterful interior design. The Capitol Historic Site also hopes that someday it may serve as a laboratory in which students can learn about Gilbert's approach to design.

Research continues as the state looks forward to restoring the remaining interior spaces in preparation for the capitol centennial in 2005. With the completion of each additional space, visitors will recognize even greater evidence of the relationship of design and color in the public and ceremonial areas. In the coming years visitors can look forward to experiencing a monumental public work of art that is true to its appearance in 1905 (see Figure 5-3) and continues to work, both as the seat of state government and aesthetically as Gilbert intended.

PART 3

MONUMENTALITY IN NEW YORK

CHAPTER 9

THE IMAGE OF THE CITY:
THE WOOLWORTH BUILDING AND
THE CREATION OF THE NEW YORK SKYLINE

Gail Fenske

By 1915, New York had developed a distinctive urban identity as a "skyscraper city." Subsequently, images of the new skyline were circulated worldwide—in etchings, illustrated views, photographs, tinted photographs sold as picture postcards, and fanciful compositions such as the 1926 cover illustration for *King's Views of New York* (Figure 9-1). In the illustration for *King's Views,* the Singer and the Woolworth towers are exaggerated in height, making them appear even more towerlike, and the ship in the harbor is given a grand, intimidating presence. Such an illustration, tailored for tourists and popular audiences, makes clear how New York's business interests wished the city to be seen by the United States and by the world at large—as a modern capital of commerce, industry, and finance. New York was competing as an international economic power, and they used the technological audacity, scale, and artistic distinction of the modern skyscraper as a way of making their preeminent financial position known.

The principal shapers of New York's new skyline were hardly the monarchical powers of former eras, seeking to enhance the order and the beauty of the urban realm.[1] Instead, they represented a new breed of modern enterprising speculators, development syndicates, and corporate potentates determined to garner publicity, both commercially and socially, by projecting before urban spectators and the world-at-large landmarks symbolizing their rise to success. The city's buildings, one observer noted, were "more or less reflective" of "such an obtrusive individuality."[2] Cass Gilbert and Frank Woolworth—neither of whom was a native New Yorker—epitomized this

type. Gilbert was an architect and Woolworth a merchant, but both were shrewd about business affairs and both were popularizers. Gilbert designed his colorful and lavishly ornamented Beaux-Arts public buildings to appeal to a broad spectrum of observers among New York's heterogeneous urban crowds, and Woolworth tailored his retailing enterprise to satisfy America's sidewalk shoppers. In creating the Woolworth Building, both assumed a central role in defining the popular skyline image of New York. Gilbert later wrote that "the changing skyline of New York is one of the marvels of a marvelous age. . . . skyscrapers were born of the necessities of time and space, under the urge of modern life, and they are expressive of its commercial conditions and the enterprise of our epoch."[3] Woolworth pointed out that his skyscraper brought fame not only to itself but also to New York.[4] Both considered skyscrapers America's newest and most distinctive form of urban monumental architecture.

Gilbert arrived in New York in 1880, to begin his apprenticeship with the architectural firm McKim,

9-1. Cover illustration showing the Singer and the Woolworth towers, in *King's Views of New York* (New York, 1926). (Collection of the author)

Mead & White at 57 Broadway, and Woolworth arrived in 1886, to establish a headquarters for his rapidly growing retailing enterprise at 104 Chambers Street and shortly thereafter, in the Stewart Building at 280 Broadway. Both worked near the heart of New York's business district, and so both were in the position to witness the city's newly developing and increasingly controversial modern skyline. By the end of the century, illustrations comparing New York's old and new skylines commonly appeared in journals such as *Harper's Weekly* and *Scientific American* (Figure 9-2). Their purpose was not only to call attention to the city's burgeoning growth but also to heighten a reader's awareness of the city's changing urban image. Skyscrapers replaced the steeples of churches to command skyline views. New York had begun to develop, critics noted, an architectural identity, that for better or worse, signified a powerful center of spirited entrepreneurial activity, corporate consolidation, and high finance. In the 1890s, the demand for offices in lower Manhattan mushroomed. Of the nation's 185 largest industrial enterprises, chief among them railroads and steel, 69 chose to establish headquarters in Manhattan before 1900.[5] By the middle of the decade, the word *skyline* came into common use to describe the profile view of the city's tall buildings, many of which were built to house new headquarters and so carried company names. The skyline view replaced the older harbor views as the convention for "picturing" the city.[6]

Not everyone agreed that the skyline view was worthy of the nation's new economic capital or indeed, that the city's increasingly powerful commercial status merited such bold architectural representation. In 1896, a writer for *Scribner's Magazine* (probably Russell Sturgis) observed that "there is, of course, no architectural merit" in the skyline.[7] A year later, Montgomery Schuyler noted that for the European visitor to the city, the first impression of the skyline may not be "agreeable," but it was nonetheless "tremendously forcible. . . . it seems to him [the visitor] that he has never before seen a water-front that so impressively and exclusively 'looked like business.'" For the inland American visitor, by contrast, the skyline represented an "index of the national prosperity" and for some, a prosperity "acquired somehow at the expense of the interior." Schuyler concluded that although the skyline projected a singular image of brashness, the view was devoid of *ensemble,* or the Beaux-Arts-inspired compositional order desired by designers of cities after the World's Columbian Exposition of 1893. The only hope for the view's improvement, Schuyler thought, lay in the efforts of "artistic-minded" designers who, in imagining the view of the city from across the river, might give the silhouette, as much as they could, "of spirit and of picturesqueness."[8] Ideally, wrote the critic A. D. F. Hamlin that same year, architects would design the skyscrapers as isolated towers.[9] Both Schuyler and Hamlin seemed to be suggesting that the tower form offered the most satisfactory artistic solution for the city's newly vertical construction, particularly if the distant view was to be appreciated for the quality of picturesqueness.

With the creation of Greater New York in 1898, proponents of New York's artistic improvement, or what they called after 1902 the City Beautiful, joined in the discussion of New York's skyline image. John De Witt Warner wrote in *Municipal Affairs* that today's New Yorkers bore the responsibility for "building the world's capital for all time to come."[10] He and other champions of the City Beautiful began imagining the city as a Europe-inspired imperial capital, graced by magnificent buildings—another Paris, London, or Vienna. While they focused on the design of a civic center at City Hall Park, the City Beautiful's chief theorist and spokesman, Charles Mulford Robinson, wrote in his *Modern Civic Art* of 1903 that the view of a city from a distance also should be emphasized as an urban focal point. In assessing what he called the "water approach," Robinson called attention to the well-known views of Boston from the harbor or Venice from the sea. Such an approach, he emphasized, revealed at a glance for the visitor and native alike the dreams, aspirations, and progress of the city's inhabitants. It constituted the most important "picture" of the city and should be the pride of citizens. New York's water approach, Robinson added, was marred

in the nearer view by flimsy docks and piers. But the "far-off picture," or the skyscrapers as viewed from a distance, "clustered like a forest of silver birches gleaming in the brilliant light," marked the city with an "unmistakable personality." Robinson further suggested that it might be possible to create from the skyscrapers' chaotic arrangement the impression of an "artistic whole."[11]

Gilbert was uniquely prepared as an architect to contribute to the shaping of New York's skyline view, or "city of towers," as writers and critics frequently described it after the completion of Ernest Flagg's Singer Tower in 1908. Gilbert established his office in New York in 1899, shortly after receiving a commission there for his first skyscraper, the Broadway Chambers Building. During his many study

tours in Europe, Gilbert time and time again sketched or painted isolated towers, among them his *Tower of the Palazzo Vecchio, Florence* (1880). Equally often, however, he recorded profile views of cities, such as his *Towers from the City Wall, Nuremberg* (1897). There he carefully observed the visual contribution of towers to the picturesque character of the city's composition (Figure C-15). Ultimately, Gilbert would aspire to reconcile the skyscraper, which he envisioned as a tower standing free in its surroundings and so appearing "picturesque," with the City Beautiful's most basic assumption that all urban architecture should be conceived as an ensemble. Gilbert's concern for the ensemble was grounded in his Beaux-Arts education at MIT and his apprenticeship with McKim, Mead & White. By 1900 he assumed a leadership role in designing the City Beautiful—he proposed City Beautiful plans for

9-2. "The Skyline of Buildings below Chambers Street, as Seen from the Hudson River," in *Harper's Weekly* 41 (March 20, 1897): 296–97. (Library of Congress)

Washington, D.C. (1900) (see Figure 3-2); for St. Paul, Minnesota (beginning 1902) (see Figure 12-1); and, with Frederick Law Olmsted Jr., for New Haven, Connecticut (1907–10) (see Figure 12-5).[12] Gilbert deeply understood the complementary relationship between a singular work of architecture and a particular urban setting. His didactic essay of 1900, "Grouping of Public Buildings and Development of Washington," for instance, focused on compositional strategies for interrelating buildings, among them axes, vistas, alignments, and focal points.[13] When designing his Ives Memorial Library for New Haven in 1907, Gilbert argued for the virtues of harmonizing new buildings with the "traditions of their site."[14] As an architect, then, Gilbert had not only a natural predilection for the picturesque but also a strong commitment to the ideals of urban order and unity espoused by advocates of the City Beautiful.

Gilbert's earliest designs for skyscrapers, the Brazer Building in Boston (1894–96; see Figure 1-16) and the Broadway Chambers Building in New York (1896–99) (see Figure C-5), were originally conceived as medieval towers with picturesque crowns. His West Street Building (1905–7) followed the pattern, sporting a seven-story tower that emerged from a lower office block (Figure 9-3). Gilbert's client for the project, General Howard Carroll, vice president of the Starin Transportation Company, chose a building site on the Hudson River waterfront; he wanted to ensure that his skyscraper would be visible to river traffic. Carroll's company transported freight across the Hudson by car floats. The floats left the Delaware, Lackawanna & Western Railroad Company yards in Hoboken, New Jersey, and arrived at Pier 20, directly in front of the West Street Building. Significantly, the West Street Building would stand out conspicuously in the view of lower Manhattan shared by the more than 100,000 ferry passengers who traveled to the city daily from New Jersey. Carroll anticipated attracting tenants who, like himself, were seeking highly conspicuous quarters on the Hudson.[15]

When Gilbert began designing the West Street Building, he placed a new emphasis on finding the proper architectural "character," in the Beaux-Arts sense of the term, for the headquarters of an Ameri-

can commercial enterprise. For inspiration, he turned to the secular Gothic architecture of Flanders—notably to its *hôtels de ville,* cloth halls, and belfries (Figure 9-4). The monuments of Bruges, and the Belfry in particular, held a special interest for Gilbert (Figure 9-5). Flemish cities were thriving centers of trade during the Middle Ages. Bruges, which reached the heights of prosperity during the thirteenth and fourteenth centuries, was one of the great harbors of Europe. As the center of the northern European textile industry, it imported and spun English wool and supplied the world market at the time. Gilbert traveled to Flanders for the first time in 1897; his interest in the region, as documented in his diaries, an essay, and travel drawings, was well established at the time of his West Street commission in 1905.[16] Later, Gilbert argued for the importance of a "civic or commercial" compositional prototype, inspired by the Flemish Gothic tradition—that is, a low blocky mass joined to a prominent tower—in conceiving the headquarters for an American commercial enterprise.[17] Other architects, from Gilbert's Beaux-Arts-trained predecessors in New York to the French

Beaux-Arts theorist Julien Guadet, similarly emphasized the "emblematic" connection between the towered structures of medieval cities and qualities such as "municipal dignity," grandeur, and wealth.[18] If Gilbert found in the architecture of medieval Flanders the proper character for a modern commercial building, then it is likely that he appreciated the tradition's implications for New York's urban character as well. He may well have regarded the nation's chief commercial metropolis as a comparable prospering and ambitious international center of trade.

Gilbert's vision for the West Street Building as an emblem of commercial enterprise was compromised when Carroll chose not to build the skyscraper's seven-story tower. Still, Gilbert was able to bring the spirit of Flanders to his design. For the crown, he detailed in terra cotta a bristling repertory of medieval gables, crockets, and tourelles, drawn in part from sources such as the *hôtel de ville* in Audenaarde. Gilbert's detail was especially appreciated by Schuyler, who praised it in views of the city from the Hudson River. Schuyler, inspired by John Ruskin, described the crown's "misty masses of multitudinous pinnacle and

OPPOSITE
9-3. West Street Building, original design, 1905. (Wurts Collection, 111013. Museum of the City of New York)

ABOVE
9-4. "The Seven Wonders of Bruges," attributed to P. Claeissens the Elder, c. 1550, Benguinage, Bruges (Institute Royale du Patrimoine Artistique–Koninklijk Instituut voor het Kunstpatrimonium, Brussels)

THE IMAGE OF THE CITY

diademed tower," adding that "relieved against roof or sky" it was especially evocative visually "from up and down the river," as well as in the distant view from afar (Figure 9-6).[19] Schuyler's continued interest as a critic of the city's evolving skyline was paralleled by its growing appeal as a subject for artists and photographers as well as illustrators and producers of picture postcards. Furthermore, New York, now in the process of becoming the nation's major tourist center by receiving up to 200,000 visitors a day, was developing an enhanced awareness of itself as a marketable attraction.[20] Critics such as Schuyler, along with the producers of the urban views, took an active role in shaping the popular perceptions of the skyline as an emblem of the city.

The social meanings of the newly popular skyline, however, continued to perplex informed observers. On one hand, it signified a business community vigorously engaged in the shared activity of white-collar work. Boston architect and planner Sylvester Baxter described New York's skyline in 1906 as marked for "the effect of collective activity" that accompanied "a common impulse in a given direction."[21] On the other hand, that very activity was inextricable from what amounted to a new social order, described by Henry James during his visit to New York in 1904 as "a vast, crude democracy of trade."[22] The single-minded pursuit of profits at any cost, others argued, compromised the ideal of community for the sake of individualistic gain. Hence, for Montgomery Schuyler writing in 1907, the skyscrapers, regardless of the merits of the view, suggested

independent individuals "merged in a riot." Altogether, they were "bewildering and stupefying in the mass, with no ensemble but that of strife and struggle."[23] For the editors of *American Architect and Building News,* the skyline represented no less than a "vaunting of sheer materialism."[24] If the skyline generated mixed feelings, then for many it also signified a peculiarly "American" character. The skyscraper, the critic Mary Fanton Roberts argued, was "the first absolutely genuine expression of an original American architecture." New York's skyline, consequently, had the capacity to convey potent messages about Americans as a "busy people" engaged in "fearlessly building" to suit the most basic and ordinary needs.[25]

Gilbert produced fantasy designs for both his Broadway Chambers Building (1899), which he described as "a good deal higher than the moon," and his West Street Building (1905), which in a sketch soared skyward to 150 stories.[26] Such projects, more than a sign of personal eccentricity or excessive ambition on Gilbert's part, vividly manifested the spirit of the time. Other designers, Charles Rollinson Lamb, R. H. Robertson, Theodore Starrett, and Ernest Flagg among them, similarly suggested the construction of skyscrapers as modern towers to 100 stories, 650 feet, 1,000 feet, and comparably daring heights.[27] Taken together, the projects suggested future New York as a breathtakingly vertical city. The sheer innovative energy of the city, it seemed, fostered the impetus to test the potentials of modern steel construction. A modern city was in the making—"simply bursting its bonds," observed *Harper's Weekly* in 1902—"it is as if some mighty force were astir beneath the ground, hour by hour pushing up structures that a dozen years ago would have been inconceivable."[28] The desire to build also manifested itself in the frenzy of construction activity surrounding the city's infrastructure. The city's engineers and contractors were at the time tunneling under the Hudson River and the East River; spanning those waterways with the Williamsburg, Manhattan, and Queensborough Bridges; excavating beneath streets for Manhattan's extensive subway system; and digging underground corridors and electrifying tracks for the Grand Central and Pennsylvania

9-5. Sketch of the towers of Bruges, showing the Belfry, c. 1905. (Library of Congress)

railroad terminals. Gilbert, who harbored the ambition to build the world's tallest towers, aspired to become similarly engaged with the energetic process of restructuring the city.

Ernest Flagg's Singer Tower, completed in 1908, represented the boldest expression to date of New York's ambitious dynamic of vertical construction. Flagg's slender pinnacle amazed architectural critics such as Schuyler, who judged the Singer Tower "among the most interesting of our experiments in skyscraping," and popular audiences alike.[29] With a quantum leap in height, the Singer Tower nearly doubled the threshold of the former skyline. Flagg, previously known as an outspoken critic of the skyscraper, now viewed his daring feat of construction as a model for skyscraper reform. Flagg's tower also suggested a city of the future, described by the project's engineer Otto Francis Semsch as a "veritable city of towers" (Figure 9-7).[30] The future city, as Flagg envisioned it, would be composed of tall, thin campanile-like skyscrapers that occupied only one-quarter of a site's buildable area and ascended upward over carefully proportioned commercial blocks to dazzling and previously unconquerable heights. The office blocks would combine to create an ordered urban ensemble, but the isolated towers—memorable, unique, and artfully disposed—would suggest in their freer arrangement, Flagg thought, a "picturesque, interesting, and beautiful" skyline with a European flavor. Their construction in steel, moreover, would signify a

thoroughly modern city, in which the elevator and the steel frame had been carried to a logical conclusion, in Flagg's words, a "City of the Twentieth Century."[31]

The Singer Company had its own reasons for building Flagg's tower. When it undertook the project in 1906, it was undergoing the final phase of a prolonged period of vigorous expansion in the world market for sewing machines. It had dominated that market since the Civil War and controlled nearly 80 percent of it by 1890.[32] Consequently, the Singer Tower, designed by Flagg in his distinctive "modern French" idiom, would serve as the symbolic headquarters of an expansive international empire. It would function equally efficiently as memorable advertising and as a powerful public relations tool. Singer, as a retailer that dedicated multiple outlets to the distribution of its product, had an important relationship to forge and to maintain with the consumer. Moreover, the monopolizing tendencies of big businesses such as Singer received harsh criticism during the early years of the century, following the great wave of merger activity that began in 1897. If the city's crowds could be dazzled with a technologically adventurous, highly ornamental cynosure that suggested dreams other than those of an aggressively consolidating commercial enterprise, then those crowds might in turn view the Singer Company in a more favorable light.[33]

Flagg's Singer Tower was an overnight architectural sensation. John Van Dyke applauded it as both

9-6. View showing the West Street Building and the Singer Tower from the Hudson River, postcard photograph by Irving Underhill, c. 1908. (Collection of the author)

THE IMAGE OF THE CITY

beautiful and outrageous in *The New New York,* his paean to the modern city.[34] Even architectural critics responded favorably. The editors of *Architectural Record* hailed the tower as a spectacular skyline feature, whose completion marked the "breaking through of another stratum of ether" to create a striking profile for the city.[35] For Harrison Rhodes, writing in *Harper's Monthly Magazine,* the newly towered skyline embodied "the romance of the future."[36] Joseph B. Gilder confessed in *Putnam's Monthly Magazine* that although he opposed skyscrapers, if treated as towers they might number among "the chief architectural ornaments of the new New York."[37] Flagg's creation was especially appreciated for its contribution to the views of the city from the water. Van Dyke compared the approach to New

contrast to the dignified architectural groupings espoused by the advocates of the City Beautiful—suggested a futuristic and memorable image for the city, which called it out as distinctive among the metropolises of the world.[40]

Given the ongoing process of picturing and debating the views of the city, the ground was prepared by 1910 for Gilbert's design of the Woolworth Building as a striking and spectacular Gothic tower, a skyline feature that would powerfully influence the shaping of New York's new urban identity (Figure 9-8 and see Figure C-6). Frank Woolworth requested at his first meeting with Gilbert that his skyscraper have a "great tower" modeled on the Victoria Tower of the Houses of Parliament in London.[41] Woolworth admired Gothic architecture generally, and especially that of the cathedrals. The Victoria Tower, however, with echoes of an imperial grandeur, provided Woolworth with a Gothic exemplar of precisely the sort that he was seeking for the new

9-7. Ernest Flagg, "Future New York as a "city of towers," 1908, in *A History of the Singer Building Construction,* ed. O. F. Semsch (New York, 1908), 9. (Library of Congress)

York with that of Constantinople.[38] A writer for *Living Age* responded in 1909 that "a towered city" on the water, recalling Venice or ancient Tyre, would indeed provide New York with an unmistakable urban identity. "The dead skyline of the future city will not rise extravagantly high, but above it, like particular peaks upon a chain of mountains, will be towers and domes and pinnacles, through which the sun may shine and the breezes blow. New York will be a towered city. And then of course this style of architecture will be imitated all over the world. . . . the towers of New York will be reckoned as characteristic as the minarets of a Mohammedan city, as the bell towers of Russia, as the pillar-towers of India . . . or as the campaniles of Italy."[39] Joseph Pennell prominently featured the Singer Tower in his etching of 1908, "Unbelievable City," and Alfred Stieglitz, in his photogravure, "City of Ambition," of 1910. For New Yorkers and visitors alike, the startlingly vertical commercial tower, all dazzle, modernity, and show—by

headquarters of F. W. Woolworth & Company's international chain of stores. The chain incorporated 318 stores scattered across the United States and Canada, along with a new group of stores in England.[42] Woolworth, in transposing the Victoria Tower from its Thames waterfront site to a highly visible site in lower Manhattan, hoped to impress the city's crowds with a work of architecture that they expected to see—a marvelous, enchanted European image, as Gilbert put it, "noted for its beauty."[43] Woolworth's choice of the Victoria Tower had another advantage. It differentiated his project from the Singer Company's recently completed "modern French" urban cynosure. As a consequence, F. W. Woolworth & Company would have its own distinctive symbol on the New York skyline.

Gilbert's process of designing the Woolworth Building was complicated. The project's many designs reflected no less than his and Woolworth's intensified awareness of the skyscraper's potential for strongly influencing the ever-changing urban image of New York. The first design rose twenty stories, but as the project progressed, Gilbert and Woolworth repeatedly reconceived its scope in response to their shared ambition to build a skyscraper of increasingly greater height. As Julia Gilbert put it, the two eventually "conspired together with the result that it was decided to make the skyscraper the highest office building in the world."[44] Woolworth initially was competing with the 612-foot height of the Singer Tower, but as the project evolved, the 700-foot Metropolitan Life Insurance Tower, designed by Napoleon LeBrun & Sons and completed in 1909, served as the benchmark to surpass. Moreover, Woolworth's proposed corporate merger of November 1911, after which he would monopolize the five-and-ten-cent retailing industry with a significantly expanded empire of nearly six hundred stores, strongly suggested a "beacon of worldwide publicity," or a landmark headquarters of unassailable height.[45]

As Woolworth's skyscraper grew increasingly taller, to reach after construction a final height of 792 feet, Gilbert carefully studied the exterior's verticals. He initially conceived the verticals as a modern treatment for his West Street Building elevations, but now he further refined them to take on a new structural prominence and visual sophistication. Rhythmic and syncopated, they were tense with energy. As if to accentuate a modern city in the making, they shot dynamically upward from the sidewalk toward the sky. The composition of the Woolworth Building, which recalled a Flemish cloth hall or belfry, showed that Gilbert had continued to value the secular Gothic tradition of Flanders. While the lower office block, at twenty-eight stories, was hugely disproportionate in size, Gilbert was able to calibrate its height nonetheless, or to align it with that of adjacent skyscrapers; ultimately his design strengthened the order of the city. He shaped the tower's silhouette with setbacks, tourelles, and an ornate crown, to enhance the skyline's picturesque qualities in distant views. Altogether, his design showed a sophisticated understanding of the relationship between a single skyscraper and the larger, indeed panoramic, composition of the city's skyline. Gilbert responded on one

9-8. Woolworth Building, 1910–13. Alfred B. Mullet's old federal courthouse and post office is at center. (Library of Congress)

hand to the City Beautiful ideal of a coherent urban ensemble and on the other, to the criterion of picturesqueness long esteemed by those who documented and assessed the city's profile views.

As construction of the Woolworth Building neared completion, critics, photographers, and view makers instantly recognized Gilbert's design as a significant addition to New York's skyline, which now sported a series of distinctive contrasting towers (Figure 9-9) (also see chapter 10). Two more prominent towers—Trowbridge & Livingston's Banker's Trust Building and McKim, Mead & White's Municipal Building—rose to completion at the same time.

Together the towers contributed to the skyline's picturesqueness, but in their isolated arrangement they also brought a new order to the skyline. This further enhanced the quality of ensemble that earlier critics were searching for. Schuyler praised the new view of the city, which he now understood as the fortuitous consequence of inspired labors by many individual designers. "It will be admitted that all these towers are shapely, worthy of the attention which they compel, credits to their designers, ornaments to the city."[46] Schuyler especially admired the Woolworth Building, by proclaiming "how worthy the tower is of its pre-eminence." In distant views, it was to him "but a 'fair attitude,' a gracious and commanding shape, an overtopping peak in the jagged sierra that calls itself the skyline of lower Manhattan."[47] Gilbert, Schuyler pointed out, had assumed a key role in shaping the new skyline view. The makers of picture postcards and topographical illustrations instantly recognized

the aesthetic potential of the view, and through their process of imaging, Gilbert's design was incorporated into a widely shared perception of the composition of the city. New York, the newest images seemed to proclaim, had at last developed a forceful urban identity.

For some artists and writers, the Woolworth Building, along with New York's vertical construction in general, signified a modern city in the making. The avant-garde artist John Marin, for instance, perceived forces latent in the Woolworth Building's verticals that signified the city's dynamism and futurity. They seemed to cause the entire building to fling itself vigorously skyward, "pushing, pulling, sideways, downwards, upwards" in Marin's words, as if to free itself from the historical city of a quickly disappearing past.[48] Henry Adams described those same energies in a more circumspect tone when

he traveled through New York in 1904: "the outline of the city became frantic in its effort to explain something that defied meaning; power seemed to have outgrown its servitude and asserted its freedom; the cylinder had exploded, and thrown great masses of stone and steam against the sky."[49] The skyscrapers, in Adams's mind, stood for processes of change that had escalated far beyond human control.[50] One reason the City Beautiful's European models continued to hold such high significance was that they offered a compensating paradigm for New York's unbridled forces of modernity, insofar as they signified the promise of restoring order to the city. With the continued construction of steel-framed towers to breathtaking heights, however, the fate of New York as a twentieth-century vertical city was sealed.

Only a few years earlier, in 1903, New York's Municipal Art Society proposed a scheme for a new civic center at City Hall Park (Figure 9-10). Designed for Mayor Seth Low by the engineer Gustav Lindenthal, along with the architects George Post and Henry Hornbostel, it featured a proposed new municipal office "campanile," which was to be constructed to a record-breaking height of 650 feet.[51] The campanile rose nearly twice as high as the Park Row Building, at that time the tallest skyscraper in the world, prominently sited at the opposite corner of the park. The designers' purpose, reporters noted, was to "dwarf" the skyscrapers in the neighborhood.[52] With the construction of such a prominent campanile, the city would secure at long last a collective symbol of the community, as opposed to commerce, on the skyline. Daniel Burnham had similar aspirations for the dome of his city hall, illustrated in his *Plan of Chicago* of 1909—it, too, was to rise above all surrounding commercial construction as a powerful symbol of civic order and unity. Although New York's municipal campanile was never built—Mayor Low thought it required too large a financial investment, and the city's subsequent mayor, George McClellan, thought it too closely tied

9-9. View of lower Manhattan skyline, c. 1915, postcard. (Collection of the author)

with the reforms of the Low administration—it nonetheless powerfully signified the City Beautiful's aspirations for identity of the city.[53]

New York, however, was already in the process of becoming a modern commercial city. By 1915, the imposing height of the city's newest spate of skyscrapers impressed that fact on New Yorkers and visitors alike. Popular photographers and illustrators continued to be at once fascinated and perplexed by the city's newly modern character. In grappling with the challenge of representing the city, they frequently fell back on the filter of the earlier City Beautiful conventions. They would frame towers as symmetrical compositions or show them as if paired to flank the Brooklyn Bridge, giving the illusion of the City Beautiful's highly esteemed "portal" to the city (see Figure 10-12). In the latter case the skyscrapers, striking in their extremity of height, suggested an especially exhilarating entrance because they were appropriately scaled to the experience of approaching the city from the one-mile-long roadway of the bridge. A writer for the *Independent* declared in 1910 that New York, rather than a "City Beautiful," must instead become a "City Majestic."[54]

Gilbert, long a leading designer of the City Beautiful, was now arguing instead for the "City Practical," and he had few reservations about envisioning the future New York as a picturesque as well as modern "city of towers."[55] He made a sketch of the New York skyline in 1912, as the Woolworth Building neared completion (Figure 9-11). In the letter of which the sketch formed a part, he wrote, "[T]he view of New York as I saw it today is I believe the most picturesque thing in the whole world. As we went farther and farther away it seemed to swim in the atmosphere like a dream city of towers and pinnacles—its color was fascinating and its silhouette enchanting."[56] Joseph Pennell chose a similar view for his etching, "New York, from Brooklyn," of 1915

(Figure 9-12). Both Gilbert and Pennell accentuated the height of the Woolworth Building (to make it more towerlike), placed it close to the center of the view, played down the Singer Tower, and rearranged the city's other skyscrapers to make the skyline appear still more picturesque. Their drawings, while part of the same aestheticizing process, also reflected a continuing desire to shape the architectural profile of the city, if only through the comparatively ephemeral device of the image. The towers in both Gilbert's and Pennell's views complemented and contrasted with

one another to enhance the impression of a European, yet new and modern city on the water. As Gilbert put it, "[T]hese are masses seen nowhere else, and possible under no other conditions."[57]

Significantly, in his drawings Gilbert placed the Brooklyn Bridge as a prominent feature adjacent to the skyscrapers. The drawing echoed his earlier watercolors of towered cities in Europe, but by contrast he associated the American skyscraper with the world of engineering and indeed with all great works of heroic construction. His modern epoch, Gilbert later reflected in 1928, had "produced the submarine boat and the airplane, the telegraph, the telephone and the radio in rapid succession; developed electric light and power, forged steel by machinery, spanned rivers and

9-10. Proposal for a New Civic Center, New York, George Post and Henry Hornbostel, 1903, in *Architects' and Builders' Magazine* 4 (August 1903): 485. (Library of Congress)

THE IMAGE OF THE CITY

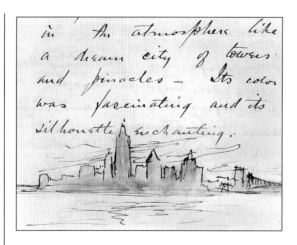

in the atmosphere like a dream city of towers and pinacles— Its color was fascinating and its silhouette enchanting.

valleys with bridges and viaducts of unprecedented size, joined the Mediterranean to the Red Sea and the Atlantic Ocean to the Pacific, had explored the Arctic and the Antarctic. . . ."[58] New York's skyline view for Gilbert embodied the spirit of American daring, pragmatism, and can-do. As such, it was an emblem of an authentic American character, the creation of a "bold, adventurous people."[59] Consequently, the skyline as an image of twentieth-century modernity and progress—as represented in actual views as well as the depictions of them— Gilbert thought ultimately carried the most significant cultural meanings.

After the completion of the Woolworth Building, the popularity of New York's new skyline overwhelmed any significant earlier criticism of it. Gilbert, along with Ernest Flagg, Trowbridge & Livingston, McKim, Mead & White, and other architects, had fashioned lower Manhattan into a modern and spectacular "city of towers." In doing so, they shifted attention away from the questionable practices of big business toward larger and also more widely shared popular cultural ideals—novelty, excitement, glamour, and the breathtaking spectacle of the twentieth-century city. By 1910, moreover, it was obvious that New York had little chance of becoming another London, Paris, or Vienna. In the absence of the significant architectural traditions that characterized those cities, New York's commercial skyscrapers presented themselves as an especially powerful tool for shaping the identity of the city. That identity, inseparable from the nation's identity, not only recalled the medieval cities of Europe but also evoked a twentieth-century futurity. As such, it presented the ideal subject for still further commercialization by view makers, who aggressively advertised the city in a plethora of dazzling skyline images they circulated throughout the United States and the world.

9-11. Sketch of lower Manhattan skyline, 1912. (Library of Congress)

9-12. Joseph Pennell, "New York, From Brooklyn," 1915. (Library of Congress)

CHAPTER 10

IN THE CAMERA'S EYE:
THE WOOLWORTH BUILDING AND AMERICAN
AVANT-GARDE PHOTOGRAPHY AND FILM

Mary N. Woods

Cities are places of unexpected and even strange encounters. Alfred Stieglitz described one such encounter that took place at his 291 Gallery during an exhibition of John Marin's works:

"It was before the Armory Show in 1913. Marin's new exhibit at 291 was creating a sensation. He had produced a series of several pictures, calling the group as a whole *The Woolworth Building*. The building had been erected not long before, and Marin had fallen in love with it at first sight.

"A man—well-built, well-dressed—came into the gallery soon after the Marin show opened. He went straight to the wall on which the Woolworth paintings were hung and stood, barely moving, for a long while. He looked so serious, so sad, as though he had lost his last friend. I approached him: 'Is something troubling you?'

"'Something is,' answered the man.

"'I supposed this kind of work startles you,' I said, 'but if you are at all acquainted with Chinese or Japanese art, these pictures should not be so very strange, even though they are not directly related to either. This series of Marins has been inspired by the Woolworth Building, a passion of his.'

"The man's expression remained sad, his face immobile. 'So this is the Woolworth Building.'

"'Yes,' I replied, 'it is the Woolworth Building in various moods.'

"The man shook his head slightly and repeated, 'The Woolworth Building's various moods.' Whereupon he turned around and left the room, I accompanying him to the elevator. He quickly said, 'Thank you,' and disappeared.

"When I returned to the room, someone who had heard the conversation laughed: 'Stieglitz, don't you know who that was?'

"'No, I have no idea. But the man seemed desperately sad. I wonder why?'

"The visitor still laughing, told me, 'That was Cass Gilbert, architect of the Woolworth Building.' I never met Mr. Gilbert again. I wonder whether, had he come upon those same Marins later, would he have seen them with different eyes? Would he have enjoyed them, or would he have been still sadder?"[1]

Although Gilbert and Stieglitz were contemporaries—the former was fifty-four and the latter forty-nine when they met in 1913—they came from strikingly different worlds. The completion of his Woolworth Building in 1913, then the world's tallest building, made Gilbert the most celebrated architect in the United States, if not the world. Fourteen years after his arrival in New York from the Midwest, he was a pillar of the American establishment, acclaimed in both artistic and business circles. Although steeped in ideas of the Beaux-Arts, Gilbert was a hardheaded businessman who organized his office as a modern corporation and decried the City Beautiful movement's neglect of what he called the City Practical. Architects, Gilbert argued, could not forsake the workaday world of tall office buildings and factories for an aestheticized, classical idyll of monumental buildings and public art in squares and parks. Instead he fused the City Beautiful with the City Practical in the Woolworth Building, creating a speculative office building that was also a civic and personal monument.[2]

Stieglitz's milieu was another world, the American avant-garde, where he was artist, critic, editor, impresario, and mentor. His passion was photography, and he saw himself as its savior, redeeming the medium from the degrading commercialism of American practice and recasting it as the preeminent art form of modern life. Far from embracing commercial realities, Stieglitz recoiled from them. Wealthy, educated, and refined amateurs like himself were—he contended in his publications *The American Amateur Photographer* (1893–96), *Camera Notes* (1897–1902), and *Camera Work* (1903-17)—key to photography's rejuvenation as a fine art. He exhibited photography with painting, sculpture, and other works on paper at his 291 Gallery.

Although Stieglitz introduced Americans to successive waves of the European avant-garde—Auguste Rodin and Paul Cézanne, then Pablo Picasso and Henri Matisse, and finally Francis Picabia and Marcel Duchamp—he also promoted distinctly American modernists—Edward Steichen, Marsden Hartley, John Marin, Georgia O'Keeffe, Paul Strand, and Charles Sheeler. In 1914 Steichen wrote that progress

at 291 was due "not to a gradual process of evolution but to sudden and brusque changes caused by eager receptivity to the unforeseen."[3] Stieglitz's own work reflected the "sudden and brusque changes" at his gallery. Reinventing his photographic work, Stieglitz moved away from his early intimate portraits and romantic landscapes to scenes of modern urban life and the machine age. Eventually a new style accompanied this change of subject matter as Stieglitz abandoned the impressionist forms and handworked plates of pictorialism for the crisp focus and high contrast of straight photography before 1910.[4] If Gilbert tempered modernity with tradition in his art, Stieglitz preferred to see himself as a revolutionary.[5]

The 1913 Marin exhibition at 291 was the one time Gilbert and Stieglitz met. But John Marin's "passion" for the Woolworth Building was not unique; the skyscraper also resonated with the young photographers whom Stieglitz nurtured at 291. Alvin Langdon Coburn and Karl Struss, in fact, photographed the building in 1911 and 1912, possibly inspiring Marin in his choice of subject.[6] Paul Strand and Charles Sheeler featured the Woolworth Building in their 1920 film *Manhatta,* the first American avant-garde film. Sheeler also returned to the Woolworth Building in his still photography. Francis Picabia, Albert Gleizes, and Marcel Duchamp—European avant-garde artists who gathered at 291 during their self-imposed exile from Europe during World War I—also celebrated the Woolworth Building as a touchstone of modernism. Seeing the Woolworth Building in the commercial landscape inspired Duchamp to claim it as one of his "readymades," an artwork created when he displaced an artifact from its context.[7]

Does it really matter what a small group of avant-garde photographers and filmmakers made of the Woolworth Building? I think it would have mattered to Gilbert. He was, in my estimation, a "proto-postmodern architect" because he grasped the importance of image and understood the need to shape and control it. Correspondence in the New-York Historical Society collection shows him deeply involved in creating and granting access to both visual and textual information about the Woolworth Building. The Woolworth Building became the focus of an enormous media event, and Gilbert orchestrated its image and promotion. He carefully monitored the reproduction rights of Woolworth images, at one point in 1910 restricting them to Hearst newspapers, and copyrighting Hughson Hawley's watercolor perspective in 1911 (see Figure C-6).[8]

Photography played an important role in this media campaign; Wurts Brothers, Tebbs-Hymans, and Underhill and Underhill, all leading commercial photography firms in New York, documented the building under construction and once completed.[9] Spectacular images taken by Tebbs-Hymans from temporary scaffolding erected around the tower depict the elaborate Gothic terra cotta details against views of the city below, creating dramatic—even surreal—juxtapositions of scale between the near and the far (Figure 10-1). Featured in a special issue of *Architectural Record* devoted to the Woolworth Building in 1913, these photographs, Gilbert proudly noted, could never again be duplicated. He also presented portfolios of Woolworth Building photographs to the Ecole des Beaux-Arts and European museums.[10]

Critics and historians of photography describe such commercial images as "standard solutions" at best and "architectural eye candy" at worst.[11] During the early morning hours, photographers for firms like Wurts Brothers and Tebb-Hymans typically used a wide-angle, sharp-focus lens from a nearby tall structure to produce clear images where the building stands out from its context (Figure 10-2). Or they used a long-focal-length lens to capture crisp close-up details (Figure 10-1). Yet their work shares certain formal qualities and attitudes with contemporary art photographers who focused on the city.

The Tebbs-Hymans photograph taken from the scaffolding around the Woolworth Tower emphasizes the bowler-hatted figure gazing out between the Gothic finials to the city below. It recalls, probably inadvertently, Charles Nègre's depiction of his fellow photographer Henri Le Secq contemplating the new Paris from atop the cathedral of Notre-Dame. Taken together, the two images trace the distance—chronological, architectural, and sociological—between

10-1. Tebbs-Hymans, Detail at the 51st Story, The Woolworth Building, in *Architectural Record* 33 (February 1913): n.p. (Library of Congress)

10-2. Tebbs-Hymans, Rear View of the Woolworth Building, in *Architectural Record* 33 (February 1913): n.p. (Library of Congress)

10-3. Power Plant, Woolworth Building Subbasement, photograph, c. 1913, Wurts Brothers Collection. (Museum of the City of New York)

10-4. Workers shoveling coal, Woolworth Building Subbasement, photograph c. 1913, Wurts BrothersJ157 Collection. (Museum of the City of New York, New York City)

medieval and modern cities and between cathedrals of God and those of commerce. Coburn, Struss, Strand, and Sheeler structured their images around this spectatorial gaze over the city too. While they eliminate the gazing figure from their images, their photographs still allude to us, the viewers gazing at an image. As Jan-Christopher Horak wrote, such "self-reflexity of the audience's reception . . . [is] a goal central to all modernist art."[12] Here both commercial and avant-garde photographers play with the idea of multiple viewers caught in the act of viewing.

Mechanomorphism, imagery derived from the look of machines, was another modernist fascination. It was a passion the American avant-garde shared with Europeans like Picabia and Duchamp. In 1914 Stieglitz described New York as "unspeakable . . . fascinating . . . like some giant machine."[13] Although they praised skyscrapers as machines, these artists evinced no real interest in the actual mechanical systems of the buildings. Their skyscraper imagery stayed on the surface, focusing only on the facades. But commercial photographers did penetrate, at Gilbert's behest, into the mechanical heart of the skyscraper. The Wurts Brothers revealed its workings, descending into the Woolworth Building subbasement and photographing the gleaming machines of the electrical generating plant and workers shoveling coal into the boilers (Figures 10-3 and 10-4).[14] Since these images appeared in *The Cathedral of Commerce,* a 1916 tourist brochure for Woolworth visitors, it is possible Fritz Lang saw them when he became fascinated with skyscrapers during a 1924 visit to New York. These photographs of the Woolworth Building recall the imagery of *Metropolis,* his 1927 film, where workers tend fearsome machines in an underground city far below the skyscraper towers (Figure 10-5).

Strand, Sheeler, Picabia, and Duchamp were interested in the modern commercial vernacular. Duchamp made commercial advertising and mass-produced urinals and bottle racks his art, dubbing

10-5. Fritz Lang, "The Machine Room," *Metropolis,* 1927 (Museum of Modern Art/Film Stills Archive)

them "readymades." Strand and Sheeler also supported themselves as commercial photographers. Strand
was a stringer cameraman for Hollywood newsreels,
and Sheeler worked for advertising agencies and shot
conventional architectural photography for publications like *The Arts*.[15] Surely, these artists were aware of
the commercial photography of skyscrapers like the
Woolworth Building. The media campaign orchestrated by Gilbert and Woolworth was inescapable.
Even art photographers like Stieglitz, who shunned
commercialism, would have had difficulty avoiding it.

When juxtaposed with the work of Stieglitz,
Coburn, Struss, Strand, and Sheeler, the commercial
photography Gilbert commissioned reveals unexpected affinities and disjunctures between art photography and the Woolworth Building in particular and
the avant-garde and the architectural establishment
in general. Considering the Woolworth Building
through its depictions in American avant-garde photography raises several issues. First, why did Gilbert's
historicized building with its Gothic facades and
tower and Byzantine vaulted lobby appeal so strongly
to American avant-garde photographers? The Woolworth Building remained, we will see, a constant even
as the 291 Gallery photographers moved from pictorialism to straight photography to mechanomorphism. Second, Stieglitz's question, would Gilbert
ever have appreciated Marin's works or would they
have made him "sadder still," also can be asked about
the still and moving images of the Woolworth
Building the Stieglitz circle created. Third, how differently did the photographers in Stieglitz's circle and
Gilbert understand the Woolworth Building and the
modern city?

Such questions highlight the afterlife that buildings generate following their completion. This afterlife is the history of the built environment architectural critics and historians usually dismiss or overlook
in favor of the architect's "history" of her or his building.[16] Critics and historians need to look more widely and carefully at images, whether commercial photography or art photography and film. Both types of
images are artifacts and just as worthy of our study as
buildings, drawings, models, and archives. Photography is evidence, not simply a tool for illustration,

helping us to construct a more inclusive history of the built environment. The rich and varied afterlife of the Woolworth Building captured in photography does not diminish Gilbert's achievement; it enhances his accomplishment, underscoring the power of architecture like the Woolworth Building to resonate beyond its immediate purpose and context.

Stieglitz never photographed the Woolworth Building, and I have no evidence to explain its conspicuous absence from his skyscraper oeuvre. In the early 1900s he photographed the Flatiron Building and the Singer Tower. But when the Woolworth Building was completed in the teens, Stieglitz seemed preoccupied with promoting younger artists like John Marin, Georgia O'Keeffe, and Paul Strand at his 291 Gallery. When he returned to photography in the 1920s and 1930s, his skyscrapers were uptown where he had relocated: the RCA Building near An American Place, his gallery at 509 Madison Avenue, and the Shelton Hotel, where he and O'Keeffe had an apartment on Lexington Avenue between 48th and 49th Streets.[17] Nevertheless, Stieglitz later wrote admiringly of the Woolworth Building's "extraordinary [form] . . . shooting into the sky," making his earlier love, the Flatiron Building, now appear "rather unattractive to me."[18] Moreover, he established the conventions for other photographers' depictions of the Woolworth Building when he photographed the Flatiron Building in 1903 (Figure 10-6).[19]

Stieglitz's fascination with the skyscraper was not shared by many during the early 1900s. The tall buildings bewildered and repelled many New Yorkers. Coming upon Stieglitz photographing the Flatiron Building in the middle of Fifth Avenue, his own father exclaimed, "Alfred, how can you be interested in that hideous building?"[20] Others shared the senior Stieglitz's opinion. While Henry James dismissed the lower Manhattan skyline as "extravagant pins in a cushion," William Dean Howells used a metaphor of death and decay, likening it to "a horse's jawbone with the teeth broken or dislodged." Architect Charles F. McKim and artist William Merritt Chase saw the skyscraper as proof of American greed, crassness, and materialism. In 1909 McKim wrote that the new

Metropolitan Life Insurance Tower on Madison Square had "the merit of bigness and that's all. I think the skyline of New York grows daily more hideous."[21]

But Stieglitz believed artists had to embrace skyscrapers as uniquely American forms of modern life. He and other artists, as Wanda Corn observed in her essay "The New New York," coped with the "unprecedented visual and physical fact" of the modern city by "evoking images of the sublime, the picturesque, and the exotic." They were *flâneurs* whose experience of the city was ambulatory, episodic, and impressionistic; they interpreted the city through *fin de siècle* stylistic conventions of asymmetry, muted light, subtle tones, and blurred contours.[22] In photographic terms, Stieglitz made the skyscraper a subject for pictorialism, the turn-of-the-century movement that extolled photography as a projection of the photographer's personal vision and a unique, handcrafted art object.[23] His 1903 Flatiron photograph paradoxically married the skyscraper, exemplar of industrial production and technological innovation, to pictorialism, a rarefied aestheticism. The skyscraper was simultaneously light and solid, dissolving and emerging, natural and man-made, timeless and modern in Stieglitz's image.

It was landscape, a traditional symbol of antiquity, nationalism, and monumentality in American art, that allowed Stieglitz to encompass the contradictions of combining the skyscraper with pictorialism. He evoked the Flatiron's natural rhythms: photographing it at a particular time, in a particular light, and in a particular season. Furthermore, he captured a particular moment, placing a snow-encrusted tree in the foreground and on axis with the building's prow, visually rhyming the tracery of boughs with the flatiron shape of the skyscraper. The Flatiron was also a masonry cliff rising into an overcast sky. A tiny, silhouetted figure is the only human intrusion into this mysterious landscape, making the skyscraper seem more a natural rather than a human phenomenon.

In his early photography Stieglitz wanted to fix on film what Ian Jeffreys has called "the moment intensely apprehended; the moment as figured in the emergence of a trope."[24] The intensity of Stieglitz's vision established ways of seeing and understanding

OPPOSITE
10-6. Alfred Stieglitz, *The Flat Iron—New York*, 1902. (Bequest of William P. Chapman Jr., Class of 1895. Herbert F. Johnson Museum of Art)

the skyscraper as art. Alvin Langdon Coburn acknowledged this, observing that he followed in Stieglitz's footsteps when he composed his own Flatiron images. Coburn was a member of pictorialist circles in both New York and London, and Stieglitz published his photographs in *Camera Work* and exhibited them at his 291 Gallery.[25] When Coburn turned to the Woolworth Building in 1911–12, he again drew on Stieglitz's trope of the skyscraper as urban landscape (Figure 10-7). Coburn wrote he was equally fascinated by "natural views from high altitudes like Mount Wilson and the rim of the Grand Canyon . . . [and] the man made views from the top of New York's skyscrapers." In fact, Coburn photographed the Woolworth Building the year after he had made pictures of Yosemite, Mount Wilson, and the Grand Canyon.[26]

But Coburn was no genteel *flâneur,* eying the skyscraper from street level like Stieglitz or Steichen. To depict skyscrapers he ascended them and experienced the city from the unique vantage points they provided. In the catalog for a 1913 London exhibition "New York from Its Pinnacles," which featured the Woolworth Building, the Municipal Building, and Liberty Tower, he wrote, "How romantic, how exhilarating it is in these altitudes few denizens of the city realize."[27] *The House of a Thousand Windows,* Coburn's 1912 photograph of Liberty Tower (Figure 10-8), at 55 Liberty Street to the southeast of the Woolworth Building, was taken from the observation balcony of the Singer Tower (1908).[28] At thirty-three stories, the Liberty Tower designed by Henry Ives Cobb (1909–10) was publicized as the "tallest building in the world on so small an area of ground." Its height, verticality, Gothic details, white terra cotta cladding, and copper-sheathed pyramidal roof made it one of the predecessors to the Woolworth Building.[29] Coburn represented both it and the Woolworth Building as white towers proudly rising above the city.

Photographing from atop tall buildings posed certain technical and physical problems for Coburn. First, he used a large and heavy view camera because it allowed him to compose his pictures out to the edge. What he saw in the camera viewfinder was the same size, except upside down, as what he got in the

10-7. Alvin Langdon Coburn, *Woolworth Building,* 1911–12, platinum print. (Courtesy, George Eastman House)

10-8. Alvin Langdon Coburn, *The House of a Thousand Windows,* 1912. (Courtesy, George Eastman House)

final print.[30] The slow films and lenses of the early twentieth century, combined with the overcast or nocturnal light conditions favored by pictorialists like Coburn, necessitated long exposure times. This was definitely not "hit and run" photography. It is no wonder that Coburn compared photographing skyscrapers to depicting the Grand Canyon or Mount Wilson. Both subjects required physical strength and mental concentration.

For his photograph of the Woolworth Building (see Figure 10-7), Coburn became the building's equal, positioning himself atop a tall building, probably the Singer Tower again, to the south. While Stieglitz rooted the Flatiron Building in a grove of trees, Coburn levitated the Woolworth Building above the city, a great white cliff swaddled by steam clouds with darker, heavier earth-bound buildings below. As Merrill Schleier noted, Coburn's Woolworth now literally "occupies a separate realm" from other buildings. Similar images appeared in Woolworth advertising materials like H. Bruce Addington's *Above the Clouds & Old New York,* a 1913 tourist brochure (Figure 10-9).[31] But here an artist's drawing more easily creates the effect of Coburn's hard-won photograph.

In London Coburn exhibited with the Linked Ring, a photographic society influenced by symbolist and Swedenborgian ideas of correspondence between physical and spiritual worlds.[32] Coburn's Woolworth photograph is a symbolist representation of transcendence. The skyscraper rises above its mundane function, what Gilbert called in 1900 "merely the machine that makes the land pay," and apotheosizes into the "cathedral of commerce" suspended above the workaday world.[33] Like Stieglitz's photograph of the Flatiron Building, Coburn's Woolworth encompasses the contradictions surrounding the skyscraper: light and dark, air and mass, and now cathedral and commerce.[34]

Coburn's London experiences suggest another influence on his Woolworth Building photograph: James McNeill Whistler's art and aesthetics. Coburn knew Whistler's works intimately; he had photographed Charles Freer's Whistler collection in 1907.[35] Furthermore, oriental composition fascinated both Whistler and Coburn and profoundly affected their art. Whistler, who like Coburn was an American living and working in England, took the city as his subject matter, transforming London views into visual tonal poems. Coburn, who described himself as the "Whistler of photography," created a Whistlerian "symphony in white" when he depicted the Woolworth Building, a white building wreathed by steam clouds against an overcast sky.[36]

Whistler's influence is also evident in Karl Struss's photograph *Brooklyn Bridge: Nocturne* of c. 1912–13 (Figure 10-10). Four years younger than Coburn, Karl Struss met him in the early 1900s through Clarence White, a leading pictorialist photographer and teacher. White taught both men photography and the oriental compositional principles of abstraction, simplicity, and asymmetry later seen in their photography. Struss also knew Stieglitz and regularly visited the 291 Gallery; he and Stieglitz photographed in the same locations, lower Manhattan and Madison Square, during the 1900s.[37] But it was Coburn, the most persistent photographer of skyscrapers among the pictorialists, who inspired Struss's large body of New York work.[38]

Struss's twilight scene of the Brooklyn Bridge and lower Manhattan skyline explicitly recalls Whistler's London "nocturnes." These crepuscular views of London docks and bridges dissolve urban forms and transform them into asymmetrical, abstract compositions of subtly calibrated tones. Like Whistler, Struss also drew on Japanese woodblock prints of bridge spans. The arch of his Brooklyn Bridge forms a vignette around the now fabled skyline of Manhattan's towers, beckoning like a modern day Oz. The Woolworth Building is not immediately apparent, eclipsed almost completely by the bridge pylon. But its distinctive setbacks and pyramidal roof can eventually be picked out. Perhaps Struss wished to visually link the bridge's pointed arch portals and

10-9. Cover, H. Bruce Addington, *Above the Clouds & Old New York,* c. 1913. (Library of Congress)

10-10. Karl Struss, *Brooklyn Bridge, Nocturne,* c. 1912–13, palladium print. (P1983.23.75, Copyright 1983, Amon Carter Museum, Fort Worth, Texas)

nineteenth-century technological daring with the twentieth-century Gothicism and engineering marvels of the Woolworth Building. But here the nineteenth-century bridge is dominant. Viewed from the Brooklyn side, Gilbert's proud monument is reduced to a triangle barely disengaged from the bridge pylon, its identity submerged into the older structure. Struss celebrates the horizontal expansion rather than the vertical rise of the modern city.

Unlike Stieglitz or Coburn whose images discussed here focused on a single building, Struss composed a sweeping panorama of the new vertical city. But he still framed this modern metropolis in landscape terms, emphasizing the city as sky, water, and skyscraper peaks. The dominance of the Brooklyn Bridge emphasizes the city as an island. According to many early twentieth-century writers, approaching Manhattan by water provided the most picturesque and artistic view of the city. Writing in a 1911 issue of *Camera Work,* Coburn observed, "New York is a

vision that rises out of the sea as I come up the harbor on my Atlantic liner, and which glimmers for a while in the sun . . . but which vanishes, but for fragmentary glimpses, as I become one of the grey creatures that crawl about like ants, at the bottom of its gloomy caverns."[39]

I do not know whether Gilbert ever saw these pictorialist photographs of New York and his skyscraper. Since the Marin images of the Woolworth Building saddened and puzzled Gilbert, the Struss nocturne might have angered him, given its reduction of the Woolworth Building to a mere appendage of the Brooklyn Bridge. Frank W. Woolworth might have bristled at this diminution of his personal monument. But the Coburn image of a pure white building suspended above the city might have pleased both Gilbert and Woolworth. Focusing on the building, it celebrated the skyscraper's ascendancy like Woolworth promotional materials such as *Above the Clouds & Old New York* or the thirty-by-seventy-three-inch rendering commissioned from artist Hughson Hawley (see Figure C-6).[40] Furthermore, Gilbert might have responded to Coburn's artistic and technical virtuosity in highlighting a white building against a white background.

Putting Gilbert's taste in art aside, there is a more significant connection between him and these pictorialist photographers. They were all alchemists, creating works of art out of base materials. While Gilbert's base material was the "machine that makes the land pay," the pictorialists' was the camera, again a machine. Commercialism had debased both the skyscraper and photography. Thus, they were the ultimate artistic challenges for architects and artists. As a *Camera Work* critic observed in 1905, if you were a true artist, "you may succeed in the almost impossible feat of combining your thoughts with railroads yards, locomotives, and skyscrapers."[41] Just as architecture critics and civic reformers marveled at how Gilbert had transformed the skyscraper from speculative real estate into a civic monument, Stieglitz's father wondered how he could produce such a beautiful picture out of anything so ugly as the Flatiron Building.[42] Coburn recognized this special affinity between the skyscraper and pictorialist photography: "Photography born of this age of steel seems to have naturally adapted itself to the necessarily unusual requirements of an art that must live in skyscrapers, and it is because she has become so much at home in these gigantic structures that the Americans undoubtedly are the recognized leaders in the world movement of pictorial photography."[43] The Woolworth Building, in particular, embodied the same conflicting forces of technology and spirituality, art and materialism surrounding photography in early-twentieth-century America. Skyscrapers resonated for Stieglitz, Coburn, and Struss, symbolizing their struggle to make art out of both photography and modern life.

But skyscrapers were also irresistible subjects for these photographers as they redefined pictorialism. They wished to break away from the intimate and precious landscapes, interiors, and portraits that heretofore had characterized pictorialist photography.[44] The skyscraper was vital, raw, male, and mod-

ern. It was the new New York, the perfect metaphor for Manhattan because it was a city under one roof. The eight thousand Woolworth tenants never needed to leave the building; it had a bank, shops, bars, restaurants, a club, swimming pool, and subway connections. In the subbasement, coal-fired boilers furnished steam heat, a power plant generated electricity for lights and elevators, and a well provided a secondary water source if city supplies failed.[45]

Since pictorialist photographers were transforming the modern city into a work of art, their aims might seem similar to those of City Beautiful proponents. But pictorialism, in fact, subverted architects' and planners' conception of the City Beautiful. Disturbed by class, racial, and ethnic conflicts that divided the modern city, City Beautiful reformers envisioned a new urban order created through the supposedly transcendent, universal, and inclusive forms of historicized architecture, Beaux-Arts planning, and public art.[46] Gail Fenske observed that City Beautiful theorists, designers, and advocates "naively believed they could transform the quality and character of urban life through art."[47] Charles M. Robinson, one of the first journalists to call himself a "city improver," wrote that public buildings (like city halls, churches, and courts) open to all social groups were the "truest reflections of the people." Since such public art supposedly humanized the masses, Fenske wrote, Robinson and other City Beautiful reformers argued it eased ethnic tensions and class conflicts. In their minds, social reform and municipal art and architecture were interchangeable.[48]

Although the City Beautiful movement influenced Gilbert in work like the Minnesota State Capitol, he still criticized its retreat from the real city into what he considered a romantic and sentimental idyll. In the Woolworth Building, he fused what he called the City Practical with the City Beautiful. As Fenske stated, before the Woolworth Building, "unbridled skyscraper construction, propelled by economic forces" contradicted the City Beautiful "notion that the city should become a work of art."[49] Standing across from City Hall Park (the focus of a City Beautiful campaign for a new civic center in the early 1900s), the Woolworth Building demonstrated

10-11. Frame enlargement of Woolworth sequence from Paul Strand and Charles Sheeler's *Manhatta*, 1920. (Museum of Modern Art; © Aperture Foundation Inc., Paul Strand Archive)

that skyscrapers could be civic monuments. Sacrificing rentable space to its setbacks and tower, the Woolworth was less greedy than skyscrapers like Graham, Burnham and Company's Equitable Building (1912–15), rising forty stories straight upward from its site on lower Broadway. As Fenske noted, the Woolworth Building "seemed to reconcile the common good and reckless individualism." An illustration for a 1913 City Beautiful exhibition at the New York Public Library signals the change in thinking about the tall building after Gilbert's design; two skyscrapers, the Municipal Building (1909–14) and the Woolworth Building, stand to either side of the Brooklyn Bridge, creating a monumental ensemble from the East River (Figure 10-12).[50] The temporary White City of the 1893 World's Columbian Exposition, which so inspired the City Beautiful reformers, was now made permanent through the conjunction of public and private skyscrapers in New York.

But in Coburn's and Struss's photographs, the Woolworth Building represented art for art's sake, not art for civic order's sake. Coburn abstracts and uproots the Woolworth Building from the city fabric. Suppressing the horizon line, he gives the viewer no way to judge its scale or relate it to the surrounding urban context. We enter into a world governed solely by Coburn's vision. Imposing his style on the Woolworth Building, the city, and the viewer, Coburn disrupts and subverts the City Beautiful vision of creating urban order through universal and transcendent forms. Struss's nocturne offers an even more extreme abstraction of the Woolworth Building. It is Struss who constructs or, in this case, reconstructs the skyline according to a highly personalized vision.

Gilbert commissioned painters and sculptors to embellish the facades and interiors of the Woolworth Building, creating the desired City Beautiful synthesis of all the fine arts.[51] He expected these artists to defer to his architectural conception in order to create order and unity. But the city was not about order and unity for Coburn and Struss. Despite the soft focus and subtle tones of their photographs, they celebrated the pedestrian's fragmentary and disorienting perceptions of the city. Looking down from atop the skyscrapers or from afar at the skyline, they compressed and flattened space with their long-focal-length lenses.[52] Human scale and traditional perspective were lost in the abstract patterns they created. While reminiscent of Whistler's white symphonies and tonal nocturnes in privileging art rather than documentation, their photographs, as Bonnie Yochelson argued, also challenge "their audience to experience more intimately the city's chaotic sensation."[53]

Critics have often charged pictorialist photographers with a failure of nerve or creativity for still clinging to *fin de siècle* stylistic conventions in depictions of the modern city.[54] So-called straight photography seemed to exemplify the modern aesthetic missing from pictorialism: sharply focused, well-lit, black-and-white images created without technical manipulation or handwork. Paul Strand and Charles Sheeler tried to depict the modern city in a style that was influenced by cubist and futurist painting and was true to the mechanical nature of the camera and contemporary life.[55] In Strand and Sheeler's film *Manhatta* of 1920, the Woolworth Building emerged from the steam and twilight in which Coburn and Struss had bathed it. Furthermore, the images of the city now moved, collapsing space into time.

Filmed and edited over several months in 1920, *Manhatta* was shot in a five-block radius around Battery Park, the Staten Island ferry docks, Wall Street, Broadway, and Trinity Place. Although it has no narrative, it is a highly structured film, depicting the life of lower Manhattan in four movements from morning until dusk, a day in the life of the city.[56] The four movements recall a symphony, and in fact, *Manhatta* inaugurated the avant-garde film genre of "city symphonies" like *Berlin: Symphony of a Great City* (1927) and *Man with a Movie Camera* (1929). But the symphonic structure also indicates the lingering traces of Coburn's and Struss's Whistlerian city symphonies.

The Woolworth Building first appears in the intertitles, in an extreme long shot of lower Manhattan skyscrapers from the Hudson River. As Jan-Christopher Horak noted, this image is the only clear and comprehensive depiction of spatial relationships in the city. The other film frames are fragmented, disorienting views of the city, more than half filmed by either gazing up from the streets or looking down from the skyscrapers.[57] Like the pictorialists, Strand and Sheeler present a pedestrian's incomplete, splintered view of the new vertical city. They are also, like Coburn, fascinated with views from atop the skyscrapers and with the steam clouds vented by the buildings. Many shots track the steam as it moves across the sky, a veil sometimes cloaking and sometimes revealing the skyscrapers. When screened in Paris, the film was called *Fumée de New York.*[58]

The Woolworth appears in the second movement of *Manhatta,* immediately following an intertitle with verses from Walt Whitman's poem *Mannahatta*: "High growths of iron, / slender, strong / splendidly uprising / toward clear skies."[59] But it is almost unrecognizable in this sequence, which lasts only a few seconds (Figure 10-11). Strand and Sheeler behead the Woolworth Building, robbing it of its distinctive and glorious crown. They also tilt the camera down the decapitated building until it disappears from view, perversely denying us the thrill of rushing up the building facade and soaring into the heavens. Strand and Sheeler embed the Woolworth Building, now looking decidedly grimy and weathered only seven years after its completion, into a forest of buildings. The lens compresses and compacts the city space, collapsing the buildings into one another and

10-12 "City Planning Exhibition," poster, 1913, in *American City* 9 (December 1913): 504. (Library of Congress)

flattening them into the abstract patterns Coburn and Struss had first explored. Strand and Sheeler also suppress the horizon line, like the pictorialists, enfolding the Woolworth Building completely into their cinematic vision. They transform it from a unique, heroic form into part of a dense cubist collage of the urban vernacular.

Yet Strand and Sheeler fuse the city with nature in other sequences of *Manhatta.* Cubist collages of the Woolworth and other buildings alternate with lyrical footage of sky, water, steam, light, and shadow as the city moves from day to dusk. Their *Manhatta,* like Struss's nocturne, is about the city as an island. They capture on film what Lewis Mumford felt Stieglitz first discovered in photographs of New York: "nature in its most simple form, the wonder of morning and the night," finding the sky "in the cracks between buildings" and trees "in the surviving cracks of the pavement." The natural rhythms that Stieglitz first depicted in the Flatiron Building animate *Manhatta,* and Strand and Sheeler, like their mentor, still romantically yearned for a harmony of nature and technology in the modern city.[60]

10-13. Gargoyle, Woolworth Building lobby, in *Architecture* 27 (June 15, 1913): pl. 55. (Library of Congress)

Gilbert was concerned about his identification with the Woolworth Building. When Gunvald Aus, the engineer for the building, wrote articles on it, Gilbert fretted that his own contributions might be overshadowed.[61] In 1924 he requested that the Woolworth Company have his name carved on the building. (His request was apparently not honored.)[62] Gilbert's concerns seemed justified. In 1933, the year before his death, an editorialist in *Architecture* wrote that Gilbert's name had been forgotten, eclipsed by the fame surrounding the building.[63] In the gargoyle portrait of Gilbert in the building lobby, he holds a model of his skyscraper tightly in his embrace (Figure 10-13). But the fame of the Woolworth Building that Gilbert orchestrated through photography and the media attracted other artists. Coburn, Struss, Strand, and Sheeler recast Gilbert's image of the Woolworth, inscribing it with new and different meanings. Buildings like the Woolworth inspire complex and paradoxical narratives their architects, owners, and critics can never foresee or control, narratives that testify to their enduring power.

CHAPTER 11

"GREAT GRAY BUILDINGS": THE UNITED STATES ARMY SUPPLY BASE

Sharon Irish

In the fifty-two-year career of architect Cass Gilbert, what he described as "the great gray buildings" of the United States Army Supply Base (1918–19) were remarkable because of their austere appearance as well as their singular use of reinforced concrete (Figure 11-1). The base was all the more prominent in his practice because Gilbert was best known for his adaptations of historical styles in stone, terra cotta, and brick. Architecture is an unpredictable art, however, and Gilbert creatively adjusted his designs to a range of contingencies, from the political challenges of using a non-local stone on the Minnesota capitol, for example, to the dilemma of creating a firm foundation on a water-logged site for the West Street Building in New York City. World War I tested Gilbert yet again, not only demanding much of the architect and his family (his son was at the front in France) but also affecting real estate, construction, engineering, and design in the United States while producing human tragedy around the globe. The poignant fact is that the interior of Warehouse B at the Army Supply Base, a stunningly sublime space that easily holds its own against other commercial and industrial designs of the twentieth century, resulted from efforts to service the devastating war in Europe. The Army Supply Base provides a compelling example of the systematic organization of labor, transportation, and freight handling by a team of civilian and military experts. The resulting physical plant elicited praise from a range of architectural commentators, including modernists like Le Corbusier and traditionalists like Russell Sturgis. Much else of interest remains embedded in those formerly gray walls. This chapter briefly explores some links between civilian industries and endeavors and their counterparts in the U.S. military, recognizing that the rapid manner in which the military could mobilize national participation was due in large part to innovations in industry before 1914.

After the Civil War in the United States, the wholesale store, the warehouse, and the factory were sometimes one and the same but came to be differentiated as expanded and specialized businesses.[1] With the rise of the department store and changes in buying habits, not only were ample open spaces needed for storage, but also buildings that could display large quantities for a wholesaler were in demand.

St. Paul, Minnesota, where Cass Gilbert began his independent career, was first a river town, then a railroad center, with expanding needs for infrastructure and buildings. The boom in growth experienced by both Minneapolis and St. Paul provided opportunities for builders, contractors, and architects alike, although competition was fierce. Gilbert began his practice in 1883 at the crest of the St. Paul boom. Other chapters consider his Minnesota career, but to

Building and the Hanan Building—were admired by architect and critic Russell Sturgis and offered as models for future construction.[3] He defined the characteristics of the type: they were "obviously utilitarian," with little ornament; no additional money had been spent beyond the needs of everyday use.[4] Gilbert went beyond Sturgis's analyses and recognized warehouses as units in a larger system. He had a canny sense of what was essential in each building type. In an essay written about 1919 he commented, "The modern storage warehouse should no more be regarded as a *tomb* for merchandise than the modern high pressure boiler as a *tank* for water. If merchandise does not flow through freely and easily, it is stagnant and unprofitable. It is worse than that, it is an 'aneurism' on traffic."[5] Gilbert's savvy about the ways in which physical space could enhance organizational performance helped him succeed when he moved his practice from Minnesota to New York City in 1899, where he continued to design warehouses in addition to the civic monuments and skyscrapers for which he is better known.

The knowledge that Gilbert brought from Minnesota and the lessons learned on the job in New York City were used in Gilbert's design for the Austin, Nichols and Company warehouse starting in 1909 (Figure 11-3). Built by the Henry C. Turner Construction Company for a grocery wholesaler, the Austin, Nichols warehouse departed from the brick construction of the De Vinne and Hanan Buildings and confidently asserted the strength of reinforced concrete construction.[6] This workaday building is made exceptional by grouping windows into sets of three up the six-story facade, emphasizing the corners by reducing the fenestration to pairs of slots, and flaring the roofline. One critic called this "an excellent example of the modern adaptation of Egyptian architecture to the present-day requirements of commercialism."[7] Thus by 1909, Gilbert was collaborating with Henry Turner on reinforced concrete facilities for industrial

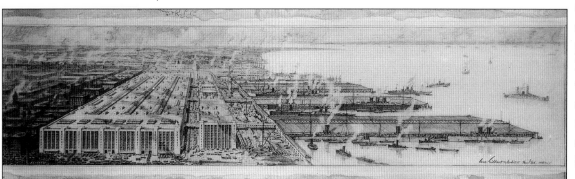

11-1. An early scheme for the U.S. Army Supply Base in Brooklyn, New York, depicts the relationships among warehouses, piers, and the East River. By May of 1918 the warehouse on the left (Warehouse B) had been reduced in size. This graphite drawing by Hugh Ferriss was done for Cass Gilbert in February 1918. Approx. 18" by 42." (© Collection of the New-York Historical Society, neg. #74415)

place the Army Supply Base in perspective, two of Gilbert's early warehouses deserve mention here. They were relatively small in scale and located in the central business districts of St. Paul and Minneapolis. The Paul H. Gotzian Building (1895), near the Mississippi River just south of downtown St. Paul, was a combined warehouse and wholesale store (see Figure 1-14). For that reason, its appearance was formal and carefully wrought, attractive to visitors. On a corner site, the building addressed two public streets. It had big windows to illuminate goods for the wholesalers who visited the store, whereas a later warehouse for the U.S. Realty Company in Minneapolis (c. 1895-1907) had few windows in its brick facade because ample light was unnecessary in such a storage facility (Figure 11-2).[2]

Two New York City industrial designs of 1885 by Babb, Cook & Willard—the De Vinne Press

11-2. Cass Gilbert's Fireproof Storage Warehouse for the U. S. Realty Company (1902) was located near downtown Minneapolis, Minnesota, in *Western Architect* 2 (December 1903). (Minnesota Historical Society)

11-3. Cass Gilbert designed this reinforced concrete warehouse in 1909 in New York City for the Austin, Nichols and Co. Warehouse ©Collection of the (New-York Historical Society, neg. #71535)

purposes, essentially what he would do in the next decade for the army, but on a much larger scale.

In 1918 Gilbert was well positioned to design an enormous warehouse complex for the U.S. Army in Brooklyn, New York.[8] Variously known as the United States Army Supply Base (the name that will be used here), the U.S. Military Ocean Terminal, and the Brooklyn Army Terminal, the group of five buildings and four piers was constructed in 1918–19. The United States had entered World War I on April 6, 1917, and at that time it was thought the war would

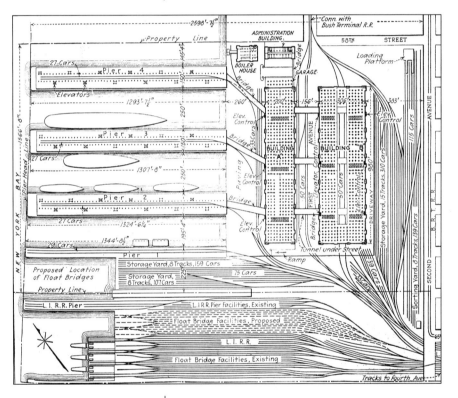

11-4. This layout of the U. S. Army Supply Base (1918–19) in Brooklyn, New York, depicts the orientation of the piers, the railroad tracks, and the warehouses. The bridges connecting the piers and Buildings (Warehouses A and B) are clearly indicated. Reproduced from *Engineering News-Record* 83 (September 18, 1919). (Library of Congress)

continue for at least another two years. Early in 1918, in response to a request from the military, Congress appropriated funds for five enormous terminal storage plants to be built along the Atlantic Coast, and one along the Gulf Coast, at New Orleans. The terminal at Brooklyn was to be the largest of these facilities for the storage and shipment of Army supplies to forces in France.[9] Gilbert sketched the situation: "[I]t was necessary to establish at once a system of concentration points at the Atlantic ports; . . . The Government had taken over the Bush Terminal [in Brooklyn] with its vast system of warehouses and piers, and the

Hoboken [N.J.] piers of the North German Lloyd and Hamburg American Steamship Companies. . . . The great Army Supply Base in South Brooklyn, then, was considered as part of a system of transportation, assembly, and shipment."[10] The army figured that five tons of supplies per person were needed to support the troops in France, and that it was likely that there would be one and a half million Americans in France. The need for storage facilities and freight-handling facilities was thus acute.[11]

The United States Army Supply Base in Brooklyn was exceptional in its physical scale and in the organization of both its construction and operation. The team of army personnel and civilian architectural and construction firms put in place systems intended to produce satisfactory buildings efficiently and economically. For example, the structures were built primarily using the recently patented concrete construction methods of Claude Allen Porter (C. A. P.) Turner. (As far as I know, Henry Turner and C. A. P. Turner were not related.) Not only had Gilbert built warehouses throughout his career, but also he had collaborated with the contractors, like Turner, and manufacturers who had close ties to the military men in charge of construction during World War I. The Brooklyn Army Supply Base then, while a remarkable design, is not a remarkably deviant one in Gilbert's practice. Rather it demonstrates Gilbert's and his colleagues' willingness to use novel building techniques and materials to satisfy practical needs. Writing for the 1919 *Construction Completion Report* for the army, Gilbert described the supply base: "The great gray buildings rise above the streets and waterfront like some vast medieval city's wall. Their scale and strength dominates [*sic*] the landscape and gives one the impression of power, strength and use. The observer feels that they represent 'the facts in the case' as they truly are and that impression of strength and truth together with the beauty of mass and the play of light and shade, and local color all combine to make the remembrance of the buildings of the Brooklyn Army Base an impression not soon to be forgotten."[12]

The choice of the site in Brooklyn is a story in itself. Most of the acreage was owned either by industrialist Irving T. Bush, chairman of the War Board of the Port of New York, or by the Thompson-Starrett Company, a major construction firm. The area was available for immediate development. The diaries kept by the Army's acting quartermaster general, George W. Goethals, give some clues about the real estate fever that arose around site selection. Goethals commented to C. M. Leonard: "[C]ontractors and engineers are on par with real estate agents, without patriotism when the dollar is in sight. . . ."[13] Located in southern Brooklyn (between 58th and 64th Streets) the approximately one-hundred-acre site was adjacent to existing rail lines and near Bush Terminal, which had already been leased by the War Department. Fronting on a deep water channel (forty feet deep, fifteen hundred feet wide), the site made it possible to transfer goods from rail to water and back (Figure 11-4). Construction began in April of 1918 and was completed in September of 1919, when the war had already been over for ten months. (The armistice was signed on November 11, 1918.) The total cost was $36 million, with Gilbert receiving a fee of $60,000.[14]

Erected in reinforced concrete to save money and steel, the eight-story (plus basement) Warehouse B was the largest ever built in this material up to that time (Figure 11-5). It provided fifty-two acres of floor space within its 980-by-306-foot perimeter. (Warehouse B had story heights of 12 feet because it was thought that after the war the building might be used for light industry, for which higher ceilings would be useful.) There were eight other structures on the site, including Warehouse A (980 by 200 feet), an administration building, a boiler house, a repair shop, and the four piers. Bridges connected the piers to the warehouses, and bridges between the two warehouses allowed for continuous circulation on the third floor as well as on the ground floor (Figure 11-6). The warehouses were connected by subterranean tunnels as well. The facility was designed to handle fifteen hundred tons per hour of outgoing freight at peak operation, with warehouse storage for five hundred thousand tons of supplies. Because the Army Supply Base was only completed after the war's end, however, its full capacities were never tested. [15]

Construction in reinforced concrete in the United States had revolutionized the factory in the first decade of the twentieth century.[16] Innovators in techniques and concepts included O. W. Norcross, Ernest L. Ransome, C. A. P. Turner, and Albert and Julius Kahn. Concrete structures were favored because they were relatively quick to build and fireproof, and the necessary materials were readily available. By 1919, it was recognized that reinforced concrete construction not only was economical but also could be treated attractively.

To execute the reinforced concrete construction, the army hired experienced contractor Henry C. Turner, who had specialized since 1902 in industrial construction using reinforced concrete.[17] An innovator in large-scale concrete construction, Turner had developed techniques for working with concrete in freezing weather, for example. Because Turner's firm had been working in the New York area for more than a decade, they had a large, trained labor force at their disposal. To keep up morale on the project, the army produced a weekly newspaper, "Brooklyn Army Supply Base Mixer," although after the armistice there were strikes by carpenters, dock builders, steam fitters, plumbers, laborers, tugboat workers, and electricians. There were also six fatalities on the project. As the army's report noted in 1919, "[T]he completion . . . required that a force of one thousand carpenters and twenty-five hundred laborers begin the reinforced concrete work immediately. . . . [I]t was most fortunate that the location of the Base and the number of old [trained] men available made it possible to start with experienced gangs. . . ."[18]

Unlike wood or steel, each of which can be delivered and assembled, huge quantities of concrete

11-5. Warehouse B of the U. S. Army Supply Base in Brooklyn, New York. The base resulted from a team effort by civilian companies—the architectural firm of Cass Gilbert and the Henry Turner Construction Company, among others—and the military to rapidly complete terminal facilities at the end of World War One. (©Collection of the New-York Historical Society, neg. #71540

had to be prepared at the site. Building in concrete, therefore, is rather like manufacturing, requiring continual quality control not only in the assembly but also in the mix of materials. (For example, the ratio of concrete mixture used for the columns was 1:1½:3, cement, sand, and gravel.) In addition to stone, sand, and cement, approximately 2 percent of the cement mix for the base was a gray powder called Toxement, which increased the water resistance of the concrete.[19] Concrete hardens by hydration, a chemical process whereby Portland cement and water react to form compounds called calcium silicate hydrates. These hydrates then form a mass that on a submicroscopic level resembles crumpled sheets; they in turn bind to each other's surfaces. Toxement was a compound that made the hydrates more dense, minimizing openings through which water could enter.[20]

Lumber for the base was stored and the forms were fabricated at Sheepshead Bay, approximately

11-6. Hugh Ferriss used graphite to make this perspective of the U. S. Army Supply Base for Cass Gilbert. The East River is to the far right, through the arcaded bridge. The arched bridge connecting Warehouse A on the right to Warehouse B on the left is also visible. ©Collection of the (New-York Historical Society, neg. #74416)

eight miles from the Brooklyn construction job. Sometimes as many as fifty carloads of lumber arrived at the Sheepshead Bay yard. The workers then matched and dressed the forms for the exposed concrete surfaces. Forms for an entire story were completed and shipped; each form was used nine times as a cost-saving measure.[21]

Reinforced concrete construction on this scale was rare. The mixing and placing of concrete was described in the *Construction Completion Report*:

The sand, stone and cement was [*sic*] hauled to the various concrete mixing plants [located at twelve places within the warehouses] from a central or receiving station and dumped into the receiving bins. From there it was conveyed to the mixers, where 10 revolutions of the drum were required after all the materials had been assem-

bled in the mixer. After being mixed it was dumped into a bucket and hoisted [to] the desired height where it was dumped into a hopper, from which it was poured into concrete buggies and wheeled to the desired location. All concrete poured was wheeled by hand, and well spaded in the forms. . . . Government inspectors were stationed at each mixer and each material bin. . . . All concrete was sprinkled and kept wet for four days.[22]

Each of the concrete plants was operated electrically and each was equipped with a hoisting tower, so that the plants were independent of the others. According to Turner, "There was never a time when any part of the concrete work was held up for concrete materials."[23]

Prior to the war, Turner had worked with both Gilbert and industrialist Bush. For the Army Supply Base, Turner, Gilbert, and engineer Kort Berle of the Aus Company used a patented system of two-way reinforced concrete girderless slabs supported on spirally reinforced columns. C. A. P. Turner had developed this system in 1905 and patented it in 1908. The majority of the reinforcing rods were corrugated bars, but when those became scarce, the Turner Company used round and square high-carbon bars. The supply base team was thus up-to-date in its concrete production as well as in the use of C. A. P. Turner's patented design for concrete column and slab construction.

The combination of flared column capitals with flat slabs was the prototype for all major subsequent slab construction through the 1930s. This mushroom system, as it was called because of the shape of the reinforcement around the column heads and its rapidity of construction, allowed ample natural light into the interior because no girders blocked the daylight. The columns on the ground floor, spaced twenty feet on centers, were three feet in diameter with five-foot mushroom capitals on the ground floor. Each floor was designed to carry live loads of three hundred pounds per square foot.[24]

The importance of the Army Supply Base to concrete building technology is, first, as an extensive application of Turner's column and slab system.

Second, the scale and speed of construction required a thorough understanding of the materials and careful coordination of experts. The contractor engaged the materials testing laboratory at the University of Illinois in Champaign to test sample concrete elements. He also had the aggregates and concrete elements tested in a Manhattan laboratory of the Public Service Commission, which had overseen New York City subway construction.[25] Further, inspectors visited each of the quarries and sand companies supplying the material. Reinforced concrete construction thus was associated with engineering experts rather than with less skilled workers.

University departments of engineering were important contributors to the base of knowledge about reinforced concrete as well as to the pool of experts who entered industry. Concrete testing was well understood by 1900, but the scale of the tests changed "almost exponentially" after that date, including, for example, refining information about the setting of concrete or the appropriate mixtures for floors or columns.[26] The Laboratory of Applied Mechanics at the University of Illinois, which opened in 1902, acquired sophisticated testing equipment with funds from the state legislature. Professor Arthur Newell Talbot played a key role at the University of Illinois as head of the Engineering Experiment Station after 1903.[27] The station conducted "some of the most influential research being done on reinforced concrete" in the early twentieth century.[28] It was Talbot's prominence in the field that probably brought him to Turner's attention by 1911.

Turner had been working with Talbot for nearly a decade, as indicated by correspondence in the University of Illinois Archives. In 1911, Turner encouraged Talbot, saying his tests would "have a very beneficial effect in this part of the country in the introduction of girderless floor construction."[29] Further, the Army Supply Base column footings were designed according to recommendations made in a University of Illinois bulletin published by Talbot's laboratory.[30] For a project on the scale of the supply base, then, the architect and contractor wisely had design prototypes tested at the very reputable laboratory in Illinois.

With the production of buildings such as the Brooklyn supply base, or early-twentieth-century skyscrapers for that matter, we see the transition from a craft-based approach to building to a routinized method that relied on a hierarchy of personnel. Not only were experts consulted on engineering and design, but also construction supervisors gathered data on all kinds of details, so that labor efficiency and economics determined behavior. Seemingly every move by every worker was scrutinized and documented. One example out of many is an account of scows being unloaded: "Auto trucks were used to deliver the aggregate to the mixers, . . . capable of holding 4.5 yards of aggregate. . . . Trucks were able to make an average of 3.5 trips per hour per truck on a haul averaging one mile to the round trip. As a rule when the maximum amount of concrete was being placed, thirty trucks were able to haul on an average of from 4000 to 5000 yards per day."[31] Similarly, the unloading of cement barges utilized trucks backed up to electrically driven belt conveyors that ran from boat to dock. Three boats were usually unloaded at a time, eight men placing bags on the conveyors, one man at the truck end, and a foreman watching the "conveyor gangs."[32] The modernism that the Brooklyn terminal represents, then, is not a superficial style but rather an approach becoming firmly established in the organizations and culture of America. Characteristic of this modernism is labor stratification, with experts directing workers, and rational planning for and analyses of efficient movement of goods, traffic, and people.[33]

To build such a complex for the army required a great number of people working closely and, in this case, quickly to complete the job. An appendix to the army's *Construction Completion Report* showed the way in which the architect's office interfaced with others. At the top, Gilbert was one of a trio, which also included Turner and, for the army, Lieutenant Colonel Herbert S. Crocker, the constructing quartermaster.[34] Under Gilbert, John Rockart, an employee of Gilbert's since 1891, coordinated with Dene E. Polglase, the chief mechanical engineer; Franklin H. Keese, the architectural specifications writer; R. D.

Read, head of the clerical force; Kort Berle and Stephen F. Holtzman of the Gunvald Aus Company; and the consulting engineers from the railroads. The Aus firm had been involved with Gilbert's office since 1900, gaining prominence for their contributions to the Woolworth Building. Rockart was assisted by Charles A. Johnson and Eugene Ward, another longtime Gilbert employee.

Outside of the architect's office, the government created a new Construction Division in March of 1918 to replace the Cantonment Division and handle all the war building programs. A civilian board, headed by Professor Talbot, who was then president of the American Society of Civil Engineers, was charged with making the contracts "profiteer proof."[35] General George W. Goethals, who had overseen the construction of the Panama Canal earlier in the decade (1907–14), was appointed acting quartermaster general, but the day-to-day work on the supply base came under the Division of Purchase, Storage and Traffic. During his tenure, Goethals reorganized that division and practically eliminated his own office through consolidation.[36] According to George C. Nimmons, writing in the *Architectural Record,* "The reason that the Construction Division succeeded in accomplishing such wonderful results was owing to the fact that it drew to its organization the best and most capable engineering and executive talent in the country who had been instrumental in building up the industrial and commercial life of the nation."[37] Nimmons' praise included not only the army but also the civilian architects, engineers, and contractors who joined with the military in a team effort.

A document from Gilbert's office reveals initial decision-making processes. An early meeting with Goethals was held in February of 1918 in Washington, D.C. (Gilbert had met Goethals once before, in 1917, at Delmonico's in New York City). Major F. B. Wells also attended, along with Irving Bush, the attorney Julius Kohn, Henry C. Turner, and a Turner associate, J. H. P. Perry. "I showed the drawings that had been prepared in my office showing the key plan and perspective illustrations rendered by Ferriss."[38] The group then left Goethals and met with Major Wells to work out the details. Goethals reported in

his diary that "we were open-minded concerning terminal facilities at the Port of New York."[39]

Late in February 1918, Gilbert and Turner described the scheme at that point: The complex was to be of reinforced concrete, nine stories high, with six passenger elevators and thirty-three freight elevators. Auxiliary buildings, such as a barracks, mess hall, power house, and garage, were mentioned.[40] By March, plans were in full swing, with frequent meetings among architect, contractor, and army personnel, even though Gilbert still didn't have a contract and would not have one until June 1918.[41] Initially in February and March of 1918, the program required six million square feet of warehouse space, with three double-decked piers (150 feet by 1,200 feet long), one open pier, and a storage yard for thirteen hundred railroad cars (see Figure 11-1). By May 1918, the warehouse square footage requirement was reduced to four million.[42] In the May reduction, Gilbert chose to add a basement but eliminate two courts and two wings from the original Warehouse B, resulting in the single courtyard through the center.[43] This visually impressive courtyard conveyed much of the meaning of this warehouse complex: to organize the efficient and economic movement of goods (Figure 11-7). When the architectural design conforms to its function so completely, as it does here, the result is elegant indeed.

Photographer Walker Evans accompanied his photoessay on warehouses with the commentary: "The warehouse exists because all the interminable shoving and hauling and parking and ticketing of materials has to have a place of operations somewhere near shipping and railroading."[44] Gilbert conceived the warehouse as a nexus, the link between systematic handling of freight and maritime and rail transportation.[45] Gilbert's "planning . . . of all facilities of handling freight make it a practical achievement of notable character; and demonstrate that the work of the trained architect in organization of a practical plan is of the highest value."[46] While Gilbert was firmly committed to the participation of architects like himself in large-scale projects, he also knew when to seek advice. For example, Gilbert worked closely

with railroad engineers to design the rail yards. At his request, L. V. Morris, chief engineer of the Long Island Railroad (LIRR), was called in for a consultation. H. M. North, an engineer with the Army Construction Division, assisted.[47] Some shipments arrived by car floats and used the LIRR float bridge facilities. The remainder arrived over the Hell Gate Bridge. After some maneuvering, the cars were stored in the yards.

To assist in solving the project's challenges, Bush in January of 1918 asked automobile manufacturer Henry Ford to "loan him one of his expert operating engineers to confer with him on the subject of elevators, conveyors, etc. . . ."[48] In May 1918, two men (one from Gilbert's office—Polglase—and the other from the office of B. F. Cresson—who was himself a warehouse traffic expert) went to the Ford Motor Works in Detroit and met with Ford engineer C. W. Avery. They observed the operation of the traveling overhead cranes, among other aspects of the Ford

plant. Avery, in fact, suggested the use of cranes and cantilevered balconies in the central court of the Brooklyn warehouse. As a result of his advice, the staggered balconies projecting into the 740-by-66-foot court of Warehouse B helped shape one of the great interior spaces of twentieth-century architecture in the United States.

Gilbert's office invested substantial time and energy analyzing freight handling at the Brooklyn terminal.[49] Time studies were made, the ratio of elevators to square footage was examined, and delivery systems were scrutinized. The Construction Completion Report described the hustle and bustle: "The first floor of Warehouse B is the main receiving floor where the freight is received from motor trucks and trains. Motor trucks discharge their loads at all four sides of Warehouse B. The trains discharge their freight in the court of Warehouse B. . . . Running on a track at the roof level of the court are two five-ton travelling cranes operated by electric power. On the

11-7. This view of the interior of Warehouse B at the U. S. Army Supply Base shows the cantilevered balconies and the railroad tracks in the courtyard of the reinforced concrete structure. (Photograph by Pamela Hepburn)

east and west walls of the court are cantilever balconies, . . . staggered in plan so as to permit direct overhead loading without interference from the balcony above."[50] Another method of freight delivery was to use carts drawn in trains by storage-battery tractors in a continuous circuit, to five-ton-capacity freight elevators, then to storage areas, and back again. The large elevators (nine feet by seventeen feet) made the movement of goods more efficient, accommodating four carts at one time.[51] Telephones at every landing allowed freight handlers to contact an elevator dispatcher when needed; otherwise elevator schedules were pre-set. There was a total ninety-six elevators at this terminal. The idea was to avoid rehandling material, to move it from the point of origin to the point of final disposition quickly and economically. This efficiency coincided with industrial streamlining and systematic management in many areas of production across the country.

The U. S. Army Supply Base stands out in Gilbert's practice as an exceptionally severe design, but it was not an anomaly in Gilbert's career. Rather, it shared with his other designs a monumentality, an awareness of Beaux-Arts planning, and some historicist motifs. Russell Sturgis commented that industrial designs gave the impression of medieval fortifications, "so natural and obvious a device."[52] Gilbert's work in Brooklyn promoted the image if not the substance of what Francis Onderdonk called "a new type of Gothic. . . . As Gothic was based on the unity of material—stone—so the new style will be characterized by ferro-concrete prevailing from foundation-pile to roof-balustrade, from chimney-flue to wall-tracery."[53] Good proportions and design coherence gave the concrete army base a monumental presence.

Gilbert believed that the single material of concrete offered architectural opportunities, but he never became exclusively committed to its use. Further, he did not view concrete's possibilities as deriving from its wet state. "Concrete is not a plastic material," Gilbert wrote. "It is no more plastic than cast iron, and less so than terra cotta."[54] Instead, he viewed the massing and variations in light on a single color to be the source of new ideas. Of the Brooklyn scheme,

Gilbert commented, "[T]he stairs [are placed] in such a location as not to obstruct the traffic lines inside the buildings and incidently [sic] forming an important buttressing to the walls. . . . [T]hey provide strong vertical salients which give the main walls an effect of majestic strength and of light and shade that would have been impossible otherwise."[55]

Critics of many persuasions agreed with Gilbert on the terminal's success. In *Ports and Terminal Facilities*, Roy MacElwee wrote that the Brooklyn "terminal is the finest example of warehouse construction that can be found. . . . It is safe to say the the good architectural treatment did not increase the cost of this huge base one dollar."[56] Arthur McEntee noted in *Architecture*, "What is probably the simplest and most striking group of concrete buildings ever constructed is the U.S. Army Supply Base, Brooklyn, N.Y. The buildings are without any decorative detail whatsoever, and possess a quiet dignity and character which is at once apparent."[57]

Certainly part of the reason for the success of the army terminal was Gilbert's familiarity with nineteenth-century exhibition planning and Beaux-Arts ideals. Gilbert and other American mainstream architects had thoroughly absorbed the eminently teachable system of the Beaux-Arts and put it into practice in the early twentieth century. By then, Beaux-Arts tenets served a wide variety of designers, from progressive French urbanists to Frank Lloyd Wright to Gilbert. Briefly, Beaux-Arts assumptions included the ideas that various types of buildings were best served by certain types of plans; that a building was planned from the inside out, from the plan to the elevation; and that the exterior of the building reflected the interior layout and functions. Also of importance were the relationships of buildings to each other, usually organized around major and minor axes.

The Army Supply Base put into practice ideas of Beaux-Arts planning and modern technology that were consistent with Gilbert's other work in government and commercial architecture. Beginning in 1901, for example, Gilbert had chaired the site plan committee for the Louisiana Purchase Exposition in St. Louis, which opened in 1904. Certainly, the grand scale and axial planning in relation to water, whether in St. Louis or Brooklyn, derived from Beaux-Arts schemes. Gilbert also helped several of his staff, including John Rockart, a key staff member on the Brooklyn base, to study at the Parisian school in the decades before the First World War. The base echoed the Beaux-Arts in its ensemble planning, careful massing, and few historicist elements.

The classical idealism of Beaux-Arts schemes, using traditional forms and thoughtful planning, gave polish to the gritty reality of wartime. For example, an arcade led from the administration building to Warehouse A and allowed views from the loading areas through the arches to the water, so that the movement of freight from water to warehouse and back could be monitored (see Figure 11-6). The arcade framed the view of modern functions, a traditional form in the service of efficiency. Further, the profiles of the arched bridges that joined the upper floors of the two warehouses were elliptical, reminiscent of the Venetian Renaissance. As MacElwee noted, "If a Cass Gilbert is the architect, the bridges across the streets, albeit of iron and cement, may have the beauty of line of a Bridge of Sighs. . . ."[58]

Gilbert's army project in the end also had similarities to Le Corbusier's ideas about the city as a machine. Recall that the layout of the supply base was determined largely by careful studies of efficient traffic circulation through the complex. Each warehouse was designed for optimum use, with elevators, bridges, and interior balconies combined with cranes located to support freight handling. Flat slab construction allowed for ample light. While Gilbert remained skeptical of always applying Beaux-Arts methods to design problems in the United States, he clearly was partial to the planning and rendering skills of Beaux-Arts-trained men. Compared to the linear control of some of Le Corbusier's schemes, for example, Gilbert had the operations of a busy port dramatized. Hugh Ferriss, who had worked for Gilbert for a short time, created renderings of the base between February and May of 1918.[59] Here dexterous use of conté crayon gave the complex a romance, with highlights, shadows, and steam enlivening the concrete surfaces (Figure 11-8).

Architect and critic Russell Sturgis viewed industrial architecture as instructive for all other design: "There is something to be said for the theory broached now and then by the persons not enamored of our present architecture of mere pretense, that the designers should be restrained to square masses and sharp corners and plain windows for twenty years to come."[60] Gilbert, however, remained enamored of historical styles that could be adapted for modern building needs. He reduced his supply base designs to bare essentials because it was expedient, owing to wartime shortages and the necessity for rapid construction. Sometimes the paring was done at the insistence of others on the team. Despite intervening levels of bureaucracy, Goethals kept a close watch on the port projects. In August 1918, he noted in his

11-8. Architectural drawing from Cass Gilbert's office, 1918, shows U. S. Army Supply Base in Brooklyn, New York. (©Collection of the New-York Historical Society, neg. #69618)

diary: "Instructed Mr. [B. F.] Cresson to inform Cass Gilbert that I do not like design of pier ends: that they must be plain in the extreme. . . ." Two weeks later Cresson brought in a design of a "perfectly plain pierhead," which Goethals approved.[61]

The architect was not often forced to change. In September 1918, Brigadier General R. C. Marshall supported the architect when others in the Construction Division wanted to lower the height of the parapets (from six feet to three and a half feet): "Mr. Gilbert . . . has expressed himself as very strongly opposed to any change in the height of the parapet walls and the Construction Division does not wish to take the attitude of overruling so competent an architect whose judgment and opinions are entitled to full respect and consideration."[62] Gilbert's firmness on the parapet issue was probably prompted by his efforts to achieve good proportions: "To add further to the massive appearance the stair wells are set out from the face of the walls to form towers, the four corner ones rising above the parapet wall to form turrets. This design is quite appropriate for a building to be used for war purposes."[63]

In general on the Brooklyn project Gilbert emphasized practicality, utility, and planning, but he did not use these words polemically. Gilbert was not a proponent of a warehouse aesthetic but rather was simply willing to use new techniques because they were economical and quick. Still, he was able to appreciate the spareness of the result: "All work is of an extremely practical character demonstrating that ornamental detail is not necessarily a feature of architectural design where vast spaces predominate. In fact, ornament of any kind would seem flippant and trivial in so great and impressive a mass; architecture in its best sense, for works of this type, can safely rely upon good, reasonable, logical planning from the standpoint of utility. . . ."[64]

Despite his appreciation of "utility," Gilbert continued to choose from a variety of architectural approaches. He was no modernist. Similar to the methods of Albert Kahn, Gilbert's design ideas were framed by the building type, material, and specific situation. As indicated already, the supply base was representative of a broader modernism in its use of experts, its systematic approach to construction and freight handling, and its innovations in concrete technology. Kahn himself praised the result: "Nothing could be finer in mass, more straightforward or more direct. It is almost bald in its simplicity, certainly ornamentation plays no part in the design and yet by a masterly vertical sub-division of pylons, piers and mullions, all in proper relation to each other, all splendidly proportioned not only in width and height, but also in relative projection, we have a work of the highest architectural merit."[65]

Yet for reasons listed by Kahn—simplicity and good proportions, among others—the Brooklyn supply base was a source, however unintentional, for the "capital-M" modernists. Le Corbusier and Richard Neutra, for example, saw its scale and concrete gray masses as inspiration for their own works. Le Corbusier used an overall view of the terminal as an example of modern industrial design in his *Vers une Architecture* (1923), which appeared first in English in 1927 as *Towards a New Architecture*. Richard Neutra in his book, *Amerika: Die Stilbildung des neuen Bauens in den Vereinigten Staaten* (1930), also used an illustration of Warehouse B at the Brooklyn base.

Builders and architects alike at the beginning of the twentieth century found that new materials—or materials used in new ways on a large scale—could produce compelling new forms, if the material was allowed to express itself. Even the traditionalist Gilbert wrote in 1923, "Concrete must . . . be treated in accordance with its own nature, and so treated it is a highly useful building material, with many yet undeveloped possibilities in design."[66] But precisely because the Army Supply Base was not created to support a theory, it helps expand and diversify what we mean by early-twentieth-century modernism, a trend at once broader culturally and economically, as well as less rigid, than the modernists would have wanted us to believe. Reyner Banham predictably said it well: "Piecemeal, the dynamics of building in a market economy at a time of rapid technological advance would produce every aspect of an architectural revolution except the revolutionary intent."[67] For doctrinaire architects, Gilbert's stylistic flexibility and willingness to adapt modernist aesthetics as one approach in a panoply of approaches could easily have prompted Le Corbusier's warning: "Let us beware of American architects."[68] Le Corbusier's contempt aside though, the U. S. Army Supply Base demonstrated the possibilities of reinforced concrete in a convergence of military and civilian expertise made urgent by the frenzy of World War I. Rather than furthering a revolution in architecture, the supply base instead gave physical form to a consolidation of management and engineering trends in industry and in the military.

PART 4

IDEALS IN PLANNING

CHAPTER 12

A "NEW" NEW ENGLAND:
PROPOSALS FOR NEW HAVEN AND WATERBURY,
CONNECTICUT

Barbara S. Christen

In 1920, the *Architect's Journal* of London reported that

> No American architect enjoys a higher reputation among us than Mr. Cass Gilbert. . . . He is of the rare type of those who do all things well. In this respect, he is a true scion of the great house of McKim, Mead and White, whose miscellaneousness was their astounding quality. It takes a great man to be as various as [he] has been—his work ranging from a monumental building to a humble cottage—and on the quality as well as on the variety of work, it is not an abuse of words to say that . . . Gilbert is a great man, coming as near to genius as any architect that the Continent of America has yet produced. . . . Concerning the Woolworth Building, the chief thing to take into account is not its gigantic size, but its embodiment of a very successful attempt to invest a skyscraper with architectural character.[1]

Such was the praise about Gilbert by his peers before the rise of modernism and before he completed his last major work, the United States Supreme Court (1928–35). Clearly, Gilbert was a talented and respected designer in his own day. Yet the dynamic between the architect and client or close advisor had an impact on his projects and proposals at certain junctures throughout his career, including those for New Haven and Waterbury, Connecticut, the subject of this chapter. The end result of these designs (and as might be argued, with most architectural designs) was not a perfect solution delivered by "genius"—as implied by the above quotation. Rather, it was the product of a complex process involving interactions about the needs and desires of the client or advisor, cost, reception in the community, and other mediating economic, social, and political factors.

Gilbert was extremely familiar with trends in comprehensive planning at the turn of the century, particularly the City Beautiful movement. His design for reshaping the core of Washington, D.C. (see Figure 3-2) was influenced by his exposure to such ideas presented at the American Institute of Architects (AIA) and under the guidance of AIA Secretary Glenn Brown. He further experimented with grand,

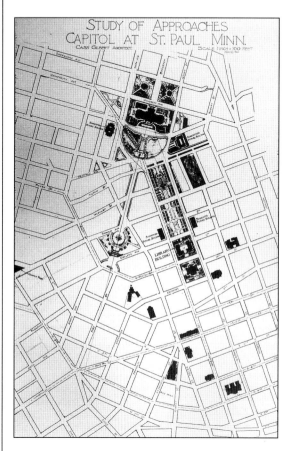

axially placed boulevards and hierarchically arranged building groups in his proposals for the Minnesota State Capitol Approaches (Figure 12-1), a project that was to occupy his interests from 1902 through the early 1930s. Similarly, his campus plans for Washington University (1899) (see Figure 16-1), the University of Minnesota (1907–10) (see Figure 15-8), the University of Texas (1909–14) (see Figure 13-8), and Oberlin College (1904–15) (Figure 12-2) reflect Gilbert's interest in planning large groups of buildings harmoniously arranged and designed to contribute to a greater whole. In each of these projects, the interplay between designer and client or advisor played a significant role in the development of his proposals.[2]

In the case of New Haven and Waterbury in the early twentieth century, this interplay took shape in the context of an idealized romantic revival of the sights and associations of an "historical 'old' New England."[3] This yearning for the past was manifested by painters, craftsmen, and decorative artists as well as architects. This model is useful in considering Gilbert's artistic sensibility and the context of his projects. His work in New Haven and Waterbury provides intriguing examples as to questions of style and how the dynamic between architect and client or advisor contributed to the design process.

Both sets of projects by Gilbert for New Haven and Waterbury rely heavily on use of the Federal style (which roughly corresponds to developments in

12-1. "Study of Approaches: Capitol at St. Paul, Minn.," plat, November 13, 1902. (Minnesota Historical Society)

12-2. Oberlin College Administrative Group with Tower, n.d. [c. 1915]. (© Collection of the New-York Historical Society)

American architecture between approximately 1780 and 1820) or precedents of the Federal style—seventeenth- to mid-eighteenth-century English sources from the Georgian period. As a point of reference, Charles Bulfinch's Massachusetts Statehouse (1795–98) is an often-quoted Federal example that represents a re-interpretation of such earlier English sources as William Chambers' Somerset House (London, completed 1780). Similarly, Ithiel Town and Asher Benjamin's Center Church at New Haven green (completed 1814) harkens back to James Gibbs's St. Martin-in-the-Fields (London, completed 1726). Characteristics of the neo-Federal or neo-Georgian style in Gilbert's day included the primary use of red brick with structural elements such as columns or quoins in white stone (or wood painted white); clearly defined geometric components in massing; and columnar details often articulated in a wiry, taut, and attenuated fashion.[4]

Gilbert showed an appreciation for Federal-era (and loosely colonial) art and architecture when he saved from demolition the portico of the Judge William Bristol House constructed in New Haven in 1803–4 by a Connecticut builder, David Hoadley (Figure 12-3). Gilbert later donated this portico to the Metropolitan Museum of Art and used details from it, such as arched molding, in his own historic summer residence, the Keeler Tavern, also known as the Cannonball House, in Ridgefield, Connecticut (Figure 12-4). Notably, Gilbert filled this eighteenth-century house with colonial-period furniture and examples of decorative arts. He also expressed interest in early American architecture by contributing to a campaign at the turn of the century to restore Thomas Jefferson's Monticello.[5]

Gilbert's use of late-eighteenth- to early-nineteenth-century Federal style and neo-Georgian aesthetic—a neocolonial style in the loosest sense—has much to do with two civic leaders: George Dudley Seymour (1859–1945) in New Haven and Henry Sabin Chase (1855–1918) in Waterbury. Both of these men were committed to reshaping their respective towns in substantive ways. They championed Gilbert's work at various levels of development, although they did not always agree with the architect's ideas.

In New Haven, when Seymour and Gilbert met in 1906 during a campaign to build a new public library on the New Haven green, Seymour was emerging as a distinguished leader in civic affairs. He would continue in this role for much of his life. Although he was trained as an attorney who practiced patent law for more than sixty years, his deepest commitment lay in pursuing municipal improvements for downtown New Haven at the turn of the century. In the course of this second career, he was chairman of

12-3. David Hoadley, Judge William Bristol House: portico, New Haven, Conn. 1803–4, in *Old Houses of Connecticut*, ed. Bertha Chadwick Trowbridge (New Haven, 1923), opening plate. (Ryerson and Burnham Libraries, Art Institute of Chicago)

12-4. Keeler Tavern (Cannon Ball House), Ridgefield, Conn., c. 1915. Wurts Brothers Collection. (Museum of the City of New York)

the New Haven Municipal Art Commission, vice president of the Society for the Preservation of New England Antiquities, and secretary of both the city planning commission and the committee for a new library. He also wrote widely about the colonial history of the region. In fact, he became an expert on the life and history of Nathan Hale.[6]

Seymour and Gilbert probably first met through Gilbert's attempts to design a new railroad station in New Haven for the New York, New Haven and Hartford Railroad, including dozens of proposals for the project, including one fashioned in a Georgian mode (see Figure C-11). It is not surprising that Gilbert was chosen for such a commission, since he had recently completed several designs for smaller

Commission (of which Seymour was secretary in name and functionally the leader) commissioned Gilbert and Frederick Law Olmsted Jr. to produce a detailed study of the city, including recommendations for making the area more viable as an urban entity. In 1906 Gilbert had just published for St. Paul a similar report for the Minnesota State Capitol Commission.[9] In the early stages of discussion for New Haven, Gilbert and Olmsted entertained the possibility of working with a third specialist, namely Charles McKim of McKim, Mead & White. It soon became clear that McKim could not join them, at which point Walter Cook (from the architectural firm, Babb, Cook & Willard) was proposed. Seymour decided ultimately to work only with Gilbert and Olmsted.[10]

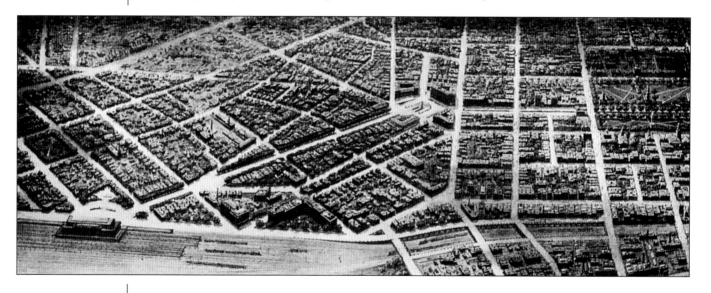

12-5. Cass Gilbert and Frederick Law Olmsted, Jr. "New Haven Improvement Perspective," in *The Relations of Railways to City Development* comp. Glenn Brown (Washington, D.C., 1910), pl. after p. 48. (Library of Congress)

passenger stations for the railroad.[7] With the advent of the company's absorption of various rail entities, the railroad company had gained control of the sole route into southern New England for both passengers and freight service. Gilbert, who had worked for McKim, Mead & White in the upper Midwest on the Northern Pacific Railway, had impressed Northern Pacific executive Charles S. Mellen, who later became president of the New Haven line.[8]

After Gilbert's involvement with the railroad, however, three other New Haven projects in 1907 began to coalesce rapidly: the development of a comprehensive city plan, the building of the public library, and proposals for a courthouse and other buildings. First, the New Haven Civic Improvement

It was Seymour's vision to develop a plan for new public buildings for roughly the north and east sides of the green. In working mainly with Gilbert, Seymour made this civic improvement report his rallying cry for reshaping the city's core. Gilbert's drawings and his consultations with Olmsted indicate their treatment of the city as an organism, with interconnected systems for traffic, sanitation, and recreation as well as residential and commercial growth. Gilbert and Olmsted wanted to convert the area around the green into a civic center, leaving the historic core as open space. They proposed creating a wide boulevard approach to connect the new railroad station with Temple Street, the route along which three early-nineteenth-century churches were located

12-6. Ives Memorial
Library: perspective,
photoreproduction of
plate from Cass Gilbert
and Frederick Law
Olmsted, Jr., *Report of
the New Haven Civic
Improvement
Commission* (New
Haven, December
1910), no. 23, p. 52.
(©Collection of the
New-York Historical
Society, neg. #74378)

12-7. Byers Hall, Yale
University, New Haven,
Conn., 1905 postcard.
(©Collection of the
New-York Historical
Society, neg. #74379)

(Figure 12-5). Gilbert and Olmsted also considered the impact on New Haven environs of changes that were expected to occur because of increasing industrialization and population growth.

As part of the New Haven plan, Gilbert alone was engaged in late 1907 to design a new public library on the property of the Bristol House, mentioned earlier. This site was located along "Quality Row," a series of distinguished houses that had been built in the early to mid-nineteenth century but by 1900 had begun to show signs of decline. Funded by a generous gift from a New Haven widow, Mary E. Ives, the library was the first structure to be built as part of the new civic center on the north edge of the green. Most important in terms of the dynamic between Gilbert and Seymour, who in this case was an interested inside advisor (and not a direct client),

work so the New Haven citizens "should then begin to recover for New Haven something of its old time air. . . ."[12] Seymour eventually commemorated Hoadley with further study, articles, and installation of a tablet at the United (North) Church.

Gilbert was excited about the prospect of designing the library. He expressed his commitment to the project when he promised library committee member George D. Watrous that he would give the library design his close personal attention and hoped it would "express the refinement and purity of style to which its purpose, its location, and its importance entitle it."[13] He also wanted to make the building "distinctive and monumental and at the same time . . . preserve the proportions of spirit of the fine old architecture of New Haven."[14] Gilbert's design for the library (Figure 12-6) also nearly copied the proportions and massing of Byers Hall at Yale University. In fact, his files for the New Haven project contained a period postcard depicting the building (Figure 12-7).

12-8. Elevation of New Haven building group: Records, Courthouse, Bank, Hotel. n.d. [c. February 1907]. (©Collection of the New-York Historical Society, neg. #72879)

was that the style of the new structure was to be neo-Federal or neo-Georgian. It was, Gilbert and Seymour agreed, to be designed in harmony with the United (North) Church, which was designed by Hoadley approximately ten years after he completed the Bristol House. Gilbert regarded this church as one of the finest examples of colonial architecture, one worthy of preservation and documentation with historic record drawings.[11] Gilbert and Seymour also worked to restore Center Church (Ithiel Town, architect; ca. 1815), located next to the United (North) Church on the green, which like the neighboring church had been painted and "disfigured" in the mid-nineteenth century. Seymour, in fact, wrote eloquently about hoping to restore both churches to their original appearance of red brick with white wood-

In the third component of the busy 1907–1908 season, Seymour advocated the development of designs for a county courthouse to be built on a site near the library. Initially he had hoped that Gilbert would produce a complex building group that would include the Hall of Records, a courthouse, a bank, and a hotel (Figure 12-8). In early 1907, Gilbert appeared to oblige Seymour by trying out various building arrangements and treatments of the tower. In one sketch, Gilbert included a note to his draftsmen to modify the dome to look more like those of Christopher Wren's Royal Naval Hospital at Greenwich, England (completed 1707).

Like Wren, Gilbert was intrigued by the concept of the vista and how his buildings would be perceived from afar. However, it appears that soon after these early sketches were completed, Gilbert and Seymour realized that the library would be dwarfed by such a complex building group, not to mention the complications in obtaining necessary land and building funds. Gilbert responded to this concern with a few proposals, including a presentation drawing, which balanced the library and courthouse in a more equitable (and simpler) arrangement (Figure 12-9). He went so far as to prepare other elaborate presentation drawings based on the architectural vocabulary of Independence Hall in Philadelphia (1732–48 and later), perhaps because he hoped to benefit from being on the inside track with Seymour (Figure 12-10). This latter plan was designed, as Gilbert explained to Seymour, "to go with" the design of the library nearby.[15]

Gilbert did not refine the designs for the New Haven County Courthouse further, however, because between February and early March 1909, a controversy broke out that reflected as much about Seymour's alliance with Gilbert as it did about the state of the architectural profession at that time.

given the commission and compensation that was 1 percent lower than that recommended by the AIA guidelines. The building commission conceded on four of the complaints, the architects withdrew three, but the most objectionable one—no professional specialist or jury to judge the competition drawings—remained. This protest was supported not only by Seymour but also by prominent members of the commission and the community, including former Connecticut Governor Rollin S. Woodruff; John K. Beach, the leader of the New Haven County Bar Association; George D. Watrous, library committee member and president of the Connecticut Bar Association; several Yale University faculty; and members of both the Chamber of Commerce and the Women's Civic Club.[17]

Their detractors most forcefully included Jacob D. Walter, who was a career politician and county

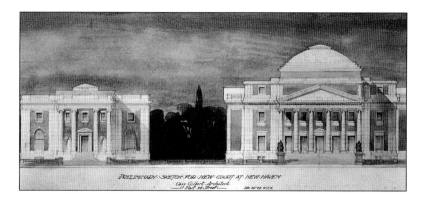 

Gilbert's firm was one of seven that were invited by the courthouse building committee to participate in the competition. But Gilbert's firm, along with two others, Tracy, Swartwout & Litchfield from New York and L. W. Robinson from New Haven, protested that their design proposals would not be judged by a professional. At issue were the reputations of Gilbert and his colleagues, members of the AIA, who were honor-bound to follow the professional code of ethics, specifically Rule 17, which required peer review in such competitions.[16] The architects issuing complaints believed that the competition was faulty on eight counts, with the most important issue being the lack of peer review. They also contested the fact that the winning architect might or might not actually be

commissioner between 1895 and 1923.[18] Walter argued that since the city was paying for most of the building costs (which eventually totaled half a million dollars), the city commissioners should have been able to set their own guidelines and not have been directed by the demands of non-New Haven, or "outside," architects. The controversy escalated when patent attorney John K. Beach resigned from the building commission in support of Gilbert's protest.[19] The New Haven County Bar Association lodged its own complaint with the legislature, and still later, a group of New Haven taxpayers filed an injunction to halt the award of contracts for work on the building's interior. Thomas Gilbert White (1877-1939), a young and inexperienced artist, had been lined up to

12-9. "Preliminary Sketch for New Court House at New Haven," W. J. S. renderer, January 25, 1909. (©Collection of the New-York Historical Society, neg. #72877)

12-10. Courthouse: later proposal, n.d. [c. 1910], in George Dudley Seymour, *New Haven* (New Haven, 1942), 651. (Library of Congress)

A "NEW" NEW ENGLAND

do this courthouse work at what was reportedly an exorbitant price, and taxpayers were outraged.[20]

This latter action caused the controversy to reach fever pitch. County Commissioner Walter claimed that Gilbert had bribed him to make changes in the competition process for selecting the architect of the project. Walter is said to have replied imperiously to Gilbert's supposed bribe that "he was not yet ready to go into his neighbor's hencoop and steal chickens and that when he did, he wanted to go with gentlemen."[21] Gilbert responded swiftly to this serious allegation and engaged a law firm to represent him, although it appears the matter was eventually dropped. He also referred to the ordeal as the courthouse "fracas," which he and Seymour did well to let die down before embarking on another phase of their civic improvement goals for the city.[22]

The building commission did not accede to Gilbert's request, resulting in the selection of William Allen and Richard Williams's proposal. Their design was noted variously in local newspaper editorials as "provincial," a step backward into the "dark ages of architectural competitions," and "a grave error in judgment."[23] It was generally felt that with the Allen and Williams courthouse design, the standards of public building had been compromised. As the Reverend Anson Phelps Stokes of Yale noted, this attitude would have prevented Boston from getting its beautiful public library and Providence its state-house.[24]

After the county courthouse controversy abated, Seymour had less initiative to lead the cause of civic improvement in New Haven. His correspondence with Gilbert reveals both fatigue and frustration at having passed from "youth to age" in the process of dealing with the concerns of the New Haven Civic Improvement Commission. By 1916, Seymour was all but fully discouraged, feeling that his hopes for a comprehensive city plan were dashed.[25]

Nonetheless, Seymour was central to Gilbert's role in designing a remarkable cluster of buildings for the New England city. It is evident in this project—perhaps more than in most—that Gilbert did not operate in a vacuum when developing new designs. He was lucky to have found in Seymour such an enthusiastic, committed, and intelligent colleague. Their joint efforts to create a civic building group that would have linked together key sections of the city were indeed admirable, even if the entire plan was not realized. Today, the only reminders of this grand scheme are the Ives Memorial Library and the railroad station, each suggesting the stylistic consistency of the Federal and neo-Georgian modes that both men revered and celebrated for its historical significance to New Haven.

In Waterbury, northwest of New Haven by thirty-eight miles, Gilbert's experience was quite different. At the turn of the century, Waterbury was on the verge of a great population expansion. In less than twenty years, the number of the town residents would more than double. The industrial needs of the town's companies that manufactured brass, buttons, pins, clocks, and so on would be competing for access to the Naugatuck River, a valuable water supply. With Henry Sabin Chase's lead, the city in 1909 reconstructed and widened main thoroughfares, including Grand and Meadow Streets, at the intersection of which McKim, Mead & White had completed the town's Union Station in the same year.[26] Other improvements at this crossroads of the town included eliminating South Willow and Cedar Streets. It is on and near Grand Street that an unusual group of municipal and private buildings came together, as the National Register of Historic Places report has noted, in "a remarkable combination of topography, street evolution, civic and corporate responsibility and co-ordinated city planning and design."[27] It was Chase's vision, and later that of his younger brother, Frederick Starkweather Chase (1862–1947), that Grand Street in true City Beautiful tradition would provide a suitable entry into town.

These two brothers and other members of their family were respected for their contributions to the civic appearance of Grand Street, and specifically for their work with Gilbert on both public and private projects. Henry Chase was a financier and manufacturer who had taken charge as president of the brass and metal works that his father had begun in 1885, one of the largest brass manufacturing concerns in

the Naugatuck Valley.[28] Henry's brother Frederick was an industrialist and brass manufacturer who, with Henry, in 1917 merged the Chase metals triumvirate (the Waterbury Manufacturing Company, the Chase Rolling Milling Company, and the Chase Metal Works) into a powerful national business concern.[29] (The company even went so far as to change the course of the Nangatuck River in order to acquire the land necessary for expansion.) By 1923 they and other family members (including sisters Helen Elizabeth and Edith and brother Irving Hall Chase) contributed more than $100,000 to changing the face of downtown Waterbury.[30] Gilbert's work, however, occurred mostly with Henry, Frederick, and Irving, in chronological order.

Years later a Waterbury citizen described their alliances on several buildings (the city hall, a social welfare house, private offices and stores, a bank, a medical dispensary, a town park and fountain, and fire drill tower among other projects) as an attempt to make " 'a Cass Gilbert town.' "[31] By this time, Gilbert had also designed the Waterbury Club (1914–18), and proposals were being entertained for a theater, an armory, and women's housing for the Scovill Manufacturing Company. He would soon be asked to design a temporary entertainment pavilion for Library Park as well as cemetery headstones for the Chase family and a tablet commemorating Connecticut builder David Hoadley. The unfolding of the largest projects, the Waterbury Municipal Building, the Chase Companies offices, and the Waterbury National Bank, provides a distinct example of the interplay between architect and client or advisor in the design process. This process reveals much in terms of stylistic decisions as well as, in one case, the public's reception of a particular building or area. In the case of the Municipal Building, a surprise voice came on the scene.

On April 22, 1912, when a fire destroyed the existing town hall located on West Main Street on the

12-11. Waterbury Municipal Building: competition design, in *Architecture* 28 (October 1913): 230. (Library of Congress)

green, the city's leaders were quick to respond with plans for a new municipal building. This building would further embellish the new great entrance to the city, begun by street widening and McKim, Mead & White's railroad station. A Chamber of Commerce pamphlet boasted that a new $600,000 municipal building would be the "dominating feature" of the civic center, making the entrance to the city "one of the most impressive in the country."[32] In short order, a building commission was formed, and a national competition was conducted by Warren Powers Laird, an architecture professor at the University of Pennsylvania.[33] Gilbert won the competition with a neo-Federal design, suggesting the use of red brick and white marble as the main materials for the exterior (Figure 12-11). This stylistic envelope ultimately housed a complex building program that included the mayor's office, other town offices, fire department, police department and jail, assembly chambers for town aldermen, a town courtroom, and facilities for such city officials as the town engineer, health inspector, and parks commissioner.[34] While it remains unclear who Gilbert's competitors were in the building competition, it is evident that the guidelines prepared by Laird stipulated the use of brick and stone because the building commissioners were impressed by the aesthetics of the New Haven Public Library.[35] It is also clear that Gilbert received an early vote of confidence from Henry Chase, whom Gilbert had known socially since at least 1911. Although Chase was not a member of the building commission, he offered to help Gilbert if the architect needed someone "familiar with local conditions."[36] This offer laid the foundation for future discussions.

What is curious about the Municipal Building project is that Gilbert, in further refinements of his design, had other ideas for this structure and the look of the new downtown. A couple of months after the competition design had been accepted and published, he continued to wrestle with a desire to use more purely late-eighteenth-century English Georgian sources. Although Henry Chase was a strong supporter of Gilbert in this general project, in this aspect of design refinement it was, surprisingly,

New Haven's George Dudley Seymour with whom Gilbert discussed such stylistic issues at length. When Gilbert planned to send Seymour the competitive design, Gilbert believed that the design was just what Seymour might like. Gilbert admitted that he thought of Seymour and his point of view "many times while the drawings were underway."[37] Seymour was delighted with the general proposal and described the small cupola as "exquisite, large enough for its intended purpose and [it] counts as a jewel—'a fine ring on a large hand.' "[38] In subsequent studies (which were numerous), Gilbert indicated his concerns about cost, and he truncated the gambrel roof, an aesthetic decision with which Seymour agreed.[39] In later correspondence with John P. Elton of the Waterbury building commissioners, Gilbert explained that he wanted to design a bell tower as well as McKim, Mead & White had done in the New York Herald Building, "with bronze figures modeled by a real sculptor like Paul Bartlett." But the architect did not dare suggest it because of the additional expense.[40] Because of pressure from nearby business owners not wanting to be disturbed and because of concerns that its ringing would disturb the delicate instrumentation at the fire department, a simpler bell (made by the Meneely Bell Company) was installed ultimately at Union Station. This decision was applauded by Henry Chase.[41] Seymour responded to other aspects of the design when he wrote, "It pleases me to have all of the arches in the basement alike, all of the main window openings in the main building alike & all of the pilasters of the same size. These repetitions produce an effect of solidity and quietness and ease. The entire effect is wonderfully refined—I do hope you won't have to use any limestone. I don't so much object to limestone in France or in England or anywhere when it occurs tho. to my eyes it is not a beautiful stone except in rare instances."[42] Seymour's criticism of the use of limestone was extensive, and it provided him with a platform for addressing more philosophical issues. He wrote that even when fine limestone was used, such as that at Yale's Woolsey Hall, it

is not and never will be domesticated and it does not "belong." Kendall [of McKim, Mead & White] tells me that beauty is the first consideration—that he may be put down as an extremist when it comes to that. But there is something more than external beauty in architecture—there is the greater beauty of fitness—of propriety. You architects—excuse my abuse—are so absorbed in the execution of your designs in beautiful materials or in materials that you fancy, that you don't always consider the graver side, the moral side, if you please. Nor will an ever increasing facility—of transporting building material over the surface of the earth destroy my principle that the use of locally fit material is the soundest practice. Limestone in New England [thus] must always be an anomaly. Mr. Taft laughs at my outrageous maxims but I can't discard them.[43]

Gilbert did not answer this vehement letter but continued to consider how the design might best be implemented. The issue of local materials troubled Seymour, as he explained in a more general context: "Our public architecture will certainly become arbitrary and fanciful if we go on building without any reference to the local material, and I think we shall never be on a sound foundation as to public architecture until the material is selected in advance, and the competitions framed accordingly."[44]

By July 1914, Gilbert more hotly debated this issue with Seymour, specifically because he, Gilbert, changed course and wanted to use marble for the entire exterior midsection of the building. He chided Seymour for strongly recommending to building commissioner Elton that brick be used for this entire central section. Gilbert wrote, ". . . I am writing to you this personal note to ask that if any of my friends in Waterbury talk to you again about it that you should tell them to follow my lead in this matter. You know my own admiration for brick that I strongly backed your suggestions for its use in the New Haven Library where it is so aesthetically successful."[45] Gilbert went on to say that he felt justified asking the building commissioners to avail themselves of the opportunity to use more marble, because the contract bids had come in approximately $200,000 less than the original estimate, a saving that he believed would easily allow for an extra expenditure on better-quality stone. Gilbert explained that he had used as the

main motif an adaptation of Robert Adam's Sir Watkin Williams Wynn House in London (completed 1776) (Figure 12-12), a thoroughly Georgian example of British residential architecture of this period. Gilbert further explained,

> That is to say, it is a building of three stories, the lower story having round arched windows, the wall being very low, delicate rustication, and the 2nd and 3rd story being pilastered with arches between the pilasters in the 2nd story and small square windows above. . . . It is built entirely of light stone, I think either Portland or Bath stone.

No brick was used in it. I have been studying a number of English examples of the Georgian period and find so many in which the material was either all brick or all stone that I am justified in quoting this one as typical.[46]

Gilbert's greatest concern was for the proportions of the design and the overall effect of the materials. In this same (extensive) letter to Seymour, he explained, "I find that the wall spaces are necessarily so small in area (because of the practical requirements of the frequent window openings) that the whole surface of brick would be so little that it will not have the

12-12. Robert and James Adam, Sir Watkin Williams Wynn House, London, 1772–76, in Arthur T. Bolton, *Works in Architecture by Robert and James Adam, 1758–1794* (London, 1922), 104. (National Gallery of Art)

12-13. Chase
Companies Head-
quarters: as built,
1917–19. (Cass Gilbert
Collection, Archives
Center, National
Museum of American
History)

breadth of effect which we secured in the New Haven
Library. . . . In short, I am very anxious lest it should
have a vibrating effect of white and red that would be
highly disturbing and very unsatisfactory."[47] He thus
pleaded with Seymour to contact Elton to convince
him that the commission should accept this design
change. As a final effort, Gilbert used one more argument—that of New York's City Hall by Joseph-
François Mangin and John McComb (completed
1812). He wrote, "Imagine the old City Hall in New
York alternating with marble pilasters and brick in
the narrow space between those pilasters and the windows and you would have what I hear will be the
result of our present arrangement. I cannot change
the marble to brick and my only hope is to change
brick to marble. I think they [the building commis-
sioners] would be willing to do it and they certainly
ought to."[48] Needless to say, it appears that Seymour
did not write to Elton to influence the building
commission, and Gilbert's plea went unanswered.
Although the outcome of this decision was not what
he expected, Gilbert nevertheless must have been

pleased later to find out that his city hall at
Waterbury had influenced proposals for the city of
Lexington, Kentucky, and possibly Mt. Vernon,
Ohio. He must also have been pleased to discover
that sculptor Paul Barlett, whose work he admired on
the New York Herald Building, proclaimed the
Waterbury Municipal Building as "one of the most
beautiful buildings in the United States."[49]

To set aside this issue of the dynamic between
Seymour and Gilbert at Waterbury, one can see other
details on the interior that Gilbert employed from the
sources that he mentioned in his extensive letter. The
central stair pays homage to Mangin and McComb's
building and the coffering in the main hallway was
influenced by Robert Adam's detail of the design for
the morning room of the Wynn House in London.

With the early designs of the new headquarters
for Chase Companies, which Gilbert began
in 1916, Gilbert's vision for a unified complex was
consistent with the initial expectations of Henry
Chase. Located directly across from the new Water-

bury Municipal Building, the Chase Companies' headquarters as Gilbert proposed was to be made of brick and pale stone (Figure C-18), because Henry Chase first indicated his preference for this type of Georgian-inspired, loosely colonial building.[50]

By mid-1917, however, Henry Chase changed his position and objected to Gilbert's echoing certain aspects of the Municipal Building's design. Specifically, he objected to the brick and stone combinations and the balustrade that articulated the cornice line of the structure because it would make the new building look too much like the city hall. The elder Chase wrote, "I cannot get out of my mind the impression that our new office building is going to be too much like the city hall in appearance, for it would seem a presumptuous attempt on the part of private citizens to imitate and share the dignity of city hall. The position that we hold in the cummunity [sic] is such that we dislike very much having this impression exist."[51] Gilbert proceeded to take Henry Chase to different sites around midtown and upper Manhattan, to inspect the use of stone and brickwork in various buildings.[52] Although the exact nature of their discussions on this tour is unknown, the matter was left undecided, with Frederick joining the debate and taking his brother's side when he made the plea that marble not be utilized as it had been in the town's building across the street.[53] By summer, the issue of materials was still being debated, as Henry Chase's correspondence with Gilbert indicates: "We have been most carefully considering the question of the exterior of the building for some time. The marble and brick never really did appeal to us and for many reasons we [now] do not want it. We feel that with ivy and other green things on the building or about it and with such balconies or other iron or bronze or gilt ornamentation and carving, etc. as your own skill and taste will suggest that we will get the building that we want. We have perfect confidence that you can do this."[54] Although Henry Chase understood Gilbert's viewpoint about using marble and brick, or at least limestone and brick, he reminded the architect that in the end "of course we [the Chases] must be the deciders. . . ."[55]

The resulting building was rendered in a Renais-sance-revival style, and not the colonially inspired design that Gilbert had envisioned (Figure 12-13). As for the Chases' concern that the companies' head-quarters would be misconstrued as city hall, it was anyway, as depicted in a cartoon from a company brochure published on the fiftieth anniversary of the firm (Figure 12-14). In an ironic twist, the company sold their building in 1963 to citizens interested in preserving it, and three years later it was sold to the city of Waterbury for use as city offices.[56]

After the major decision about exterior materials was made, on Gilbert's side, he was able to convince the family that they should accept the proposal of a wrought-iron fence and entrance gate for their property based on what McKim, Mead & White had done for John Pierpont Morgan's library in 1906 in New York.[57] Although the design and scale of this feature at the two buildings differ, the impetus is the same: to surround the compound with a distinctive boundary of high-quality materials and design. For the Chase building, this wrought-iron fence, along with bronze sconces on the exterior and some interior metalwork, was carried out by the heralded metals craftsman Samuel Yellin of Philadelphia.

they think it's the city hall

Up in Waterbury, Conn., people come in and ask to be married. They think they're in the City Hall but they're not. They are in the central offices of the Chase Companies, built of limestone and marble by Cass Gilbert who designed the Woolworth Building.

The Chase offices are really beautiful and we are proud of them for they mark a half century of successful service to the brass industry.

Chase Brass

The other striking feature about the Renaissance-revival design was noted frequently in period journals about the Chase family's building: the architectural reference of the Temple of the Winds in the central section of building. This reference harkened back to James Stuart's design of the same name in 1780 at Mt. Stewart, Ireland, itself based on the Roman Tower of the Winds in Athens of the second half of the first century B.C. Although it remains unclear whose idea it was to employ such a reference, it was likely Gilbert's. He owned and

12-14. Cartoon from fiftieth anniversary brochure of Chase Companies, November 1925. (©Collection of the New-York Historical Society, neg. #74408)

WATERBURY
NATIONAL BANK
CASS GILBERT ARCH'T.

12-15. Waterbury National Bank, Waterbury, Conn., 1920–21. (Cass Gilbert Collection, Archives Center, National Museum of American History)

utilized copies of Stuart and Revett's *Antiquities of Athens,* along with other mainstays of the study of classical architectural monuments such as the nineteenth-century volumes by Letarouilly and d'Espouy.[58] On the interior, by contrast, Gilbert used Adamesque details in prominent areas such as the ceiling of the vestibule. Clearly, if he could not create a neocolonial exterior, Gilbert at least was able to sport a few examples on the inside where the public's perception of the building was not as much at stake.

On a final note, the choice of location for the Waterbury National Bank (1919–22), at the corner of Grand and Field Streets, directly across from the Municipal Building and diagonally across from the Chase offices (Figure 12-15), reflects Gilbert's influence on Henry Chase. Before Chase died in 1918, he had planned to sell his property on this site to the YMCA, which needed expanded facilities close to downtown. Chase wanted Gilbert to design the building, but the YMCA president and building committee favored the hiring of an "expert architect" skilled in designing such structures, that is, not Gilbert.[59] However, representatives from the Y understood Chase's desire to request Gilbert. Although Gilbert was interested in the prospective work and in designing a red-brick structure (suited to the context of the Municipal Building as well as the nearby brick Social Welfare and Lodging Building and the Lincoln House that he had also designed for the Chase family), Gilbert confidentially wrote to Chase with a new idea. He suggested that Henry reserve this plot and not build anything on it until Chase could see the trend in real estate development after the Chase headquarters was completed. Gilbert ultimately advocated that the site should be used for a banking and corporate office center. He elaborated, "We used to think that the location of a court house or a public building on a street would increase its business value. As a matter of fact it does not do so

.... [In fact,] the presence of the YMCA would that much more isolate it [the property] from the business center."[60] Chase did not give in easily, because as he explained, "the public wants it [the YMCA] there ... and you should be the architect.... We don't want some botcher to get in on that lot of mine and muss all up our Grand St. dream."[61] To add to these issues, there was a fiscal problem: the YMCA had only approximately half the funds they needed to put up the kind of building they wanted. Even though Gilbert eventually was unanimously selected to be the architect, he refused to take the job because of the financial problems. In the end, the deal fell through, owing to complications with the Y's building committee. Henry Chase died suddenly a mere two months later, after this final blow. It is likely that Irving Chase (1858–1951), brother of Henry and Frederick, had heard of Gilbert's thoughts about the use of this property for a financial building, as the Waterbury National Bank, of which Irving was president, purchased the property several months later and proceeded to engage Gilbert to design a five- or six-story building, with bank space at street level and rental space above.[62] With this second Renaissance-revival structure on Grand Street, it is likely that Gilbert willingly chose to build in this idiom (and not a colonial one) to echo the Chase family's business headquarters and to distinguish it from city hall, the issue that had so concerned the family with their new offices.

In conclusion, both Seymour and several members of the Chase family were intimately involved with Gilbert in making design decisions for the many projects that were undertaken in their respective cities. In New Haven, by late 1917, the library had been completed and construction of Gilbert's railroad station was finally underway. Other discussions were pursued for a post office, a hotel, and other buildings, none of which were realized by Gilbert. But for Gilbert's first New Haven building, the Ives Memorial Library, Seymour had unstinting praise. Seymour expressed this admiration when he wrote, "... I had no idea how stunning the building was going to be.... To say I am pleased with the building is to express very inadequately how I feel about it. I am confident that no building that will ever be put up on the Green will surpass it in beauty, for it combines the solidity of a monumental building with a perfect grace and justness, an essential combination of qualities ... almost never achieved."[63] Henry Chase and his brothers were similarly satisfied in their roles as actively involved advisors and clients, although they never expressed themselves as eloquently as Seymour did.

Surely the interplay between architect and advisor or client is not the only determining factor in the development of architectural design. But for the projects in New Haven and Waterbury, Connecticut, both an advisor and a set of clients played a significant role in the architect's proposals for different kinds of municipal plans. In New Haven, Gilbert and Seymour were close allies, in agreement about major contextual issues such as responding to Hoadley's Federal-style United (North) Church. In Waterbury, when Gilbert tried to follow a similar formula as buildings were added by accretion at the behest of the Chase family, he was pressed to develop a different, Renaissance-revival idiom because of family members' concern about how their building might be perceived by the public. This decision further affected choices made with subsequent buildings, such as the Waterbury National Bank. Despite these differences in situation, geography, and milieu, however, Gilbert, Seymour, and many of the Chases all shared an engaging interest in creating new civic identities for their changing cities.

CHAPTER 13

THE UNIVERSITY OF TEXAS: VISION AND AMBITION

Lawrence W. Speck

During his thirteen-year tenure as campus architect, from 1909 to 1922, Cass Gilbert made a seminal contribution to the University of Texas that would have a profound and far-reaching impact on the development of that institution. From his very earliest sketches, Gilbert portrayed an image of the university that was far more ambitious and sophisticated than had been imagined previously. In his schemes for a campus master plan, his studies for a variety of campus buildings, and the two buildings he completed on the campus, Gilbert developed a fresh new architectural vision for what the University of Texas might become both as an entity and as a place. Gilbert's vision had enormous staying power, fundamentally influencing the architects who followed him and strongly affecting a large ensemble of buildings that was completed between 1922 and 1950. This ensemble represents one of the most coherent and well-planned groups of buildings on any American university campus. Though later architects such as Herbert M. Greene and Paul Cret made important contributions, it was Gilbert's selection of materials, his general stylistic vocabulary, and his orderly arrangement of axes and quadrangles that determined the shape of the distinguished campus that would eventually evolve.[1]

When Gilbert's involvement with the University of Texas began, the school's twenty-seven-year-old campus was a hodgepodge of mismatched buildings strung across a hilltop just north of Austin's central core.[2] The Old Main Building, begun in 1882 and placed near the center of the forty-acre campus, had been designed by Frederick E. Ruffini in a Victorian Gothic style that was common among American university buildings of the 1870s and 1880s.[3] Just east of Old Main was Brackenridge Hall, which originally was built as a plain-brick men's dormitory and later remodeled to incorporate a prickly series of towers with steeply pitched caps and elaborate ornamentation. A series of three buildings designed by San Antonio architects Charles A. Coughlin and Atlee B. Ayres shortly after the turn of the century rejected the Victorian vocabulary of earlier structures in favor of a variety of more contemporary idioms.[4] The Women's Building (1903), the Engineering Building (1904), and the Law Building (1908), individually and taken together, failed to define any clear architectural vocabulary that might direct the future development of the campus.

Though Coughlin and Ayres had prepared a formal campus master plan for the university when they began their work in 1903, the motley collection of buildings completed by 1909 was not built in accordance with any larger planning vision. The 1903 plan depicted a row of pavilion buildings around the southern half of the forty-acre campus, with a large tree-filled commons between the peripheral structures and Old Main at the center of the campus.[5] The scheme was rural in feeling and very unsophisticated compared with the plans that had been generated for other American campuses such as Stanford University and Columbia University a decade earlier. Little stock was put in the Coughlin and Ayers plan, even in the placement of the three buildings completed by the university between 1903 and 1908. Though the Women's Building could have been enlarged to comply with the scheme, both the Engineering Building and the Law School were sited in locations not in keeping with the master plan.

Dissatisfied with the piecemeal and disappointing results that they were getting from local Texas architects, President David Houston and Regent George Brackenridge began in early 1907 to search for a new campus architect who had the ability to provide greater architectural cohesion for the university and to incorporate sound campus planning principles. They settled on Frederick M. Mann, who was then head of the Department of Architecture at Washington University in St. Louis.[6] That university had held a widely publicized competition for their own campus master plan in 1899, which had been won by the firm Cope & Stewardson, beating out Cass Gilbert's own entry (see chapter 16). Mann had been involved in the implementation of that plan, establishing his own reputation as an advocate for campus design of high quality. Mann's plan for the University of Texas, completed in early 1909, maintained a large, open green space as its central feature, just as the 1903 plan had done.[7] Mann's college commons, however, was open to the city on its south face and had a more strongly defined, tree-lined axis at its center, connecting the university's main building visually with the state capitol on the hill beyond. The east, west, and north sides of the forty acres were much more densely developed than those in the 1903 plan. Uniform ranks of three-story buildings with hipped and gabled roofs defined a range of different courts and quadrangles on three flanks of the campus. Essentially walled off from the city except to the south, the scheme had a strong inward focus with specific quadrangles designed for natural sciences, engineering, visual arts, and language arts. Circulation between these tightly defined areas was minimal and somewhat mazelike.

Mann retained only the two most recent campus buildings in his own master plan, proposing the replacement of Old Main with a new structure that would become the architectural focus of the campus. The new building was capped by a monumental polygonal lantern that stood well above the roofs of surrounding buildings. University President David Houston had requested that the architectural character of the campus buildings be responsive to the Spanish legacy of Texas. The new main building met this criterion by combining a range of Spanish motifs drawn from Romanesque and baroque traditions.

Mann built only one building on the campus, the Power House at its western edge made of heavy limestone pavilions capped by red-tile roofs with very deep overhangs. He also completed, however, two private commissions across the street from the campus, the University Methodist Church to the northwest and a building for the YMCA midway along the university's western edge. Like the Power House, these buildings had a striking Mediterranean character with strong Romanesque roots. The church even had a polygonal lantern not unlike the one depicted in the master plan for the new main buildings of the campus.

Gilbert's energetic early sketch, conceived almost a year before he actually won the commission at Texas, illustrates the striking difference between the vision he conjured for a new university campus and the very timid-by-comparison visions that Coughlin and Ayers and Frederick Mann had for the University of Texas. Gilbert's sketch was influenced by the modest diagram of Thomas Jefferson's campus at University of Virginia but was expanded into a larger-than-life ensemble full of pomp and grandeur. As he commenced discussions with university officials, it was evident from the start that Gilbert was an architect with sweeping vision who sought to create a university of the first class.

13-1. Bird's-eye-view sketch and plan of South Mall, University of Texas, February 15, 1909. (Library of Congress)

Frederick Mann's work for the university did not provide the overall vision for the University of Texas that its leadership had sought. Even as drawings for Mann's scheme were still being completed, representatives of the university were making queries on its behalf in search of a new architect. Gilbert would have been a logical candidate on any well-conceived short list for such a position. Though Gilbert had been unsuccessful in his submission for the comprehensive plan for Washington University, by 1908 he had bolstered his campus planning credentials by winning the well-publicized competition for the University of Minnesota. As early as February 15, 1909, Gilbert made a conceptual sketch for the Texas campus (Figure 13-1) that had strong roots in his work for the Minnesota campus. The sketch illustrated a broad mall stepping up the hill to a very grand, domed University Hall. The mall was lined on either side by perpendicular, rectangular buildings similar to those in his Minnesota master plan. A monumental University Hall with its enormous flanking towers bore a strong resemblance to a similarly domed composition that was present in early versions of the Minnesota plan.

In June 1909 Gilbert responded to an inquiry from Colonel Edward M. House, brother-in-law to recently appointed university President Sidney E. Mezes.[8] (House was also a friend and advisor to President Woodrow Wilson and the client for a distinguished Shingle-style house in Austin designed by New York architect Frank Freeman.) Gilbert outlined his ideas about campus planning and architecture in broad strokes in his correspondence with House. In October of the same year, President Mezes visited Gilbert's office in New York, and the following month Mezes recommended that the university commence preparing a new general plan with a new architect. He advised, in fact, the creation of a new position of university architect and recommended that the best-qualified architect in the country who could be secured should be selected for the position. The following January, Gilbert made his first trip to Austin. He discussed with university officials his ideas for a new library, which was the highest priority for the university at that time. (Gilbert was, at that point, in the midst of designing both the St. Louis Public Library and the Ives Memorial Library in New Haven.) He investigated the forty-acre site, making a series of preliminary sketches for the campus and especially for a new University Hall at the top of the hill. On January 10, 1910, the Regents' Building Committee recommended Gilbert for the position of university architect, and he commenced design officially on both a new campus master plan and a new library building.[9]

At the age of fifty, Gilbert was at the peak of his career when he accepted the commission in Texas.[10] Recent projects in Ohio, Minnesota, Michigan, and Missouri as well as on the East Coast had established him as a nationally known architect. Beginning in 1908, he started to serve a term as president of the AIA. The University of Texas, after several abortive attempts, finally had found an architect of ambitious vision and national reputation capable of creating an enduring image for the campus and for the university.

Back in 1907 Gilbert had been invited to participate in a limited competition for a new central library for St. Louis, which he won after two stages of submissions. His scheme, though quite innovative, was based significantly on McKim, Mead & White's Boston Public Library (1888–95), which in turn had been based on Henri Labrouste's Bibliothèque Ste.-Geneviève in Paris.[11] The libraries in St. Louis, Boston, and Paris took the Italian Renaissance *palazzo* as a starting point, placing more mundane library functions on a ground floor behind heavy walls with simple, spare openings. Reading rooms and other more gracious library spaces were lifted to an upper *piano nobile* with high ceilings, tall arched windows, and monumental exterior treatment. Having worked for McKim, Mead & White in their New York offices (1880–82), Gilbert was well equipped to elaborate on and refine the Boston scheme in his St. Louis project.

The Texas library, which Gilbert began to conceive in 1909, was much more modest in scope than either the Boston or St. Louis municipal works. The budget at St. Louis was almost two-and-a-half times that of the Texas project, and its program required four major reading/display rooms, whereas the university library needed only one. From his earliest soft-pencil sketches, Gilbert conceived the Texas library as a *palazzo* but of a very different sort than what might have been the prototype for St. Louis. Its smaller scale allowed the building to sit as a free-standing pavilion rather than filling an urban block. Its hipped tile roof became a distinctive cap for an object building rather than another horizontal layer in a broader composition. Deep shadowy roof overhangs distinguished the Texas library from its more northern counterparts,

and a more festive, lively character—even present in early drawings—indicated a distinctly different feeling from the dour edifices in Boston and St. Louis.

A watercolor rendering of the library's east elevation, dated March 19, 1910 (Figure 13-2), illustrates a well-proportioned, two-story building with a rusticated stone base punctuated by eight rectangular windows and an arched central entry portal. A more elaborate upper floor was articulated with a series of nine tall arched windows alternating with pilasters that supported an ornate frieze under broad eaves. Ornamental balconies topped a dominant stringcourse, which separated the two floors on the facade, and lanterns of similar treatment flanked the doorway. A later perspective drawing (Figure 13-3) indicated the same general approach but with some significant changes and refinements. The two floors

received identical stone treatment without the heavier base that had been indicated in the earlier scheme. Seven, rather than nine, arched windows punctuated the facade with proportions more robust than in the previous version. The pilasters disappeared but were replaced by an ornamental treatment along the arched portion of the monumental windows, similar to that employed at the Boston Public Library (and very different from the window treatment at the St. Louis Public Library). Rondels, similar in size and placement to those employed in the entry portal at St. Louis, were located on each side of the arched openings. Terra cotta tiles were also added in the deeply recessed upper floor openings around the windows. Detailed ornament in the tiles was matched by a

13-2. Watercolor rendering of east elevation of Library (Battle Hall), University of Texas, March 19, 1910. (©Collection of the New-York Historical Society, neg. #59039)

13-3. Perspective view from the southeast of the Library (Battle Hall), University of Texas. (©Collection of th4e New-York Historical Society, neg. #74380)

highly articulated, bracketed soffit under the building's dominant roof cap. The exuberance and delicacy of the ironwork balconies and terra cotta ornament and the ornate treatment of the eaves set the Texas library apart from its counterparts in Boston and St. Louis. The cream-colored Texas limestone used for its construction was also softer and gentler than the granite employed in the earlier buildings. The feeling of this new scheme was fresh and original, more southern in character with its deep shadows and bright colors to counterbalance the bleaching effect of the strong sun; less tough and urban than its big-city precedents.

As built, Gilbert's Texas library, named Battle Hall in 1973 after Dr. William J. Battle, longtime chair of the university's faculty building committee, was almost identical (Figure 13-4) to the perspective rendering. The only substantial change was that the proposed balustraded terrace in front was never constructed. The terra cotta window surrounds were executed in lively greens, yellows, and blues and depict-

ed appropriate iconographical images for a library, including open books, torches, and lamps of enlightenment. The owl, which Gilbert had used in the attic story of the St. Louis Public Library, was employed repeatedly, both in the terra cotta surrounds and to support the brackets of the deep eave overhangs. The signs of the zodiac (which Gilbert also had employed in St. Louis) provided the theme for the twelve rondels, beginning with the start of the calendar year on the south side of the building, working sequentially around the east facade, and terminating on the north face (Figure 13-5).

Inside, a low barrel-vaulted passageway led from the east entry through the front volume of the T-shaped building to a well-lit stair hall. Winding marble stairs, with a gracefully detailed wrought-iron balustrade, ascended to a compact, polygonal delivery hall. Located at the very center of the building, the delivery hall was capped by a domed glass skylight. West of the stairway and delivery hall, and completing the rear leg of the building's T shape, were the

library stacks. The most elaborate interior space was the reading room on the upper floor of the east wing behind the great arched windows (Figure 13-6). Its plain limestone walls were topped by elaborate wood-faced trusses, very similar to those Gilbert had proposed for the interior of the Finney Memorial Chapel at Oberlin College in 1907 (see chapter 14). Similar in character to many Spanish and Italian Romanesque buildings, the Battle Hall trusses employed elaborate ornamental brackets and exposed metal straps to provide a robust, tectonic feeling. They were colorfully stenciled with largely geometric patterns, including lone stars like that on the Texas flag.

The east wing of Battle Hall was constructed of load-bearing masonry walls with limestone quarried in nearby Cedar Park. Openings were filled with terra cotta tiles and wood windows. The deep eaves under the hipped red-tile roof were made of a combination of wood boards and carved wood. The wing of the building containing library stacks was constructed as

a steel cage with low floor-to-floor heights and structural marble slabs as the complete floor/ceiling assembly. The very different exterior treatment of the more utilitarian volume was evident elsewhere in Gilbert's work. The west facade of Battle Hall (now covered) originally had vertical strips of windows alternating with stone piers, very similar to the treatment used on the north-facing stack wing at the St. Louis Public Library.

Battle Hall currently houses the Architecture and Planning Library and a portion of the School of Architecture at the University of Texas.[12] The building's exterior has been very well maintained and is in excellent condition, with the current paint carefully matched to the original colors. Interior functions have remained similar to those initially planned for the building, with offices, conference rooms, and special collections on the ground floor and primary library functions operating from the reading room and delivery hall on the upper floor.

13-4. View of Library (Battle Hall) from the east, University of Texas, 1911. (Photograph by Debbie Sharp, 1984)

By the end of 1910 Gilbert had completed and submitted the first version of his master plan for the University of Texas campus, including a sparely drawn ground plan and a bird's eye perspective (Figure 13-7). A very similar, but more detailed ground plan is documented in a drawing dated August 15, 1914 (Figure 13-8). Unlike the Mann scheme of 1909, most existing buildings on the campus were retained and cleverly integrated into the new plan. One significant removal, however, was Ruffini's Old Main Building, which was replaced by a new University Hall accommodating administrative offices and a large assembly room. The dominant new structure at the center of the forty acres was a linchpin for the plan, serving as the terminus of four axes that divided the campus into roughly equal quadrants. The south axis was clearly primary, introduced

by a wide main plaza in front of University Hall. Gilbert's new library created the western edge of the plaza and was matched by a projected building of similar massing to the east. Perpendicular to the main plaza was a broad tree-lined south mall that created the critical visual connection between University Hall on the north end and the dome of the state capitol on the south end of a grand urban axis.

The southwest quadrant below the new library was the only area unencumbered by existing structures. For it, Gilbert proposed an almost square courtyard with long, thin buildings on each of the four sides. The two westernmost corners were filled with small squarish structures while the easternmost corner buildings projected farther out to create anchors at the edge of the south mall. The new library and a companion structure on the north side of the quadrant similarly defined the border of the west mall that connected a major campus entry point on Guadalupe Street to the end axis of University Hall.

The southeast quadrant began with a similar approach but was altered to accommodate two very oddly positioned existing buildings. The 1908 Law Building became the centerpiece for a composition of new buildings that took the general spirit of the parallel face of the southwest quadrant and repositioned its elements slightly. The result was a well-balanced and compositionally strong southern edge of the campus with a new image that incorporated the Law Building as an integral part. Brackenridge Hall at the northern edge of the same quadrant was used similarly to create a minor north-south axis that became the focus of a new courtyard on its south side. Although the east axis of University Hall was located so as to just miss the northern end of Brackenridge Hall, it was here that the strain of incorporating existing buildings into the new plan became most evident. Dealt with very cleverly, Brackenridge Hall was still a bit awkward in relation to the east mall.

In the northeast quadrant, Mann's L-shaped Power House formed one corner of a courtyard that Gilbert completed with two similar L-shaped structures and the existing 1904 Engineering Building. Mann's building, in fact, became more natural and appropriate in Gilbert's master plan than it had been

13-5. Exterior detail of east facade of Library (Battle Hall), University of Texas, 1911. (Photograph by Debbie Sharp, 1984)

13-6. View of Reading Room of Library (Battle Hall), University of Texas, at end of construction. (©Collection of the New-York Historical Society, neg. #74381)

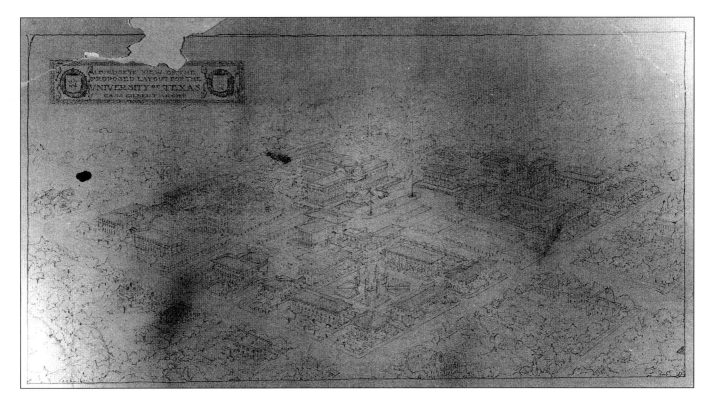

in his own. The northwest quadrant similarly incorporated two existing buildings with three new L-shaped structures and one linear building to form a fourth well-defined academic court. For all three quadrants with problematic existing buildings, Gilbert created a seeming inevitability out of difficult exigencies and demonstrated his extraordinary skill in responding to local conditions without allowing them to destroy his larger conceptual framework.

The strength of that conceptual framework has proved very potent indeed. The powerful monument at the focus of well-defined linear public spaces gave an appropriate civic grandeur to the campus that the University of Texas needed. And yet, the smaller-scaled courtyards at each of the four corners, defined by a series of more modest and variable buildings, provided the campus with intimate personal spaces for individual collegiate components. Both as a whole and in individual parts, Gilbert's master plan had great dignity and presence. It was sophisticated without being intimidating. It was visionary but also very practical. Even ninety years later, the original site remains fundamentally organized according to Gilbert's ideas of what a campus for the University of Texas should and could become.

Active planning for the second building designed by Gilbert for the University of Texas did not begin until 1915, and it was not completed until early 1918. It was a general-purpose academic building located in the southwest quadrant of the campus on the north side of what was to be an academic court in the master plan. Although the 1914 master plan rendering indicated flanking projections at each end of the north face of the building, the final version became a simple long rectangle with a double-loaded corridor down the center and a perpendicular entry hall at its midpoint. Despite the fact that the Education Building was very near Gilbert's recent library, there was, curiously, little functional or formal relationship between the two. The library faced east toward the proposed new main plaza, with only a basement door on the south side toward the newer building. The Education Building faced south, toward the projected academic court and distinctly away from the library to the northeast (Figure 13-9). Because of the topography in this area, the Education Building also sat a full twelve feet lower than the library, which had been placed near the top of the hill.

In an undated watercolor rendering of the elevation of the Education Building (Figure 13-10),

13-7. "Bird's-eye-view of the Proposed Layout for the University of Texas," n.d. [c. 1911]. (Center for American History, The University of Texas at Austin)

THE UNIVERSITY OF TEXAS

Gilbert included nearly all of the elements that would eventually constitute the structure. These included a smooth stone ashlar first floor with arched openings; a second and third floor of contrasting material (perhaps stucco in the rendering); an even rhythm of regular rectangular windows in the center of the long facade syncopated by a more highly ornamental vertical stack of windows on each end; a colorful, highly articulated frieze of ornament under the eaves with heavy brackets; and a red-tile roof with deep overhanging projections. The building as built differed from the rendering, however, in several important ways. The material on the second and third floors of the Education Building became a distinctive textured brick of variegated color ranging from tan to ochre, orange, and brown. The number of windows in the midsection was increased from ten to eleven, and the entry portals stretched from two to three openings, creating a more classic odd number of bays. An elaborate terra cotta attic treatment was created to encompass the midsection windows on the third floor, and balconies were transferred from second-floor windows up to the third floor.

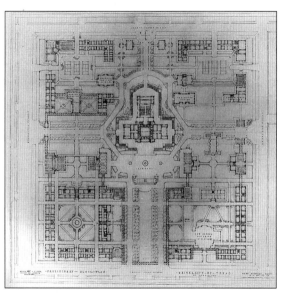

13-8. "Preliminary Block Plan: University of Texas at Austin," del., Phillips, August 15, 1914. (© Collection of the New-York Historical Society, neg. #59142)

Later named Sutton Hall for William Seneca Sutton (who was the first dean of the School of Education), the new building added a distinctly different vocabulary to Gilbert's vision for the campus, beyond that established by the library. Both buildings relied on the Renaissance palazzo as a precedent but differed substantially in scale, material usage, color, and detail. Although the scale of the library was elevated by the huge double-story windows and the unified facades made of large limestone blocks, the scale of the Education Building was diminished by the use of several different wall materials, both horizontally

and vertically. The brick and terra cotta as well as paint colors on the Education Building were much darker than those on the library, and the rough texture of the brick produced a ruddier, less refined building character. The stone selected was from a quarry in a different part of Texas and had a much darker, grayer hue. Even the roof tiles were a deeper red and more variegated in color than those on the library. The construction methods used for the Education Building differed as well. The exterior walls on the bottom two floors and on the ends of the third floor were load-bearing masonry, whereas the interior support of the building and the exterior support in the midportion of the third floor were provided by a reinforced concrete frame.

The School of Architecture at the University of Texas currently occupies Sutton Hall, which was renovated substantially in 1980.[13] The general structure of rooms opening off a wide central corridor was carefully retained in that renovation, though the exact partitioning of spaces was altered. Two grand rooms with vaulted ceilings at each end of the third floor were recovered for use as open studios. The only substantial changes to the exterior were the addition of a new entry portal on the north side of the building, which generally resembles the original south-side entry, and a dormer window on the north face of the roof to provide natural light for newly occupied space in the attic. In 1998 the exterior of the building was completely restored, returning finishes and details to near-mint condition.

Several hundred surviving documents illustrate Gilbert's various proposals for other campus buildings between 1909 and 1922. Besides the library and the Education Building, the single element most frequently depicted in those documents is Gilbert's unrealized University Hall, which was to be the centerpiece for the campus. Three distinctly different approaches to the building were studied. In the February 15, 1909, sketch noted earlier (see Figure 13-1), University Hall was rendered as an ornate domed structure with a monumental portico on the front and enormous towers to either side. The composition was distinctly baroque at a grand scale.

13-9. Education Building (Sutton Hall), University of Texas, from the northeast at end of construction. (Cass Gilbert Collection, Archives Center, National Museum of American History)

13-10. Watercolor rendering of south elevation of Education Building (Sutton Hall), University of Texas, n.d. [c. 1916]. (©New-York Historical Society)

University of Texas – Jany 2 1910

13-11. Sketch of south
elevation for University
Hall, University of Texas,
January 12, 1910.
(Library of Congress)

University Hall lorded over the buildings on the south mall below. A simpler, though still quite grand dome with more restrained classical roots capped the version of University Hall depicted in a 1911 colored cross-section drawing taken through the entire campus and indicating Gilbert's new library beside the central monument. As late as a pencil sketch dated October 5, 1920, Gilbert revisited the dome as a focus for the campus, this time flanked again by towers.[14]

A second approach by Gilbert created a pedimented temple at the center of the campus, a notion he had used in his entry for the University of Minnesota competition. In a sketch dated January 12, 1910 (Figure 13-11), University Hall was portrayed as a mammoth structure, three times the height of the library to its side and festooned with elaborate ornament above a giant colonnade. The temple version of University Hall was elaborated in a number of other studies, including some that depicted a two-tiered building with a large gabled volume at the scale of the

city and a lower pedimented portico scaling down to adjacent campus structures.

The third distinct approach Gilbert experimented with for University Hall was a single very tall tower. In a small pencil sketch from 1920 (Figure 13-12), he portrayed a hefty shaft rising from a low, flat base not unlike Bertram Goodhue's Nebraska state capitol that had been conceived the previous year. A similar undated sketch of probably the same period depicted a tower with a pointed peak and a prominent clock at its top. By the 1920s Gilbert had become famous for his towers. The Woolworth Building in New York, which he completed in 1913, was the tallest building in the world until 1930, and his Union Central Life Insurance Company Building in Cincinnati was the fifth tallest building when it was constructed.[15]

Clearly, Gilbert's studies for University Hall and also his sketches for other projects (such as a gymnasium and an outdoor amphitheater) depict a very broad architectural vocabulary that he imagined for the campus. Just as the Education Building was quite different from the library, both of them were very different from his proposals for University Hall. Gilbert's vision for the whole campus therefore was inclusive, encompassing existing campus buildings of disparate styles as well as a range of new building expressions designed in reaction to functional and site dictates. This attitude was consistent with his work on the Oberlin College campus in roughly the same period. Gilbert portrayed the college campus, not as a cookie-cutter, military-style collection of uniform buildings but as an assemblage of diverse structures, related and carefully coordinated with each other but not constrained by an artificial stylistic code.

In 1922, the regents decided not to renew Gilbert's contract, and for almost a decade, the role of university architect was filled by Herbert M. Greene and his firm, Greene, La Roche & Dahl, from Dallas.[16] Greene's excellent work in this period followed both general and specific intentions that Gilbert had established. Garrison Hall of 1925, for example, was placed opposite the library, creating the eastern edge of the main plaza as outlined in the master plan. Its architectural character was very similar to that for the Education Building, with a stone base, brick upper stories with generous terra cotta ornament, and a red-tile roof. In the spirit of Gilbert's acceptance of diversity, Greene created an iconographic palette for Garrison Hall which was very different from that of the library or the Education Building. Built for the history department, the building's ornament depicts the heritage of Texas with names of political heroes, branding irons from historic ranches, and emblematic symbols like longhorns, bluebonnets, cacti, and lone stars. Gilbert's hand was clear in the building's general orchestration, but Greene had the freedom to customize as well.

In the ten or so buildings Greene designed, there is a broad range of stylistic liberty but still a conscientious effort to create a coherent whole. His men's gymnasium of 1930, for example, was designed in a sober Lombard style[17] with no bright terra cotta ornament, but its use of a variegated brick similar to that of the Education Building made it comfortably a part of the larger campus. Although two new versions of a

campus master plan were produced in 1923 and 1926 by James M. White of the University of Illinois, the proposals were not influential. Even the Greene-designed buildings that were built after the late 1920s (e.g., Waggener Hall and the Chemistry Building, both 1931) were placed according to Gilbert's scheme rather than White's.

In March 1930 the university appointed Philadelphia architect Paul Phillipe Cret as a consultant to design a new library. At the time, French-born and Beaux-Arts-educated Cret was teaching at the University of Pennsylvania as well as heading a thriving

practice. The university had outgrown the 250,000-volume capacity of Gilbert's library and had decided that expansion of it was not feasible to meet long-term needs. During the 1930s Cret designed sixteen buildings for the university and in 1933 created a new master plan (Figure 13-13) that guided the development of the campus through the 1940s and well beyond the original forty acres. What Cret pro-

13-12. Sketch of south elevation for University Hall, University of Texas, October 1920. (©Collection of the New-York Historical Society, neg. #59038)

THE UNIVERSITY OF TEXAS

13-13. Paul Cret, Bird's-eye-view from the southwest of campus master plan, University of Texas, 1933. (Paul Phillipe Cret drawings, The Alexander Architectural Archive, The General Libraries, The University of Texas at Austin)

posed for the area Gilbert had planned was remarkably similar to Gilbert's own scheme. A main building of grand scale was placed at the focus of four axes, creating four roughly equal quadrants. Cret admired Gilbert's "plaza in front of the Main Building and the South Mall approach" and reiterated these two features almost verbatim. He even lined the mall with perpendicular buildings alternating with courts, almost exactly like those Gilbert proposed in his earliest schemes but modified somewhat in later versions. In each of the four quadrants, Cret created an academic court, with each court taking its own distinct character just as Gilbert had suggested. Cret's east mall and west mall were narrower than Gilbert's but retained essentially the same location and role in the larger plan.

The vocabulary of Cret's buildings certainly owes a debt to Gilbert's in their general character and materials. But, perhaps more significantly, Cret also adopted Gilbert's liberal attitude about the range of styles and building forms that should energize the campus and keep its development lively and progressive over time. Some of Cret's designs, like that for the lower part of the main building, are strongly influenced by the same kind of monumental Mediterranean classicism that inspired Gilbert's library. Others, such as the Geology Building and the Physics Building, owe a great deal to Gilbert's Education Building with their stone base, second and third floors in variegated buff brick, and red-tile roofs. Still others, such as the Union and the Architecture Building, were rendered in more picturesque, vernacular styles with asymmetrical massing punctuated by towers and characterized by varied, sometimes irregular fenestration. Original versions of these buildings even had rubble stone walls and crafted wooden balconies, very different from, but compatible with, the clear, regular *palazzi* Gilbert designed nearby. By the end of the 1930s, Cret had completed an Art Deco gem, the Texas Memorial Museum, which related strongly to the rest of the campus in placement, scale, and materials. It also substantiated by its clean, modern lines Cret's desire for the campus vocabulary to allow for progress and innovation. Cret's centerpiece for the campus, the University of Texas Tower, also has Art Deco touches in its shaft but is crowned by a classical lantern. In its vertical punctuation atop a low horizontal base and in its bold scale, it was comfortably aligned with Gilbert's earlier schemes for a tower as the focus for the campus.

The forty or so projects that were designed according to the intentions of Gilbert, Greene, and Cret from 1909 to the end of the 1940s represent an extraordinary campus ensemble of great character and vitality. These buildings have created a distinctive and highly valued image of the university that helps to define it to this day. Though Cret is often given great credit because of the number of buildings he had a hand in, Cass Gilbert was the seminal and sustaining design force in the development of the University of Texas campus. The vision, sophistication, and ambition he brought to his service as campus architect left an indelible mark on the University of Texas.

CHAPTER 14

OBERLIN: THE GRAND COLLABORATION

Geoffrey Blodgett

In January 1903 fire destroyed the old chapel that stood on the campus green of Oberlin College in northern Ohio. That fire proved to be the catalyst for an early-twentieth-century building program that left the college with the most distinctive cluster of Cass Gilbert buildings anywhere. This happy outcome resulted from a grand collaboration between Gilbert and Henry Churchill King, Oberlin's president from 1902 to 1927.

Gilbert and King, while differing from one another by background and calling, belonged to a generation of educated Americans for whom culture was a seamless web, and shared a conviction that an attractive visual environment was crucial to the nurture of a virtuous life. King graduated from Oberlin in 1879, the same year Gilbert finished his brief architectural training at MIT. Oberlin carried into the twentieth century a proud tradition of missionary education that celebrated coeducation, temperance, racial equity, and academic striving among its salient values. The aesthetic dimension of campus life had not loomed large among these values over the first half-century since the college was founded in 1833, and its architectural deposit remained offhand and ordinary. King changed that. An ordained minister, he joined the faculty in 1884 to teach mathematics and later philosophy and theology. Early on, his colleagues began to think of him as an obvious presidential prospect. A vigorous foot soldier in the Protestant Social Gospel movement of the 1890s, he also had a knack for persuasive leadership that would make his presidency the longest in Oberlin's history.

Soon after his inauguration, King set to work on the college's most urgent building needs—a new chapel, an administration building, and (owing to the recent gift of a large private art collection) an art museum. He was determined to achieve architectural coherence and quality—the best the college could afford. First he asked the Olmsted Brothers of Boston, sons of the pioneering landscape architect Frederick Law Olmsted, to prepare a campus master plan. The Olmsted report, delivered in June 1903, guided campus development into the future with impressive clarity. It called for removal of all buildings from the central campus green, where the old chapel had stood with several other obsolete structures, turning the green into a thirteen-acre open "pleasure ground," later called Tappan Square, to be shared by town and gown. New college buildings were to front the square on all sides, and a quadrangle of academic buildings—including a new chapel—was to be developed west of the square, with dormitories and athletic facilities to the north and south of that. The Olmsteds envisioned a rectilinear campus landscape in line with the urban planning ideas emerging from the Chicago World's Columbian Exposition of 1893, their father's last important public project.[1]

With the Olmsted guide in hand, King invited Frederick Norton Finney, son of Oberlin's famous nineteenth-century evangelist, Charles Grandison Finney, to suggest an architect for the new chapel that the son, a prospering western railroader, proposed to donate as a memorial to his father. Finney did not know much about architecture, but he believed in getting the best. He sent King two names, "Kim" and Gilbert. "Kim" turned out to be Charles McKim of McKim, Mead & White, the country's leading architectural firm. Gilbert was a "very artistic fellow," Finney wrote, whose reputation stood high among the country's younger architects, owing to his surprising victory (over McKim, Mead & White, among others) in the competition for the United States Custom House, a five-million-dollar Beaux-Arts monument then rising in lower Manhattan.[2]

When King invited both Gilbert and McKim, Mead & White to enter a competition for the Oberlin chapel commission, both promptly declined, but Gilbert added that he would consider an outright offer of the job if its working budget promised a substantial building of permanent quality. Gilbert's self-confident candor impressed King. After winning assurances from Finney about an adequate budget, he went to New York in April 1904 to talk the matter through with Gilbert and wound up handing him the job.

During this meeting Gilbert made a pencil sketch of a building that closely resembles the chapel he completed for the college four years later. His basic design survived one of the roughest relationships he ever endured with a donor, since Finney objected repeatedly to the cost and wisdom of his design decisions, notwithstanding earlier assurances. Despite the donor's bullheaded behavior, the years from 1904 to 1908 also launched a collaboration between Gilbert and King that spanned two more decades and produced several more Gilbert buildings for the college, an architectural legacy that dominates the campus to this day.

King's leadership skills were tested from the outset by rival priorities at issue in the program for the new chapel. His on-campus building committee, responding to pressures from the college's conservatory of music, stressed the chapel's use for musical performances and was pleased that its dimensions would match almost exactly those of the new music hall in Boston designed by McKim, Mead & White. Donor Finney, who placed a $100,000 ceiling on building costs, wanted a building that could seat some two thousand people, easily filled and emptied, with good acoustics, of which visiting speakers could say, "Here is the best audience chamber on the continent." Gilbert himself worried about the conflicts he detected in the building's functions. He told King, "It is not difficult to make a design for a chapel *or* for a music hall, but it is difficult to make a design for both chapel and music hall in one, in which the chapel shall not be submerged in the music hall. . . . [A] place of worship should assume the ecclesiastical aspect which bears out the association of long usage and tradition, all of which means that a church should look like a church and not like a place of amusement."[3]

14-1. Normand Patten, Warner Gymnasium, 1900, Oberlin College. (Photograph by Geoffrey Blodgett)

Stylistic issues also vexed the planning process. A number of influential Oberlinians favored the Gothic, hoping to bring some coherence to the highly eclectic post–Civil War accumulation of campus buildings. Finney cared little for external appearances but admitted his affection for the old Greek-revival meetinghouse on the northeast corner of the square, where his father the evangelist had preached for forty years. Gilbert's reputation rested on his known mastery of Beaux-Arts neoclassicism, but for Oberlin he reached for something altogether different. During his first visit to the campus in 1904, its architecture dismayed him. He privately called it "fussy" and "stupid." An exception was a new gymnasium (1900) near the chapel site, designed by Chicago architect Normand Patten (Figure 14-1). Its rectangular footprint, buff sandstone walls, round-arched fenestration, and low-pitched red-tile roof were to Gilbert's eye "quiet, simple, and well-proportioned." He decided to translate these traits into his design for the chapel.[4]

For historical inspiration he reached back to the twelfth-century Romanesque churches of northern Italy, including those at Assisi and Perugia that he had contemplated during a journey to that region years before. The Romanesque had for him the virtues of pliability and relatively modest cost. In contrast to classical and Gothic architecture, the Romanesque allowed exterior ornament to concentrate at particular focal points, leaving broad surfaces elsewhere unadorned. "In short," he wrote, "it is the simplest and most straightforward type of architecture, absolutely without affectation." This resonated with what he had learned so far about Oberlin's institutional mood.[5]

The focal point in Gilbert's design for Finney Chapel was the front entry at the base of its great gabled eastern facade (Figure 14-2). The entry resembled the portal of St. Bartholomew's Church in New York City, designed by Gilbert's former mentor Stanford White in 1902. White's portal had been inspired in turn by the porch entry to St. Gilles du

Gard in Arles that he had visited on a tour of southern France in 1878. Gilbert expressed vast enthusiasm for White's design. But his entry for Finney Chapel is much more compacted and modestly ornamented than that for either St. Gilles or St. Bartholomew, thus adding strength to his chapel's gabled face as a whole (Figure 14-3).[6]

By early 1906 Gilbert was confident that his detailed plans were ready for final approval. "I feel very enthusiastic about the design," he wrote. "It is just the kind of building I would like to build. It is quiet, serious, and strong. It will be impressive by its simplicity." However, the college had given the donor veto power over the design, and Finney proceeded to exercise it quite willfully. He told King that Gilbert's chapel was "very heavy and unfinished," and that its interior arrangements were inferior to those of Oberlin's First Church meetinghouse, which his father had helped design sixty years before. Some of his proposed changes staggered Gilbert. He called for a fan-shaped building with semicircular seating. He raised the seating capacity to three thousand while maintaining the original budget cap. He favored exterior walls of yellow brick rather than stone to reduce costs. He wanted the bell tower enlarged, shifted, or removed. He wondered why the steel trusswork under the ceiling had to be covered with wood.[7]

Finney was not the most ornery donor Gilbert had ever experienced. A dozen years earlier, another western railroader, James J. Hill of the Great Northern and other railways, had insulted him by demeaning his work for the campus of St. Paul Seminary in Minnesota (see Figures 1-11 and 1-12), but the architect had come some distance since that youthful encounter. He now responded to Finney's critiques with cool professional reserve. Here are some of his rebuttals: "These are questions of design to which I have given thoughtful study, and are not matters of chance or whim." "I suppose that my clients presume that I will not design that which can not be built." "If I am to design the building you must leave matters of this kind strictly to me, for otherwise I can be of no service to you." Gilbert indicated that he could make the chapel as plain as a warehouse of brick or galvanized iron but could not be held responsible for the results. Finney remained undeterred by these shafts, and only after Gilbert as architect, Oberlin as client, and Finney as donor each had announced at one time or another withdrawal from the project was an agreement struck among them at last in April 1907 to build according to Gilbert's favored design—provided the chapel was completed by commencement in June 1908, the seventy-fifth anniversary of Oberlin's founding. Gilbert had survived with his professional authority intact but with only thirteen months to finish the job.[8]

In its own way, the commencement deadline proved to be highly constricting on Gilbert's hopes for the chapel. From New York he lashed the building's contractor whenever he heard of delays. "The

College must have," he wrote, "and IS GOING TO HAVE this building for use at the time provided in your contract. If your further progress and management of the work is not improved in the near future, . . . the work will be completed by other parties and at your expense."[9]

Meanwhile details of ornament and color preoccupied him. When Cleveland sculptor Stephen Gladwin, hired to prepare capitals for the columns of the main entry, sent photos of them to New York for Gilbert's inspection, the architect replied by telegraph, "Not satisfactory in any respect." His instructions for improvement were precise. He wanted "the leafage to be much sharper and more accented . . . ,

14-2. Finney Chapel, 1908, Oberlin College. (Oberlin College Archives, Oberlin, Ohio)

the spaces between the volutes and back of the leaves to be very sharply and deeply cut . . ., the eagle and the foliage to be strong and vigorous." Gladwin met expectations on his second try.[10]

Gilbert urged the college to seek out alumni gifts to brighten the chapel interior with stained-glass memorial windows, bronze plaques, carefully selected mural tones, and geometric figures in gold, green, blue, and red on horizontal trusses overhead, the latter to be modeled after the trusswork in the Church of San Miniato in Florence. "[T]his building is so simple in its form," he wrote of his chapel, "that the interior without color would be very barren and uninteresting." The college failed to fund any of Gilbert's recommendations, and shortly before the

14-3. Entry, Finney Chapel, 1908, Oberlin College. (Photograph by Geoffrey Blodgett)

chapel opened for use, its interior walls were painted an institutional off-white. They remained that way for the next seventy-five years, barren and uninteresting. In 1976 architect Robert Venturi perceptively described Finney Chapel as a "Protestant auditorium," though he went on to acknowledge that from the perspective of the 1970s the quality of workmanship and materials in Gilbert's Oberlin buildings was "enviable."[11]

Gilbert's climactic frustration was the fate of the rose window planned for the chapel's great gable. Finney suggested a tracery window, "something such as Tiffany would be apt to get up," for about five hundred dollars—an unrealistically low figure. Gilbert

much preferred a window to be designed by his artist friend Kenyon Cox, rich in color and biblical imagery, rather than "the work of a commercial stained glass establishment." Finney backed away from both Cox's cost estimates and his religious symbolism, and so this last stand-off between architect and donor was never resolved. Over the years Oberlinians came to regard the dark glass hole where the rose window was intended as a normal part of the chapel's somber Protestant mood.[12]

Both Gilbert and President King came away from the creation of Finney Chapel chastened by its troubles, but also with a deepened respect for one another. Gilbert grudgingly admired King's patient negotiation skills—so crucial to the broader success of his presidency—while King noted the efficiency of Gilbert's office and the high caliber of the work that came out of it. He also appreciated Gilbert's keen interest in the Oberlin campus. In 1911, for example, while vacationing on the Maine coast, Gilbert sent King an unsolicited series of building sketches showing what could be created for the campus if Oberlin were to purchase the arches and ornament left over from the recent demolition of Henry Hobson Richardson's Cincinnati Chamber of Commerce building. This brilliant suggestion died in committee, but four months later, with strong support from key trustees, King decided to make Gilbert the general architect of the college, with the authority for campus planning and the design of all important new buildings.

Gilbert promptly recommended that the college once more retain the Olmsted Brothers of Boston as landscape design consultants. King agreed. Together Gilbert and the Olmsteds proceeded to refine the recommendations made by the brothers a decade earlier into a new master plan for campus development. They proposed a highly architectonic plan, reminiscent of plans for the Mall in Washington, D.C., that Gilbert had helped formulate years before (see Figure 3-2), and of Daniel Burnham's plan for downtown Cleveland—both inspired by Chicago's White City of 1893. Long navelike vistas, lined with Olmsted plantings, mostly elms, would take off from Tappan Square toward adjacent quadrangles, terminating in major new campus buildings, all to be designed by Gilbert.

The first of these was a new administration building, tucked between Finney Chapel and towering old Peters Hall along the square's western edge— a location Gilbert accepted only after assurances that Peters would soon come down. The building was named for Jacob Dolson Cox, an Oberlin graduate famous in his day as a Civil War general, governor of Ohio, secretary of interior under Grant, five-term Ohio congressman, and finally a university dean and president. One of Cox's sons was the artist Kenyon Cox; another was Cleveland industrialist Jacob Dolson Cox Jr. The latter gave the money for the administration building. In striking contrast to the donor of Finney Chapel, he remained a virtually invisible presence during the creation of the structure commemorating his father. Cox Administrative Building, the smallest of Gilbert's Oberlin buildings, is an oblong box of smooth-cut sandstone, two stories high with a red-tile hip roof (Figure 14-4). Size aside, it is similar in external appearance to the library (now Battle Hall) (see Figure 13-4) that Gilbert completed for the University of Texas in 1911.

The east entry to Cox is among Oberlin's most attractive. Its history is complex. Gilbert had ordered from Italy a Venetian Byzantine doorway, which on arrival was found to be cracked along its upper edge. Even with repairs it would be vulnerable to Ohio weather, so Gilbert had it placed in storage for future indoor use and instructed Stephen Gladwin to carve a doorway for Cox similar to the Venetian import.

Next Gilbert invited Samuel Yellin of Philadelphia, a Jewish immigrant from Poland soon to be recognized as America's preeminent decorative metalworker, to fashion a wrought-iron grille for the transom over the entry. Yellin's gratitude for this commission was life-long. When Gilbert died in 1934, he wrote to Gilbert's son, "You will be interested to learn that when I have established my workshop some 25 years ago,—it was your dear father who gave me my very first opportunity (for the Oberlin College). . . . May God give you the strength to bear your great loss, and to carry on the high standard of truly beautiful work created by that great master: Cass Gilbert."[13]

For the vestibule inside the entry, Kenyon Cox painted two lunette-shaped murals, rich in symbol

and allegory, in honor of his father and mother. For the same space he also designed a bronze plaque celebrating his father's civic achievements, the plaque executed by Frances Grimes, a student of Augustus Saint-Gaudens. In the building's lobby, Gilbert changed the design of the stairway as construction proceeded, replacing plans for a pierced ornamental balustrade with a simple round-edged cement staircase and smooth brass handrail, lending a modern touch to the lobby. While the office spaces in Cox have proved rather inelastic over the years, it remains a satisfactory administrative headquarters. Since the 1960s it has been the building of choice for seizure by student demonstrators, but its interior has never been damaged.[14]

No sooner had the administration building been completed in 1915 than Gilbert plunged happily into his next Oberlin commission, Allen Memorial Art Museum. Trustee Dudley Peter Allen was one of those who believed that Gilbert's Finney Chapel was "a great success" despite the adverse conditions he had grappled with. Allen, son of an Oberlin doctor, had graduated from the college and gone on for medical training at Harvard University before returning to practice in Cleveland, where he married the daughter of a Standard Oil millionaire. As early as

14-4. Cox Administration Building, 1915, Oberlin College. (Cass Gilbert Colledtion, Archives Center, National Museum of American History)

14-5. Allen Memorial
Art Museum, 1916,
Oberlin College.
(Oberlin College
Archives, Oberlin, Ohio)

1908 he told Gilbert that he wanted to confer about the future development of the campus. The art museum he had in mind was well along on Gilbert's drawing boards when Allen died in 1915. He had warmly approved the architect's design, and his widow Elizabeth saw to it that the building proceeded with a generous budget. When President King told Gilbert that the museum "ought to be certainly one of the most beautiful of our buildings," Gilbert promptly replied, "[S]o far as it lies within me I propose to make it so." The building met that mark. Facing Finney Chapel across the square, it is among the most colorful and inviting he ever designed anywhere. Its style is perhaps best described as Mediterranean Renaissance (Figure 14-5).[15]

A low, square, tan sandstone building under a broad, low-pitched, red-tile roof, the museum rests gracefully on its site. A central clerestory block rises above the roof to cast natural light down into the main sculpture gallery. The entry to the sculpture gallery is reached through a vaulted loggia (Figure 14-6) inspired by those of Brunelleschi's fifteenth-century *Spedale degli Innocenti* (Hospital of the Innocents) in Florence, and probably influenced as well by McKim's splendid courtyard in the Boston Public Library, completed in 1895.

The museum extends to the rear past an arcaded open-air fountain court to classroom space beyond. The fountain court provides the building's most Mediterranean ambiance (Figure 14-7). Gilbert's attraction to mission-style architecture may have influenced its look. A trip to California with wife Julia in May 1914, just as he was refining his final design for the museum, included a stay at the Hearst family ranch, Hacienda del Pozo de Verona. "I am perfectly entranced with it," Julia wrote. "It is difficult to believe that I am in America. The house is like a Spanish Hacienda with a picturesque patio for an entrance surrounded by a charming colonade; in the center of the patio is a wonderful fountain which gives the house its name." Cass did not record his reaction to this characteristic hacienda arrangement, but the resemblance to his Oberlin fountain court is striking.[16]

The architectural critic I. T. Frary qualified his otherwise admiring review of Gilbert's museum by regretting the brilliance of some of its colors: they were too intense, too "ardent." Gilbert himself worried that Elizabeth Allen would find the color contrasts between his tan sandstone walls and their red sandstone patterned trim too strong, and promised they would grow more "quiet" over time. But in Mrs. Allen he had found a donor who fully shared his fondness for chromatic flourishes—the blues in the rafter ends and della Robbia roundels in the frieze below the red-tile roof overhang, the red-brick approach walks, and the blue and gold mosaics in the vaulting of the loggia. Gilbert's interior sustains the mood more moderately. The entering visitor is greeted by ochre gallery walls rising from a floor of variegated red bricks, brightly polished and laid in patterns that Gilbert hoped would call to mind a picturesque Italian courtyard. In the passageway from the main gallery to the library, he installed the imported Venetian doorway he had placed in storage during the construction of Cox Administration Building.[17]

For decorative iron gates and stairway and window grilles, Gilbert turned once more to Samuel Yellin. When the contractor's construction superintendent balked at Yellin's cost estimates, Gilbert took the issue straight to King: "Mr. Yellin's work is of very superior artistic quality, so superior that every item of it is really a museum piece. There is no iron worker in the country that I know of that can compare with him in ornamental iron work and I want the Art Museum to have the finest example that can be purchased for the money we have available however simple the work may be." King agreed, and Yellin's metalwork remains among the treasures of the museum to the present day.[18]

The didactic inscriptions for the museum were in their own way as insistent as the ornament. Over the entry loggia is a confident statement by the socialist craftsman William Morris: "The Cause of Art is the Cause of the People." This was not Gilbert's choice but rather that of a revered Oberlin English professor, Charles Wager. Closer to the architect's outlook are the Beaux-Arts thoughts flanking the loggia on either side: "The Fine Arts, A Heritage From the Past," and "The Fine Arts, A Gift to the Future." High on the walls of the central sculpture gallery are verses of the poem "Enosis" by the American transcendentalist Christopher Pearse Cranch. In retrospect, its third and fourth stanzas

might be read to anticipate the impending fate of the Beaux-Arts architectural tradition in America:

> Heart to heart was never known;
> Mind with mind did never meet;
> We are columns left alone,
> Of a temple once complete.
>
> Like the stars that gem the sky,
> Far apart, though seeming near,
> In our light we scattered lie;
> All is thus but starlight here.

14-6. Loggia, Allen Memorial Art Museum, 1916, Oberlin College. (Oberlin College Archives, Oberlin, Ohio)

After the completion of Allen Memorial Art Museum, the mesh between Cass Gilbert's aspirations and those of President King would never be as smooth again. The museum was dedicated as Gilbert received an honorary degree in the commencement ceremonies of June 1917, shortly after the United States entered World War I. More than any other event, the war deflected the collaboration of Gilbert and King toward the shadows it entered in the 1920s.

By the beginning of that decade the drawing boards of Gilbert's New York office had generated plans and renderings for a dozen fresh additions to

STUDY FOR OBERLIN TOWER. Cass Gilbert Alt 1916

14-7. Fountain Court, Allen Memorial Art Museum, 1916, Oberlin College. (Oberlin College Archives, Oberlin, Ohio)

14-8. Proposed Bell Tower (not built), graphite sketch, 1916, Oberlin College campus. (Oberlin College Archives, Oberlin, Ohio)

the Oberlin campus. Chief among these was a tall bell tower (Figure 14-8), to be visible for miles around, rising from the site of the cavernous Peters Hall, which Gilbert repeatedly insisted, and King repeatedly promised, would soon disappear. The proposed bell tower would unite the quadrangle of the academic buildings that Gilbert planned for the western edge of Tappan Square, and would punctuate a central campus vista crossing the square from the east. A large Gilbert-designed auditorium was already being planned to face the bell tower from the east across the square.

World-famous now as creator of the soaring Woolworth tower in Manhattan, Gilbert urged the bell tower on King with just the slightest edge of condescension: "It is over twelve years since I first began to work for Oberlin College and though its buildings heretofore have been small and relatively unimportant I have found it a very interesting, not to say inspiring work and I devoutly hope to see this consummation." But the bell tower, lacking an urgent practical function, never found a donor, and Peters Hall, too useful and too costly to demolish, never met a wrecking ball. In the mid-1990s, Oberlin spent seven million dollars to renovate Peters, now its oldest campus building and the object of warm alumni nostalgia, as an international language center.[19]

Frustrated by these obstacles to his master plan, Gilbert felt his Oberlin work to be less compelling as the postwar years set in, and both he and President King began to age. On his return from high-level war and postwar service overseas, King found that he no longer commanded quite the presidential clout he had enjoyed before the war, and he soon began to suffer from the neuromuscular ailment that would ultimately force his retirement. Meanwhile, Gilbert was running one of the busiest firms in the country without partners, and the relatively slow pace of his Oberlin work was beginning to tell. He listed Oberlin among the chief offenders when he wrote in his diary: "I have had so many works stopped and postponed that it has to some extent discouraged me. It is not fruitful to make designs that are not built. . . ." Evermore frequent bouts of poor health and lassitude began to plague him. "Jaw hurts—arm hurts—tired out," a diary entry ran in 1922. "Sometimes I think I cannot keep on much longer." But his Oberlin work was far from over.[20]

Aside from the promised auditorium, two more campus buildings remained for him. The first of these was a small hospital, funded by yet another bequest from the estate of Dr. Dudley Peter Allen, to be owned by the college and shared with the town. Back in 1916, hospital planners had retained a Cleveland architect, Charles Hopkinson, to design the facility. When he produced a design in the popular eighteenth-century red-brick Georgian idiom, which would have clashed with Gilbert's architectural themes for the campus, college trustees balked, insisting that the hospital be done by Gilbert. Gilbert's interest in the job wobbled, but his design finally arrived in 1920. Owing to postwar inflation, cost estimates ran far above funding. Dr. Allen's widow, now Mrs. Prentiss after remarriage, came through once more. While Gilbert's bell tower had not interested her, the hospital did, and with her big fresh donation, construction got underway in 1924. A low one-story building with a red-tile roof and walls of white stucco decorated by colorful roundels, Allen Memorial Hospital had a welcoming Spanish mission look about it (Figure 14-9).

Gilbert's personal oversight of the hospital's construction was looser than for his earlier Oberlin buildings. He put his thirty-year-old son, whose architectural talents were no match for his own, in charge of building the hospital. "Cass Jr. leaves for Oberlin Monday afternoon," he told his wife. "Quite an undertaking for the boy—but I am deliberately putting responsibility on him. . . . For Cass Jr. to go out to Oberlin alone to handle this matter is quite a step forward." The son proved not entirely up to it. When the father came to Oberlin to inspect the work as it neared completion, he was heard to ask his son why certain things were done the way they were. When Cass Jr. replied that he did not know, Gilbert snapped, "Damnit, you should, for this is your building." That overheard remark brought on the first serious breach between Gilbert and his Oberlin sponsors.[21]

News of the exchange between father and son spread and lingered among college administrators and trustees. When President King finally retired in 1927, his successor, Ernest Hatch Wilkins, ordered a campus survey of Gilbert's buildings so that trustees could evaluate his service. One trustee responded with a view now widely shared, "I am not for keeping Cass Gilbert, Inc., for our architect. I am afraid it is mostly the 'Inc.' whose services we get and I haven't been happy over the tremendous cost of our buildings which, after we get them, are so hard to adapt to the uses for which we built them. I do admire the exteriors." Here and there a dissenter noted that the college had rarely drawn up adequate programs for its new buildings, often lacked the money needed to proceed with Gilbert's plans, and changed its instructions and

priorities for the architect with some frequency. Like most colleges, Oberlin could not afford to be a model client.[22]

Gilbert's early plans for his last Oberlin complex—the Graduate School of Theology, a large quadrangle planned for the northern edge of Tappan Square—also dated from before the war. They gathered dust throughout the 1920s for lack of adequate funding, until 1929 when John D. Rockefeller Jr. provided $300,000 for the project. A year later, at the request of the college, Gilbert himself visited Rockefeller and coaxed an additional $100,000 from him, and construction finally began.

14-9. Allen Memorial Hospital, 1925, Oberlin Ohio. (Oberlin College Archives, Oberlin, Ohio)

The theological quadrangle was designed to provide Oberlin's divinity students with a small campus of their own, complete with chapel, library, classrooms, dining hall, and dormitories. As completed in 1931, a central Romanesque tower rises above the chapel and its classroom wings, all in Indiana limestone and graced with hand-carved medieval entries facing Tappan Square (Figure 14-10). Dormitories to the rear, finished in dark-red brick, enclose a cloistered yard. Connecting the living space to the classroom wings are two colonnades, one of them decorated by the faces of distinguished religion professors implanted in the capitals of its columns—a unique and charming arrangement relating architectural ornament to the local past (Figure 14-11).

14-10. Theological Quadrangle, 1931, Oberlin College. (Oberlin College Archives, Oberlin, Ohio)

Gilbert's office staff, working from his sketches, refined the close details while he vacationed in Scotland. And again his son carried out most of the on-site negotiations, which were often testy. Professor Clarence Ward, head of the Art Department and himself a trained architect, criticized the plans "in a very nasty way," the son reported. When Ward asked what the style was supposed to be, young Gilbert replied that "the stonework was American, the character was based on Northern Italy, and the style was 1930 Cass Gilbert." "Mr. Ward left the meeting apparently in not good humor," he concluded. A year

later the son asked President Wilkins for additional money to make the student lounge and library the "finest interiors in the Middle West." Wilkins replied that the budget was fixed and that Gilbert was not authorized to raise any more money in the name of the college. Then he looked at his watch for his next appointment. "I was with President Wilkins about four minutes," the son wrote. After yet another trip to Oberlin he told his father, "President Wilkins was not in Oberlin. Thank heaven!" He called Wilkins "the world's worst for giving information." Clearly as the Great Depression set in, the new president, while more sympathetic than Professor Ward to Gilbert's ambitions for Oberlin, had begun to share a widening sense that those ambitions were too costly. The theological quadrangle, like Finney Chapel a generation earlier, was completed with a look of strong, sound permanence but with few amenities. The chapel windows, for example, were left unfinished, not to be filled with stained glass for another twenty-five years.[23]

It was in this atmosphere that Gilbert waited for the college's acceptance of his climactic offering: the large auditorium he had been hoping to build since 1914. The story of promise, delay, and ultimate rejection of his auditorium design is a tale etched with embittering ironies. These underscore not only the growing stress in Gilbert's Oberlin connection but also the rout of his Beaux-Arts historicism before the advance of the modern.

The story begins in an Oberlin family woodshed, where in 1886 Charles Martin Hall, a minister's son and chemistry student who had graduated from the college the year before, discovered the electrolytic process of turning bauxite into aluminum, thus radically reducing the cost of that metal. With encouragement and legal advice from college classmate Homer Johnson, a Cleveland lawyer, Hall proceeded to exploit his experimental breakthrough by organizing what became the Aluminum Company of America (ALCOA) in 1907. Hall and Johnson profited handsomely from ALCOA's earnings, and both soon joined the Oberlin College board of trustees. When Hall died in 1914, his will, drawn up with Johnson's help, directed a major portion of his ALCOA stock to his alma mater, along with a bequest for a large auditorium in his mother's memory. The will named Gilbert as the desired architect and Johnson as executor with power of approval over the auditorium's design.

President King had gotten on well over the years with Johnson, finding him a vigorous troubleshooter. As early as 1908, relations were close enough for King to express personal concern when Johnson's older son Alfred caught a fatal illness. After Alfred died, Homer Johnson was left with a single remaining son, Philip—the Philip Johnson who would one day become a famous architect. Homer Johnson helped King through the business negotiations that led to Gilbert's selection as campus architect and to the construction of Cox Administration Building, Allen Memorial Art Museum, and Allen Memorial Hospital. But with Hall Auditorium, relations between King and Johnson began to cool. When King tried to impose a religious definition on the auditorium, Johnson, a religious skeptic who was fond of poking friends with jokes about their afterlife, opposed this definition, and after a careful reading of Hall's will, his fellow trustees agreed, rejecting King's solution in 1924.

Johnson then resigned from the board of trustees in order to put his lawyer's skills to work for the president of ALCOA, his close friend Arthur Vining Davis, who wanted to improve his control of the company against rival stockholders. To this end Johnson persuaded Oberlin's trustees to sell a major chunk of the college's ALCOA stock back to Davis at current market value. When ALCOA stock then took off in the wild Wall Street boom of the late 1920s, Oberlin's trustees decided they had been taken and threatened a lawsuit for fraud unless the stock was returned to the college.

Alarmed over Davis's reputation as well as his own, in 1930 Johnson grudgingly agreed to an out-of-court settlement that returned the stock. Outlawyered by the college trustees, he was permanently alienated from them by this turn of events, which called both his honor and his professional competence into question. His embitterment shaped his

behavior as executor of Hall's auditorium bequest for the next twenty years. His power of approval over the auditorium's design gave him the weapon he needed to nurse his grudge, and he used it with maddening tenacity. Along the way, under the influence of his son Philip, he became an avid student of contemporary architecture.[24]

Gilbert's earliest designs for Hall Auditorium, a larger and more lavishly ornamented Romanesque elaboration of Finney Chapel, dated from 1916, the

year before American entry into World War I (Figure C-14). Postwar recession, President King's declining presidential energies, and trustee procrastination combined to postpone the auditorium across the 1920s. Matters worsened when Wilkins replaced King in 1927, and worsened further after the stock market crash of 1929.

In 1929 Philip Johnson, now a young millionaire by virtue of ALCOA stock inherited from his father, graduated from Harvard and joined New York

14-11. Theological Quadrangle: colonnade, 1931 ff. Capital depicts Religion Professor Clyde Amos Holbrook. (Photograph by Geoffrey Blodgett)

City's new Museum of Modern Art as head of its architectural department. In 1932, with Henry-Russell Hitchcock, he organized the museum's famous exhibition about modern architecture, which introduced the so-called International style to America. Homer Johnson was impressed. Relations between father and son were not altogether serene, since the father regretted Philip's sexual orientation and his career decision to pursue the arts instead of law. But the father learned about the modern idiom from the son and proceeded to apply what he learned to Gilbert's design for Hall Auditorium.

Gilbert's latest plans came up for approval at a trustee committee meeting in 1933. Johnson joined the meeting as guardian of the Hall will. The minutes record his architectural critique: "Mr. Johnson thought that the proposed auditorium, as planned by Mr. Gilbert, looked too much like a church; that it resembled too closely the general idea of Finney Chapel; that it was not in line with the trend of architecture in the modern world. . . . Mr. Johnson further suggested that we now delay some more in the construction of it because the times require it." In the meantime, Johnson said, Gilbert should forget what he had already done and come in with a new design that had "brightness, colorfulness, sparkle, snap." In later years Johnson would acknowledge that his call for a new design was mainly a tactic to force the college to end its commitment to Gilbert and look elsewhere for a more satisfying architect. As time passed, Johnson's son Philip became for his father an ever more promising prospect.[25]

Just as Johnson was aiming the first of his many vetoes at the design of Hall Auditorium, Gilbert wrote a letter to an admiring lawyer in Little Rock, Arkansas, that summed up his Oberlin frustrations:

Your letter also speaks of some time visiting Oberlin College. I fear if you do that you will have some disappointments. The buildings which I have designed there are of a picturesque type, and quite different from the style of the Detroit Public Library, the Supreme Court and the other works with which you are familiar. They have never allowed me money enough for any of their buildings and the matter has strung

along for nearly thirty years in which time I have struggled, sometimes ineffectively, to create an environment suitable for a college that would give some impulse toward architectural beauty and distinction and which would possibly have a good influence upon the student body. I have had but little encouragement there in this direction since President King retired.[26]

Seven months after composing this glum obituary on his Oberlin career, Gilbert died in England while trying to recover his health. The college dropped its ties with Gilbert's firm soon thereafter. During the next decade, Homer Johnson effectively vetoed three more designs for the auditorium, including one by Eliel Saarinen that proved too modern for many trustees. Then in 1946, Wall Street lawyer William Stevenson succeeded Wilkins as president and promptly set about to solve the auditorium problem. He stroked the aging Homer Johnson at every opportunity and engaged the help of Davis, still head of ALCOA, whose friendship with Johnson back in the 1920s had been at the heart of Johnson's break with the college. When Davis suggested that Wallace K. Harrison, chief designer of the United Nations complex in New York who was building a new headquarters for ALCOA in Pittsburgh, be hired to design Hall Auditorium, Johnson seemed pleased and suggested in turn that his son Philip, just then gathering praise for his Glass House in New Canaan, Connecticut, might have some ideas for Harrison about the auditorium. Johnson's pride in his son was not lost on Stevenson. "I would conclude that Mr. Homer Johnson will not be difficult to handle," he noted, "so long as Philip Johnson is satisfied." A few weeks later, with Harrison's agreement, Stevenson arranged for Oberlin trustees to hire Philip Johnson as a design consultant for Hall Auditorium. The trustees agreed to this tactic, though some expressed reservations about Philip's "known preference for modern architectural design."[27]

Stevenson then proceeded to resolve, one by one, several longstanding objections by Homer Johnson about the auditorium's function, size, and cost and finally brought the eighty-six-year-old lawyer to the dotted line. Forty years after Gilbert had been named architect of Hall Auditorium, Harrison's version of it was completed at last, with Homer Johnson's consent and some help from his son (Figure 14-12). In an interview twenty-five years after that, Stevenson was asked why he had not tapped Philip Johnson himself for the job, as his father clearly desired. "Well you see," Stevenson replied with a smile, "back in [1948] his son hadn't become the greatest architect in the world. His father had thought he was going to be . . . , but on the face of it I had never heard of Philip Johnson."[28]

Gilbert's Oberlin career ended in disappointment in 1934, and his campus master plan was never realized. In retrospect his dream of a twentieth-century campus of planned uniformities, harmonized by a single designer, was doomed at Oberlin—as it was at the University of Texas and the University of Minnesota. Both the emerging diversities in American higher education and the ever more assertive individualism swelling among top American architects worked against campus harmonies. But the influence of Gilbert's thirty-year connection with Oberlin did not disappear. In his time, with President King's strong support, he had instilled in Oberlin the habit of wanting the best architecture the college could afford. That habit survived.

Harrison was just the first of a sequence of distinguished building artists to be called to the campus after World War II, a list that includes Minoru Yamasaki, Hugh Stubbins, Robert Venturi, Gunnar Birkerts, Charles Gwathmey, and the "green" architect William McDonough. Their buildings, each very different from the others, inevitably defy the older traditions of beauty and continuity implanted by Gilbert a generation earlier. Each reaches aggressively for its special campus distinction. Nevertheless, taken together in all their variety, they build on Gilbert's quest for excellence.

Moreover Oberlin itself began to honor Gilbert's local legacy as his national reputation emerged to glow again across the 1980s. The college spent millions to restore and renovate his major campus buildings. In 1982 during a renovation of Finney Chapel that brought fresh color to the building indoors and out, its interior was repainted at last in harmonic shades of rose—an approximation of the color scheme Gilbert originally had in mind, as indicated by a wash drawing from his office discovered in deep storage. In 1992 a stained-glass abstraction in brilliant tones of flame red, silver, and blue by artist Robert Mangold filled the round hole in the chapel's great gable, thus resolving the dispute over a rose window dating from 1908. In Cox Administration Building the large second-floor conference room, long cluttered with office desks, became a conference room again, renamed the Cass Gilbert Room. Flanking its entry is an exhibition of Gilbert's drawings, many of them given to the college by Cass Gilbert III in 1984. And in 1999 Allen Memorial Art Museum

received an urgent comprehensive restoration that saved its structural shell from serious decay.[29]

Thus, eight decades after President King first engaged Gilbert's talent for Oberlin, the college embraced his major gifts to the campus-the finest architectural cluster of his long career—with the guarantee of their survival.

14-12. Wallace K. Harrison, Hall Memorial Auditorium, 1954, Oberlin College. (Photograph by Geoffrey Blodgett)

CHAPTER 15

A BRITISH RESPONSE TO AMERICAN CLASSICISM:
CASS GILBERT AND CHARLES REILLY

Joseph Sharples

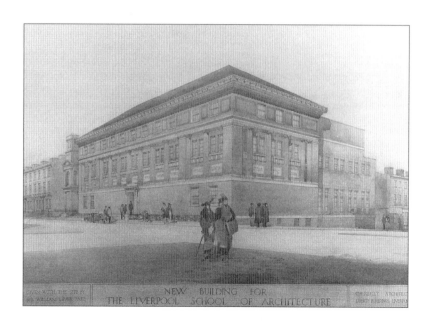

NEW BUILDING FOR THE LIVERPOOL SCHOOL OF ARCHITECTURE

When Herman Melville's *alter ego* Redburn sailed into Liverpool from New York, he was at once struck by a depressing lack of architectural display along the city's waterfront. The Old World seemed as humdrum as the New: "Looking shoreward, I beheld lofty ranges of dingy warehouses which seemed very deficient in the elements of the marvellous; and bore a most unexpected resemblance to the warehouses along South Street in New York. . . . these edifices, I must confess, were a sad and bitter disappointment to me."[1] Some sixty-five years later, in 1914, these two great maritime cities facing each other across the Atlantic presented a very different appearance to those arriving by sea. A Cunard poster (Figure C-17) dating from about this year shows Cass Gilbert's recently completed Woolworth Building soaring above the majestic bulk of the liner SS *Aquitania,* advertising the splendors of New York and America to European travelers. While still under construction, the Woolworth Building had already been praised in the British architectural press as likely to be "the most beautiful as well as the highest building in the world,"[2] and it stood as an apt symbol of the wealth, ambition, and technological achievement of the United States.

At the opposite end of the *Aquitania*'s transatlantic route, in Liverpool, architects also had transformed the city's waterfront since Melville's day, albeit on a more modest scale than in lower Manhattan. During the course of the nineteenth century, Liverpool had grown immensely rich on the profits of its shipping. It was Britain's second port after London, and through its seven miles of docks on the River Mersey passed the raw materials that supplied the country's industrial heartland and the manufactured goods that Britain exported around the world, as well as a vast number of passengers. At the center of this line of docks is the Pier Head, a large open public space where trams and railways once converged and where ferries and ocean liners arrived and departed, comparable in some respects to New York's Battery Park. The Pier Head was the hub of Liverpool's regional, national, and international transport links, the "Gateway of Empire," and for many travelers it afforded their first or last impression of the city. In

1900, George's Dock, on the landward side of the Pier Head, was closed and subsequently filled in, thus creating a superb site for three huge office buildings (Figure 15-1) that would express architecturally the city's self-confident prosperity. First to be built was the domed headquarters of the Mersey Docks and Harbour Board (Arnold Thornely, architect, 1907), immediately followed by the Royal Liver Buildings (Walter Aubrey Thomas, 1908–10), a miniskyscraper with a pair of extravagant clock towers. The size of these buildings is absolutely exceptional by early-twentieth-century British standards. Passengers arriving in Liverpool on the *Aquitania*'s maiden voyage would have been greeted by these two swaggering baroque giants, but between them they would have seen the third of the Pier Head buildings, still under construction in 1914, the markedly different Cunard Building (Willink & Thicknesse, 1913–15), head office of the *Aquitania*'s owners. Its powerfully battered and rusticated basement and its imperialist pro-

15-1. Pier Head, Liverpool, c. 1920. (Liverpool Record Office)

A BRITISH RESPONSE TO AMERICAN CLASSICISM

gram of sculptural decoration might have evoked in the careful observer memories of Cass Gilbert's United States Custom House in New York.

With its emphatically square outline, elegant proportions, and general air of restraint, the Cunard Building suggests that a significant shift was taking place in architectural taste in Liverpool around this

15-2. Charles Reilly, photograph by Edward Chambré Hardman, 1924. (Board of Trustees of the National Museums & Galleries on Merseyside: Walker Art Gallery, Liverpool)

15-3. *Mind and Matter*, Edward Carter Preston, 1920, watercolor on paper. (Board of Trustees of the National Museums & Galleries on Merseyside: Walker Art Gallery, Liverpool)

time, and indeed other buildings in the city bear out this view. What brought about this change of taste? To some extent it was a reflection of a wider trend in British architecture, a general move away from late Victorian and Edwardian heaviness toward greater refinement. More importantly, though, it was due to the presence in the city of Professor Charles Reilly (Figure 15-2), an enthusiastic advocate of contemporary American classicism.

In 1904, at the remarkably young age of thirty Charles Reilly (1874–1948) moved to Liverpool from London to take up the post of Roscoe Professor of Architecture at the University of Liverpool.[3] At that time, schools of architecture in Britain were few in number and apprenticeship was the normal route into the profession. The School of Architecture and Applied Art at the University of Liverpool was, as its name suggests, a creation of the Arts and Crafts movement, in which architecture was taught alongside metalwork, carving, modeling, and other practical skills, in accordance with the principles of John Ruskin, William Morris, and William Richard Lethaby. Reilly despised this Ruskinian, medieval-inspired approach to design with its emphasis on—as he saw it—ornament, variety, sentimental reverence for the past, and small details at the expense of the bigger picture. (Soon after his arrival in Liverpool, the teaching of crafts became the responsibility of the city art school, and Reilly was able to concentrate exclusively on teaching architecture.) More generally, he rejected what he perceived as the chaotic indiscipline of much Edwardian architecture, its willful eclecticism and its frequent failure to take account of the wider urban setting. To Reilly, the Pier Head buildings offered a glaring illustration of these shortcomings. "Liverpool," he wrote, "offers one of the best or worst examples in the world of excessive individualism in architecture. I refer to the group of the three big buildings at the Pier Head. No one looking at them as a group, whatever their respective merits or demerits, can fail to realise their gigantic disharmony; a disharmony in the main brought about by the excessive individualism of their designers . . . if there had been any great restraining tradition, as in the culminating periods of architecture, no such diversity would have come about."[4]

Reilly made it his mission to reestablish a "great restraining tradition" and to promote it through the Liverpool School of Architecture, as the former School of Architecture and Applied Art came to be known. To accomplish this task he directed his students' attention toward the severe Greco-Roman public and commercial buildings of the earlier nineteenth century in which Liverpool was—and is—particularly rich, and toward the understated elegance of her Regency domestic architecture. But he also took as his models contemporary American classical architecture and American architectural schools, and for nearly thirty years he made the Liverpool School of Architecture the most important channel through which the influence of architects like McKim, Mead & White and Gilbert reached England.

It would be difficult to exaggerate the reverence with which Reilly and his associates regarded American classicism. A satirical drawing by the Liverpool artist Edward Carter Preston, *Mind and Matter* (Figure 15-3), includes a caricature of Reilly's bookish second-in-command, Lionel H. Budden, constructed out of drawing instruments. He stands before a Doric temple, the stylobate of which is inscribed with the names of celebrated architects of the classical tradition: Ictinus and Callicrates, Percier and Fontaine, and—on the topmost step—McKim, Mead & White. "America," Reilly wrote, "is the new power in world architecture . . . the great American architects are the heirs of the Old World, and well are they using their heritage."[5] Again and again in his published writings, he described how American architects had made themselves masters of the European architectural tradition, and how this had resulted not in undiscriminating eclecticism but rather in scholarly correctness, sobriety, restraint, and self-effacement. The Americans appeared to have evolved what European architects had been seeking throughout the nineteenth century, a viable, modern, international style, and where America led, he believed Britain should follow.

Reilly's conversion to American classicism was fueled by a three-month trip to the United States in 1909. The journey was financed by William Hesketh Lever (1851–1925), the immensely wealthy soap manufacturer and art collector whose factory was close to Liverpool and who was himself deeply interested in American architecture and planning. Reilly toured the cities of the eastern seaboard, visited architectural schools, and established friendships with leading architects that were to pay dividends later. On his return he wrote excitedly to the architect Reginald Blomfield, "I am back from America with a new scale for life,"[6] and it is fair to say that he was charmed by the glamour and wealth of the country as well as by the quality of its architecture.

He brought back two packing cases full of drawings and photographs of American work to hang on the studio walls and inspire his students. Sadly, only one of these drawings has survived the vicissitudes of twentieth-century architectural taste (Figure 15-4). It is a design for a Monument to Admiral Dewey dated 1907, by a Philadelphia student named G. A. Holmes

working under the pseudonym "Dreadnought," and it resembles the Palais de Justice in Brussels superimposed on the Rock of Gibraltar. Many of Reilly's students emulated the overscaled, impractical, and almost comically nationalistic character of such designs, producing elaborate drawings for fantasy projects such as a Monument to the Universal Adoption of the Greenwich Meridian and a Monument to the Glory of the British Navy. They also prepared more convincing designs in the American manner, and a large number of these are reproduced in four "sketchbooks" of his students' work that Reilly published between 1910 and 1920.[7] The 1913 volume contains a design for a Picture Gallery in a Public Park that so closely echoes the triple-arched entrance of Gilbert's design for the St. Louis Public

15-4. G. A. Holmes, Design for a Monument to Admiral Dewey, 1907, watercolor on paper. (University of Liverpool Art Galleries and Collections)

A BRITISH RESPONSE TO AMERICAN CLASSICISM

Library (see Figure 16-11) that it must have been based on it. The 1920 volume has a design for a University Assembly Hall (Figure 15-5), which conspicuously recalls McKim, Mead & White's Low Library at Columbia, a building Reilly particularly admired. A critic reviewing an exhibition of Liverpool students' work held in 1912 commented, "It is, in fact, evident that the United States furnishes either the model or the inspiration for the composition, and even detail, of nearly every essay in design. But it is also clear that this enthusiasm for American achievement has behind it sound knowledge of classic forms, and is not ill-considered or superficial in its nature. . . . the manners of . . . Charles Follen McKim, Hornbostel, Cass Gilbert and Van Buren Magonigle are the chief favourites."[8]

A VNIVERSITY ASSEMBLY HALL
NORTH ELEVATION

A master of advertising and public relations ahead of his time, Reilly produced lavish prospectuses for his school, illustrated in color, that were directly inspired by the prospectuses of Cornell and other American schools of architecture. He strove to develop the school library along American lines, and if circumstances had allowed, he would have employed an American lecturer, the Beaux-Arts-trained Thomas W. Ludlow (1881-1929), who offered his services.[9] Beyond the confines of the school, he promoted the cause of American classicism to a wider public through lecturing and through his highly readable journalism for the professional and popular press. He

15-5. Wesley Dougill, University Assembly Hall, 1919. *The Liverpool University Architectural Sketchbook,* eds. C. H. Reilly and L. B. Budden (London, 1920), 27.

was being uncharacteristically reticent when he told the Anglo-American architect and journalist Francis S. Swales, "American architecture is your field in English journalism."[10] It is true that Swales wrote a series of lavishly illustrated articles on contemporary American architecture (concluding with a major piece on Gilbert) for the *Architectural Review* between August 1908 and January 1912, for which Reilly supplied him with photographs. But Reilly was more prolific, wrote for a very wide range of publications, and was able to exert his influence in an editorial capacity on such periodicals as *Country Life* and the *Builders' Journal.* Among numerous examples is a piece entitled "Some Thoughts on Modern American Architecture" in *The Builder* of July 30, 1920. It rehearses Reilly's by-now-familiar arguments about America leading the world in forging a new international architecture, based on knowledge of the past but addressing modern needs, and it is illustrated with a photograph of a rendering of Gilbert's design for the Theological Seminary at Oberlin College.

Reilly's vivid and amusing impressions of New York, originally published in the *Liverpool Daily Post,* appeared in book form as *Some Architectural Problems of Today* in 1924, and in the same year he brought out *McKim, Mead & White,* the first monograph on the celebrated practice to appear in Britain. His introductory essay to this book explicitly holds up the works of McKim and his partners as models to be studied and imitated in Britain: "Vast tracts of America from east to west have long been under their sway, and in England to-day and for the last ten years or more most of us have been consciously or unconsciously influenced by their work and outlook. Indeed, some of us have paid them the sincere flattery of direct imitation."[11] In that same year the AIA elected Reilly an honorary corresponding member, and Harvey Wiley Corbett, fresh from designing Bush House in London, told his colleagues at the AIA's fifty-seventh annual convention that Reilly believed "the success of American architecture—and he recognises America as . . . the leading country in architecture—is the combination of the Beaux-Arts idea in architecture plus the American open-mindedness and the American intelligence."[12]

Reilly's students were not entirely dependent on published sources for their knowledge of contemporary architecture across the Atlantic. In the 1920s, through his friends and contacts in the American profession, Reilly was able to send a handful of his best students each year to spend their summer vacation working in the offices of leading architectural practices in New York. This program of work placements began in 1920 with the help of Benjamin W. Morris,[13] and in subsequent years students from Liverpool worked for John Russell Pope, Raymond Hood, Shreve, Lamb & Harmon, Flagg & Chambers, and—most frequently—Thomas Hastings. The scheme continued until the Wall Street crash of 1929, and even afterward a number of students made the transatlantic journey. A breezy letter of introduction to Paul Cret in Philadelphia, written by Reilly on behalf of his student Alwyn Sheppard Fidler, shows that the point of such placements was not just to gain practical experience but also to enjoy at first hand the glamour of the American architectural scene: "One of my best fourth year students has, in spite of the depression America, like we ourselves, is suffering from, secured a place for the six months of his long vacation in the office of your friends Messrs. Zantzinger, Borie & Medary. . . . I want him to meet you so that in after life he can say he has met the great Paul Cret. I still feel like that myself you know. He is a very keen Welshman who has won scholarships to bring him to Liverpool. Let him see some of your great schemes and drawings."[14]

Some of these Liverpool students had the opportunity to participate in highly prestigious projects during their time in America. Gordon Stephenson, who later held professorships at Toronto and Perth, Western Australia, drew the presentation plan of Corbett, Harrison & MacMurray's first, unexecuted design for Rockefeller Center, and Fidler, who was to become city architect of Birmingham, England's second city, worked on the U.S. Department of Justice building in Washington, D.C. Joseph Stanley Allen, later professor of town and country planning at the University of Durham, worked for Donn Barber on the New York Cotton Exchange and collaborated with Ezra Winter on the murals that decorated the

trading room on the top floor. These murals represented great cotton ports of the world, the painted vistas of Bombay and Alexandria contrasting with the actual view of New York harbor from the adjacent windows. One mural (Figure 15-6), now known only through photographs, showed a magnificent panorama of Liverpool and the River Mersey busy with picturesque—if somewhat anachronistic—sailing ships. It serves as a vivid reminder of the commercial and

architectural ties that existed between Liverpool and New York at that date.

Back in England, the very ambitious designs of Reilly's students for buildings in the American classical style did sometimes progress beyond the drawing board. Herbert J. Rowse (1887–1963) trained under Reilly before going to Canada, where he worked as assistant to another ex-Liverpool architect, Frank

15-6. Ezra Winter and Joseph Stanley Allen, *Liverpool*, photograph of a mural formerly located in the New York Cotton Exchange. (Ezra Winter Papers, Archives of American Art, Smithsonian Institution)

Simon, on the Manitoba State Legislative building. Rowse traveled back to Liverpool across the United States and spent the rest of his career practicing in the city in a thoroughly American style. His masterpiece is the former headquarters of Martins Bank on Water Street, a steel-framed, stone-clad block, eleven stories high, on an island site in the center of the business district. With its set-back upper floors, its penthouse and roof garden, and its majestic, top-lit, arcaded banking hall rich with travertine and bronze (Figure 15-7), it would be entirely at home in Manhattan or Montreal. Writing in 1934, H. S. Goodhart-Rendel observed that this style of building

> has been brought to a pitch of rare perfection by the multiple firms of architects that supply the needs of American commerce, and has generally proved beyond the scope of architects having only English experience. That an Englishman should have produced single-handed a specimen equal to America's best is undoubtedly gratifying, although the flawless magnificence of Martin's Bank at Liverpool may evoke in us admiration unmingled with affection. . . . Whatever may be true of its class, this particular specimen is no near-architecture, but architecture itself, excellently planned and consistently worked out in all its elaborate and variously derivative details.[15]

Reilly held strong views on bank design. He contrasted what he saw as the typical British bank, subdivided like a pub by mahogany and glass partitions, with the characteristic American model, centered on the imposing, cathedral-like space of the banking hall.[16] Reilly was the judge in the competition for Martins Bank, and it is not surprising that he awarded the commission to his former student, whose design embodies his teaching so completely.

There is no evidence that any of Reilly's students worked in Gilbert's office, but it seems very likely from their subsequent correspondence that Gilbert was one of the New York architects whose acquaintance Reilly made during his 1909 trip to America. Shortly after his return to Liverpool, Reilly obtained from Gilbert photographs of his plans for the University of Minnesota (Figure 15-8) for publication in the *Town Planning Review,* the newly founded quarterly of the Liverpool School of Architecture's Department of Civic Design. The Minnesota drawings duly appeared in the second issue in July 1910. Much of the *Town Planning Review* was written by Reilly and by Stanley Adshead, head of the Department of Civic Design, and it was very much a vehicle for pushing their ideas about the merits of modern classical architecture and City Beautiful planning. Its pages were filled with reports from around Britain and from continental Europe, Australia, and especially North America, about the planning of new towns and the improvement of old ones. Indeed, Reilly's 1909 visit to the United States was undertaken with the specific intention of researching American approaches to town planning. The following year Adshead too was in America ("helping to lay out a new town on Long Island!"[17] in Reilly's typically sweeping words), and in February 1911 he published "A Comparison of Modern American Architecture with That of European Cities" in an American journal, the *Architectural Record*. The same year, the *Town Planning Review* contained a review of "Some Recent American City Reports and Plans," including Gilbert's report on New Haven, published in 1910.

Reilly had an obvious motive in publishing Gilbert's ambitious University of Minnesota designs. At that time the University of Liverpool occupied an elaborate Gothic revival building of 1887–92—the aptly named Victoria Building—designed by Alfred Waterhouse, with an exterior of hard, red terra cotta and an interior lined with glazed ceramic tiles. Reilly despised its romantic medievalism and its harsh materials. He described it as "out-Nuremberging Nuremberg . . . in its efforts to be picturesque" and recoiled from its "colours of mud and blood,"[18] and he was keen to persuade the authorities to plan the university's further expansion along classical lines. From 1906 the university had been preparing to construct a new arts building on a site next to the Victoria Building. At first Reilly was on the building committee, but he resigned in circumstances that are unclear. In 1909 the local architects Briggs, Wolstenholme & Thornely won a limited competition that called for the design of the new building to be "in harmony" with the Victoria Building; then, in 1911, they were invited to

submit new plans, and this time the committee expressed its preference for a classical design. Reilly later said that "by making [him]self obnoxious," he believed he had been responsible for bringing about this change of style.[19] Whatever the details of the affair, it is certain that for a man of Reilly's tastes,

OPPOSITE
15-7. Interior of Martins Bank, Liverpool, photograph by Stewart Bale, 1932. (Board of Trustees of the National Museums & Galleries on Merseyside: Archives Department)

15-8. University of Minnesota, Minneapolis: Plan and Section, [W. P.] Foulds, del., October 1909. (University of Minnesota/Twin Cities, University Archives)

15-9. O. Newbold, Plan for the University of Liverpool. *Town Planning Review* 3 (1912): pl. between pp. 80 and 81. (By courtesy of the University of Liverpool Library)

15-10. Stanley Davenport Adshead, "New University with a facade on Public Gardens," 1910, watercolor on paper. (Board of Trustees of the National Museums & Galleries on Merseyside: Walker Art Gallery, Liverpool)

American campuses were ideal models for the development of British universities, and Gilbert's Minnesota scheme on the bluffs of the Mississippi River was particularly relevant to Liverpool because of its own sloping site.

In 1912 a competition was held among students in the Liverpool School of Architecture and the Department of Civic Design to explore ways in which the University of Liverpool might be extended and replanned. Prizes were awarded by William Hesketh Lever, and the report published in the *Town Planning Review* says that the subject of the competition was Lever's own idea.[20] However, it is difficult to believe that Reilly was not behind this eye-catching contest, which must have had more to do with encouraging his students and colleagues to think on an ambitious scale than with developing realistic proposals for the expansion of a young, provincial, and not particularly rich university. The *Town Planning Review* described the site—"a triangular area situated

between Mount Pleasant and Brownlow Hill. . . . This area has a gentle slope . . . and is occupied by mean streets and buildings"—and gave the following extract from the competition conditions:

"It is proposed that the whole of this area be reserved for Collegiate buildings and open spaces, laid out in a monumental manner. The eastern end of the site is to be occupied by new University buildings in detached blocks, extending down Brownlow Hill and Mount Pleasant. The lower end, which forms the approach from Lime Street, is to be kept open as public gardens; isolated blocks may be erected here, provided that the general open character is preserved. It is suggested that on the main axis of the site there be a monumental approach to the new University buildings, the different levels being reached by monumental flights of steps."

The perspective of the winning design published in the *Town Planning Review* (Figure 15-9) shows the

site stretching uphill, away from the city center, with the Gothic tower of Waterhouse's Victoria Building just visible to the left of the new quadrangle with its commanding dome. Gilbert's plans for the University of Minnesota clearly offered a useful lesson in the treatment of such a site, although the winning design appears rather fussy in comparison with Gilbert's simpler and more elegant proposal.

The 1912 competition and the New Arts Building were not isolated attempts by Reilly and Adshead to promote the idea of an American-style campus of classical buildings for the University of Liverpool. In 1910 Adshead had produced an imaginative drawing (Figure 15-10) of a "New University with a facade on Public Gardens," published in the *Town Planning Review* in July of that year, in a style very much influenced by the contemporary work of McKim, Mead & White at Columbia University. Reilly later praised that institution's Low Library effusively in his book about McKim, Mead & White, describing it as

"forming the kernel and centre of a university group as a library should," lamenting the fact that no British university had yet commissioned such a building, and asking "who would now design a central library for a modern university, after seeing McKim's great dominating Roman solution for such a universal theme, in an Elizabethan or Jacobean manner?"[21] In 1914 Reilly himself designed a new building for the Liverpool School of Architecture that paid homage to McKim, Mead & White's Robinson Hall, home of the Harvard University School of Architecture. Unlike Adshead's stimulating but impracticable drawing—one of a series in which he aimed to show how Liverpool might be replanned along American City Beautiful lines—this building could and should have been realized. Lever initially agreed to provide the site and pay for the building, but World War I intervened, and at the same time a rift developed between Lever and the university, leading to his withdrawal of the necessary funds. All that we have of Reilly's ambi-

15-11. Charles Reilly, architect; Harold Chalton Bradshaw, perspectivist, *New Building for the Liverpool School of Architecture,* watercolor on paper. (University of Liverpool Art Galleries and Collections)

tious design is a fine watercolor prepared by Harold Chalton Bradshaw, one of the school's outstanding students, which was shown at the Royal Academy in 1915 (Figure 15-11). A much later instance of American-influenced, Reilly-inspired classicism is the geology building of 1929 by Arnold Thornely, but this, like the New Arts Building and the Students' Union designed by Reilly in 1909, stands in isolation, unrelated to any comprehensive plan for the university as a whole. The University of Liverpool never did achieve the sort of unified layout Reilly wished it to have, and in his 1938 autobiography he observed that in general the founding of new universities in Britain in the first half of the twentieth century had been an

15-12. Emley & Williamson, The University of the Witwatersrand, Johannesburg, 1922 onwards. (By courtesy of the University of Liverpool Library)

educational success but not an architectural one: "unlike the corresponding movement in America, far too little attention has been paid to the sites, the layout and the general appearance of the buildings with the result that these newer seats of learning . . . are in their material environment almost wholly unworthy of their high object."[22]

To find a direct comparison with Gilbert's Minnesota scheme and American campuses in general among the work of Reilly's students, one has to look beyond Britain. Students came from British colonies and dominions all over the world to attend the Liverpool School of Architecture, and a large

number of the school's graduates pursued their careers overseas. Frederick Towndrow's description of Reilly's school as "an Empire centre of artistic culture"[23] was no exaggeration, and working in private practice in Shanghai or Singapore, or as government architects in Cairo or Baghdad, Liverpool graduates had the chance to build on a scale that would have been difficult to match in Britain. Frederick Williamson studied at the school between 1913 and 1921 and was one of the first batch of Reilly's students who spent their final summer vacation in New York in 1920. The following year he went to South Africa, to collaborate with the Johannesburg architect Frank Emley on the University of the Witswatersrand (Figure 15-12).[24] This massive complex of classical buildings, symmetrically arranged about a principal axis that leads to the central, pedimented portico, is closer than anything in Britain to the classical university campuses and civic centers of contemporary America. The plan had been established in 1919, before Williamson's arrival, but it seems clear that Emley chose Williamson as his partner because of the Liverpool-trained architect's familiarity with this style of building and this scale of project. The firm Emley & Williamson went on to design other important classical buildings in South Africa—notably the triumphal arch of 1923 at Hartbeespoortdam, which again evokes memories of McKim, Mead & White—before turning to modernism in the 1930s.

One of the most outstanding students from overseas who came to study architecture in Liverpool was the South African William Holford.[25] He became one of the leading official architects and planners in post–World War II Britain, and like others of his generation, under the influence of European modernism he came to reject the decorative trappings of the classical style in which he had been trained. In 1925, fresh from school in his native Johannesburg, he had gained his first practical experience of architecture by working for Emley & Williamson on the great portico of the University of the Witswatersrand. Some forty years later he had the job of planning an entirely new university himself, the University of Kent at Canterbury, in southeast England. An early sketch plan by Holford for this project (Figure 15-13) shows a hemicycle of buildings toward the top of the gently sloping site, aligned with the distant view of the towers of Canterbury Cathedral. The buildings are modern and functional in style, and there is a strong asymmetrical accent in the form of a twenty-story Science Tower at the east end of the hemicycle. Nevertheless, the plan is predominantly symmetrical about the axis of the central lecture theater and the cathedral, and in this, as well as in the way it relates to the slope of the site, it is the heir of numerous eighteenth-century country houses whose curved wings reach forward to embrace their landscape setting. At the same time, it is equally clearly descended from the symmetrical, Beaux-Arts university campus schemes of Gilbert and others, which Holford had studied in Liverpool under Reilly. The University of Kent eventually was built to a rather different layout, though the axiality of Holford's initial proposal survives. It shows how the comprehensive planning that Reilly had identified as lacking in Britain's new, urban universities of the earlier twentieth century made a belated appearance in those built on rural sites in the 1960s and 1970s, and it illustrates the faint but persistent influence of American classicism in the country's post–World War II reconstruction.

For Reilly personally, the culmination of his enthusiasm for American classicism was probably his collaboration with Thomas Hastings on Devonshire House, a prestigious block of flats above shops and showrooms, opposite the Ritz hotel on Piccadilly in London. According to Reilly, he was asked by the owner of the site, J. B. Stevenson, to recommend the best American architect for the job.[26] He suggested his friend Hastings, and Stevenson appointed Hastings and Reilly as joint architects. The two men made the initial designs in 1924 (an illustration appeared in the *Year Book of the Architectural League of New York* the following year), but according to the account in Reilly's autobiography the scheme was subsequently revised without his direct involvement.

Devonshire House was completed in 1927. Among the more interesting contemporary comments it elicited are those of Charles Rennie Mackintosh, who wrote to his wife about it from the south of France in the summer of that year.[27] Mackintosh had

private reasons for intensely disliking Reilly, but the views expressed in these letters are striking for more than just the bitterness of their personal invective. Mackintosh recognized that Devonshire House was essentially an American building transplanted to London. He condemned its classical detailing as unimaginative and backward-looking, and voiced his despair at the pervasiveness of American influence in Europe— not just the influence of American architecture but the more general trend toward commercial values that he identified as coming from across

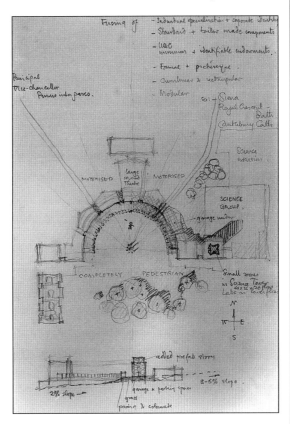

the Atlantic. According to Mackintosh, the American way was to offer the mass of people the standardized product they seemed to want—whether in architecture, moving pictures, or even tobacco— and in the case of architecture, this inevitably devalued the uniquely personal vision of the creative individual. For Reilly, this process of standardizing and depersonalizing—of avoiding "excessive individualism" — was exactly what had drawn him to American classicism in the first place. He saw it as a corrective to precisely the kind of "queer *Art Nouveau*" (Reilly's words) practiced by Mackintosh's circle.

15-13. William Holford, Initial sketch for the University of Kent at Canterbury, 1962–63, graphite on paper. (By courtesy of the University of Liverpool Library)

A BRITISH RESPONSE TO AMERICAN CLASSICISM

Maxwell Fry, a former student of Reilly's who had worked in the office of Carrère & Hastings, claimed that the disgust he felt at the sight of Devonshire House under construction—its steel frame irrationally disguised under a veneer of classical stonework—was what turned him into one of Britain's pioneering modernists.[28] The year the Devonshire House was completed, 1927, was also the year in which the first English translation of Le Corbusier's *Vers une Architecture* appeared, and developments in continental Europe made the classicism of Gilbert and McKim, Mead & White look less and less like the modern, international style Reilly had proclaimed it to be, and more like a continuation of worn-out nineteenth-century historicism.

Surprisingly, during the next few years Reilly adjusted with remarkable ease to this new climate of taste, and following his retirement in 1933 he stopped advocating classicism altogether in his public pronouncements and became an out-and-out modernist. It is interesting to compare his admiration for Rowse's classical Martins Bank (1927–32) with his enthusiastic response to William Lescaze's Philadelphia Saving Fund Society building a few years later. Here was a bank, he said approvingly of Lescaze's building, that did not "in any way rely upon the fancy dress of other epochs" and was "no temple, mausoleum, church or banquetting hall, but a place of work . . . as bright and clean as an operating theatre."[29] One interpretation of this apparent *volte face* is to see Reilly as an opportunist with no firm convictions, who recognized the new architecture as an inevitable development and wanted to be an opinion former within the movement rather than a reactionary criticizing it from the sidelines. An alternative view, and perhaps a fairer one, is that some of the qualities Reilly had most admired about the classicism of Gilbert and his American contemporaries—its restraint, its scholarly attention to the smallest details, its lucid planning, and its avoidance of eccentric individualism—had come of age in the buildings of the modern movement, stripped of "the fancy dress of other epochs."

PART 5

GILBERT AND THE PUBLIC DOMAIN

CHAPTER 16

ST. LOUIS: PUBLIC ARCHITECTURE, CIVIC IDEALS

Ingrid A. Steffensen

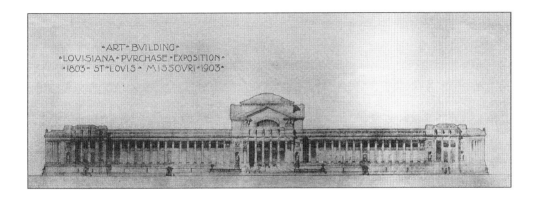

Cass Gilbert left an indelible imprint on the public face of St. Louis, Missouri, with his designs for the 1904 Louisiana Purchase Exposition and the St. Louis Public Library. Perhaps more so than for any other major U.S. city, St. Louisans identify the international exposition of 1904 as a signal event in their history. Rightly or wrongly, their associations with that event and the setting it provided for the Judy Garland movie version of *Meet Me in St. Louis* still shape both residents' and visitors' impressions of the city. As recently as 1997, the president of the Missouri Historical Society wrote in an introduction to a photographic work about the Louisiana Purchase Exposition, "The memory of that experience became a part of our community, an event whose meaning expanded in the stories shared through generations. . . . [T]he Fair and its aura have remained in the memory and the history of St. Louis."[1] Gilbert, as architect of both the temporary centerpiece of the fair, Festival Hall, and the only permanent survivor of the ensemble, the St. Louis Art Museum, may claim an association with St. Louis that is stronger than most individual architects can claim for any entire city. Add to his designs for the fair Gilbert's St. Louis Public Library, and one has a single architect shaping the cultural and very public face of a city. Gilbert's ideals for important public buildings, especially those with a high cultural mission, are especially well reflected in his St. Louis buildings, and one may follow his design processes, his high ambitions, and thoughts on architectural appropriateness and the urban milieu through the three important structures he gave to the city of St. Louis.

16-1. Peabody & Stearns, St. Louis Museum of Fine Arts (destroyed), Nineteenth and Locust Streets, St. Louis, Missouri (1879–81), in 1904. (Missouri Historical Society, St. Louis)

Gilbert's association with St. Louis began somewhat inauspiciously with his unsuccessful entry into the competition for the campus plan for Washington University in 1899.[2] Near the end of the nineteenth century, St. Louis was experiencing the same growing pains that many American cities, particularly in the Midwest, were experiencing. Formerly adequate downtown locations for such institutions as Washington University and the Museum of Fine Arts were feeling the strain as both the city and the institutions grew. Indeed, the area between Seventeenth and Nineteenth Streets and between Lucas Place and Washington Avenue, which was home to the loosely grouped buildings of the Washington University campus, was also the site of the original St. Louis Museum of Fine Arts (Figure 16-1). This museum housed the St. Louis School of Fine Arts.

By 1893, the decision to move the university to more spacious quarters west of the original downtown location had been made. One hundred and three acres of land, and later an additional fifty acres, were purchased at the northwest corner of St. Louis's largest urban parkland, Forest Park, which was opened to the public in 1876. Not coincidentally, this was also to be the site of the 1904 world's fair and the new St. Louis Art Museum. The university's board of directors, following its initial resolution to hire a landscape architect to provide a plan for the layout of the proposed university buildings, hired the foremost firm in the field: the senior Frederick Law Olmsted's Boston firm of Olmsted, Olmsted & Eliot.[3] Based on the oblong shape of the university's parcel of land, this firm's preliminary campus scheme of 1895 consisted of a single dominant axis dividing the rectangle lengthwise. The university buildings were shown lining this dominant axis and facing a large, mall-style green along the center. This scheme was reproduced and circulated for fundraising purposes, which were successful such that in 1899, six architectural firms were invited to participate in a paid competition for the designs of the university buildings. The invitees were Carrère & Hastings of New York; Cope & Stewardson of Philadelphia; Eames & Young of St. Louis; McKim, Mead & White of New York; Shepley,

Rutan & Coolidge of Boston, Chicago, and St. Louis; and Gilbert.

The milieu thus established was one of the most distinguished pools of competitors that could be found at the turn of the century; certainly the commission for the designs for an entire university campus was an architectural plum. Shepley, Rutan & Coolidge had recently designed the campus for Stanford University and Charles McKim had designed, de novo, the campus plan for Columbia University.[4] In the era of the World's Columbian Exposition, the rise of the City Beautiful movement, and the ascendancy of the Ecole des Beaux-Arts and its design methodology, the university campus held a significant cultural and aesthetic place in the turn-of-the-century cultural constellation. It is most certainly not coincidental that the convergence of the new university campus, the Louisiana Purchase Exposition, and the construction of the new city art museum occurred at this time and place.

Gilbert's entry into the Washington University competition reflected the current thoughts and ideals of architecture and planning, especially as taught at the Ecole des Beaux-Arts in Paris. Although he followed the general suggestions of the Olmsted, Olmsted & Eliot plan, Gilbert's submission (Figures 16-2 and 16-3), in both design and execution, outstripped by far the rather modest, comparatively informal proposal submitted by the landscape architects. In a tradition mindful of the ensemble at the Court of Honor at the World's Columbian Exposition in Chicago, and reflective of the kind of drawings produced by Prix de Rome competitors at the Ecole des Beaux-Arts (for an example, see Figure 16-9), Gilbert's scheme was organized around a highly dominant central axis and two large, open quadrangles. In the center of the larger, western quadrangle was a university chapel, and surrounding this were groupings of residential buildings forming minor quadrangles with their own separate subaxes. The smaller, eastern quadrangle held the appropriately denser grouping of academic buildings, with the main administration building closing one end of the composition, and all focusing on a monument or fountain at the center. The intricate yet balanced

weaving together of major and minor axes and cross-axes, and the hierarchical disposition of buildings (chapel at the center, loosely grouped residential buildings, and tightly grouped academic buildings) make the scheme highly logical, "readable," yet also very formal and rather rigid. Gilbert's facade for the Brookings Building, the main administration building, bears a generic resemblance to his recent Minnesota State Capitol and also to certain structures at the World's Columbian Exposition, especially the Fine Arts Palace by Charles Bowler Atwood. His proposed centerpiece and gateway for the university

16-2. Block Plan, Washington University Competition, St. Louis, Missouri, 1899. (Washington University Archives, St. Louis, Missouri)

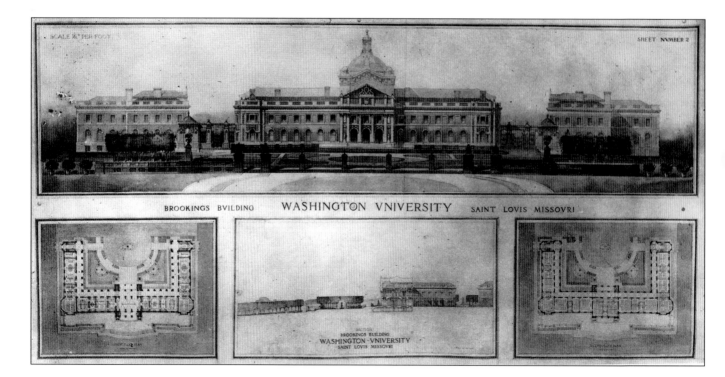

BROOKINGS BVILDING WASHINGTON VNIVERSITY SAINT LOVIS MISSOVRI

SECTION
BROOKINGS BUILDING
WASHINGTON·VNIVERSITY
SAINT LOVIS MISSOVRI

16-3. Elevation of the
Brookings Building,
Washington University
Competition, St. Louis,
Missouri, 1899.
(Washington University
Archives, St. Louis,
Missouri)

would have boasted a low dome and a pedimented portico overlying a triple arched entranceway.

Gilbert's overall campus design was more compact than, for example, the submission by McKim, Mead & White, and less insistent on grandiose landscape effects than the Carrère & Hastings submission. Although Gilbert's entry was probably the best design based on the original Olmsted plan, the jury preferred the design by Cope & Stewardson despite its divergence from the landscape architects' original scheme. Cope & Stewardson, who had also worked on the campuses of Bryn Mawr College, Princeton University, and the University of Pennsylvania, submitted a plan that was less reflective of the ideals inculcated by the Ecole des Beaux-Arts. But their plan was also less rigid and less symmetrical and had the advantage of an agglutinative construction pattern that would allow it to appear complete at almost any stage of construction. Their plan in fact has withstood the test of time better than most plans created by this generation of architects. It accommodated changes into the twentieth century to a greater extent than almost any of the grand plans that were inspired by Prix de Rome exercises.

Notably, Gilbert's foray into the university competition (aside from its relation to his later, successful competition entry for the University of Minnesota in 1908) defined his idea of the appropriate space and style for the high cultural and educational mission of a university. Collegiate Gothic and Georgian buildings were being built on many American college campuses at that time and in subsequent years. Gilbert, and all of his fellow competitors save Cope & Stewardson, however, saw the blank canvas of the Washington University competition as one on which to write the highest ideals of the "City of Learning." This phrase, used by the contemporaneous Phoebe Hearst–sponsored competition for what would become the University of California at Berkeley, proposed a vision of the university campus as a complex entity. It would be complete unto itself and would look inward rather than engage the outside world. The plan would be logically laid out, as orderly and rational as a textbook. In appearance, it would be noble, and above all it would be classical in style. These ideals, which were first brought into reality at the World's Columbian Exposition, would later be embodied in some of the most ambitious projects of the City Beautiful movement. Gilbert's vision of architectural appropriateness and what urban, architectural America could and should be subscribed to this formula in his completed projects in St. Louis.

Despite his lack of success with the Washington University competition, Gilbert's participation granted him familiarity with the locale of Forest Park, not only home to the university but also the site of the Louisiana Purchase Exposition. A hilly, forested, picturesque location, Forest Park was in some respects an ideal site for the grand effects envisioned by the creators of both the university and the exposition. It was chosen not despite but because of its relative remoteness from the congested downtown area. Forest Park was in 1901—the year the site was chosen for the exposition—at the westernmost edge of the growing city of St. Louis, where development could already be seen to be in the offing, and some stately streets and large homes were already built along its edges. Forest Park thus would present to visitors the city's best possible face. It should be noted too, however, that the location was less than ideal for those who treasured the park's trees and open spaces. For better or worse, it was a blank slate on which the fair designers could build an entire exposition city from scratch. The notion of converting wilderness into a shining, if temporary, city was greatly to the liking of the engineers and architects of the era, and they responded by creating the largest world's fair in U.S. history.

Late-nineteenth and early-twentieth-century Americans loved a fair. Between 1853 and 1915, major international expositions were held in New York, Philadelphia, Chicago, Buffalo, St. Louis, and San Francisco.[5] The temporary architecture that blossomed for these events was a spectacle relished by throngs of visitors who came to be impressed, educated, and entertained by the latest developments in all fields of human endeavor. Many came solely for the architectural showcase itself. Because of the impermanent nature of the architecture, fair buildings were constructed with relatively inexpensive materials, and they could be erected, as well as disassembled, with ease. Early fair buildings were functional, prefabricated structures of ferrovitreous materials. Later exposition construction began with metal frameworks that were covered with staff, a paintable mixture of plaster and fiber (horsehair or plant material) that could assume any conceivable shape or style

with ease. The evanescence of these ensembles bred a unique brand of fantasy architecture, as the huge scale—most of the buildings were measured in acreage rather than square-foot capacity—and display function seemed to call for a correspondingly spectacular architecture. Architects took advantage of this quality of exposition architecture to create monumental yet playful designs for these fairs. When called on to design permanent structures in conjunction with these exposition buildings, however, Gilbert and others adopted an entirely different, more serious architectural tone. Permanent monuments, such as the art museums built in conjunction with several of the world's fairs of the late nineteenth and early twentieth centuries, begged for a more restrained treatment than the ephemeral confections that comprised the spectacle of the expositions.

The Philadelphia Centennial Exposition of 1876 was the starting point in America for subsequent international expositions in this country. This fair was a large and complex undertaking, with numerous buildings, each of which was devoted to a different branch of human achievement and understanding.[6] The Philadelphia exposition was the first to construct a building specifically dedicated to art. Exhibiting countries would only send valuable artworks if they could be assured of security from theft, fire, and water damage. The Art Building, therefore, had to be built using more solid materials than what was used for the larger and more temporary exhibition buildings for, for example, horticulture and industry. An iron and glass dome was constructed over the crossing of the Art Building, with the remainder of the structure built from permanent materials and with traditional load-bearing masonry construction techniques. Indeed, the Philadelphia fair's Art Building, designed by Hermann Schwarzmann, still survives in Fairmount Park and houses the Park Commission and other recreational offices. Innovative, too, for Philadelphia in 1876 was Schwarzmann's adoption of a Beaux-Arts classicism that presaged the stylistic innovation to take place at the next major world's fair to be held in the United States, the World's Columbian Exposition of 1893.

After 1876, expositions and the cities that hosted them seized the opportunity to build permanent art galleries or museums in conjunction with the structures built exclusively for the fair. This strategy was the case, for example, at the World's Columbian Exposition in Chicago.[7] Atwood's Art Building was originally conceived as a temporary structure and was composed of fireproof brick walls with a staff covering. This much-beloved structure still serves as the Field Museum, although its impermanent staff covering had to be replaced by concrete in the 1930s. Simultaneously, however, what is now the Art Institute of Chicago was also being built, with the express purpose of serving as a conference site during the exposition, and as the city art museum thereafter. As at Philadelphia, a significant stylistic difference existed at Chicago between the impermanent (or what was intended to be impermanent) architecture and the permanent structure. The fair as a whole was conceived as an exercise in Beaux-Arts classicism. Atwood's Art Building—with its low, saucer dome, "quotations" from such ancient Greek monuments as the Parthenon (Acropolis, Athens, 448–432 B.C.), caryatids from the Erechtheion (Acropolis, Athens, 421–405 B.C.), and the Choragic Monument of Lysicrates (Athens, 334 B.C.)—was a supreme example of scholarly classicism. Sculptor Augustus Saint-Gaudens praised the design as the finest classicizing building in the world "since the Parthenon."[8] Despite this academic approach, Atwood's Art Building offered festive ornamentation with its abundance of columns, sculptural decoration, and its water approach, which was accessible by gondolas during the exposition. In contrast, the Art Institute of Shepley, Rutan & Coolidge was more "pure" or severe in both outline and ornamentation.[9] Because the latter was intended to serve as a permanent "memorial" to the exposition as well as a key cultural monument for the city of Chicago, the museum is a great deal more restrained than Atwood's fantastical Greek interpretation.

An even greater stylistic disjunction between the temporary and the permanent was witnessed at the next great world's fair to take place in the United States: the Pan-American Exposition in Buffalo of 1901. The ostensible purpose of the Buffalo fair was to celebrate pan-American unity.[10] There, too, an art museum was planned to serve first as a venue for the fair's art exhibitions and later as a city museum. Successful businessman and artistic philanthropist John J. Albright, eponymous founder of the Albright Art Gallery, donated money to build a gallery that was to serve as a memorial art building for the fair and for the people of Buffalo thereafter. The milieu of the Pan-American Exposition, however, was to look quite different from that at the World's Columbian Exposition in Chicago. To set the Buffalo fair buildings apart from the famed "White City" of Chicago, the architects of the Pan-American Exposition proposed a "Rainbow City" executed in what they termed a "Free Renaissance" style. Here, too, the permanent art building differed greatly from the fair buildings in the purity of its stylistic execution. The firm of Green & Wicks designed the impermanent Machinery and Electricity buildings at the fair, as well as what survives as the Albright-Knox Art Gallery. The fair buildings were executed in Spanish baroque or mission style, as the architects described it, and brilliantly painted in red, yellow, and green. The art gallery, on the other hand, was executed in "noble" white marble, with a pure Greek hexastyle portico as the centerpiece. It was flanked by pavilions bedecked with not one but two recreations of the Porch of the Maidens from the Erechtheion on the Acropolis, with caryatids executed by Augustus Saint-Gaudens. The colorful, even playful, effect of the fair buildings was, as one observer described it, "panoramic, festal, even gay,"[11] whereas the Albright Art Gallery, with its permanent, serious, even scholarly demeanor, was a great source of civic pride. As a local journalist reported, "The glories of the Pan-American Exposition will pass, but out of it all, and independent of it, Buffalo is to receive a group of permanent structures, of great beauty and of lasting credit to the city. Chief in importance is the Albright Art Gallery, a classic building of white marble."[12]

The stylistic gap between impermanent exposition architecture and permanent art museum architecture was nowhere more apparent than at the Louisiana Purchase Exposition, where Gilbert managed to secure a brilliant commission (see chapter 17). Both the temporary centerpiece of the fair,

Festival Hall, and the new permanent home for the St. Louis Art Museum represented this dichotomy.[13] The Louisiana Purchase Exposition marked the centennial anniversary—as with the World's Columbian Exposition, one year later—of Thomas Jefferson's remarkable acquisition of territory in 1803. In an era still unquestioningly optimistic about both cause and effect of expansionism, this was an event of great moment. In his Opening Day speech, President Theodore Roosevelt claimed, "This work of expansion was by far the greatest work of our people during the years that intervened between the adoption of the Constitution and the outbreak of Civil War. . . . [T]he greatest feat of our forefathers of those generations was the deed of the men, who, with pack train or wagon train, on horseback, on foot, or by boat upon the waters, pushed the frontier ever westward across the continent.[14]

In keeping with the ebullience of President Roosevelt and the zeitgeist of the turn-of-the-century United States, the Louisiana Purchase Exposition was conceived and executed as the largest American world's fair ever built, before or since. In all, the fair covered 1,272 acres of land, with a perimeter of five and one-half miles—necessitating a small, intramural railroad to service the often foot-weary visitors. As with previous fairs, the grounds were divided hierarchically into the main educational exhibits, which formed the Court of Honor and the fair's architectural and landscape centerpiece, and various secondary groupings, including the "Plateau of States," the international pavilions, and the famous "Pike" or Midway. The most important design task was the Court of Honor, and it received the grandest treatment that its designers were capable of imagining.

Together with several local firms, Gilbert was assigned the task of creating the overall scheme of the Court of Honor. Their labors resulted in a fanlike organization of buildings that took advantage of the most distinctive topographical feature of the park, the sixty-foot elevation that would later be named, in honor of the fair's only permanent structure, "Art Hill." Previous American world's fairs, most notably the World's Columbian Exposition and the Pan-American Exposition, had relied on rectangular mall-

style compositions, much as had most of the Washington University competition plans. This new arrangement was more exuberant, more baroque in its conception, and the architecture that would conform to the site would respond to this quality as well.

The crown of the hill served as an obvious focal point, both topographical and architectural. One architect pointed out that "in this hill Nature bestowed a favor that has not before been granted to the designers of expositions."[15] From the start, the architectural centerpiece of the Court of Honor was clearly the central node from which the fan radiated, and this centerpiece was originally intended to house the art exhibitions for the fair. After a complex series

of negotiations between representatives of Washington University (whose grounds were adjacent to and partially used by the fair), the city art museum, and the fair, the art exhibits eventually were housed in a separate, permanent structure, behind the architectural focal point of the Court of Honor: Festival Hall (Figure 16-4).

Gilbert was, perhaps, the most prominent architect associated with the fair from its beginnings, and it is therefore not surprising that he should have

16-4. Festival Hall, Louisiana Purchase Exposition, St. Louis, Missouri, photograph by Official Photographic Company,1904. (Missouri Historical Society, St. Louis, Missouri)

VoL. XI., No. 5.

COPYRIGHT, 1901, BY BATES & GUILD COMPANY.

16-5. "Studies and Sketches for the Festival Hall," in *Architectural Review* 11 (May 1904): pl. 23. (Library of Congress)

secured the commission for the design of the most prominent structure of the fair (for the political machinations behind the appointments see chapter 17). With the baroque axiality of the fan-shaped ground plan, a visitor's eyes would naturally be drawn immediately to the building at the crown of the hill. Together with the landscape program and the water effects, Festival Hall could be viewed as both the terminus at which every visitor would arrive, and the origination point of the entire design. Festival Hall eventually took shape as a large domed auditorium covering two acres in area. It was the venue for the numerous musical events at the fair, and held a great pipe organ which was featured in daily concert performances. At two hundred feet high and two hundred feet in diameter, it was frequently boasted to have a dome larger than the dome of St. Peter's in Rome. Flanking Festival Hall was the colonnaded "Terrace of the States," more than a quarter of a mile long. As a guidebook to the fair rather freely asserts,

"The curved lines of the Colonnade . . . at once suggest the majestic approach of St. Peter's at Rome."[16] Each end of the colonnade terminated in a circular restaurant pavilion, each of which was also domed and measured more than a hundred feet high. These were not designed by Gilbert, but by the chief of design at the fair, E. L. Masqueray. The guidelines imposed by the fair company specified only "Free Renaissance" as the style for all of the buildings, and the result was an exuberant Beaux-Arts confection. Gilbert's Festival Hall featured an enormous arched, rusticated entrance, an engaged colonnade, and a great deal of statuary celebrating the states and territories formed by the Louisiana Purchase. One architect who was associated with the designing of the fair would later term Festival Hall a "huge wedding cake," and indeed, the shape and elaborate decoration do bear a resemblance.[17]

Gilbert arrived at his design through a series of refinements that are documented in a group of drawings he published in a 1904 issue of *Architectural Review* (Figure 16-5). Here, we may follow his design process, as he progressively made the proportions of the building taller and narrower—more baroque than Renaissance in profile—and added decorations such as the round-headed or "oculus" dormers in the attic story. The overall conception draws from numerous sources. The most obvious, already referred to by contemporary descriptions, was the dome of St. Peter's Basilica in Rome (Michelangelo, 1546–64; dome completed by Giacomo della Porta, 1590), with its colonnaded drum and high, ovoid profile. The Albert Hall in London (H. G. D. Scott and Godfrey Sykes, 1867–71), a vast, circular, concert auditorium, provides another logical point of comparison in terms of shape and use. The closest source, both chronologically and functionally, however, is probably the Petit Palais des Champs-Elysées at the Universal Exposition in Paris for 1900, designed by Charles Girault (Figure 16-6). Though different in form, the Petit Palais had a high dome and a great arched entrance undoubtedly influential to Gilbert's conception. Even the radiating ribs decorating the dome and the oculus windows find precedence here. Gilbert's design, however, embodied a more serious approach than the somewhat florid, slightly exaggerated, and very free treatment of the Parisian exposition building of a few years earlier. Though certainly ebullient in a fashion then only deemed suitable for temporary architecture, Festival Hall nevertheless radiates the kind of confidence that comes from a pedigree descended from Michelangelo.

The water effects provided a spectacular setting for Festival Hall. Flowing from the top of the hill were three separate cascades that emptied into the lagoons surrounding the main exhibition buildings. The organization of the fountains, the sculptural decoration, and the cascades made it appear as if the water actually originated within Festival Hall itself. The effect of the ensemble is perhaps best described by a guidebook to the fair, which boasted of the

> three series of cascades, each bordered by fanci-
> ful sculptural groups and suggesting some-
> what—though on a far grander scale—the
> famous cascades at St. Cloud, near Paris. At the

foot of the hill, the Grand Basin with its fountains will reflect the picture. Ninety thousand gallons of filtered water per minute will be discharged into the Grand Basin from the three cascades when they are in full operation. . . . The projected arrangements for illuminating at night the Festival Hall, the Colonnade, the Cascades and the stately Exhibits Palaces bordering on the lagoons, in addition to the many-colored and constantly changing electrical fountains in the Grand Basin, will afford a spectacle of such brilliance as never in this world has been seen before![18]

As a spectacle, it must have been unsurpassed. For visitors accustomed to the rather grittier reality of life in the Midwest at the turn of the century, the vision of the fair must have been jaw-droppingly grand.

The extravagant nature of the fair certainly allowed its other architects a great deal of freedom of expression. Not to be outdone by Gilbert's Festival Hall, notable architects including Van Brunt & Howe (Palace of Varied Industries), Carrère & Hastings (Palace of Manufactures), James Knox Taylor (United States Government Building), and a number of prominent Missouri architects flexed their creative muscles on other gargantuan structures. Contemporary views of the lagoons and the main exhibition buildings provide an impression of a positive sea of columns, towers, domes, bridges, balustrades, and statuary. One contemporary, seduced by the grandeur, described his impression of the effect as "ivoried masonry surmounted with balustrades, rival[ing] dreams of Oriental splendor."[19] Although most observers delighted in the grandeur and variety of architectural expression at the fair, there were some who looked

16-6. Charles Girault, Petit Palais des Champs-Elysées, Universal Exposition, Paris, 1900, in *Exposition Universelle Internationale de 1900 —Vues Photographiques,* pl. 11. (Avery Architectural and Fine Arts Library, Columbia University in the City of New York)

16-7. St. Louis Art Museum, St. Louis, Missouri, 1904, in *Architectural Review* 9 (July 1902): pl. 38. (New York Public Library)

upon it with an indulgent, if not somewhat critical eye, such as one architect who referred to the "general bridecake look of these exposition buildings."[20] The perhaps strident net result was not entirely lost on other writers, one of whom tactfully observed, "The buildings of the Fair are of uniform height and color, but beyond this individual fancy has run riot. A certain impression of discord results."[21] This playfulness, this freedom, provides a telling contrast to the altogether more serious approach Gilbert adopted for the permanent structure of the St. Louis Art Museum.

Still standing atop Art Hill and overlooking the ghosts of the lagoons and the grand exposition halls is the only structure remaining from the panoply of Louisiana Purchase Exposition buildings. Gilbert's St. Louis Art Museum was conceived with the notion that the fair would provide the city with a new art museum while the art museum provided the fair with an art exhibition venue. By the time the planning for the fair had begun, the art museum had outgrown its

downtown building and location, just as Washington University had. Like the university, the museum desired a location that allowed not only for greater space and growth but also for a grander, more dignified architectural treatment than its old building provided. Museum officials had already decided to construct their new museum in Forest Park, so that when the park was also chosen as the exposition site, plans coincided perfectly for housing the art exhibitions at the exposition and leaving behind a "memorial" art museum for the city. In fact, the planning allowed a permanent art building to be fully completed in time to serve as the art venue for the fair, and so the alignment between art museum and exposition coincided here perfectly for the first—and last—time.

The museum originally had been housed in a well-proportioned and executed, but rather modest structure of 1879–81 designed by Peabody & Stearns of Boston (see Figure 16-1). Designed in the then-fashionable Richardsonian Romanesque, the original art museum facade was dominated by three large, blind arches, and enlivened by a richly textured masonry surface and a decorative hipped roof. Further surface enrichment was provided by high-relief portrait busts, bas-relief panels on the upper level, and richly carved swags and acroteria on the cornice. By 1900, this style had fallen out of fashion, as the eclectic mix of styles, textures, and ornamentation gave way to the more rigorous stylings of the Beaux-Arts classical. This historic building was a casualty of the changing face of downtown St. Louis; it was destroyed in 1919 as the area became increasingly industrial.

In contrast to both the original art museum and the fanciful, festive splendor of the impermanent fair buildings, Gilbert's St. Louis Art Museum (Figure 16-7) is a sober exercise in "correct," even scholarly,

the central pavilion below the cornice line. The lower galleries flanking the central pavilion are spare in ornamentation, relieved solely by aedicules with sculpture niches and a narrow clerestory near the cornice line.

Following the aesthetic preferences of museums like the Albright Art Gallery, Gilbert originally had specified pure white marble for this palace of art. Construction of white marble appears in itself to have been a symbolic marker of architectural and cultural seriousness. Not only its expense but also its associations with ancient Greece, Renaissance Italy, and Victorian morals seemed to have contributed to its desirability as the hallmark of monumental building materials. Gilbert, however, was disappointed when gray limestone was substituted as a cost-saving meas-

ancient design. Shedding the neobaroque exuberance of his own Festival Hall, Gilbert adopted what he termed a "Graeco-Roman" style for the art museum. Its architecturally authoritative appearance is indebted to the great central sculpture hall based on the Baths of Caracalla and dominated by the signature Diocletian windows. The entrance features an unpedimented Corinthian hexastyle portico, enlivened by classicizing, pedagogical statuary representing the requisite great ages of art from Egyptian to modern, as interpreted by the scholarship of the time. To either side of the entrance are sculpted allegorical figures representing Sculpture, by Daniel Chester French, and Painting, by Louis Saint-Gaudens. A Greek key motif accents the otherwise blank wall of

ure; the rear facades are brick. The permanent museum building for St. Louis was not nearly large enough to house all the art exhibits for an international exposition, so Gilbert was also called on to design two complementary, temporary buildings flanking the permanent one, these to be constructed of brick, with exterior accents of staff.

As with the origins for Festival Hall, Gilbert in this art museum project drew on several sources and modified the design numerous times before he arrived at the final design. Because of the vicissitudes of the commission and the debates over which parts of the fair ensemble would be permanent and which temporary, his plans took more than one year to solidify (see chapter 17). Once again, his process may

16-8. Study for Art Building/Art Museum, Louisiana Purchase Exposition, St. Louis, Missouri. *World's Fair Bulletin* 3 (November 1901): 11. (Library of Congress)

be followed in designs published before he arrived at the final stage. The original conception for this part of the fair was that the art museum and the fair's art exhibition building be one and the same. Working under this impression, Gilbert produced a design for the art building, reproduced in the *World's Fair Bulletin* in 1901, that appears to combine the approaches to design that would later go their separate ways (Figure 16-8). The central, domed structure that would become Festival Hall here appeared much more classical, with a central pavilion that combines the Roman thermal bath idea with the low saucer dome of the Pantheon. The columned portico merges with the extended colonnades, and all terminate in very restrained, low, end pavilions.

16-9. Eugène Bigot, "Un Etablissement d'Eaux Thermales et Casino," *Grand Prix de Rome, Ecole des Beaux-Arts* (Paris, 1900). (Avery Architectural and Fine Arts Library, Columbia University in the City of New York)

The determination to separate the two designs resulted in a very different aspect for the art museum building itself. It appears that Gilbert's fancy took flight with Festival Hall, while the art museum became more scholarly and restrained. His inspiration for the thermal bath form, as well as some of the grand planning effects of the fair in general, may have come from designs executed for the annual Grand Prix de Rome competition at the Ecole des Beaux-Arts in Paris. Specifically, the Prix de Rome project for 1900 was for "Un Etablissement d'Eaux Thermales et Casino" (a spa and casino resort complex). Its winner, Eugène Bigot, produced a design that featured a Roman thermal bath structure as the central

feature of his ensemble (Figure 16-9). That Gilbert may have eyed these designs is further suggested in the resemblance of Gilbert's Festival Hall to the two low, domed structures on either side of Bigot's Roman bath. Clearly, however, the realities of St. Louis in 1904 required a much more modest, controlled, and compact plan than the sprawling gargantuan fantasies prompted by the Prix de Rome, and the end result was really quite different and original. Architectural critic Montgomery Schuyler praised the art building as "substantial and dignified, ... of a classic severity."[22] Indeed, the museum's look may well be described as severe, especially in comparison to the fanciful concoctions of the fair. At least part of the stylistic shift may be attributed to cost-cutting necessities. Recreating elaborate staff decoration in stone would have been prohibitively expensive, but it also would have been as inappropriate as a Paris hat on a Midwestern schoolmarm.

Not only the difference in styles between the Festival Hall and the Art Museum, but also the placement of these two buildings in relation to one another is telling of attitudes toward the appropriate application of these various styles. Interestingly, and somewhat controversially, the size and location of Festival Hall had the effect of preventing the Art Museum from participating in the panorama of the Court of Honor. No photographs of the main fan-shaped group of buildings show the Art Museum. This was apparent to many observers, for example, one in the *American Architect,* who noted, "It is . . . to be regretted that the costly and well-designed Art Building should be cut out and wasted as an effective element in the architectural grouping."[23] Schuyler, too, noted this odd arrangement wherein the art museum was screened from what he termed the "vulgar gaze" of the fair-goers.[24] The art building, originally conceived as the focus of the fairgrounds and placed at the top of Art Hill to dominate the composition, became essentially invisible from most vantage points within the main avenues of the fairgrounds. "The main [art] building is not," the critic maintained, "of an 'expositional' character, and its gravity might have struck a sterner note than would have comported with the Fair. But it seems a pity, all the same, that it should have been hidden to make a local holiday."[25] The concept of the "vulgar gaze" of the fair-goers privileges the Art Museum as belonging to an entirely different realm from the remainder of the buildings at the fair. The fair architecture, presumably, was designed with a more popular audience in mind and therefore would please the less architecturally sophisticated hordes who attended the fair in order to gawk at technological and cultural novelties from the world over. As patronizing as such a notion may be, the placement and styles of the two buildings and their single designer indicate that some such thought process was in effect.

For the art building, a more "refined" style would be deemed appropriate, and Gilbert not only provided the style but also secluded the building from the rest of the built ensemble so that it would have to be actively sought out. Contained within a courtyard formed by the impermanent structures, there was a

fair architecture. Whereas the cotton-candy confections of the fair have all vanished, the art museums remain as monuments to cultural dignity and architectural good taste. Gilbert's inspiration was guided by the era's concern for proper decorum and in a sense, architectural etiquette. One may loosen one's tie when designing a bauble to please merry-making fair-goers, but a stricter dress code applies to the business of high culture and architectural monuments graven in stone.

Gilbert's vision of what an art museum ought to be—its relationship to the urban milieu and its cultural importance—sought fuller expression more than a decade after the close of the Louisiana Purchase Exposition. In 1915, the museum commissioned Gilbert to create a plan for the future expansion of the museum to approximately ten times its

formal, gently sunken garden, a further indication of seclusion and difference from the rest of the fair. From this one may judge that he, like Schuyler, agreed that the cultural requirements of the fair versus those of the Art Museum were very different indeed and needed to be addressed through commensurately formulated styles of architecture. As another contemporary observed, the "festive and ephemeral nature of exposition architecture tends to loosen the bonds of restraint which should be felt in designing a permanent structure."[26] The high seriousness with which the era regarded the cultural agenda of the art museum is reflected in its architecture, and at St. Louis, as at Chicago and Buffalo, the architect responded to this perceived necessity with a learned classicism in direct contrast to the playfulness of the

then-current size, including greatly increased gallery space, collections storage, and offices, as well as two lecture halls, a cafeteria, and conservation studios, among others (Figure 16-10). In addition, Gilbert was requested to provide a landscape plan for the area fronting the museum and comprising the distance originally covered by the major axis of the world's fair exhibition buildings. Here was Gilbert's chance to create a truly grand composition on the same scale as the Prix de Rome competitions—and one that stood a good chance of being executed.

The resulting plan generated a mall-style, axial procession from the park's entrance at the base of Art Hill through a tree-lined promenade, over four bridges spanning the River des Peres, around a remodeled lagoon (which was originally the Grand

16-10. St. Louis Art Museum Expansion Plan [detail], St. Louis, Missouri, 1916. (St. Louis Art Museum Archives)

Basin of the fair), up a vast Grecian open-air theater, and crowned by an expansive new art museum of which the original structure would be a mere kernel of a grand new complex. The plan for the new museum developed upon the Roman thermal bath, expanding the theme with six additional Diocletian windows along the facade. The expansion program was based on J.-N.-L. Durand's eighteenth-century Ecole des Beaux-Arts project for a museum, which forms a large square twice bisected with galleries, thereby forming four interior courtyards and a central rotunda (in this case, the fourth side of the square is missing). Gilbert's rotunda for the St. Louis Art Museum plan featured an ambitious saucer dome elevated on a drum for distant visibility. A cross section reveals that the dome was to have been coffered on its interior, much like the Pantheon in Rome. To balance the increased size and height of the new building, he added colonnaded end pavilions at the corners.

The grandeur of the proposed expansion is undeniable. The scale revived the glories of the 1904 exposition, and the ensemble effects might even have surpassed those temporary structures. A contemporary, clearly under the spell of the plan, noted, "The project contemplates the most ambitious and enterprising scheme of improvement ever projected as a single municipal park improvement in the United States and will give to St. Louis a recreation ground that . . . will outrival in beauty and artistic design any city park in this country."[27] In 1917, the date of this statement, the City Beautiful movement was still enjoying ripple effects in both architectural and popular circles.[28] Such architects as Gilbert, Daniel Burnham, and the firm of McKim, Mead & White, along with others, adopted ideals from the Ecole des Beaux-Arts and combined them with contemporary visions of the role of the United States on the world stage and how the American city should look. In order to rival cities like Paris, they believed, the United States needed planners and architects to create grand civic ensembles with monumental, classicizing public buildings and appropriately grand framing spaces. They envisioned baroque-style boulevards, axial planning, long vistas, and elegant settings for the grand public buildings they dreamed of design-

ing. Gilbert's vision for the expanded St. Louis Art Museum, had it been realized, would have been one of the greatest achievements of the City Beautiful movement.

For better or worse, neither Gilbert's plan for the St. Louis Art Museum nor most of the grand civic ensembles dreamt of by his generation of architects ever came to fruition. Far too costly, far too large, and far too time-consuming, most of these plans remained strictly on paper. In this respect, Gilbert's 1916 expansion plan was no different from several other equally grandiose plans for late-nineteenth- and early-twentieth-century art museums. These included Richard Morris Hunt's grand plan for the Metropolitan Museum of Art in New York (1895); McKim, Mead & White's for the Brooklyn Institute of Arts and Sciences (1893) and the Minneapolis Institute of the Arts (1911); Guy Lowell's for the Museum of Fine Arts, Boston (1907); and John Russell Pope's for the Baltimore Museum of Art (1925).[29] Beautiful as they appeared on paper and as glorious as they might have been in reality, these plans remained largely as futuristic visions of a generation gone past.

In terms of civic pride and cultural ambition, perhaps the only building to rival the pride of place of the art museum is the central public library. There can be no question that for the United States at the turn of the century, the central public library stood for culture, learning, and the highest civic ambitions of any urban area. As such, the library merited the greatest attention to placement in the city plan and seriousness of architectural treatment as well as functional design. "Related as it is with limitless associations, it demands the expression, in the highest sense, of art and science; and of all that stands for culture and the gift of civilization," one observer noted.[30] In the St. Louis Public Library, Gilbert was able to achieve perhaps the fullest realization of his architectural and civic ambitions for St. Louis (see Figure C-4).

In 1901 St. Louis was without a true, separate public library. The gears for a new building were set in motion that year, when steel magnate Andrew Carnegie donated one million dollars for St. Louis public libraries: half a million for branch libraries, and half for the new central library building. The site was provided by the city, and the remaining money needed for construction was provided through library funds. The St. Louis Public Library thus benefited from one of the greatest philanthropic endeavors of the era: the Carnegie libraries.[31] Carnegie donated millions of dollars of his fortune to build branch libraries and large central buildings in small towns and large cities across the nation. It was his belief that libraries were the best means of improving the lot of the laboring classes, immigrants, children, and the poor. Despite a philosophy that rings paternalistic today, Carnegie remains one of the single most influential—and most generous in terms of dollars—philanthropists ever to have lived. His legacy, and the gratitude felt by St. Louisans toward him, may be read quite literally on an exterior inscription of the St. Louis Public Library, which quotes his tenet: "I choose free libraries as the best agencies for improving the masses of the people because they only help those who help themselves. They never pauperize. A taste for reading drives out lower tastes."

Following the Carnegie gift, the library organized a competition in 1907 to choose the architect for the new building. Such competitions were a particularly thorny issue for the architectural profession around the turn of the century: they were fraught with political, technical, and professional difficulties. Representatives of the St. Louis Public Library conducted an especially well-administered and fair competition. They decided to run the competition by invitation only, to pay the competitors one thousand dollars each, to make the competition short (one month in duration), and to require very minimal drawings (block plan, floor plans, elevations, and two sections) of small size (no larger than twenty by thirty inches). Of the nine invitees, approximately half were local firms and half were nationally recognized. The local firms were Barnett, Haynes & Barnett; Eames & Young; Willam B. Ittner; Mauran, Russell & Garden; and Theodore C. Link. Outsiders included Carrère & Hastings; Palmer & Hornbostel; Albert Randolph Ross; and Gilbert.

The drawings were judged by a jury that consisted in part of three prominent architects chosen by the competitors themselves: Frank Miles Day, Philip Sawyer, and Walter Cook. Although the program for the competition did not specify any particular architectural style, it appears to have been taken for granted that the building would be classical. One indication of this was in the program, namely, that the drawings should show "positions provided for such works of sculpture and mural painting as will lend proper beauty and dignity to a building of this nature."[32] In the language of the day, a building of "dignity," decorated with sculpture and mural painting, was understood to embody City Beautiful and Ecole des Beaux-Arts ideals. That the submissions should have been uniformly classicizing was perhaps inevitable, as one architect argued who made a speech

before the Illinois Library Association in 1903: "Let an architect suggest Romanesque or Gothic or early French Renaissance or Byzantine, and he is, especially in the smaller cities, met with a cold, stony smile, plainly saying, 'You may think because I don't live in Chicago I don't know anything about architecture, but you may as well understand that I am quite up-to-date, and know what is the proper thing in library styles.' Any other style [than neoclassical] is practically fatal to an architect's chances."[33] What a dim view of one's patrons! One of the competitors, Tom P. Barnett, rather pointedly referred to the situation in 1913 when in an article, he was able to vent his frustrations in having to relinquish this local plum of a project to an out-of-towner. "We all know," he wrote, "that there is a great number of prominent architects in New York City . . . [who have] an intolerance toward any other architectural style."[34] Barnett may perhaps be forgiven his sour grapes. "There has been weeping and wailing in St. Louis," one architect wryly averred when the local architects failed to win such a prominent local commission.[35]

Clearly, the competitors for the St. Louis commission understood the cultural requirements of the central public library to be serious and uplifting

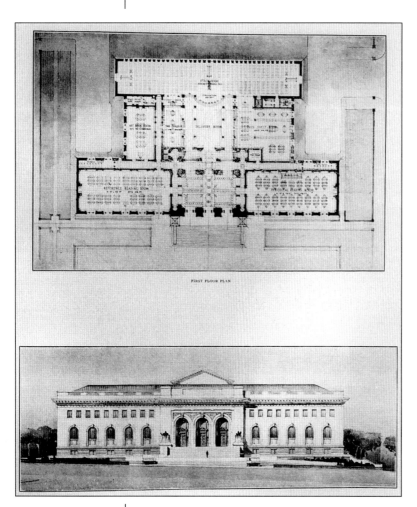

FIRST FLOOR PLAN

16-12. William B. Ittner, St. Louis Public Library Competition, St. Louis, Missouri, First-floor plan and front elevation, 1907, in *Western Architect* 10 (August 1907): n.p. (Minnesota Historical Society)

through a classical idiom, especially in light of such highly influential buildings as the Boston Public Library (McKim, Mead & White, 1888–95) and the New York Public Library (Carrère & Hastings, 1897–1911). Gilbert's winning entry (Figure 16-11) was, in fact, a rather severely edited version of those other renowned structures. It combined the arcaded facade of the Boston Public Library with the triple-

arched entrance portico of the New York Public Library. With the entrance pavilion constituting the only protruding element of the facade, Gilbert's design had a more simplified massing than the New York library, and there is very little in the way of sculptural or landscaping adornment. Numerous contemporary observers, indeed, commented on the design's severity. The *American Architect* saw the relationship of the design to the New York and Boston libraries thus: "It is not surprising to find that our three great libraries represent the work of men who are of the highest standing in their profession. The buildings they have designed typify in a sense the cities in which they are built. . . . No other building in Boston better represents that city than its public library. Likewise in the St. Louis facade we may discern a city possibly more modest, but substantial, conservative and powerful."[36]

Possibly the most notable aspect of Gilbert's stylistic treatment is its lack of elaboration. Numerous sources observed its great simplicity, which was nevertheless greatly admired and viewed as quite modern. Again, the *American Architect:* "If to the French mind this simplicity approaches poverty, it must also appear to unify the whole. We do not hesitate to say that its simplicity, repose and placidity; its dignity, strength and refinement, place this building among the most successful facades of modern times."[37] Another writer commented that the "principal feature" of the library was "its extreme simplicity. . . [T]he building will present a plain, but massive view, conspicuous in its lack of large and towering columns. The absence of columns will add very much to the beauty of the building."[38] Even the normally reserved Gilbert was sanguine about the effects of his building, writing to a librarian that the future building constituted "what I hope to make one of the best of my architectural works."[39]

In the St. Louis Public Library competition, designs from all the high-placing competitors survive, and from them we can gauge both the reactions to the competition program from the competitors themselves and the reactions of the jury to the submitted designs. Local architect William B. Ittner earned second place with his design, which bears a very strong resemblance to the New York Public Library as well as Gilbert's own submission (Figure 16-12). In fact, competitor Barnett's criticism that "in competitions for public work, you will find one design so like the other that it almost appears that they are taken off by hectographic process," gains some validity with this submission.[40] Third place was awarded to the actual architects of the New York Public Library, Carrère & Hastings, who appear to have been penalized for doing something different (Figure 16-13). In this case, their design, which they may be excused for not broadly publishing, is considerably weaker than their masterful design for New York's main library. Featuring an awkwardly placed and questionably appropriate saucer dome over the delivery room, and too-small end pavilions terminating an undistinguished entrance facade, the surprise here is that they ranked as highly as they did. Despite the chagrin generated locally by the out-of-town winner, Gilbert's design appears as the most boldly handled and competent of the submissions.

That St. Louisans saw the library as an important part of their city plan as well as their civic identity may be seen in a work published contemporaneously with the library competition: *A City Plan for St. Louis,* published by the Civic League of St. Louis in 1907. This tract, firmly rooted in the City Beautiful tradition and rhetoric, noted its desire to "bring civic orderliness and beauty" to St. Louis through a group plan for municipal buildings, a park system, small civic centers, street improvements, and a municipal art commission. *The Plan for St. Louis* envisioned a group of grand public buildings as the centerpiece of its program, comprising a major boulevard with city hall at one end and such key civic structures as a courthouse, police headquarters, and not least, the new public library grouped along its borders. The plan proposed to serve as a blueprint for future construction in the area between Thirteenth and Fourteenth Streets, and from Olive Street to Clark Avenue, encompassing the library's present location at Fourteenth and Olive. The plan thus created would tie "the civic group together and balanc[e] in its mass and majesty of location the beautiful Library which must soon occupy the magnificent site, and which

will stand ready to lend itself to this proposed scheme for the betterment and uplifting of our city."[41]

The City Beautiful movement was not merely an aesthetic movement. Its adherents believed that municipal improvements would bring about economic and social change, as well. As the *Plan for St. Louis* asserts, a thriving, orderly, and beautiful city "invites into its gates visitors, retail merchants, and shopkeepers from the surrounding country and travelers from everywhere. In order to have them tarry awhile and return again the city must be made attractive, which means clean streets, pleasant homes, good transportation facilities, parks, boulevards, and stately public buildings."[42] Even more important than the monetary aspect, however, was the social impact that beautiful public architecture and educational institutions were believed to have on the populace in gener-

al. The author of a guide to the library phrased it best when he wrote, "That a library contributes, as nothing else, to the education, culture and refinement of the community, and that in addition to the education obtained from books is that which comes from surroundings of quietude and refined good taste. That a love of beauty is an element of good citizenship and that to inculcate this lesson is a proper part of the general educational function of the library."[43] No grander ideal could be upheld for an edifice of brick and stone, but it is an ideal toward which Gilbert's St. Louis buildings proudly aspire.

16-13. Carrère & Hastings, "The St. Louis Public Library competition, Olive Street Elevation, St. Louis, Missouri, 1907, in *St. Louis Times,* July 10, 1907, p. 8. (St. Louis Public Library Archives, Special Collections, St. Louis Public Library)

CHAPTER 17

"A DIFFICULT AND PERPLEXING MATTER": THE LOUISIANA PURCHASE EXPOSITION

Susan Luftschein

On April 28, 1904, an article on the front page of the *New York Times* had the following headline: "Cass Gilbert Resigns and Sues World's Fair." According to the article, Gilbert, who had served on the Commission of Architects, had designed two of the fair's more important structures, and had chaired the subcommittee responsible for the fair's ground plan, alleged that the Louisiana Purchase Exposition Company owed him approximately forty-eight thousand dollars as compensation for his labor. Such a situation was not unheard of in the architectural and building trades; however, it had never before arisen in the context of a world's fair. When it came to payment, American architects had long been at the mercy of the individuals or organizations who commissioned their services, whether it was in a competition or a straightforward commission. Since its inception in 1857, the AIA as a professional organization was concerned with the manner in which its members and their clients conducted business. The AIA advocated that a percentage of building costs be standard payment for its members.[1] The figure of forty-eight thousand dollars, calculated from a percentage of the total costs of the buildings that Gilbert had designed, was no small sum and was well above the standard fee received by the other architects working at the fair. In addition to the matter of compensation, the architect cited additional reasons for his actions in his letter of resignation. What follows is an unraveling of the chain of events that led to this lawsuit.

Gilbert was one of a group of eight architects and architectural firms selected to design the fair's exhibit palaces for the Louisiana Purchase Exposition, held in St. Louis's Forest Park from April to December 1904. The architects were hired by the fair's Committee on Grounds and Buildings, one of nine standing committees that oversaw the day-to-day operations of the fair. The others were the Executive, Press and Publicity, Ways and Means, Transportation, Finance, Concessions, Insurance, and Foreign Relations Committees. In addition to these committees, the fair's operations were broken down into four divisions—Works, Exhibits, Exploitation, and Concessions and Admissions—each headed by a director. The four divisions and the standing committees reported directly to the President of the Louisiana Purchase Exposition Company.

The Committee on Grounds and Buildings met for the first time on June 22, 1901. Their first official decision was to reconvene on June 25 with a list of nine architects. At this second meeting it was further resolved that one of these architects should be a landscape architect, and that of the remaining eight, five were to be residents of the states in the Louisiana Purchase Territory. This stipulation was modeled on the architectural commission of the 1893 World's Columbian Exposition in Chicago, the obvious model for most aspects of the Louisiana Purchase Exposition. At this second meeting, telegrams were drafted to nine firms, all of whom accepted the appointment.

The eight architectural firms that formed the Commission of Architects (the landscape architect, George E. Kessler of Kansas City, was not a member of the commission) were charged with both the design of the exhibit palaces and the layout of the grounds. Although they reported directly to the fair's Committee on Grounds and Buildings through the director of Works (drawn from their ranks), they were generally given a great deal of autonomy. The St. Louis architects chosen were Isaac Stockton Taylor; Eames & Young; Barnett, Haynes & Barnett; Widmann, Walsh & Boisselier; and Theodore C. Link. All were men with important and established businesses in St. Louis, but unlike the majority of the

Chicago architects at the Columbian Exposition, they did not have national reputations. Taylor (1851–1917) (Figure 17-1), an architect of great reputation in St. Louis, was selected by his fellow architects to serve as the fair's director of Works; at Chicago it was also a local architect, Daniel H. Burnham, who served in the same position.[2] Taylor trained with one of St. Louis's prominent nineteenth-century architects, George Ingham Barnett, with whom he was later in practice. After opening his own office in 1879, he designed many of St. Louis's commercial buildings, including the National Bank of Commerce (c. 1900). Unlike Burnham, Taylor's effectiveness as a leader was questionable at best.

The nonlocal architects selected were Walker & Kimball (Omaha and Boston), Carrère & Hastings (New York City), Van Brunt & Howe (Kansas City), and Gilbert. Of these, Gilbert was arguably the best known, and his prominence secured him a pivotal place on the architects' commission as well as the most prized commission of the fair. He was selected by his fellow architects to chair the subgroup that determined the ground plan, and chosen to design what was, at the start of the planning process in 1901, considered the crowning monument of the composition, the "Art Palace," or Art Building (Figure 17-2).

17-1. Isaac S. Taylor, Director of Works, Louisiana Purchase Exposition, Photograph by Byrnes Photographic Company, c. 1903. (Missouri Historical Society, St. Louis)

Unlike the other structures designed for the fair, the Art Building from the start was to be permanent. This decision was made not by the Commission of Architects but by the Exposition Company's Committee on Fine Arts. At the close of the fair, the Art Building would serve as the new home for St. Louis's art museum. This decision was made in July 1901—so early in the planning process that the newly formed architects' commission had not yet assigned

any buildings. Once they were informed of this decision, and since they had determined that the Art Building would be the fair's centerpiece, it was only natural that Gilbert be awarded the fair's premier architectural commission.

Unlike his fellow architects who designed temporary structures that were essentially shells with no interior arrangements, Gilbert, as designer of the fair's only permanent structure, was obliged to work closely with the director of the exhibit department assigned to his building and the director of the city's art museum. Halsey Cooley Ives (1874–1911) (Figure 17-3) held both positions. As chief of the Art Department, Ives worked closely with the Committee on Fine Arts (which reported to the Executive Committee) and reported directly to Frederick J. V. Skiff, director of the Division of Exhibits. Ives enjoyed a distinguished career in museum work. He had been appointed director of St. Louis's Museum of Fine Arts in 1881, a post he would retain until his

death. He also had significant experience with exposition work, having served as the chief of the Art Department at the World's Columbian Exposition. In addition to his museum and exposition work, Ives was a member of the faculty at Washington University and had served as director of the St. Louis School of Fine Arts from 1879 to 1881. Ives's goal at the Louisiana Purchase Exposition was to create a system of exhibit classification much more detailed than had ever been used at a world's fair. He wanted a system of classification for works of fine and decorative art and examples of the mechanical and industrial arts; the latter were traditionally omitted from world's fair displays and Ives wanted to reverse this trend and dispel the bias against them. This was a goal he had set for himself at Chicago but had been unable to carry out.[3] His scheme was ambitious and untried, and relied on a building that would allow these types of exhibits to be adequately displayed. Among the building's requirements were special wall openings at the east and west ends to allow for the installation of stained glass, and side-lit galleries for the exhibition of applied art objects.

Ives was selected to act as chief of the Art Department at the same meeting of the Committee on Fine Arts during which the decision was made to erect a permanent art building. Although it was not his idea to make this structure permanent, he had been an advocate of a new home for St. Louis's art museum for some time. As Ives was already the director of the city's existing museum, it was only natural that he would continue his role in this new setting at the close of the fair. He therefore would naturally have had a strong interest in the design of the new museum, no matter who was chosen to be its architect.

Thus, the problems that Gilbert faced were threefold. First, he had to design a building that would function as the centerpiece of an elaborate and extremely large fairground (the Louisiana Purchase Exposition was the largest fair ever held in the United States) where it would occupy the place of honor in the center of the fair's main picture of palaces. (The term "main picture" was used by all individuals involved with the planning of the Louisiana Purchase Exposition, and almost all other world's fairs between 1893 and 1915, to describe the location of the primary structures.) Second, Gilbert had to design a structure that would meet the unusual needs of the fair's Art Department, as noted above. Third, he needed to design a building that would meet the needs of the city's art museum after the fair was over.

The first problem, recognized almost immediately not just by Gilbert but by all the individuals involved, was to design a building suitable as a crowning monument to the fairgrounds. Gilbert's original plan for the Art Building included an elaborate colonnade that followed the brow of the hill, fanning out from either side of the structure (see Figure 17-4, which depicts the modified colonnade flanking Festival Hall). The colonnade would frame the building and create a composition that Gilbert considered appropriate for this location. Since all the architects on the commission were charged not just with the design of individual buildings but also with the lay-

out of the fairgrounds, all considered the colonnade an integral part of the plan, as important as the building itself. However, in Ives's view, this colonnade only added unnecessary expense to the cost of the building and detracted from the real business at hand—designing suitable gallery space.

On November 16, 1901, Ives wrote an impassioned letter to Gilbert trying to impress upon him the importance of the design of the Art Building as exhibition space. He touched on many concerns, the least of which was the amount of wall space. Another

17-3. Halsey C. Ives, chief of the Fine Arts Department (seated), with Charles M. Kurtz, assistant to the chief of the Fine Arts Department. (Charles M. Kurtz Papers, Archives of American Art, Smithsonian Institution)

17-4. The Grand Basin, Festival Hall, and the Colonnade of States, Louisiana Purchase Exposition, photograph by Official Photograph Company, 1904. (Missouri Historical Society, St. Louis)

"A DIFFICULT AND PERPLEXING MATTER"

concern was the possibility that the permanent status of his building would be revoked if Gilbert could not change his design in order to bring down cost.

> Mr. [Isaac] Taylor constantly comes back to the statement that we must cut the building down. . . . I suggested to him the plan of divorcing the decorative part of the structure from the exhibit building and to change the location of the latter to another part of the grounds. . . . This would make possible the decorative scheme. . . . As to the location of the Art building, I believe that a great gain would result from placing it near one of the principal entrances to the Exposition grounds instead of a mile or more away as in accordance with the plan thus far pursued. Certainly no other exhibit section will attract as many visitors to the grounds. . . . Such a change would insure the adoption of the building as a permanent Museum structure by a responsible board willing to maintain and enlarge it.

> I have been advised within the last two days that the proposed location of the Art building on the top of the hill will lead to its being refused as the future permanent building for the Museum, as it would be so remote from car-lines as to make it almost inaccessible for years to come. . . .

> The authorities will permit the use of one million dollars in the erection of the Art building alone. While if the decorative scheme be carried out in connection with it, they will allot only one million dollars for the two together. The business-end of the Directory will not differentiate.

> Please understand that all I have written comes from a real desire to help solve the problem which I clearly see will confront us, since my interview with Mr. Taylor. If you will please telegraph the simple word 'YES' I will move at once toward two schemes as outlined. If you telegraph 'NO' I will take no action, thus letting matters take their course, however they may go.[4]

Gilbert does not seem to have replied to this plea; however, he made very clear at other times that his general disposition toward moving the Art Building was not favorable.

Undoubtedly at Ives's urging, the Committee on Fine Arts met in November to discuss the advisability of changing the location of the Art Building. Gilbert's original design, with its emphasis on decorative detail, was first and foremost a structure appropriate to provide a focus for the exposition and only secondly an exhibition structure. As Ives was quick to point out, even in a revised plan, Gilbert only provided a little more than seven thousand feet of wall space (as compared to the more than thirteen hundred provided at Chicago)—hardly enough for the expanded classification system Ives was determined to inaugurate.

Both the committee and Ives felt that Gilbert's plan included too much ornamental detail and did not pay enough attention to the exhibition needs of the Art Department. The ornamental detail alone would add significantly to the cost of the building and eat up the majority of the project's appropriation of one million dollars. Thus, not enough money would be left for an adequate exhibition structure outfitted with adequate ventilation, the necessary amount of wall and floor space, and the appropriate size and location of doors to allow for the suitable flow of traffic. Ives's budget also supported interior decoration costs, as well as insurance and other incidental expenses. Gilbert's original design called for a budget more than three times what the Exposition Company had allotted to the Art Department. What was needed was a new site that would compel Gilbert to design an exhibition structure—a building possessing less complicated features and requiring less expensive decorative treatment. The meeting resulted in the decision to find a new location for the Art Building. In a letter written to Gilbert after the meeting, Ives suggested that the solution to the problem would be to separate the Art building from the decorative scheme atop the hill. He also indicated that the building devoted to the Department of Art would be better suited in another part of the grounds, one more accessible to visitors and where the problem of construction would be much simpler and less expensive.[5] The decision reached by the committee was to move the building to the grounds of Washington University, immediately adjacent to the fairgrounds;

since some of the university's buildings were already being employed by the exposition, this was the obvious choice for a new location.

Gilbert was not happy with this decision. An office memo dated a few weeks after the Committee on Fine Arts meeting detailed a conversation between Gilbert and Walter Cope, of the architectural firm Cope & Stewardson, designers of the campus, about the design of the building. Gilbert had advised Robert S. Brookings (chairman of Washington University's Board of Trustees from 1895 to1928) not to place the Art Building on the university's grounds; if such a move were to take place, it should only be done with Cope's consent, and Cope should design it. Gilbert was adamant about Cope's not doing anything that would mar the university grounds.[6] Many of the university's buildings were used by the exposition; for example, Brookings Hall was used as the Administration Building, and Francis Field provided the venue for the 1904 Summer Olympics, which were held in conjunction with the fair.

Moving the building was no longer an option by early December 1901, when Washington University decided it did not want the Art Building because it did not harmonize with those it had recently erected. This decision forced the art committee, in its efforts to reduce the cost of Gilbert's structure, to find yet another location on the fairgrounds that could house the main part of the structure. The architects' commission, notably, was insistent on keeping Gilbert's elaborate colonnade atop the hill as part of the design. Although a site by the entrance to the fairgrounds was considered, by the end of the year discussions returned to using the hill. However, the building would be set back from the brow, behind the colonnade. As such, the proposed structure no longer crowned the fair's central building group. On December 23, the Committee on Grounds and Buildings adopted recommendations made by Ives to separate the Art Building proper from the decorative scheme of the layout of the exposition grounds as a whole. They also approved plans that provided a total of twelve thousand lineal feet of wall space and sufficient floor area for the installation in a "dignified manner" of the exhibits not requiring wall space. The

many shifts in location and the new plans approved by the Committee meant that Gilbert created a total of four sets of plans and devoted much more time to this project than he or the fair organizers originally anticipated.

Ives, as both department chief and museum director, naturally assumed an advisory role in the design process. In August 1901, immediately after his appointment, he set about preparing small-scale plans to show what he believed to be the proper arrange-

ment of galleries that would provide adequate light, ventilation, and circulation and allow him to set up his system of classification. These plans were created at the request of Taylor, and were approved by the Committee on Grounds and Buildings. Taylor then transmitted Ives's ideas to Gilbert. According to Ives, his plan was " . . . intended to set forth the necessity of certain essentials in the design, which proper experience had shown to have been invariably disregarded

17-5. Sculpture Hall, Palace of Fine Arts, Louisiana Purchase Exposition, 1904. (Missouri Historical Society, St. Louis)

at other expositions, as proper lighting, proper ventilation, and provision for the circulation of a large number of people."[7] In October 1901, Ives traveled to St. Paul to confer with Gilbert about the latter's preliminary plans. Gilbert presented Ives with designs that he found "sufficiently advanced to convince [me] that, if completed as suggested, the structure would have . . . great architectural beauty, but as has been the case with nearly every other exposition art building with which [I have] been familiar it would lack the essentials which go to constitute the successful exhibition building . . . ."[8] Ives requested that Gilbert modify his design, which Gilbert agreed to do. When the architect submitted his revised plans, Ives found that his requests had been ignored. This situation persisted through a number of revisions. It was not until April 1902, well after construction on the other exhibit palaces had begun, that Gilbert submitted plans that were acceptable to Ives.

The minutes of the April 11, 1902 meeting of the Committee on Fine Arts reveal how the final plans were accepted. Two letters from Gilbert were submitted detailing the lighting and construction of the Art Building. Gilbert was adamant that he did not want to leave the design of the Art Building to the Exposition authorities. He enclosed a copy of his appointment letter as architect of the Art Building, which made provisions for the arbitration of such matters by the Commission of Architects, but said that he was willing to undertake this procedure and abide by the decision. Isaac W. Morton, chair of the Art Committee, informed Taylor that compromises needed to be made and that Ives and the Art Committee would accept Gilbert's revised plans, in the interest of time.[9]

The St. Paul meeting inaugurated a troubled relationship between Ives and Gilbert. Both men had strong personalities and very clear ideas about what the Art Building should look like, both inside and out, and expressed these opinions often. What follows is first Ives's side of the story, then Gilbert's.

The relationship between Ives and Gilbert, not surprisingly, changed significantly during the course of their acquaintance. At first it was friendly.

After a meeting in October 1901 with Taylor and Gilbert in St. Louis, after the St. Paul conference, Ives, in his monthly report to Frederick Skiff, the director of Exhibits, wrote optimistically that "[I] was impressed with the feeling that the architect was desirous of carrying out as far as possible the ideas suggested by the exhibit department."[10] As we have seen, this was not the case. Just one month later, Ives found it necessary to explain to Gilbert and Taylor that his challenge was different from that in Chicago, and consequently, Gilbert's task was quite different than Charles Atwood's had been. He came away from these discussions with the conclusion that the only solution to the problems regarding gallery space and dollar appropriation was to move the building: "It is of the utmost importance that these various questions of site and of the extent and character of the building which I have outlined . . . be definitely settled at the earliest possible moment, as our further progress in promoting the interests of . . . [the department's] work must await such action."[11] It was also at this point that Ives's relationship with Gilbert began to sour.

In all subsequent reports, Ives makes constant reference to the delay in receipt of plans holding up the work of the department. This was no small matter. Ives urgently needed plans to show potential exhibitors in order to begin the demanding task of apportioning and assigning space. In early March 1902, Ives wrote to Isaac W. Morton, chair of the Committee on Fine Arts, "The matter resolves itself into a question of whether the architect shall sacrifice the needs of the Department to the requirements of his design as worked out . . . or shall conform to the instructions of the various authorities of the Exposition. I have expressed myself so frequently in regard to my own opinion . . . that I would be glad if it would be reported to some authority of sufficient influence to decide whether the architect is to dictate or the instructions of the Grounds and Buildings Committee be adhered to."[12] Ives obviously felt he was not getting his point across because later that same month he wrote,

It would seem, with Mr. Gilbert, that extraordinary measures must be taken in order to have the will of the Committee followed. We should not regret Mr. Gilbert's action should he decide to abandon the work. We have great admiration for his persistence and for his success in bending the will of other people to his. We can have nothing further to say in regard to this matter . . . From its inception . . . up to the present, six months time have been wasted by the persistence of the architect in going contrary to the requests of those who are concerned in our side of the work . . . . I write quite freely . . . because I feel that we have reached the point where "patience has ceased to be a virtue."[13]

At the end of the month he summed up the problem in his monthly report to Skiff:

Great delay and serious complications have resulted from the persistent refusal on the part of the architect . . . to carry out the suggestions of the officials of the Exhibit Department. . . . Several efforts [to develop satisfactory plans] . . . failed to recognize the requirements [and] were opposed by the exhibit officials until finally an agreement was reached. . . . To reach the [final building configuration] has required a gradual change of plans. . . . To accomplish this has required a period of six months, and at this writing the officers of the department cannot secure floor-plans drawn to scale upon which to base an estimate of the amount of space to be devoted to the various divisions of art work. . . .

The agreement referred to was reached on March 14, at an Art Committee meeting. Ives conveyed the results at a meeting between himself, Taylor, John Rachac (Gilbert's representative in St. Louis), and Charles Kurtz, assistant chief of the Art Department, at which Ives brought up points about traffic to and from the building, windows for naturally lit galleries, and the possibility of reversing the building's orientation. As the suggestions he made were acceptable to Rachac, he was instructed by the committee to convey them to Gilbert.[14] However, even after plans were finalized, Ives still complained about the lack of proper lighting and a decreased amount of exhibit space, both of which were absolutely essential if he was to carry out his scheme for a new classification of exhibits according to his original plan. But what of

Gilbert? What were his reactions to these constant demands, to the changes in location, to the interference of Ives?

After their initial meeting in October 1901, Ives and Gilbert met face to face only a few times. Most of the communication between them was through the mail, through Rachac, Taylor, and Emanuel Masqueray, the fair's chief of design and a friend of Gilbert's. (Masqueray's position had been created to handle the design of subsidiary structures.) In all correspondence with these individuals, Gilbert expressed his desire to solve problems and get on with the work. He wrote to Ives shortly after their first meeting, "In laying out [the] sketches, I have kept in mind the space required by you, and the general arrangement which you proposed. This, however, has somewhat hampered getting a good architectural composition, but with a little study I think we can get it into pretty good shape."[15] Barely one month later, Gilbert wrote to Taylor, "My consultation with Prof. Ives and Mr. Morton was very satisfactory, and I saw no reason at the time why Prof. Ives' suggestions could not be carried out, in fact, they appeared to be admirable from a practical standpoint, and I thought could be adopted without difficulty to the scheme then under consideration . . . . It would appear that Prof. Ives' requirements for exhibition space were certainly reasonable and proper, and I think we all should meet his views in that respect wherever possible."[16] Gilbert's skill as a diplomat is evident here in his desire to accommodate Ives. In April 1902 he wrote to Masqueray, "I realize that all exposition work is carried on under difficulties, and sometimes embarrassing conditions, and I have endeavored to eliminate the personal equation as much as possible, and to be wholly loyal to the work and to our Chief, Mr. Taylor. I only hope he realizes this, for I want to be helpful to him and I have every reason to think that he reciprocates this feeling. He has been most courteous to me in all of our relations."[17]

Other correspondence indicates similar attitudes. Gilbert seems to have been trying to accommodate Ives as best he could while still designing a structure he deemed worthy of its location within the exposition's layout, a situation he must have felt was not appreciated by Ives. However, toward the end of March 1902 Gilbert first began to express frustration over the design process, albeit in a diplomatic fashion. As he wrote to Morton, he did not want to incorporate Ives's suggestions, as any changes

> would not only be injurious to this building, but damaging to the entire exposition, and holding this view, I feel my duty to the Exposition Company as well as to myself, demands that I shall furnish a design which shall not be an injury to the enterprise. I beg to assure you . . . of my earnest desire to meet your wishes, and I regret very much if you cannot agree with me on this point. I am sure, that, personally, you like the design as it stands. I assure you it is the very best that I can do, and I am willing to stake my reputation *entirely* [Gilbert's emphasis] upon it.[18]

In a detailed letter to Morton, dated April 7, 1902, Gilbert abandoned his prior diplomacy and emphatically explained why he could not acquiesce to Ives's demands:

> I will say that I have given my very best work to this enterprise. As a business venture for myself it has not been satisfactory. The work has been in the office so long, and always in a rush, so that it has interfered materially with the progress of my other work. At the same time, it is so important, and the opportunity for doing a fine thing is so great, that I am most anxious to bring it to a successful issue. I am sure I will do so, and have entire confidence in the result, if I am only freed from the interference of Prof. Ives and given that backing and cooperation which you personally should give to me. . . . I have no doubt whatever of your good will and your fairness, and it is largely that which has kept me from presenting my resignation. At the same time . . . , you owe it to me that you should sustain my design. I feel that it is your duty to do so, and that you should have confidence in my ability to produce a suitable building. Prof. Ives is not responsible for the design of the building, and he will object to whatever is done. I am hopeless of pleasing him, and so I abandon the effort to do so.[19]

Obviously the pressure was beginning to wear on Gilbert. What is especially interesting about this letter is that it was sent to the chair of the Committee on Fine Arts, an individual with whom Gilbert had little contact during the course of these events, and a committee that had no jurisdiction over the actions of the architects. Morton must have struck Gilbert as possessing sound judgment and a sense of fair play, as well as the ability to control Ives.

At about the same time he confided in Masqueray about his interactions with Morton. He wanted to design a building acceptable to the Art Committee, but refused to acquiesce to Ives's demands:

> It seems to me that it is a matter in which the Director of Works should protect me from the interference of [anyone else]. . . . The matter has gone so far now that I shall not change my design . . . , and if further demands are made upon me . . . I shall place my resignation in Mr. Taylor's hands and ask to [be] relieved of all further connection with the work. . . . I should be very sorry to take this step, for many reasons, but I have reached this conclusion after very careful consideration and shall abide by it. At the same time I do not care to offer it as a threat of a "bluff."[20]

Gilbert's confidence in his abilities had finally overtaken his sense of diplomacy. Interestingly, his threat echoed Ives's desire that he abandon the project. It is also obvious that trying to reconcile the constant demands of Ives with his own design ideas had taken its toll. By April, even Ives had gotten tired of the fighting. He wrote to Morton, "I do not feel disposed to give any further time or thought to the situation. It is fixed beyond the control of anyone but the architect, there is nothing to do but accept it with as much grace as possible. If this is the decision, I shall accept it. . . ."[21]

As director of Works, Taylor should have been a more visible presence in this conflict. But as Gilbert indicated, Taylor did very little to intervene on his behalf. Taylor seemed to have been ineffective when dealing with stronger personalities than his own, specifically that of William H. Thompson, chairman of the Grounds and Buildings Committee (and treasurer of the Exposition Company). In what are obviously more personal than professional letters between Gilbert and Masqueray and Gilbert and Rachac, clues exist that help explain the vulnerable position in which Gilbert found himself. In September Masqueray wrote, "I have been now here [St. Louis] a week and every thing is going on smoothly, Mr. Taylor let me have my own way in matters concerning my department. Have not had any difficulty 'to get along with' him and *do not expect any. I am getting along beautifully with Mr. Thompson* [Masqueray's emphasis]. Now I think you can congratulate me! So far every thing I say 'goes.' From what I have been able to see so far Mr. Thompson is 'the Boss' and seems to own the whole thing, Taylor included."[22] Rachac also reported in this vein:

> Both E. and Y. [Eames and Young] are sore—sore to the core, naturally, claim the whole matter [of the Art Building] is managed miserably. E. suggests the Architects assert themselves and give these *countrymen* [Rachac's emphasis] some pointers how to conduct an affair like this and what Architects really are. From what I now gather there is too much 'Thompson' in the whole establishment. Both Masqueray and E. & Y. say so. Thompson seems to hold the axe over T. [Taylor] and while I really believe the latter is trying his best to carry things along smoothly, he has Thompson always at his back.[23]

Gilbert thus had the misfortune of having to deal with one very strong personality (Ives) and finding himself at the mercy of a weaker one (Taylor).

Once the decision had been made in December 1901 to separate the colonnade from the building, Gilbert was no longer designer of the fair's premier structure. The Committee on Grounds and Buildings unanimously voted to erect another building on the brow of the hill in front of the Art Building that would assume the role as crowning structure of the architectural composition. Gilbert immediately asked to be considered the designer of this structure, tentatively designated as Festival Hall (see Figures 16-4 and 17-5). By early 1902, Taylor supported this request and sent a letter to the Archi-

tects' Commission explaining the situation and asking them to approve a new structure with Gilbert as its architect. He wrote, "It is still the wish and intention of the authorities here to hold some pronounced feature in the way of structures at the ends of the axes [of the main picture], as originally contemplated in the main scheme by the Commission of Architects. . . . I believe that if we consider the general ideas that have prevailed when Mr. Gilbert was appointed

architect of the Art Building, that if the Building Committee can be prevailed upon to appoint him architect of these structures . . . , it may be a just and proper conclusion."[24] The "general ideas that have prevailed" is a reference to Gilbert's contributions to the development of the ground plan while serving as chair of the subcommittee responsible for the same. It was his idea to make the hill in the middle of the fairgrounds the focal point, and no one ever questioned

17-6. Festival Hall from the West Cascade Stair, photograph by Official Photographic Company, 1904, Louisiana Purchase Exposition. (Missouri Historical Society, St. Louis)

"A DIFFICULT AND PERPLEXING MATTER"

Gilbert's choice as the designer of whatever structure would be atop that hill. The architects' commission granted Gilbert's request with very little delay, and the process of designing Festival Hall, the new crowning feature of the display, began. ,

So how did Gilbert move from his esteemed position to suing the Exposition Company? The clue lies in an exchange between Taylor and Gilbert that began in January 1902. At the same time that he sent his letter to the other members of the architects' commission, Taylor asked Gilbert if he could not build Festival Hall for $240,000: "If I can persuade the Building Committee to appoint you architect for this building can you afford to include it in the small remuneration you get for the Art Building?"[25] Gilbert replied that he would leave the matter of compensation to Taylor and the Committee on Grounds and Buildings. This is the only mention of it in any of the correspondence.

From this point, although Gilbert had not yet been approved by the Committee on Grounds and Buildings as architect for Festival Hall, the design process for it began in earnest. As with the Art Building, Gilbert was dealing with other individuals with a vested interest in the structure—in this case both Taylor and Masqueray, who had taken over the design of Gilbert's colonnade to which Festival Hall would attach. There was much discussion over the shape of the building (round versus square), the manner in which the colonnades would attach to the structure, and the location of a fountain that would stand in front of the entrance to the building, which was also the top of the Cascades (the tripartite waterfall in the center of the architectural composition). In addition, Taylor and the Exposition Company originally requested a building with a seating capacity of four thousand people. This figure was later revised to twenty-five hundred. As a result, Gilbert again created more than one set of plans. Although it was not unusual for architects to create multiple sets of plans, this kind of situation did not often occur when designing temporary structures for world's fairs.

Although Gilbert was not officially appointed architect of Festival Hall until January 1903, he began to submit sketches as early as May 1902. In the same letter in which Taylor notified Gilbert of his official appointment, Taylor wrote, "[I]n all of this there is one paramount matter that is giving me more anxiety day by day, than anything else connected with our little exploitation out here, and that is, the supreme matter of time."[26] Later, in what seems to have been preparation for the lawsuit, Gilbert jotted a note at the bottom of this letter: "I. S. T. [Isaac S. Taylor] had my working drgs [sic] in his office for several months without taking any action therein so far as I could learn and then asked me to prepare another design which should have a higher dome the more ornate but less expensive. I prepared another complete set of designs (working and drawings) and these likewise were held several months without action and finally the work was put under contract." It was not unusual for Gilbert to make such notations. He was meticulous at record keeping, preserving copies of all letters and memoranda going in and out of the office.

By January 1904, Gilbert wrote to Taylor informing him that he had sent a letter to David Rowland Francis, president of the Exposition Company, regarding additional compensation. This letter to Francis outlined in detail the amount of work Gilbert had done for the design of two structures. Gilbert's argument, which was used in the trial, was based on the fact that he had designed the Art Building, two annexes, terraces, colonnades and gardens, and Festival Hall, "the equivalent of at least four important buildings, involving much more architectural service than originally contemplated."[27] Gilbert resigned from the architects' commission on April 5.

Gilbert had a legitimate case against the Exposition Company; the original contract between the company and the architects stipulated a set fee of ten thousand dollars for the design of one building. Each of the other architects had worked on a temporary structure without interior arrangements; they were not bound by the demands of an exhibition department. Gilbert's designs demanded extensive exterior and interior design. This meant that additional individuals would be involved in the design process, and as a result, Gilbert created more sets of plans than the other architects, and there was greater discussion about those plans.

Gilbert obviously felt it necessary to sue the Exposition Company for a number of reasons. His relationship with Ives had become so contentious that it created not only more work but also emotional distress, a condition not experienced by the other architects. His work on Festival Hall also was hindered, initially, by the constant demands and subsequent inaction of Taylor, who did not seem able to communicate his needs in a clear and concise fashion.

Taylor's behavior was part of a pattern that extended to other individuals connected with the fair. Frederick Ruckstuhl, the fair's chief of sculpture, resigned on December 16, 1902. His resignation letter cited ". . . the numerous humiliations inflicted upon me by Mr. Isaac S. Taylor . . . which are to me utterly incomprehensible except as evidence of his fixed intention of reducing me from the position of DIRECTOR [Ruckstuhl's emphasis] of Sculpture to that of a mere hired assistant of himself, and in view of the fact that my Department is dangerously in arrears on account of his strange dialatory [sic] tactics before, and since, I became . . . connected with the Exposition . . . ."[28] Ruckstuhl's resignation was also reported in the *New York Times*. In the interview he gave, he stated that his actions also were based on the matter of compensation, but in addition he cited the same poor leadership qualities that plagued Gilbert with the design of Festival Hall. Taylor would not let Ruckstuhl carry out the sculptural program that he had devised and that had been approved by the fair's Sculpture Advisory Board, composed of three of the country's most eminent sculptors (Augustus Saint-Gaudens, John Quincy Adams Ward, and Daniel Chester French). He claimed Taylor insisted that he cut down the number of sculptures without consulting the architects of the buildings, and told Ruckstuhl he was employed only "to produce the sculptures that should be ordered by the Exposition Company."[29] He continued, "I think that he began to see that the successful carrying out of an admirable scheme of sculpture would gradually make of the chief of sculpture, even in spite of himself, one of the most prominent men connected with the Exposition, and I fear that was too much for him . . . . To those who can read between the lines, all this is the result of Mr. Taylor wanting to be the Sultan of the St. Louis World's Fair."[30] Why Taylor acted in this manner is unknown.

In his resignation letter, Gilbert also pointed out some other reasons for his resignation. He cited the failure of the exposition authorities to allow the architects' commission to act as an advisory board for sculptural and color decoration as stipulated in their letters of appointment. The Architects' Commission had been asked to submit recommendations for decorative painting around the fairgrounds, and their extensive report was ignored. In addition, Louis Julian Millet (painter and the brother of Francis David Millet, a well-known painter and muralist) was appointed chief of Mural Decoration to work in consultation with the Architects' Commission, but his plan for murals and color decoration on the buildings was voted down by the Executive Committee without consulting the architects. Gilbert also referred to the Exposition Company's failure to faithfully adhere to the original ground plan designed by the architects, and to adhere to the role of the architects' commission as an advisory board for all building designs.

> I think I voice the feeling of most, if not all, of the Commission of Architects, in saying that one of the chief inducements we had in accepting such meagre compensation for the important work contemplated by our original employment was that our reputations would be enhanced by the publicity of having our respective names known as the designers of the buildings respectively allotted to us; but instead of that there has been on the part of the management a sedulous concealment of the names of those who designed the buildings in all publications which have been made concerning them, so that the world at large cannot give such credit as may be due to any one of the architects for the individual work which he has performed.
>
> I regret exceedingly that my sense of duty and professional pride compels me to take this step.[31]

The hearing for Gilbert's suit took place on March 31, 1905. Gilbert was awarded 2.5 percent of $218,184 (the final cost of Festival Hall), or $6,454.32. This was in addition to the $10,000 (and compensation for incidental expenses) received for his work on the Art Building. Gilbert expected to be paid, in addition to the set fee for the Art Building, more than three times that amount by the Exposition Company (a 5 percent fee on the cost of Festival Hall and compensation for expenses).

As Gilbert pointed out in his resignation letter, more was at stake than just fees and the terms of the architect's contracts. Since midcentury, American architects had been attempting to reinforce the idea that architects were gentlemen—artists with social standing, not just artisans or craftsmen. During Gilbert's early years in the offices of McKim, Mead & White, the three principals created a nurturing atmosphere in which their young draftsmen styled themselves as artists who worked with architecture as their medium. As American architects in the nineteenth century were businessmen as well as artists, unless they had outside sources of income they relied on the swift completion of and payment for projects undertaken in order to make a living. Therefore, in suing the Exposition Company, Gilbert was fighting both for his professional status as an artist and for his means of earning a living. Although the amount of money awarded was much less than Gilbert had hoped for, the award was a victory for both the architect and the architectural profession.

CHAPTER 18

A USER'S VIEWPOINT:
GILBERT AND HIS PUBLIC

Jeffry H. Gallet

When I was asked to write this chapter, my first instinct was to decline. What business, after all, does a mere judge have in writing a chapter in a book dedicated to architectural discussion among distinguished architectural scholars? The mumpsimus, deeply ingrained in the American psyche, that judges are the ultimate source of wisdom aside, I have no scholarly architectural credentials. But architecture is more than fodder for intellectual inquiry. It is history; it is political science; it is art; it is shelter.

Although it addresses beauty, architecture is more than a spectator sport. Unlike painting or sculpture, the end product must serve the function for which it was intended. It must serve the body as well as the soul. So, as an end-user of Cass Gilbert's work, I may have a contribution to make to this discourse among the architectural experts. In architecture, if not in other artistic endeavors, the hackneyed phrase "I don't know art, but I know what I like" may be apt.

18-1. Exterior of the United States Supreme Court Courthouse, showing "Equal Justice Under Law." (Photograph by Josh Mathes, Collection of the Supreme Court of the United States)

While it is well known that part of Gilbert's prolific output includes several significant courthouses, few know that his contribution to the American legal system goes beyond his magnificent buildings. Over the entrance to the United States Supreme Court, one of Gilbert's courthouses, are the words "Equal Justice Under Law" (Figure 18-1). At a dinner party, I once asked a group of lawyers and judges from whom the quote came. The answers ranged from John Marshall to Oliver Wendell Holmes, but not one knew that they were written by Gilbert.[1] Those words, to a great extent, have come to summarize American jurisprudence. They are also the moving force behind Gilbert's courthouse architecture.

I have had the pleasure of working in two Gilbert courthouses, the United States Courthouse at 40 Foley Square (see Figure PS-1) and the United States Bankruptcy Court in the Alexander Hamilton Custom House at One Bowling Green (see Figure 3-1), both in New York City. I have visited two others, the

United States Supreme Court in Washington, D.C. (see Figure C-1), and the Essex County Courthouse in Newark, New Jersey (see Figure 7-1). Each is a magnificent public building. Each sets the tone for the court within. Each sends a loud and clear message that important work takes place inside.

Governments send their messages in many ways. Some, such as laws or court decisions, are direct; some are indirect, by action or forbearance. One way a government sends a message is by the appearance of its public buildings and its public spaces. Gilbert was a master at sending those messages and making his buildings appropriate stages for the action within.

There is a story (probably apocryphal) told of the Manchu Emperor Kangxi, the second emperor of the Quing (Manchu) dynasty (1662–1722). Responding to a minister recommending judicial reform, he decreed

   . . . that those who have recourse to the courts
   should be treated without any pity and in such a

manner that they shall be disgusted with law and tremble to appear before a magistrate. In this manner the evil will be cut up by the roots: the good citizens who may have difficulties among themselves will settle them like brothers by referring to the arbitration of some old man or the mayor of the commune. As for those who are troublesome, obstinate and quarrelsome, let them be ruined in the law courts; that is the justice that is due to them.

An interesting observation, but what does it have to do with architecture? I remember well the day I learned the answer to that question. It was a hot, sunny, summer Sunday afternoon. My daughter Sarah and I stopped at my office to pick up a file. I was working in the New York State family court's Manhattan courthouse at 60 Lafayette Street (Figure 18-2). We were walking hand-in-hand approaching the building from the east. We stopped for a traffic light at the corner across the street from the courthouse.

My daughter looked up and exclaimed, "That building looks like Darth Vader. Do we have to go in?"

She was right. The New York State family court courthouse, the place where children and their families go at their moments of highest distress, did make me think of the "Star Wars" villain Darth Vader, the epitome of evil to generations of American children. The building is surfaced in black marble, without windows at the lower levels. It is austere and chilling. Its message is, "All who enter here give up hope, for that is the justice that is due you," not "Equal Justice Under Law."

That the building is ugly has never been seriously disputed. But at that moment, for the first time, I realized that its aesthetics ran counter to its purpose. A building that by its appearance causes dread in children, and even some adults, rather than confidence that wise decisions will be made, is not where emotionally charged cases should be heard. But that was and is exactly where they are heard.

18–2. Haines, Lundberg & Waehler, Family Court Courthouse (1976), 60 Lafayette Street, New York City. (Office of Court Administration, New York State Courts)

To the east of the family court building is the New York City Civil Court courthouse at 111 Centre Street (Figure 18-3). In an apparent effort to make it less forbidding, the architect displayed steel and glass liberally. While this building may be less threatening than the family court building, it radiates all of the dignity and permanence of a second-rate suburban office building.

The architects of these buildings missed the illusion necessary for the efficient functioning of the

18-3. William Lescaze and Matthew Del Gaudio, Civil Court Courthouse (1960), 111 Centre Street, New York City. (Office of Court Administration, New York State Courts)

judicial system. How does the judiciary, with a budget less than the cost of a new submarine, maintain its position as an equal branch of government? It looks and acts like an equal branch and therefore it is. Part of that is appearance.

Each court session is opened by the cry, "All rise." All do come to their feet as black-robed judges and justices take their raised benches, and mere

mortals crane their necks to look up to them. The form of address in the courtroom is often in the stilted and archaic language of the English common law courts of long ago. "May it please the court," "Yes, your Honor," and "No, your Honor" ring through the room. All of this pageantry is to an important purpose: to remind the citizenry that judges play an important part in society. It emphasizes that what they decide is important and that their orders must be obeyed, not only because the state enforces them but also because the rule of law is indispensable.

Gilbert understood this phantasm and his role in creating it. His courthouses and other public buildings cry out, "Important work is done here." The buildings set the tone for the business that transpires inside. Even before its citizens enter, the government has broadcast its message of authority to them.

For many years I served as a judge in several New York State courts, sitting in seven architecturally undistinguished courthouses in five counties. The last courthouse I served in before ascending to the federal bench was the Darth Vader family court courthouse. It is as bad inside as it is outside. In what I assume was an effort to make them cheery, the waiting rooms are furnished with plastic bucket chairs of various colors bolted to the floor and the walls are constructed of blocks, painted in a variety of bright colors. One of my family court colleagues once referred to this decor as "Ding Dong School modern."

The courtrooms are similarly undistinguished. They are tiny. Small, relatively low benches are surrounded by a semicircle of tables bolted to the floor, with plastic chairs, also bolted to the floor, behind them. The courtrooms are sterile and overcrowded, with the lawyers and litigants much too close to the bench and to each other. The overall impression is sterile bureaucracy. There is no mystique of justice descending from on high to resolve society's conflicts. There is only the sad impression of an inefficient bureaucracy addressing mundane disputes with quotidian answers.

Family court is known for its rather unruly crowd. Lawyers and litigants alike dress more casually than might be expected. Loud, angry voices, of both litigants and lawyers, are the norm. There is no shortage of uniformed court officers to keep the peace.

When I moved from the family court to the United States Bankruptcy Court, I relocated from the Darth Vader building to Gilbert's United States Custom House. From the first day, I felt the difference. I looked forward to working in a beautiful building. At the family court building, I ducked in and out through the rear loading dock. At the Custom House, although the back entrance is more convenient, I enter and leave through the front door. More than seven years later, a day does not pass that I do not take a minute to admire the building. Each time I enjoy looking at it and each time it reminds me of the public trust I carry.

As part of my duties as a bankruptcy judge, I have sat as a part-time appellate judge in the beautiful second circuit courtroom in Gilbert's courthouse at 40 Foley Square in New York City (see Figure PS-3). I know this courtroom well, having practiced in it as a lawyer. It is the most beautiful courtroom I have ever seen, exceeding even the beauty of the United States Supreme Court courtroom. At once, Gilbert captured both the majesty of the Court of Appeals for the Second Circuit, one of the nation's preeminent courts, and the genteel clubbiness of the appellate bar. Many of the most important cases in the United States are heard there. It is a room that reflects its purpose from floor to ceiling. It is a room in which people speak in whispered tones, even when the court is not in session.

After twenty years on the bench, I have become a courtroom people watcher. I have noticed an interesting phenomenon. Lawyers and litigants act differently in the Gilbert courthouses from the way they do in the less distinguished buildings. Every so often, I see in bankruptcy court lawyers or litigants who appeared before me in family court or civil court. The difference in their appearance and demeanor is striking. Invariably, they dress better, hold themselves more erect, and speak in a softer, less belligerent way.

This change cannot be explained by the type of cases involved. Like those in family court, the issues in individual bankruptcy cases—the loss of a home, a car, or most of one's worldly possessions—-are also

highly emotional. It is as though the building, with its dignity and visual strength, reaches out to them and restrains them. It is also worth noting that although the bankruptcy court building has a significantly smaller security presence, there are many fewer instances of vandalism and graffiti.

One example stands out in my mind. Mr. Jones (his name has been changed to protect his privacy), a New York City corrections officer, appeared before me several times in a family court proceeding regarding child support. He was loud, disrespectful, and defiant each time. After his first disruptive appearance, security officers followed him into the courtroom. His lawyer was not much better. I do not remember the lawyer ever appearing in a jacket that matched his trousers. Not once was his shirt collar buttoned or his tie pulled up to his neck. His method of addressing the court was to half rise and mumble into his papers.

Mr. Jones had two problems from which his legal troubles sprang. He was hot-tempered and a compulsive gambler. He was months behind in his child support payments and had grabbed and pushed his ex-wife when she asked him for the money. The issues before me were whether to reduce his support payments because of his gambling and whether to deduct support from his wages to ensure payment.

The case was what my law clerk referred to as a "slam dunk." The law does not allow a parent to spend or gamble away wages and reduce child support payments as a result. From the bench, I decided against Mr. Jones. His lawyer then asked me to recuse myself from any of Mr. Jones's future cases. I declined, telling him that I was the only judge Mr. Jones would ever have. Two security officers stood between Mr. Jones and the bench as he left my courtroom in his usual manner, loudly casting aspersions on my parentage. That was in early October 1993. On November 10, I left the family court for the bankruptcy court, never expecting to see Mr. Jones, or for that matter his lawyer, again.

In contrast to my Darth Vader building courtroom, my new one, designed to harmonize with the rest of the Custom House, is large and airy, with high ceilings, wood-paneled walls, and pewlike cushioned seating. The marble-topped bench is a sufficient distance from the lawyers and the parties so that they do not have the impression they had in family court that they are having an intimate chat with the judge. I love my courtroom.

In March 1994, I was preparing for the next day's calendar of consumer bankruptcies when I came across Mr. Jones's name on a petition. He had the same lawyer and was trying to get around my support order by declaring bankruptcy. This was far beyond what either the lawyer or I thought when I told him that I was the only judge Mr. Jones would see. I notified court security that Mr. Jones was coming.

Come he did. There he was bright and early the next morning. Although Mr. Jones and his lawyer could not have been pleased to see me, they acted quite properly in the courtroom. The lawyer was dressed in a suit and his shirt collar was buttoned. He rose to speak, was clean and respectful, and unlike his family court appearances, was well prepared. Mr. Jones sat quietly and left at the end of his hearing without incident. This was repeated twice more until Mr. Jones and his lawyer, realizing that they would be no more successful in bankruptcy court than they had been in family court, withdrew the case.

Those three latter appearances set me thinking. What had changed Mr. Jones's attitude and his lawyer's demeanor? There was nothing I could think of except the change of courts and courthouses. I started to watch the behavior of lawyers and litigants who had previously been before me in the New York State courts. Although the transformation was never as stark as in Mr. Jones's case, there was always an improvement in behavior and attitude.

For some years, I heard appeals as part of the Bankruptcy Appellate Panel of the Second Circuit. Our three-judge bench sat in the second circuit courtroom. Lawyers could argue their cases in person or by a remote video hookup. It is interesting to watch the differences between the lawyers in the courtroom and those arguing by video. Consistently, those in the courtroom are less flamboyant and more professional in their presentations than those presenting their case from remote locations.

Thus I am convinced that appropriate courthouses mitigate bad behavior and encourage appropriate demeanor. Most other judges agree. The courthouse and the courtroom set the tone for the proceeding. Ideally, they also convey the message that important business is taking place and that "Equal Justice Under Law" will be meted out.

The same behavioral phenomenon also applies to court personnel. British essayist, novelist, and critic G. K. Chesterton (1874–1936) complained in 1913, "The horrible thing about all legal officials, even the best, about all judges, magistrates, barristers, detectives, and policemen, is not that they are wicked (some of them are good), not that they are stupid (several of them are quite intelligent), it is simply that they have got used to it. Strictly they do not see the prisoner in the dock; all they see is the usual man in the usual place. They do not see the awful court of judgment; they see only their own workshop."[2] If "their own workshop" is a sterile, ugly, undistinguished box, how can we expect more from them? Like the litigants and the lawyers, those of us in "the system" also react to our surroundings. The family court building fed an "us against them" mentality. The bankruptcy court building, on the other hand, supports a "we are here to do something important" attitude.

Court personnel at the bankruptcy court are noticeably more polite and helpful to the public than their counterparts in the state courts. The face that bankruptcy court personnel present to the public, as compared to the one seen in the family court, speaks for itself. It is almost as though the bankruptcy court building does not tolerate surly behavior. It provides an environment that builds self-respect in the court staff and the feeling of doing an important job that is too often missing in the state courthouses in which I have worked. I would compare it to the old negotiator's trick of serving food to an adversary before the negotiator intends to say something controversial. Somehow, people are less likely to be offended while munching on a donut. Somehow, court employees take more pride in their work in a building that makes them proud to be part of the justice system. This is certainly not a surprise.

There are several messages here. The first is that what is functional goes beyond how many square feet are necessary for an office or a courtroom. Courthouses must accommodate the soul as well as the body. Beauty and majesty are not "frills" to be slashed by self-righteous bean counters allegedly watching the public fisc. They advance a court's mission.

Another is that the utilitarians are wrong. It is not necessary for a building to be ugly to be efficient. Indeed as far as public buildings are concerned, it is impossible for an ugly building to be completely efficient because its government users have to expend energy establishing the government's authority to perform their assigned functions. The utilitarian doctrine is advanced by those without the vision and the talent of a Gilbert. The family court is not utilitarian. It is ugly and its environment is deleterious to those who use it. It hampers the judges, lawyers, and court staff charged with effectuating the court's purpose of "Equal Justice Under Law."

Finally, all judges know that litigants should not only receive justice but also perceive that they have received justice. It is an unfortunate day to see a winner in a case leave the courthouse feeling that justice was not done. This happens periodically, more often in family court than elsewhere. Perhaps this is because it is difficult to separate the surroundings from the proceedings. Too often, parties depressed or even degraded by the courthouse in which they appear believe justice is impossible. Kangxi's litigants might have found justice in his court system, but the emotional price was high. So it is with New York City's family court.

Gilbert and his clients understood the need for court buildings to be more than four walls and a roof. Too many of today's architects and their clients do not. They are more concerned with the fiscal than the physical. They have forgotten that they represent justice. They have forgotten the illusion they are charged with creating.

Judges speak with the authority of the state. Their buildings should reflect that authority, and Gilbert's do. For that, and the fact that I work in two beautiful Gilbert courthouses, I am thankful.

CHAPTER 19

REPRESENTING AMERICAN JUSTICE: THE UNITED STATES SUPREME COURT

Paul Spencer Byard

The end of this volume brings us to Cass Gilbert's last major work, the United States Supreme Court, at an excellent moment, as we continue what is neither a discovery nor a rediscovery of Gilbert and his work—he has always been a big figure in American architecture—but an important re-appreciation of what Gilbert and his buildings mean when viewed in the light of the present. That light in turn reflects a rebalancing in the current public view of the architecture of the twentieth century, as we begin again to acknowledge the importance of modernism—the century's greatest architectural achievement—and to see preservation as a creative rather than a preventive paradigm.

The Supreme Court building has actually become just a little old, old enough by the standards of most preservation laws to be not just a prominent building but a landmark for its architecture. This status invites consideration of the courthouse as a work of art that has earned by its age the right to a particular kind of attention, with a new emphasis on what it is from the point of view of what I call the "interested observer," one who looks at it and other buildings for their significance as enduring works of the art of architecture. The point of view of the interested observer is the point of view of a notional being like the "reasonable" man. This notional observer is like the person Aaron Copland said he wrote his music for, the "gifted listener," the person in the audience who could see where the artist was "coming from," could "get" what the artist intended to say, and could take away from the experience something enlightening, to help the observer deal with the inescapable problem of living in his or her own time.

The object of this chapter is to look at the courthouse from the point of view of the interested observer, focusing not on the extraordinary events it has seen or stands for but on its current effects as a work of art, to see first, where Cass Gilbert was coming from, what he intended to say about his subject matter in his work of art; and, second, how the architecture of his building might be read to help us understand the issues we face today.

Most buildings are more like camels than their friends and sponsors would ever admit. They are creations of committees of special interests—sponsors in sales, bankers in loans, public agencies in particular public goods—and they stand by the road as often as not with the arrogant awkwardness of something odd that works. In most instances when a building goes up, it indeed does work: each member of its committee has got what he or she wanted and left us to figure out what that must have been.

Most buildings have architects on their committees. Like other members of the committee, architects want buildings to make sense from their point of view. They want them to get built, stand up, work for their client, and pay for their livelihood. But in addi-

tion to that—and this is the uniqueness of architects' contribution—they want their buildings to make sense to the world, to be palpably coherent, to use their commanding places in the world to say something illuminating about the human condition. How much of this architects achieve in any particular instance depends on their authority within the particular committee, the resources available, and their particular gifts as artists, their ability to create and convey meaning. Ideally, the more authority, gifts, and resources architects have, the better the architecture we get and the more we have to learn from it, to come to understand about ourselves.

In addressing this building in the 1920s—in stamping it with what he wanted it to mean—Cass Gilbert was in an exceptionally strong position. He had the smallest possible committee, one powerful, like-minded friend, Chief Justice William Howard Taft. He had significant gifts as an architect and great authority not only in his committee but in his world, based on his success in his practice and the high regard in which he was held generally. He had terrific resources, including a budget to make any architect salivate, particularly during a depression that made a dollar go farther than he might ever have dreamed. And he had an unusually clear agenda for what he wanted to use the courthouse to say.

An ambitious man, Gilbert in all probability was likeable by the standards of his times for hearty males. The letter he wrote to his wife when he won the Custom House competition, saying their ship had come in and drawing an elaborate galleon with its sails full entering New York Harbor, is particularly appealing. One could appreciate his real gifts as an artist—he was a talented watercolorist—and the exquisite work he did in buildings like the Allen Memorial Art Museum at Oberlin. But one would have liked him the wary way one likes an admirable competitor who is both very good and very determined.

How good Gilbert was is apparent right away from his first nationally important work, the United States Custom House in New York City, an example of the kind of strength and life the young Gilbert could give a building. The Custom House is a great building, rich, compact with an almost anatomical fitness of its plan to its purpose—a representation in the nation's greatest seaport of the federal interest in the fecundity of its wealth, the showering coin of custom collections that entered its front door and begat the capacity of the federal government to push and steer the growth of the nation.

How determined Gilbert was begins to emerge in any consideration of the context of the Custom House commission. Gilbert won the chance to build it in a strenuous competition (see chapter 3). He had moved to New York full of energy, strength (his Minnesota State Capitol was a big success), and a willingness to calculate and act on a determination about where he ought to be to succeed in his chosen art, bodily moving himself and family to be where the action was, among men, hearty men in men's clubs, in the east. Action he got in the form of good private commissions. But the big chance he got was a place on the list of architects competing for the Custom House project. He scrambled to get on the list for the competition. His former partner, James Knox Taylor, was the supervising architect of the United States Treasury, a position of some authority, and may have helped him get on it. He worked very hard and won, beating out architects who were possibly better than he was—Carrère & Hastings—and who were offering a very similar classical scheme. They wrestled with each other like Thomas Eakins's athletes in a relatively gentlemanly gym, and Gilbert won.

The classicism of the Custom House—the classicism one needs to start with more than a hundred years ago to understand the Supreme Court courthouse—was a Beaux-Arts classicism that was just right for its time and for Gilbert. Gilbert was launching his career at the peak of the influence of the World's Columbian Exposition in which he had participated with all the great men and women—there were actually a few women—artists of his time. The exposition was one of the defining moments in the evolution of the American view of itself, when Beaux-Arts classicism began to be adopted by the United States as the authoritative raiment for its burgeoning national ambitions. Beaux-Arts classicism was particularly useful because it was flexible and it loved size.

It could handle the ever-bigger buildings required by the vast and fast-increasing capacities and wealth of the late nineteenth century. It was fairly specifically Roman, associated with a big, powerful empire and gaining strength from two more recent emperors, Napoleon I and his nephew, Napoleon III. Its structure derived from a system of architectural education that included many rules about the proper way to do things, was strongly competitive, and explicitly gave out its grades in the form of prizes as if it were rewarding winners. It fit nicely with the kind of competitive manliness associated with Teddy Roosevelt's strenuous life and the Spanish American War—the world in which Gilbert came to play.

But Beaux-Arts classicism had higher justifications and aspirations. It fit with a great American change near the time of the exposition in 1893, as the nation turned away from the absorption of its western frontier—it was in connection with the exposition that Frederick Jackson Turner in his famous essay announced the closing of the American frontier—and began to appreciate its authority in the world and to impose it with its great White Fleet. Beaux-Arts classicism as a style, with a claim to continuity from the historic architectural style, had a further vital attribute as well, a claim of authenticity, and through that claim, a claim of right. The notion of right was a very particular late-nineteenth-century notion of right, one that went, for example, with Kipling's British imperial idea of the white man's burden. It was something muscular: you had to be strong to pick it up, but in picking it up you were rewarded, you showed yourself to be morally admirable.

This Beaux-Arts notion of right was, however, muscular in another way: it was something unmistakably willful and imposed. The facades of the buildings of the World's Columbian Exposition (Figure 19-1) were in fact plaster, hung on underlying structures, troweled on an underlying rough reality by strong men determined to impose the virtues it proclaimed and make them part of daily life. Beaux-Arts classicism went with the commitment of its times to beautification. The effort was corrective: Beaux-Arts classicism would will the world not to be the way it was, but the way its sponsors thought it ought to be.

Beaux-Arts classicism spoke of all these things—authority, continuity, right, the way things ought to be—and it was the effort, the argument, the cause with which one feels Gilbert was most comfortable. Unlike many of his important contemporaries, Gilbert did not study at the Ecole des Beaux-Arts. But it was a characteristic of architectural practice of the late nineteenth and early twentieth centuries that architects put on styles to suit their subject matter. Going through the monographs of the great offices of the time, it is wonderful to see what architects could design, usually favoring one style or another that fit with their deeper interests or the special drift of their practice—Gothic, Romanesque, Queen Anne, or Beaux-Arts. Like all his peers, the gifted Gilbert could design in lots of styles. But Beaux-Arts classicism is the one he did out of conviction because it was the style that served his deepest interest.

One can approach this conviction a little backward by thinking of Gilbert's best-known success, the

Woolworth Building. It is a terrific building—even if it is the very definition of a camel in the sense suggested earlier. It is literally a winner, the successful competitor in the competition to be the tallest building in the world, and it is a wonderful example of the match of a style to a subject matter, the Gothic to the skyscraper. It was a commission Gilbert vigorously pursued, to the extent of quickly taking passage on a steamer he found out Mr. Woolworth was on, disembarking with an approved design and a contract.

Gilbert had a highly successful commercial practice. The Broadway Chambers Building, the West Street Building, the Woolworth Building, and the New York Life Insurance Company building all were enviable commissions, but at heart he was also a civic person, helping to found the Architectural League of New York and leading the AIA. From the position on the National Commission of Fine Arts to which Taft appointed him in 1910 and in which Wilson continued him, Gilbert had an influence on the shape of the

19-1. Beautification at the World's Columbian Exposition, The Court of Honor looking west towards the Grand Plaza, C. D. Arnold, photographer, 1893. (Chicago Historical Society)

public realm in the execution of the McMillan Plan of 1902 in Washington—another aspect of his commitment to the late-nineteenth-century drive for civic betterment, to make things as they ought to be. As an actual designing architect he was clearly most satisfied by public buildings. In the vastly growing wealth and power of his times, many public buildings were being built. Some were private benefactions such as the Allen Memorial Art Museum, but others were government buildings, a market in which he had an enviable share, from the Minnesota capitol to the Louisiana Purchase Exposition, the West Virginia capitol, and the courts in New York. Many of these, one way or another, were in the Beaux-Arts idiom, the style that fit with what Gilbert thought was important about those public buildings, what needed to be said from the bully pulpit they provided.

The Supreme Court building was a dream commission for Gilbert, a chance to make a building rep-

19-2. Henry Bacon's sketch for the Supreme Court design: an evocative group held together by the portico. (Collection of the Supreme Court United States)

resenting one of the three great branches of American government—given the basic constitutional equality, he could not do better than that—to establish and make explicit in stone his understanding of the Court's connection to authority and right. In the early 1920s, the body of thought that there should be a Supreme Court building argued in part from need: Taft appealed for the move out of the Old Senate Chamber because of inadequate space for counsel to think and spread out papers. But the better part of the appeal relied on a sense that there *ought* to be a courthouse, an aspect of the same interest in betterment, the duty and will to dignify and establish the Court into what the proponents of the building thought it ought to be.

When the proposal began to become a design in 1924, Henry Bacon had the commission. Bacon was a very good architect who had designed the Lincoln Memorial and a scheme for the Supreme Court when he died. Gilbert was tactful but alert when the opportunity opened up, making his interest clear to Taft and then, when there was a good chance he would get the job, though no commitment, beginning to make sketches on "spec," like many architects close to landing a great commission.

The commission brought with it a couple of givens. One was the notion that the building should somehow reflect a single temple form. Where this came from one cannot be sure, beyond Henri Labrouste's 1824 proposal for an ideal Beaux-Arts courthouse, a scheme Gilbert admired, and what one could see in Bacon's design. As Franz Jantzen of the Supreme Court's Curator's office discovered, there apparently also was a scheme for a single temple designed by none other than Gilbert's old gentlemen wrestling partners, Carrère and Hastings, whom once again Gilbert, in a sense, was beating out. The single temple form (Figure 19-2), for these purposes, came not so much from the Parthenon and Greece but from Rome and buildings like the Maison Carrée in Nîmes, a truly seminal building because of its conjury of relevant perfections, its almost perfect unity as a form, and the authority that went with its form—the fact, for example, that its form had a clear direction, a processional authority, one way up and in toward the god within it. The little building finally had an unequaled measure of right, as represented by the exquisite perfection of all its proportions. One can see the attraction of the form as an idea for a building having to do with the Supreme Court, though one also has to remember how tiny it is—it would fit like an exhibit with room to spare in the Memorial Hall of the courthouse—and how much its idea had to be inflated, stretched, and reshaped to make a court building reflecting the ambitions of Beaux-Arts classicism.

To build a single temple-like government building associated with the enlightened perfection of the Maison Carrée was an American dream in the early nineteenth century. With his elegant mind at work

Jefferson came closest in his Virginia State Capitol in Richmond, a typically ingenious architectural device, though also awkward in its effort to compress in the single temple the multiple parts of a state government. Its obliteration of the parts in a single form contrasts, for example, with what became the standard route to an American capitol—use of a dome to pull spread-out parts together—the route that even Jefferson adopted in his own later schemes for capitols. Whatever its limitations for a capitol, the temple was a form Gilbert knew and admired—notably in Paul Vignon's 1807 Madeleine in Paris with all its authoritative associations with Napoleon's imperial majesty and with God himself—and could readily have imagined as a form for the single authoritative body of the Supreme Court.

Gilbert actually received the temple model for the Court in a subtle, graceful form from Bacon, a form far gentler than the Madeleine, with only a portico on a central pavilion to suggest the temple as the focus of a group of structures and a different way to stand up to the court's powerful adjacent architectural competitors. The first of these was the United States Capitol. Gilbert's courthouse was going to be right across the street from the most important single building in the United States and one that had achieved, during more than a century of accretion, rare architectural success in the resolution of its central issues of unity and power.

The adjacency to the Capitol was in some respects not a problem at all: it put Gilbert and his building in the best possible company. But Gilbert was also going to be right across the street from another building much more important as a problem, the Library of Congress (Figure 19-3). Smithmeyer & Pelz had won the right to design the Library of Congress in the famous competition of 1871. Burly, inventive, rich and big, started in 1871 and finished in 1897, the Library of Congress was the kind of tasteful powerhouse the post-Columbian Exposition Beaux-Arts sought to harness with style.

The problem the Library of Congress presented for Gilbert was not just the pomp of the building. More important in the end was the formal equivalence suggested by the obvious pairing of them

behind the Capitol. The Court and the library were *not* equivalents, and Gilbert had to find some way to distinguish them.

Gilbert's response to the two givens was characteristically intelligent: he argued to change the site for the Supreme Court building. Knowing the plan of Washington, he could see a way simultaneously to enhance the power and logic of the single temple form and to get some distance from the neighbors by moving the Court to the end of a ceremonial avenue on an axis east of the capitol. There the court building would be valued for itself like the Madeleine, and the trees would obscure the wings so that it would be seen as a single temple at the end of a much-enhanced ceremonial procession from the Capitol toward justice.

Gilbert was turned down, and after other sites were explored and rejected, he settled in to the problem presented by the original site. The first problem was size. The Supreme Court building did not have to be very big to function. Its program was tiny, to house nine individuals engaged in the most cerebral of tasks, big in stature but still small in actuality, even if one of the individuals, Chief Justice Taft, was about as big as humans get. For Gilbert, this absence of a necessity for much size was a real difficulty. Gilbert needed a big building, big enough to stand up to its neighbors. He needed size to permit the exercise of the power of this kind of architecture, big enough to

19-3. The cheerful pomp of Smithmeyer and Pelz's Library of Congress, 1871–97. (Library of Congress)

REPRESENTING AMERICAN JUSTICE

permit the flexing of its particular stylistic muscle to confer on the Court the authority and sense of right Gilbert felt he should be giving it. And he needed a way to differentiate it from the Library of Congress.

An extremely interesting sequence of designs (assembled by Franz Jantzen from a variety of archives) traces the evolution of Gilbert's response. The sequence begins with Bacon's scheme (see Figure 19-2) of 1923. In this scheme the single central temple was the main event, very much present in plan but subtly announced by an applied central portico

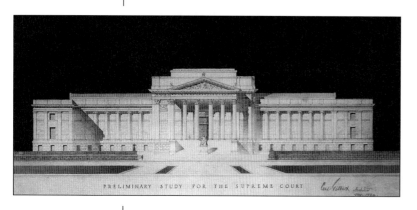

PRELIMINARY STUDY FOR THE SUPREME COURT

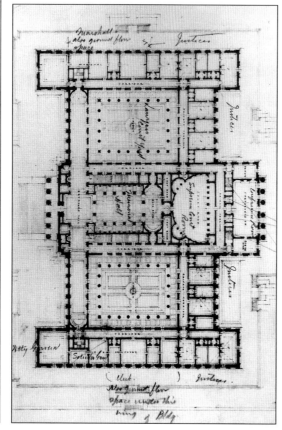

19-4. "Preliminary Study for the Supreme Court," November 1926. (©Collection of the New-York Historical Society, neg. #74417)

19-5. Gilbert's direct, processional plan (entrance at right). (©Collection of the New-York Historical Society, neg. #74417)

principally as the place where, in Bacon's view, a balanced plurality of parts came together, not as something that by its nature controlled and dominated the scheme. His scheme suggested one appealing view of the court as a device for reconciliation. Bacon's scheme also fit well with the plan of the Library of Congress, though possibly too well given the fundamental difference in the relative importance of the institutions that the two buildings served. Bacon's E-shaped plan offered a kind of tartan or plaid spread out to occupy the site around a major rectangular central space. The plan was unclear since there was no obvious courtroom on the ground floor, nor are there obvious stairs to get to a courtroom if it is on another floor. The plan, however, does make clear the balance of parts and the potential beauty—at least as the Beaux-Arts followers would have understood it—of the proposal.

Gilbert's first rendering of the elevation (Figure 19-4) stays close to Bacon's, but with the size of the central portico already increased and Bacon's balanced plurality of parts significantly altered in favor of a building that reads more clearly as one piece. Gilbert's early plan (Figure 19-5) is likewise close to Bacon's. Gilbert's next elevation drawing in May 1928 (Figure 19-6) has both a portico and a central dome.

One of the issues Gilbert was working out had to do with the location of the courtroom itself in the building. He seemed to be working with two choices. One was to put the room at the intersection of the axes of the plan. This would make the courtroom the place where things came together, the place where the ultimate brainwork went on, like the reading room of the Library of Congress, emphasizing the role of the court as an agent of reconciliation. In this position the courtroom might well be called out by a dome. The other choice was to put the room not at the center but at the end of a directional axis, as the end of the line, the ultimate authority, the final appeal—in the model of the Maison Carrée and the processional temple, the chamber of the god. This choice would argue for no dome and more temple. The plan that seems to go with the elevation with the dome suggests that the courtroom at this point was indeed under the dome, with almost nowhere else in the plan for it to be.

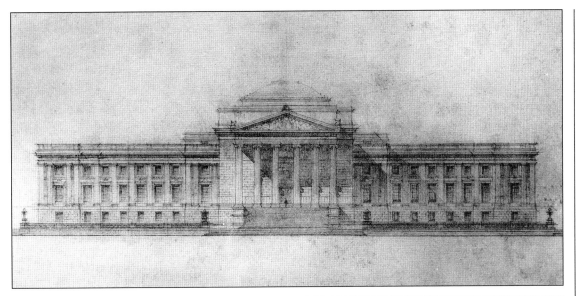

19-6. Gilbert considered a dome to bring the design together behind the portico. (© Collection of the New-York Historical Society, neg. #74412)

19-7. The central temple emerged in Gilbert's sketch from the Baltimore & Ohio. (Cass Gilbert Collection, Archives Center, National Museum of American History)

19-8. The wings further smoothed out and subordinated. (© Collection of the New-York Historical Society, neg. #74414)

REPRESENTING AMERICAN JUSTICE

Study for Supreme Ct. Nov 2[?] · 1928

19-9. This drawing depicts the stair elevating the central temple, which is also reaffirmed with end pavilions. (Cass Gilbert Colledtion, Archives Center, National Museum of American History)

A month later, after a meeting with Taft, Gilbert's choice became clear in a scheme drawn on a dining-car table as he rode on the Baltimore & Ohio railroad (Figure 19-7). Two days later, draftsmen drew up Gilbert's sketch and elaborated on this idea: the portico had increased to the size of a temple front and the wings were smoothed out, pushed down, and made subordinate to the temple behind the portico. Now the dominant central temple distinguished the Court from the Capitol and, perhaps most importantly, from the Library of Congress. This general scheme brought out the uniqueness and singularity of the Court, emphasizing the processional progress toward justice reenacted daily in its premises and making the whole very much of a monument.

The schemes that followed in 1928 and 1929 are interesting for the way they work through the choice between Bacon's balance and Gilbert's final, authoritative scheme. In August, Gilbert stayed precisely within the confines of the sketch (Figure 19-8). Within a few months, however, he hesitated and the temple went back to being a portico stuck on a box. Then the temple was reasserted but the pavilions at the ends of the wings became more pronounced. Gilbert's drawings now include a nearly definitive view of the stairs (Figure 19-9), giving it some of the power that would be so important in the final scheme. A month later, the scheme had a fairly strong cross axis intersecting with the temple, an axis that shows up in the plan (Figure 19-10), emphasizing not the courtroom but the anteroom just outside of it. By February 1929 these ideas were drawn up and there the matter sat for nearly a year and a half (Figure 19-11). Then in 1930, just before construction began, came drawings of two variants that are startling. The first was an obvious retreat toward the domed scheme. Then came a still greater surprise (Figure 19-12). What in the world had happened? Was someone else worried about the direction the design was taking? Was there still a preference for Bacon's view of the court and its approach to the site?

In any event, things settled back down, and by May 1931 the idea was ready to be built. In the definitive sequence on his limited site, Gilbert never got the procession to the temple he wanted and needed, and one senses he tried to compensate with the stairs

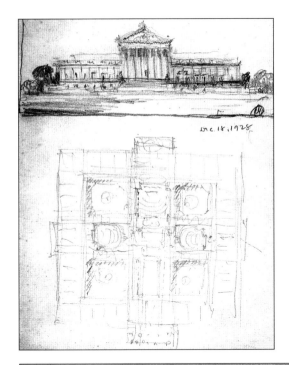

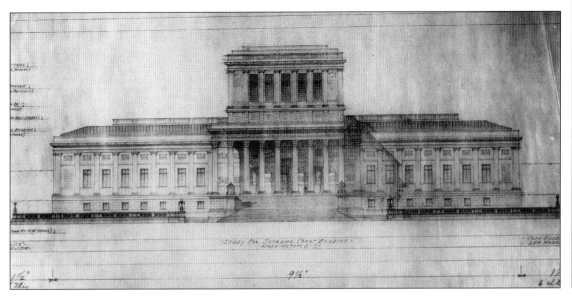

19-10. The cross-axis emphasized the first appearance of the courtroom. (Cass Gilbert Collection, Archives Center, National Museum of American History)

19-11. John Cronin, Offices of Cass Gilbert, presentation drawing of the Supreme Court west facade, "Preliminary Study for Supreme Court Building," February 20, 1929. (Asman Photo Services, Collection of the Supreme Court of the United States)

19-12. A startling retreat with a wedding cake–like design for the central portion of the building. (© Collection of the New-York Historical Society, neg. #74413)

19-13. Hugh Ferriss, rendering. The mighty stairs. (©Collection of the New-York Historical Society)

19-14. The great procession of the Memorial Hall. (©Collection of the New-York Historical Society, neg. #74421)

19-15. J. Floyd Yewall, Offices of Cass Gilbert, photograph of a presentation drawing of the courtroom, c. May/early June 1931. (Collection of the Supreme Court of the United States)

(Figure 19-13). One also sees in the glow of the drawing the importance of Gilbert's choice of material for the building: dazzling marble. He chose to distinguish the building from its neighbors by the bright purity of its whiteness, which, in some lights, makes the stairs still more awesome by making them almost too bright to climb.

Inside the door at the top of the stairs comes Gilbert's great Memorial Hall (Figure 19-14), the vessel for the great processional approach, a rectangle leading toward the courtroom. After the important enforced pause of the anteroom at the intersection of the axes, at last comes the courtroom itself. The courtroom is a square. It has no direction. It is a stable, nonprocessional destination at the end of the long procession (Figure 19-15). Like the sphere of enlightenment offered at the top of Jefferson's University of Virginia, Gilbert's perfect square, almost cube, comes at the end of his line like a decision. In final presentation drawings and in the design that was followed in construction (see Figure C-1), the central temple is strongly in charge, very different from the Library of Congress, powerfully and purely white, with the great steps up from the sidewalk setting up the progress toward "Equal Justice Under Law," presented by the building either as a fact to be found in the square of the courtroom, or as an enduring goal at the end of the procession made tirelessly and over and over again along its halls.

The question remains for the interested observer to consider what can be taken away from Gilbert's work of art as it is seen today, what can be understood from the building as a "landmark."

Two sadnesses occurred not long after the completion of design. The first was the death of Taft in 1930, when the scheme was fixed the way he liked it but before he could see it built. The second was the death of Gilbert on a trip to England in 1934, before the building was finished but after Gilbert was assured that it would come out the way he wanted.

Between these dates construction started, and the record switches from drawings to construction photographs. These immediately force a confrontation with a couple of important facts. The first is the

building's Beaux-Arts classicism: thinking of its steel skeleton and of that skeleton then acquiring its marble cladding underlines the degree to which the white classicism of the building was not inevitable. It was not the product of the logic of its construction as it would have been in first-century Nîmes. It was an expressive choice. At the same time the skeleton, by its modernity, brings out a fact not evident in the sequence of design, the extraordinary fact of the time the courthouse was designed and built. The point is not so much that both Taft and Gilbert were old when they worked on the court but that the world had changed since the second half of the nineteenth century, which formed their view of what the building should say. Gilbert worked hard, competed even, to the end. One can feel him doing it in the sequence of designs, refining the scheme, making it tighter, simpler, fighting for the purest, whitest stone, making the building just as "pure" in style as he possibly could. In the end, however, he was not competing with Carrère & Hastings; he was competing with something much more formidable—the modernists and the inescapable, irreversible passage of time.

Gilbert knew what he was up against. As he said of his building in definitive form and under construction in 1933, "I hope it will cause some reaction against the silly modernistic movement that has such a hold here for the last few years." Gilbert is clearly still competing, hoping to put the modernists in their place under his tons of marble. But his expression is a little tentative and even a little querulous. He is old and not so confident.[1]

His problem was that the modernists were on to something very important. The modernist revolution was the one that had come next after the World's Columbian Exposition, after the exposition's large, muscular, right-minded White Fleets had blown each other up in the appalling slaughter of the First World War, bringing on the cataclysmic misdirection of Soviet Russia and the mess in Weimar. The modernists thought that the world had had enough of pomp and papering over. The modernists thought one had to start fresh by seeing what was actually going on and finding a way to make sense and beauty out of that.

19-16. Gunnar Asplund's 1936 addition to Nicodemus Tessin's 1670's courthouse suggests very different possibilities for the representation of justice. (Photograph by Paul Spencer Byard)

19-17. James Ingo Freed's Ronald Reagan Building: pastiche classicism has no purpose but to look like its neighbors. (Photograph by Paul Spencer Byard)

By way of parable of the change, one can reflect on a very important, very different little court building that opened in Göteborg, Sweden, in exactly the same year as the United States Supreme Court, 1935. It was by Gunnar Asplund, an architect Gilbert might well have admired if he had been just a little younger and more flexible. Asplund worked on the Göteborg courthouse even longer than Gilbert worked on the Supreme Court, from 1913 until the building was completed, in 1936. The Göteborg project started with an existing seventeenth-century courthouse of considerable architectural importance by the major Swedish architect Nicodemus Tessin. With a confidence like Gilbert's, Asplund proposed in his winning scheme to demolish the old landmark and replace it with a new symmetrical Beaux-Arts plan dressed up in national romantic clothes. The committee for his building apparently was a little more complicated and resistant than Gilbert's. The project did not go forward right away, and when Asplund next addressed it, it had been significantly classicized, probably at the request of the committee. By the late 1920s, the notion that the old building should be replaced had gone, and the new courthouse had become an unimpeachable classical addition to the old building. Then in 1933, the addition was still more classicized and almost smoothed away into something that would be perfectly at home on Pennsylvania Avenue.

This design was in fact a tremendous anomaly for Asplund—more so than any of Gilbert's hiccups toward the end of his sequence. By the time Asplund drew his "Pennsylvania Avenue" scheme, he had evolved into a convinced and graceful modernist, famous for his work at the Stockholm Exposition, the clean, plain forms of which did so much to make the case for modernism throughout the world. The Pennsylvania Avenue scheme clearly pleased Asplund's committee—that is almost certainly why he did it—but one cannot imagine how Asplund himself could have stood to execute it. In Gilbert's position but younger, feeling the excitement of possibilities Gilbert could only regret, Asplund in fact could not stand it and in a last-minute switch presented the committee with a radical modernist scheme (Figure 19-16). With it, all the great possibilities of twentieth-century architecture began to open up. The abstraction of the addition seems not intended to impose but to draw the inside out of the old building, to explain it, to show what was going on-the formal structure of the old building exposed in the new as an abstract grid and calling out justice as a process of reason. Inside in fact are radiant, calm, top-lit spaces for the administration of a very Scandinavian ideal of justice, a styleless architecture of intelligence and integrity, fresh, surprising, and newly beautiful.

What Asplund was able to do that Gilbert could not—and could not have been expected to do—-was to explore in his courthouse the great ethical revolution of his times. Underneath the slogans—form follows function, ornament is crime—the modernists in 1935 were making a powerful ethical claim, an insistence on an engagement of reality free of pretense. This ethical claim hit Gilbert's building where it was most vulnerable, where it could be said not to be real but to be pretending. The jest about the Court's opening day—what were the justices supposed to do, ride into it on elephants?—caught the issue: not that the building was not a very good building, but that for all its strenuous effort, it was out of touch with the times. It was, arguably at least, in the then-devastating word of a modernist argument, irrelevant.

Photographs of opening day show the courthouse clean, fresh, simple, and endearing. The moment, however, was very much mixed for Gilbert's aesthetic. The building was a fine building, but by 1935 the live and athletic sense of duty and right Gilbert wanted to embody in the building was something relatively few felt or warmed to any more. The authority it meant to convey was easily confused with authoritarianism—-a confusion to which Gilbert himself contributed in his admiration for Mussolini. Its Beaux-Arts classicism, dissociated from the attitudes and times that gave it life, continued to degenerate into what came to be identified only as an oppressive index of the "official." Geoffrey Blodgett caught the sense of the moment when he described Gilbert at the end of his career as "beached," as if his architecture, and particularly the courthouse, had been lifted by some exceptional wave well after high tide and laid out as a curiosity on the upslope of the twentieth century, where the last of its intended power as a work of art seemed to have drained away.[2]

The upslope on which the courthouse was beached was the trajectory of the twentieth-century American architecture. It rose with the fierce reformist optimism of the modernists after the horrors of World War I and the general open embrace with them of the heroic possibilities of the new. This rise in turn was corrected in light of what seemed the excesses of modernism in its embrace of the new, the destructive swath of its pursuit of new solutions. The corrective included the invention of the preservation movement and the reattachment of new value to the lessons of old buildings—the lessons, for example, the Supreme Court building now offers as a landmark. The corrective went on, however, well beyond a preservationist rebalance to a wholesale discreditation of modernism, an abandonment of its pursuit of integrity and a license in its place of architectural fakery—imitation old architecture and pastiche—out of fear of the new and a blind demand for comfort.

Over the time of this rise and correction, very little was happening physically to the courthouse on Capitol Hill. It was beautifully maintained: a few draperies were hung behind the bench and over the windows in the courtroom, some new bright colors were painted on the ceiling of Memorial Hall, some gloriously inappropriate lighting was added upstairs. But as it stayed the same and the times changed around it, the courthouse was gaining the benefits age added to its inherent virtues. First, as a landmark, it lost the obligation to be anything but what it was. One no longer had to see it as something out of tune, as something that might better have been something else. Instead its observers acquired the possibility, indeed the duty, to understand it for what it was. Second, once understood as a landmark—in the licensed obduracy of every landmark's right to be itself—it became for its observers an important official point of contrast, a point of illuminating difference, to help understand their inescapably different state under the circumstances of the present.

To understand that state, to catch the particular light Gilbert and his courthouse can throw on the present, requires certain acknowledgments, first and foremost, that judgments should still be controlled, by the great ethical admonition of modernism, to see things as they are. Its corollary is the acknowledgment that the troubles that followed after modernism—the ghastlinesses of urban renewal, the horrors of highways in cities—were consequences of human imperfection, not of the modernist admonition, that fear of the new comes not from the new but from the inadequacies of human responses to it.

This acknowledgment of the ethical durability of modernism and its interest in facing the music opens the way to a different validation of what Gilbert was doing, the opportunity to face the fact, for example, that not just Gilbert but all architecture is trying to drive home lessons the way Gilbert did. This is the point Robert Venturi made in his great addition to Gilbert's Allen Memorial Art Museum in Oberlin, Ohio, collaborating with Gilbert's elegant building to show how they both were, in dramatically different ways, serving the same didactic purpose.[3] And it invites an appreciation of Gilbert's enduring contribution in light of the reality of an unhappy present, when the human gift for artifice, its ability to manipulate imagery, to interfere with perceptions of reality, to substitute realities for reality, has got humankind into possibly the greatest trouble it faces today.

That trouble is visible in the architecture of two contemporary buildings, both the work of good architects, but architects enjoying a lot less power than Gilbert had. They worked as members of committees much larger and more difficult than Gilbert's, committees themselves affected by the present, much more timid and afraid, having taken over from the preservationists their enthusiasm for the old—the way a few years earlier they had taken over from the modernists their enthusiasm for the new—and using it to serve commercial and political purposes the preservationists never intended. The preservationists themselves were watching what they had championed drown in the bath of fakery, of imitation old architecture pasted over reality to make it more comfortable, more saleable, to a world afraid of innovation, of difference, and of outcry. These architects' committees reflected the times, and without the benefit of anyone in the Taft position with a sharp eye for the problem, ready to take a little flak, to drive for an idea that would lift the whole toward something valuable.

The first building is the International Cultural and Trade Center, the Ronald Reagan Building, on Pennsylvania Avenue, completing the Federal Triangle (Figure 19-17). James Ingo Freed's neo-neo-Beaux-Arts classicism is technically rather good, full of allusions to Bramante, possibly even to Sir John Soane, but deeply troublesome in a way Gilbert's classicism makes clear. Gilbert had a purpose and a conviction about what he was doing. He was trying to use his Beaux-Arts architecture to drive home points about authority and right for the sake of the Court. At the international trade building this neo-neoclassicism has no such conviction, no purpose of its own except to look like something else, to look like the rest of the Federal Triangle, to make it look as if nothing had happened, to obscure the new and make it comfortable, to dress up what is basically a mall inside like every other mall in America, in a kind of feel-good official make-believe. However out of touch Gilbert may have seemed, however corrective, however rhetorical, he was not ever make-believe and cannot be used to justify make-believe now.

A more complicated example illustrates a slightly different version of the point. It is the federal courthouse in Concord, New Hampshire. Its plan is actually remarkably like that of the Supreme Court, but something has happened to its classicism. Its architect, Jean-Paul Carlhian, was clearly under the same pressure James Ingo Freed must have felt to make the new building familiar, at least in terms of some stereotype of courthouses. But recognizing that virtually all of the life has gone out of classicism as a vehicle, he tried to reinvent it with possible references to such eclectics as Frank Furness in Philadelphia. The chunky building has strength and presence. But if Freed's problem was the emptiness of even the highest-class imitation classicism, the problem here is the risk of pastiche, that the new derivative idea may slip over some edge and seem like a takeoff and undermine what it means to praise. Again, by contrast, in Gilbert there was a complete lack of irony and a deep respect for the seriousness of the judicial enterprise.

Photographs of the Supreme Court now offer different contrasts. In some of them the courthouse is treated with almost excess affection, swathed in blossoms, or enriched with evening shadows, a brown crepuscular light, like an ancestor. The building is now treated as officially old—even though it is not very old—and is given by the choice of light a wisdom to go with its age.

A more work-a-day, ordinary, less ephemeral view of the courthouse helps make clear its lessons for today. Good as the building seems in its own terms, one does not feel in it the old sense of right that drove Gilbert, the strenuous, almost heroic effort to correct life into what he thought it ought to be. Gilbert's "ought" is too remote and then too charged with the disappointments of subsequent history to make the building make the exact sense he once intended. But one can see in the identity and distinction he gave the courthouse, and one can feel in the effort that went into its definition and refinement—the strength of Gilbert's conviction, how hard he worked to make his point, how powerfully he set the courthouse's standard of integrity. In its rigorous classicism, in its beautiful materials, in the strict consistency of its detail, Gilbert makes a marvel of what it takes to do things right. Much current public architecture is afraid to do things right, to look them in the eye, to make beauty out of what things are, not make believe. It is a wonderful turn for Gilbert that the passage of time should be giving his artifice the authenticity to show the present's up, to invite the nation to stop fooling itself. But then he wanted to represent the Supreme Court, the part of government most nakedly and humanly engaged in the endless, arduous struggle to get things right. It is wonderful to think how importantly in this respect Gilbert and his courthouse are continuing to succeed.

POSTSCRIPT

DENNIS JACOBS

A New Yorker who looks around the city, particularly one who knows where to look, will be surprised at how great a mark has been left by Cass Gilbert. At the same time, it is astonishing how long the eclipse of his reputation has lasted. The handsome booklet published by the Alliance for Downtown New York in conjunction with the 1998–99 celebrations from which this book springs was the only available publication about the architect's group of New York contributions. Not until recently has a monograph been published about Gilbert's works as a whole.[1] Yet Gilbert's physical presence is all around, and essential. The federal courthouse at Foley Square, the finest judicial workplace I know, opens Robert A. M. Stern's section on civic buildings in *New York 1930,* with the image on the facing page (Figure PS-1).[2] This postscript addresses Gilbert's reputation: not to add a bust to a pantheon but to see his work as presented in this book, respond to it, acknowledge it, and wonder at Gilbert's remarkable posthumous ups and downs.

Gilbert's reputation seems to have suffered greatly because he projected no personal style. Art historians and creative types in general value and maybe overvalue self-expression, self-reference, and the stamp of personality on innovation. Gilbert's rich vocabulary did not overtly express his personality, except to the extent that he knew what the standards were and maintained them. His work in New York and in other regions of the country internalizes other values and drives. It evokes an era of civic ambition, reflects devotion to craft, and embodies a spirit of competitiveness and striving that is characteristically American and of his time.

In several ways, Gilbert has been fortunate to build a reputation and secure it, even though, as shown in this volume, he was unlucky in colliding with the tastemakers who were ascendant near the end of his life. He won conspicuous commissions and

rose to those opportunities. The Woolworth Building, with its full detail on all facades and its loft and confidence, acts as if it were still the tallest building in the world.[3]

Another assist to Gilbert's reputation is that he designed courthouses: three at least that are discussed in this book and the United States Custom House at Bowling Green, New York, which has become a courthouse as well as a museum, going beyond its

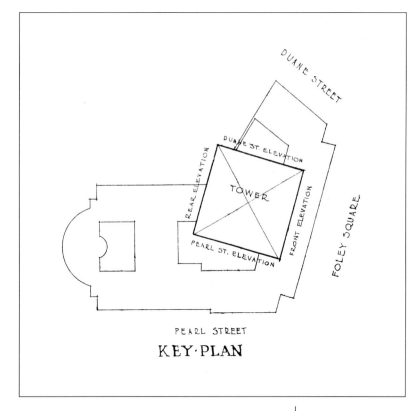

OPPOSITE
PS-1. Guy Lowell, New York County Courthouse, 1926 (left); Cass Gilbert, United States Courthouse at Foley Square, soon after its completion in 1936 (center); and McKim, Mead & White, Municipal Building, 1907–14 (right). (Library of Congress)

KEY·PLAN

PS-2. Cass Gilbert, Jr. for Cass Gilbert, Inc., Plan depicting base and tower at Gilbert's Foley Square Courthouse, 1931 (General Services Administration, New York)

original function for the U.S. Customs Service. Designing courthouses is good for one's architectural reputation because they are built to intimidate, and they tend to last.

I work in Gilbert's United States Courthouse at Foley Square in Manhattan. This building reminds lawyers what they owe the court and the law, it reminds litigants what they owe to the rule of law,

PS-3. Gilbert's court-room of the United States Court of Appeals for the Second Circuit, after restoration by General Services Administration, c. 1975, in 1998. (Photograph by Franz Jantzen, Collection of the Supreme Court of the United States)

OPPOSITE
PS-4. Life (insurance) triumphs over death: Cass Gilbert's New York Life Building, 1927, at the northeast corner of Madison Square Park. This site formerly was occupied by McKim, Mead, & White's Madison Square Garden, 1891, the rooftop of which was the scene of Stanford White's murder by Harry K. Thaw. (Cass Gilbert Collection, Archives Center, National Museum of American History)

and it reminds judges what they owe to everybody. When Gilbert had the opportunity to do something grand in a place like that, he rose to the occasion.

At the turn of the twentieth century the federal courts in New York were housed in the old Post Office Building at the southern end of City Hall Park, immediately in front of the site on which the Woolworth Building rose in 1913. A bulbous, knobby, column-decked Civil War–era building, designed by Supervising Architect of the Treasury Alfred B. Mullet, it appeared on numerous postcards and looked like the same architect's War Department Building—now known as the Old Executive Office Building—adjacent to the White House (see Figure 9-8).[4] It was described in 1931 as "old but not venerable."[5] Had it survived another decade or two, Mullet's post office and courthouse might have enjoyed the affection now bestowed on the "Old E. O. B."

The Foley Square site for a new federal court building was selected in 1923 and acquired by the

federal government in 1930. Gilbert was involved in the courthouse project from the outset. Well connected and good at getting commissions, he quickly went to work. His initial drawings for the lower six floors were adapted from drawings he did for an earlier courthouse project, the 1911 architectural competition for the State Supreme Court building immediately north of the federal courthouse site. Guy Lowell won that competition, and Gilbert was among the losers. But Gilbert was able to recycle his 1911 drawings, adapting the design to the base of the federal courthouse. And that is the face it has.

However, the federal courthouse required much more space. On paper, Gilbert tried out various ways of stacking horizontal tiers of floors on top of the base, and even ways to expand the site. The site is an odd one, irregular even for crowded lower Manhattan, and the footprint of the building crowded St. Andrew's Church, on the same block, which had to be rebuilt (Figure PS-2). The tower design gelled in 1931.

Today the courthouse in Foley Square is substantially as it was when it was completed in January 1936. The United States Court of Appeals, on which I sit, convenes still in the ceremonial courtroom designed for that court's use (Figure PS-3). It is the largest courtroom in the tower. Its proportions are intuitively pleasing: sixty-six feet long, thirty-three feet wide, and twenty-two feet high. The ceiling is painted in eleven shades of gray and tan, with gilded details. A stained-glass rose window behind the bench, visible when the door to the robing room is open, is an addition but an old one; it was designed and installed by the Rambusch Company in the 1970s.

The courthouse is very much in use, serving its intended purpose and enriching the lives of the people who work there and those who come to seek (or evade) justice in an ennobling environment.

Maybe because good courthouses are so expensive to tear down, they tend to outlive their critics. Lewis Mumford wrote of the Foley Square courthouse before it opened that it was a preeminent example of false grandeur. (He also was rash enough to suggest that he could pass judgment before the building opened: "like the proverbial eggs, you don't have to finish them to find out how bad they are."[6]) Take it from me—I go there every day, and I sit in the court of appeals courtroom: it is real grandeur, and *real* grandeur has never been out of style for long.

One of the press releases prepared for the Cass Gilbert celebrations observed that Gilbert would be well known today if only Harry K. Thaw had murdered him instead of Stanford White. This is intriguing because I just finished work on the renovation of an apartment, and some years ago I rebuilt my house, and it is sort of a wonder that more architects are not dispatched violently. But even so, the Stanford White case is special. In 1906 it was touted as the crime of the century. (Little did they know.)

In early 1996 the New-York Historical Society put on a well-attended exhibition about eight sensational New York crimes, and Thaw's murder of White was an attraction that I particularly enjoyed.

Thaw murdered White because White was conducting a liaison with Thaw's beautiful wife, Evelyn Nesbitt. A big part of the lurid appeal of the White case was that the architect was murdered on the roof garden of one of his most prominent buildings, the original Madison Square Garden. Today, Gilbert's building for the New York Life Insurance Company occupies that site (Figure PS-4).

We could try to refurbish Gilbert's reputation by starting over, and with some allowance for chronology, we could just assume that Thaw murdered *Gilbert* for entertaining Evelyn Nesbit in an apartment with a velvet swing, and that Thaw murdered Gilbert *on the grand staircase of the New York County Lawyers' Association*. That would have made a splash, would put Gilbert on a par with White as to glamour, and encourage the rethinking of his reputation and a survey of his buildings with new eyes. But since Gilbert did not conduct a dalliance with the teen-age wife of a homicidal millionaire, he cannot hope to see his reputation invigorated that way. Instead, the work falls to the scholars, preservationists, architects, judges, and writers we have heard from in this book; the grateful people who work and who do public business and private commerce in his buildings; and people with discerning eyes and a love of fine buildings.

I hope that the Cass Gilbert events, of which the 1998 symposium was one important part, will impart a permanent increment in Gilbert's reputation. On behalf of the Committee on History and Commemorative Events of the Second Circuit, and its chair for the time of these events, my colleague Judge Pierre N. Leval, we are grateful for the creativity, energy, and organizational skill—and drive—that produced the symposium that formed the impetus for this book. Gilbert, one supposes, also would be grateful; in any event, he has given us a lot and he deserves it.

NOTES

Abbreviations for frequently cited references

CORRESPONDENCE

CG   Cass Gilbert

PERIODICALS

AABN   *American Architecture and Building News*

CCR   Construction Completion Report

COLLECTIONS

BSCCP   Board of State Capitol Commissioners'
                   Papers (at MHS)

CGC   Cass Gilbert Collection (at NYHS)

CGP   Cass Gilbert Papers (at LC/MS and MHS)

HCKP   Henry Churchill King Papers (at OCA)

HIP   Halsey Ives Papers (at SLAM)

REPOSITORIES

AIA   American Institute of Architects

LC/MS   Library of Congress/Manuscript Collections

LC/PP   Library of Congress/Prints and Photographs
                   Division

MHS   Minnesota Historical Society

NARA   National Archives and Records
                   Administration, College Park, MD

NYHS   New-York Historical Society

OCA   Oberlin College Archives

SLAM   St. Louis Art Museum

SOCIETY SUBGROUPS OF CGC AT NYHS

Chron.   Chronological correspondence

CGPer.   Cass Gilbert Personal correspondence

Fldr.   Folder

LB   Letterbook

Misc.   Miscellaneous correspondence

PC   Project correspondence

PP   Personal Papers

SB   Scrapbook

MSC   Minnesota State Capitol

CHAPTER 1

1. Many thanks to Susan Roth of the Minnesota Historical Society's State Historic Preservation Office, Patricia Holsworth of the Oberlin Historical and Improvement Organization, Professor Richard Guy Wilson of the University of Virginia, and Professor Geoffrey Blodgett of Oberlin College for research assistance for this chapter.

2. According to Francis Bacon Trowbridge, *The Champion Genealogy: A History of the Descendants of Henry Champion of Saybrook and Lyme, Connecticut, Together with Some Account of Other Families of Same Name* (New Haven: printed for the author, 1891), 338, Cass Gilbert was the third of five children (one of whom lived only a year). According to Robert Jones, "Cass Gilbert, Midwestern Architect in New York" (Ph.D. dissertation, Case Western Reserve University, 1976), 3, by the time Cass Gilbert's father died, Mrs. Gilbert had three sons to raise on her own.

3. "Cass Gilbert," *Zanesville Time Signal,* August 17, 1952.

4. The *Zanesville City Directory* (1856–1857) lists Gilbert as a resident on the east side of Fourth Street between Main and Market Streets, and as being the proprietor, with Charles W. Wheeler of Wheeler's Foundry. A number of sources have confused the military record of Samuel A. Gilbert with that of his brother, Major Charles C. Gilbert who headed the 78th Ohio Volunteer Infantry and died 1903, as is noted in the *Zanesville Times Signal,* December 25, 1955. Samuel Gilbert served first with the 24th Regiment Ohio Volunteer Infantry (June to October), and in October 1861 was appointed colonel of the 44th Ohio Volunteer Infantry, with which he served until his resignation for health reasons in April 1864. He subsequently was given the brevet rank of brigadier general for meritorious services. See www.infinet.com/~lstevens/a/cw44.html (under Champion genealogy) and *Official Roster of Soldiers of the State of Ohio in the War of the Rebellion,* 12 vols. (Akron: Werner Company, 1886–95).

5. "Minnesota Winters," *Northwest Magazine* (February 1888): 36.

6. Oakland Cemetery, St. Paul, interment records and obituary, *St. Paul Dispatch,* June 10, 1868, p. 1.

7. Obituary, St. Paul Dispatch, January 16, 1897, p. 7.

8. For more about the early history of Macalester College and its predecessor institutions, see "Presbyterians Found a College" in Merrill E. Jarchow, *Private Liberal Arts Colleges in Minnesota, Their History and Contributions* (St. Paul: Minnesota Historical Society, 1973), and J. Fletcher Williams, *A History of the City of St. Paul to 1875* (St. Paul: Minnesota Historical Society, 1876; reprint 1983). Today's Macalester College has no record of Gilbert's attendance at the school. Marion D. Shutter, ed., *Progressive Men of Minnesota* (Minneapolis: Minneapolis Journal, 1897) contains biographical essays probably drafted by their subjects. The essay about Gilbert (p. 134) notes that he attended Macalester College at the old Winslow house in Minneapolis, which was then under the direction of Dr. E. D. Neill.

9. Radcliffe's name was sometimes spelled without the 'e.' An 1886 publication by Andrew Morrison, *The Industries of St. Paul* (St. Paul: J. M. Elstner and Company, 1886) reported that Radcliff had been established in St. Paul for 29 years and was "the oldest architect in the State. One third of the architects of St. Paul and Minneapolis graduated from his office. Some of the finest work in this section of the country was planned by him, amongst others, Hamline University, the Courthouse at Redwood Falls, Courthouse at Hastings, Wilder Block and Manneheimer's Block in St. Paul, Commodore Kittson's residence, Governor Hubbard's House at Red Wing, the C. H. Pettit residence in Minneapolis, the state prison at Stillwater, Minnesota, the Ladies Hall and College at Northfield, Minnesota, and many others. Mr. Radcliff makes a specialty of planning and constructing public buildings" (p. 114). Among those with whom Gilbert was associated in Radcliffe's office was another St. Paul architect, Edward P. Bassford, according to Alan K. Lathrop, curator, Northwest Architectural Archives. Letter to Pat Murphy, April 30, 1981.

10. Jones, "Cass Gilbert," 4.

11. Copy of Gilbert's official transcript, obtained from M. D. Wells, registrar, MIT, July 15, 1980.

12. Letter dated January 16, 1879, to Clarence Johnston in Clarence Johnston Papers, MHS, Fldr.:1—Correspondence, July 1878–May 1879.

13. Clarence Johnston and Cass Gilbert corresponded frequently during Gilbert's Boston and New York years, and their correspondence is revealing about Gilbert's life at this time. The two later became competitors in St. Paul, and Johnston became well established as a distinguished Minnesota architect. See Paul Larson, *Minnesota Architect: The Life and Work of Clarence H. Johnston* (Afton: Afton Historical Society Press, 1996), an excellent study that provides further insight into the Gilbert-Johnston relationship.

14. J. A. Chewning noted that in the spring of 1879 Gilbert garnered 1 of 2 prizes offered to the school's students by the Boston Society of Architects, and he speculated that "[i]t is possible that winning the prize would have seemed the culmination of a Special Student's effort, making a second year of routine study anticlimactic." Letter to the author, July 24, 1980.

15. Letter dated April 12, 1880, Clarence H. Johnston Papers, MHS, Fldr.: 3—1878–98.

16. Box: 2, General Correspondence, 1841–86, CGP, LC/MS.

17. N.d., ca. 1920, handwritten autobiographical account, Box: 17: Speeches, Articles, Notes, Poems, CGP, LC/MS.

18. Richard Guy Wilson, *McKim, Mead & White, Architects* (New York: Rizzoli, 1983), 10.

19. Cass Gilbert quoted by Walter Tittle in "The Creator of the Woolworth Tower," *World's Work* (May 16, 1927): 100–101.

20. Letters to Clarence Johnston, August 6, 1882; September 10, 1882; and November 7, 1882 in Clarence Johnston Papers, MHS. The Gilder stable project is discussed briefly in a letter from Cass Gilbert to Mr. Howard Greenley, April 28, 1921, CGP, LC/MS. The Garrett House was under construction from 1883 to 1886 and was a major project, including interior work by Tiffany, Herter, Joseph Cabus and others. The house is now the Engineers Club on Mount Vernon Square.

21. Gilbert described his work on the Winans fountain in a letter to Clarence Johnston dated September 30, 1882, Clarence Johnston Papers, MHS. Richard Guy Wilson, in *McKim, Mead & White, Architects,* includes a photograph of the fountain and several photos of the house. For a photograph and discussion of the Farragut Memorial, see Richard Guy Wilson et al., *The American Renaissance,* 1876–1917 (New York: Pantheon Books/Brooklyn Museum, 1979), 43.

22. Letter dated October 5, 1882, to Clarence Johnston in Clarence Johnston Papers, MHS.

23. Julian Ralph, "The Capitals of the Northwest," *Harper's New Monthly Magazine,* vol. 84 (March 1892): 584.

24. Undated handwritten autobiographical account by Cass Gilbert, CGP, LC/MS.

25. Letter dated August 24, 1882, to Clarence Johnston in Clarence Johnston Papers, MHS.

26. City of St. Paul Building Permit 23899, issued in 1890.

27. Lucy Fricke, "Historic Ramsey Hill, Yesterday, Today, Tomorrow," pamphlet (n.d. [ca. 1965]), MHS.

28. This group was organized in 1887 and its members included many of the wives of people who were or eventually became Gilbert's clients, including Mrs. C. P. Noyes, Mrs. G. C. Squires, Mrs. Davis, Mrs. J. Q. Adams, and Mrs. Emerson Hadley. Gilbert's mother was in attendance at the meeting of September 21, 1887. Mrs. Cass Gilbert was elected first assistant secretary at the meeting of February 27, 1889, and gave a program on December 29, 1897, on "Social Duties in the Life of a Woman." New Century Club of St. Paul Papers, MHS.

29. Later, Gilbert became a member of several of the East Coast's most prestigious clubs, again a good source of clients. These included the Century, Metropolitan, Union, and University Clubs in New York and the Cosmos Club in Washington, D.C., according to *Who Was Who,* vol. 3,

1929–40 (London: Adam and Charles Black, 1960).

30. Minnesota Club membership roster, January 1, 1888. Box: 2, Park and Family Papers, P1049 (MHS). See also Patricia Murphy, "The Early Career of Cass Gilbert, 1878 to 1895" (M.Arch.Hist. thesis, University of Virginia, 1979), Appendix III.

31. Gilbert was among the original members of the Informal Club at its first meeting in 1894, and its membership list includes many Gilbert clients. See Henry Castle, "The Informal Club," in *History of St. Paul and Vicinity,* vol. 2 (New York: Lewis Publishing Company, 1912), 483–84. Also see notes about a drinking song Gilbert wrote ca. 1884 for the Minnesota Boat Club, Box: 18, Speeches, Articles, Notes, Poems, CGP, LC/MS.

32. Box: 16, Fldr: 110, CGP, MHS.

33. Her middle name appears as "Tappen" in some sources.

34. General Correspondence—1886, CGP, LC/MS.

35. As described in Peg Meier, "Neighbors Past," *Minneapolis Star and Tribune,* January 7, 1984, p. 2C.

36. "The City House in the West," *Scribner's,* 8 (September 1890): 434. This article includes a photograph of the A. P. Warren House designed by Gilbert in St. Paul, which is incorrectly labeled as "House in Minneapolis, Minn." and does not indicate the architect.

37. "Glimpses of Western Architecture: St. Paul & Minneapolis," *Harper's* 83 (October 1891): 294.

38. Box: 1, Diaries, 1890–1934, CGP, LC/MS.

39. *Improvement Bulletin 4* (December 14, 1894).

40. Gilbert also played a role in the architectural education of another distinguished Minnesota architect, Edwin Lundie (1886–1972). See Eileen Michel's essay, in Dale Mulfinger, ed., *The Architecture of Edwin Lundie* (St. Paul: Minnesota Historical Society Press, 1995), 2–23.

41. Francis S. Swales, "Master Draftsman XVIII: Cass Gilbert," *Pencil Points,* (October 1926): 592.

42. Paul Larson's biography of Clarence Johnston contains additional information about the architectural climate of St. Paul in the early 1880s. Larson, *Minnesota Architect.* Also see Alan Lathrop, "Edward Payson Bassford, Architect (1837–1912)," *Architecture Minnesota* (February 1977): 37–40.

43. Gilbert's known independent projects from this time period include his mother's home (1882–84); the Dr. William Davis House at 409 Laurel in St. Paul (1883); the J. Q. Adams House on Crocus Hill in St. Paul (1883, since razed); the Schurmeier Rowhouse Project (1883) and the A. Kirby Barnum Summer House at Dellwood (1884; both the Schurmeier and Barnum designs were published in AABN, vol. 17, no. 473 [January 17,1885]; the F. W. Hunter Double Tenement at 268 Elm Street (1884); a storefront remodeling for Edward Searles on East 3rd Street between Robert and Jackson Streets in downtown St. Paul (1885); a house for Lucius P. Ordway at 257 Cathedral Place (1885); the J. W. White House at 460 Portland (1885); the Dr. C. E. Riggs House at 595 Dayton Avenue (1885); and the Mrs. C. S. Hall House at 381 Pleasant Street (1885). Among Taylor's independent projects were the Thomas Cochran House at 402 Laurel (1884) and the J. W. Crocker Store and Dwelling at 500–502 Laurel (1884). In 1883 Taylor and Clarence Johnston submitted an unsuccessful joint entry for a competition for the main building at Macalester College in St. Paul (see Larson, *Minnesota Architect,* 27). Johnston and Taylor also worked together on the design of a "Home for the Friendless" in St. Paul (1882–83) and the Morton County Courthouse in Mandan, North Dakota (1885); see Larson, *Minnesota Architect,* 33 and 41–42.

44. Guy Kirkham, "Cass Gilbert: Master of Style," *Pencil Points* 15 (November 1934): 515.

45. *The Record—Dayton Avenue Presbyterian Church* 1 (January 1886).

46. City of St. Paul Building Permit 8267.

47. *The Record—Dayton Avenue Presbyterian Church* 1 (March 1886).

48. Dayton Avenue Presbyterian Church records.

49. "Presbyterian Leader to Preach Today in $15,000 Church Drive," *St.*

Paul Pioneer Press, May 20, 1926.

50. City of St. Paul Building Permit 10565. The addition at the west end of the sanctuary, which creates a T-shaped plan, was made in 1922 from designs by Holyoke (who had once worked in Gilbert's office) and Jemne & Davis of St. Paul.

51. James Taylor Dunn, "Cass Gilbert and the German Presbyterian Bethlehem Church," (1968 pamphlet, probably published by the Minnesota Historical Society (MHS); and "If Gilbert Could See it Now," *Grand Gazette* 8 (November 22, 1980): 1.

52. Rev. Cass Gilbert III, interview with the author, September 6, 1980.

53. I have been unable to document any blood relationship between Cass Gilbert and Mahlon Norris Gilbert (1848–1900). Mahlon Gilbert's lengthy obituaries indicate no connection to Cass Gilbert or his family. See *St. Paul Dispatch,* March 2, 1900, and *St. Paul Pioneer Press,* March 3, 1900.

54. *AABN* 48 (June 8, 1895): 103.

55. Cited in Anonymous, "Historical Sketch of St. Paul's Church," unpublished paper written in 1945, which is part of church records.

56. *Hibbing Daily Tribune,* September 4, 1933, p. 17. See also *Hibbing Daily Tribune,* July 26, 1958, p. 71.

57. Sharon Irish, "West Hails East: Cass Gilbert in Minnesota," *Minnesota History* (Spring 1993): 200.

58. Gilbert later designed the New York Life Insurance Building (1928), which was built on the former site of Madison Square Garden in New York City.

59. Gilbert had known Bassford since the days when both worked in Abraham Radcliffe's office.

60. Gilbert's railroad projects deserve additional research.

61. Box: 1, Diaries (1890–1934), CGP, LC/MS.

62. See building specifications in Box: 4, Fldr.: 29, CGP, MHS.

63. See Larry Millett, *Lost Twin Cities* (St. Paul: Minnesota Historical Society, 1992), 137.

64. Patrick Danehy, "The New Seminary at St. Paul," *The Catholic University Bulletin* 1 (April 1895), 213–26. See also National Register of Historic Places site nomination form by Patricia Murphy, on file at Minnesota State Historic Preservation Office, MHS.

65. Fldr.: 1892, James J. Hill Papers, James J. Hill Reference Library, St. Paul.

66. Box: 15, Fldr.: 108, CGP, MHS.

67. *Improvement Bulletin* 11 (March 16, 1894).

68. Letter to Julia Gilbert, January 22, 1905, LC/MS.

69. In St. Paul Buildings—Historic clippings file, MHS.

70. *A Description with Illustrations of the Endicott and Arcade Buildings* (St. Paul, 1891), n.p., MHS.

71. Letter dated September 21, 1889, from Daniel Burnham to Cass Gilbert, CGP, Box: 5: 1887–90, LC/MS.

72. Jones, "Cass Gilbert," 66, quoting Charles King, "The Twin Cities of the Northwest," *Cosmopolitan* (October 1890): 759.

73. "Glimpses of Western Architecture," *Harper's New Monthly Magazine* 83 (October 1891): 318.

74. *New England Magazine* 11 (July 1890): 546.

75. *St. Paul* (St. Paul: St. Paul Pioneer Press, 1897).

76. Morgan, "Politics of Business," 182, fn. 22, noted that the building is almost a direct copy of Hartwell and Richardson's building for the Peter B. Brigham Estate in Boston, designs for which were published in AABN (April–June 1890), figure no. 748, p. 62.

77. *St. Paul,* 106.

78. *AABN* 51 (March 21, 1896): 135.

79. The winning entry for the American Fine Arts Society Building was submitted by H. J. Hardenbergh for a French Renaissance design at 215 West 57th Street. See Montana State Capitol Building, Box: 12, Fldr: 78, CGP, MHS. Gilbert's papers at NYHS include a Beaux-Arts Baltimore Courthouse competition sketch from 1894.

80. Box: 1, New Century Club Papers, MHS.

81. 1895 diary, Box: 1, Diaries, 1890–1934, CGP, LC/MS. Sharon Irish detailed the connections between the Brazer and Broadway Chambers Buildings with buildings in St. Paul in her book entitled *Cass Gilbert, Architect, Modern Traditionalist* (New York: Monacelli Press, 1999): 50–58.

82. Both the contractor, the George A. Fuller Company, and the terra cotta manufacturer, the Northwestern Terra Cotta Company, were from Chicago. The client was the Brazer Building Trust, which was formed to purchase the old Brazer Building and erect and manage the new one. See City of Boston Landmarks Commission, "Report on the Potential Designation of the Second Brazer Building as a Landmark," unpublished report, 1985.

83. It is probable that the family did not wish to move as long as Gilbert's mother was alive. At the time of her death from pneumonia on January 16, 1897, she was living with Cass Gilbert and his family on Floral Street (Heather Place), according to the Oakland Cemetery interment records and the obituary.

84. N.d. [ca. 1920], handwritten autobiographical account, LC/MS.

CHAPTER 2

1. The financing scheme Villard devised to assist in the takeover of the Northern Pacific Railway was the "blind pool." One of the investors in the blind pool was William Endicott, Jr., for whom Gilbert would later design five commercial buildings in St. Paul.

2. Gilbert lost all three of his draftsmen when the Northern Pacific Railway projects were completed. La Farge (son of artist John La Farge) and Heins would become partners and design the Cathedral of St. John the Divine in New York, and they would approach Gilbert about joining forces to compete for the St. Paul Cathedral. In 1899, Governor Theodore Roosevelt appointed Heins architect for the State of New York.

3. F. B. Jilson, a special telegrapher assigned to the "Villard Excursion," reported that the excursion was composed of three trains. The most prominent of the many dignitaries was General Grant. Along the route were several celebrations, including the laying of the cornerstone for the North Dakota capitol in Bismarck, at which Sitting Bull was present. The Jilson letters are in a private collection.

4. William Rutherford Mead to CG, June 12, 1883, Box: 17, Fldr.: 1882-90, CGP, MHS.

5. Wedding Invitation, Box: 17, Fldr.: 1882-90, CGP, MHS.

6. Carter Wiseman, *Shaping a Nation* (New York: W.W. Norton and Company, 1998), 37

7. Paliser & Paliser, *Paliser's American Architecture or Every Man a Complete Builder* (New York: J.S. Ogilvie, 1888), is a good example.

8. Vincent J. Scully Jr., *The Shingle Style and the Stick Style* (New Haven: Yale University Press, 1955) 29.

9. An 1883 rendering by CG, "House on Virginia Ave.," is in the collection of the New-York Historical Society. For many years, Virginia was both "street" and "avenue." It is now Virginia Street.

10. In 1882, CG supervised construction of the Ross Winans House in Baltimore, Maryland, for McKim, Mead & White.

11. J. G. Pyle, ed., *Picturesque St. Paul* (St. Paul: Northwestern Photo Company, [1887]).

12. Mark Twain, *Life on the Mississippi* (New York: New American Library, 1961), 343.

13. While in independent practice, Taylor is known to have designed the W. P. Warner House at 315 Summit Avenue in 1882 (razed), the M. M. Williams House at 583 St. Peter Street in 1883 (razed), an unidentified house in Chicago, and a greatly remodeled, extant commercial building at 500-02 Laurel Avenue for F. W. Crocker.

14. Of poverty flat's several denizens, Edwin Jaggard would become the most prominent, serving as a justice on the Minnesota Supreme Court. He traded on his friendship with Gilbert to have his office in the new Minnesota capitol properly furnished. Gilbert likely designed a cottage for

Jaggard at 2546 Manitou Island in 1893. It has been razed.

15. CG to The Tiffany Glass Company, October 25, 1887, Box: 3, Fldr.: 19, CGP, MHS.

16. Tiffany Studios to CG, January 4, 1909, Box: 20, Fldr.: 1903 CGP, MHS.

17. CG to Julia Finch, April 14, 1887, Box: 4, General Correspondence 1887, LC/MS.

18. "The Ten Best Buildings in the United States," *American Architect and Building News* 17 (June 13, 1885): 282. Richardson's buildings include Trinity Church, Boston, MA (1), City Hall, Albany, NY (7), Sever Hall, Harvard University, Cambridge, MA (8), New York State Capitol, Albany, NY, (9), and Town Hall, North Easton, MA (10).

19. White, *The Houses of McKim, Mead & White,* 60.

20. Luther Cushing represented the interests of Henry and William Endicott, Jr. and the Boston Northwest Real Estate Company as well as other Boston-based and local real estate investors. Cushing's clients provided a great deal of work for Gilbert.

21. CG to Julia Finch, July 17, 1887, Box: 4, General Correspondence 1887, LC/MS.

22. Mrs. E. F. Drake, the widow of E. F. Drake and Lightner's mother-in-law, moved into 322 Summit Avenue when the Lightners moved into 318 Summit Avenue. CG then remodeled 322 Summit Avenue for Mrs. Drake.

23. Anonymous (Club Committee), *Forty Years of the Informal Club and the Four Hundredth Meeting 1894-1934* (St. Paul: privately printed, 1935).

24. St. John's Episcopal Church to CG, July 11, 1898, Box: 14, Fldr.: 98, CGP, MHS.

25. CG to St. Clement's Church, November 3, 1906, Box: 13, Fldr.: 97, CGP, MHS. In 1896, when Gilbert was competing for the Montana capitol project, he wired Morgan for assistance in obtaining the project, and Morgan agreed to help.

26. St. John the Evangelist Church to CG, February 4, 1902, Box: 14, Fldr.: 99, CGP, MHS.

27. Harry J. Carlson to CG, November 17, 1891, Box: 17, Fldr.: 1891, CGP, MHS.

28. Architectural plans for the Placer Hotel list George Carsley and Cass Gilbert as architects.

29. Stevens Haskell to CG, March 21, 1903, Box 20, Fldr.: 1903, CGP, MHS.

30. CG to Thomas Holyoke, July 31, 1902, Box: 19 Fldr.: 1902, CGP, MHS.

31. CG to St. Clement's Church, January 5, 1911, Box: 13, Fldr.: 97, CGP, MHS.

32. CG to Reverend Dobbins at Shattuck School, Box: 14, Fldr.: 104, CGP, MHS.

33. John W. Root to CG, June 5, 1890, Box: 17, Fldr.: 1882-90, CGP, MHS.

34. T-Square Club to CG, January 20, 1899; Architectural League of New York to CG, January 21, 1899; Boston Architectural Club to CG, February 1, 1899; CG to St. Louis Architectural Club, April 3, 1899; Box: 18, Fldr.: 1899, CGP, MHS.

35. U. S. Commission to the Paris Exhibition of 1900 to CG, July 14, 1899, Box: 18, Fldr.: 1899, CGP, MHS.

36. CG to Charles Gilbert, January 17, 1902, Box: 19, Fldr.: 1902, CGP, MHS.

37. Stiles Burr to CG, July 17, 1902, Box: 19, Fldr.: 1902, CGP, MHS.

38. CG to office, November 13, 1897, Box: 18, Fldr.: 1897, CGP, MHS.

39. CG to office, November 26, 1897, Box: 18, Fldr.: 1897, CGP, MHS.

40. Luther Cushing to CG, February 21, 1910, Box: 20, Fldr.: 1906–10, CGP, MHS.

41. After the St. Paul office closed in 1911, George Carsley moved to Montana and successfully operated his own architectural practice for many years.

42. CG to J. A. Wheelock, February 4, 1904, Box: 4, Fldr.: 28, CGP, MHS.

43. F. Scott Fitzgerald, *The Crack-Up* (New York: New Directions, 1956), 69.

CHAPTER 3

1. CG to Julia Finch, October 20 and 16 and December 1886; CG, diary, 1891, CGP, LC/MS.

2. Gilbert's early political views are described in CG to John Beverly Robinson, draft, September 20, 1891, CGP, MHS. His elderly views are expressed in CG to Mnesicles Chapter, Alpha Rho Chi, University of Minnesota, December 28, 1933, CGP, LC/MS.

3. CG to William Windom, December [?], 1890; CG to James J. Hill, Dec. 20, 1890; CG to W. J. Edbrooke, April 14, 1891, LB, CGC, NYHS; W. E. Curtis to CG, June 27, 1893, CGP, MHS.

4. Robert Peabody to CG, July 8, 1893, CGP, MHS.

5. W. H. Hoffman to CG, February 24, 1894, CGP, MHS.

6. CG to Channing Seabury, March 16, 1894, CGP, MHS.

7. Neil B. Thompson, *Minnesota's State Capitol: The Art and Politics of a Public Building* (St. Paul: Minnesota Historical Society, 1974), 10–19.

8. CG, Capitol design submission (draft), September 9, 1895; [E. M. Wheelwright] to Board of State Capitol Commissioners, October 17, 1895, CGP, MHS; Channing Seabury to E. M. Wheelwright, October 21, 1895; Channing Seabury to Charles K. Cole, June 19, 1896, letters sent, State Capitol Commission Board, 1893–1909, MHS.

9. E. M. Wheelwright to CG, January 8, 1896, CGP, MHS.

10. CG to Julia Gilbert, March 7, 1893, and February 25, 1907; CG, memorandum, April 26, 1886, in CGP, LC/MS; CG to "Mr. Whitney," January 20, 1891, LB, CGC, NYHS. Plans for the Rhode Island statehouse were published in *AABN* 35 (February 13, 1892).

11. Egon Verkeyen, " 'Unenlightened by a single ray from Antiquity': John Quincy Adams and the Design of the Pediment for the United States Capitol," *International Journal of the Classical Tradition* 3 (Fall 1996): 215–16; Henry Russell-Hitchcock and William Seale, *Temples of Democracy: The States Capitals of the U. S. A.* (New York: Harcourt Brace Jovanovich, 1976), 17–203.

12. Russell Sturgis, "Minnesota State Capitol," *Architectural Record,* vol. 19, no.1 (January 1906): 31–36; *St. Paul Pioneer Press,* May 24, 1934.

13. CG to Samuel Gilbert, June 2, 1898, LB, CGP, OCA; CG to Paul Seabury, January 12, 1904, CGP, MHS.

14. For the Tarsney Act, see Charles Moore, *Daniel H. Burnham: Architect, Planner of Cities,* vol. 1 (Boston: Houghton Mifflin, 1921), 95–109.

15. Frederick Stevens to CG, December 23, 1898; James K. Taylor to CG, April 20, 1899; Stevens Haskell to CG, April 28, 1899, CGC, MHS; CG to James K. Taylor, April 22, 1899; CG to Lyman Gage, April 22, 1899, LB, CGC, NYHS.

16. James K. Taylor to CG, July 7 and July 29, 1899; [George Squires] to Lyman Gage, November 2, 1899, CGC, MHS.

17. Stevens Haskell to CG, August 29, 1899; CG to Secretary of Treasury, [September 16, 1899], CGP, MHS; CG to Julia Gilbert, September 18, 1899; Samuel Gilbert to CG, September 18, 1899, LC/MS.

18. CG to Julia Gilbert, September 22, 1899, CGP, LC/MS.

19. CG to Julia Gilbert, September 24, 1899, CGP, LC/MS.

20. CG to Julia Gilbert, October 24, 1899, LC/CGP; CG to Charles Gilbert, January 4, 1900, LB, CGP, OCA.

21. *New York Times,* November 4, 1899; New York Tribune, November 4, 1899.

22. CG to Julia Gilbert, September 24 and October 15, 1899, CGP, LC/MS.

23. Montgomery Schuyler, "The New Custom House in New York," *Architectural Record* 20 (July 1906): 1–14; Kathryn Greenthal and Michael Richman, "Daniel Chester French's Continents," *American Art Journal* 8 (November 1976): 47–58; Michele Bogart, *Public Sculpture and the Civic Ideal in New York City,* 1890–1930 (Chicago: University of Chicago Press,

1989), 74–77, 111–34; Brendan Gill, *The U.S. Custom House on Bowling Green* (New York: exhibition catalog, 1976), 4.

24. John W. Reps, *Monumental Washington: The Planning and Development of the Capitol Center* (Princeton: Princeton University Press, 1967), 84–93, 115, 136; CG to Samuel Gilbert, January 6, 1899, LB, CGP, OCA.

25. Alpheus T. Mason, *William Howard Taft: Chief Justice* (New York: Simon and Schuster, 1965), 133–37; "The United States Supreme Court Building, Washington, D.C.," *Antiques* 128 (October 1985): 760–69; CG to Willis Van Devanter, November 16, 1926; CG to William Howard Taft, November 18, 1926, March 12, 1927, and December 10, 1928; CG to George Seymour, March 4, 1927; CG to Charles Moore, September 27, 1927, CG to Harlan Stone, January 18, 1929, LB, CGP, OCA; CG, diary, May 1, June 3, November 18, and December 17, 1928, CGP, LC/MS.

26. CG to Julia Gilbert, April 10, 1929; CG, diary, December 10, 1929, CGP, LC/MS.

27. CG, diary, December 7, 1932, CGP, LC/MS.

28. CG to John W. Davis, February 28, 1934, CGP, LC/MS.

29. Geoffrey Blodgett, "Cass Gilbert, Architect: Conservative at Bay," *Journal of American History* 72 (December 1985): 634–35.

30. CG to Reginald Bloomfield, April 5, 1933, CGP, LC/MS.

31. Baker Brownell and Frank Lloyd Wright, *Architecture and Modern Life* (New York: Harper, 1938), 56, 57.

CHAPTER 4

1. Guy Kirkham and Frederick G. Stickel, "Cass Gilbert: Master of Style," *Pencil Points* 15 (November 1934): 541–56.

2. CG to George Dudley Seymour, October 30, 1908, Misc.-LB, September 1908–July 1909. Gilbert wrote a similar statement to Ralph Adams Cram, May 14, 1907, CGPers.-LB, November 1906–July 1907, both in CGC, NYHS.

3. About Japanese architecture, see CG to Mr. J. Ohta, June 21, 1910, Misc.-LB, April 1910–January 1911; for Byzantine, see CG to John Rockart, November 9, 1906, CGPers.-LB, January 1906–February 1907; for colonial, see CG to Charles Moore, October 6, 1915, Misc.-LB, June 1909–April 1910, all in CGC, NYHS.

4. CG to Thomas A. Fox, April 13, 1896, Cass Gilbert Office Book, October 1895–April 1898, CGC, NYHS.

5. CG to Thomas G. Holyoke, September 18, 1899, New York Custom House LB, CGC, NYHS.

6. CG to Stevens Haskell, July 24, 1899, Broadway Chambers LB, March 1899–January 1900, CGC, NYHS.

7. CG to Albert Kelsey, March 17, 1899, Misc.-LB, March 1899–September 1899, CGC, NYHS.

8. CG to Stevens Haskell, January 3, 1900, New York Custom House LB, November 1899–June 1908, CGC, NYHS.

9. CG to William Adams Delano, January 22, 1917, CGPers.-LB, October 1916–July 1917, CGC, NYHS.

10. Undated typescript in Misc. correspondence, 1899–1903. The list includes painters, sculptors, and architects. In total the list reads: Phidias, Ictinus, Botticelli, Giotto, Michelangelo, Raphael, Palladio, Leonardo da Vinci, Charles Garnier, Augustus Saint-Gaudens, John La Farge, Brunelleschi, Donatello, Della Robbia, Titian, Bramante, Dürer, Holbein, Rembrandt, Rubens, Velasquez, and Cellini. Gilbert was tempted to include more contemporary names but resisted. He particularly considered replacing Palladio with McKim. CG to Thomas R. Johnson, March 6, 1903, Misc.-LB, October 1902–May 1903, CGC, NYHS.

11. CG to Editor of the Brochure Series, November 12, 1898, Broadway Chambers LB, August 1898–March 1899, CGC, NYHS.

12. Ibid.

13. Ibid.

14. CG Memorandum, June 17, 1897 [*sic*], Minnesota State Capitol LB, January 1899–November 1900, CGC, NYHS.

15. Use of Spanish grillwork for elevator screens, John Rachac to CG, September 10, 1901, Minnesota State Capitol LB, February 1901–February 1902; for influence of Tomb of Galla Placidia, CG to Louis Tiffany, December 13, 1901, Minnesota State Capitol LB, February 1901–February 1902; for Venetian influence on Governor's Reception Room, CG, "Description of Capitol," n.d., Minnesota State Capitol LB, June 1904–March 1905, all in CGC, NYHS.

16. CG to Thomas Smith, April 27, 1909, Misc.-LB, September 1908–July 1909, CGC, NYHS.

17. CG to Francis Swales, June 20, 1911, CGPers.-LB, June 1911–June 1912, CGC, NYHS.

18. CG to C. H. Reilly, April 23, 1909, CGPers.-LB, February 1909–May 1910, CGC, NYHS.

19. CG to Robinson, September 6, 1918, Misc.-LB, March 1917–October 1918, CGC, NYHS.

20. CG to Arthur D. Rogers, January 31, 1918, Misc.-LB, March 1917–October 1918, CGC, NYHS.

21. CG to Dr. Edwin Wiley, Librarian, U.S. Naval War College, April 15, 1918, Misc.-LB, March 1917–October 1918, CGC, NYHS.

22. These include the Ives Memorial Library, New Haven, Connecticut; St. Louis Public Library, St. Louis, Missouri; Detroit Public Library, Detroit, Michigan; and the Beverly Public Library, Beverly, Massachusetts. I am not counting the school and university libraries designed by Gilbert.

23. Minutes of a meeting with George Bidwell, Collector of Customs, November 28, 1899, Journal 1899–1909, CGC, NYHS.

24. CG to W. S. Eames, August 30, 1909, CGPers.-LB, February 1909–May 1910, CGC, NYHS.

25. Ibid.

26. Ibid.

27. CG to George Dudley Seymour, December 1, 1913, CGPers.-LB, December 1913–December 1914, CGC, NYHS.

28. Ibid.

29. Ibid.

30. CG to Charles G. Loring, August 3, 1914, CGPers.-LB, December 1913–December 1914, CGC, NYHS.

31. CG to William Endicott, August 21, 1911, CGPers.-LB, February 1911–June 1912, CGC, NYHS.

32. CG to Warren Powers Laird, August 26, 1912, CGPers.-LB, July 1912–October 1913, CGC, NYHS.

33. CG to Irving Pond, May 26, 1915, CGPers.-LB, December 1914–December 1915, CGC, NYHS.

34. CG to Leila Mechlin, August 2, 1912, CGPers.-LB, July 1912–October 1913, CGC, NYHS.

35. CG to Paul Cret, August 3, 1915, CGPers.-LB, December 1914–December 1915, CGC, NYHS.

36. CG to George Dudley Seymour, January 15, 1909, CGPers.-LB, September 1908–July 1909, CGC, NYHS.

37. CG to Ernest Newton, September 22, 1915, CGPers.-LB, December 1914–December 1915, CGC, NYHS.

38. CG, "Indigenous Architect," undated typescript, PC, Box: Woolworth Building Correspondence, CGC, NYHS.

39. Ibid.

40. CG to Professor Roswell P. Angier, May 5, 1916, CGPers.-LB, December 1915–October 1916, CGC, NYHS.

41. CG to George Dudley Seymour, July 8, 1914, CGPers.-LB, December 1913– December 1914, CGC, NYHS.

42. CG to John B. Pine, March 1, 1916, CGPers.-LB, December 1915–October 1916, CGC, NYHS.

43. CG to Col. C. H. Graves, August 30, 1920, CGPers.-LB, December 1919–December 1920, CGC, NYHS.

44. CG to Henry Bell, February 10, 1921, CGPers.-LB, December 1920–February 1922, CGC, NYHS.

45. CG to Ralph Adams Cram, December 23, 1920, CGPers.-LB,

CHAPTER 5

1. Mark Twain, *Life on the Mississippi* (New York: Penguin Books, 1883; reprint 1984), 410.

2. C. H. Graves, "Introductory Address" in *Proceedings at the Laying of the Corner Stone of the New Capitol of Minnesota* (St. Paul: Pioneer Press Company, 1898), 15.

3. Sharon Irish, *Cass Gilbert, Architect: Modern Traditionalist* (New York: Monacelli Press, 1999), provides an indispensable overview of the architect's career.

4. For the first two state capitols, see Larry Millett, *Lost Twin Cities* (St. Paul: Minnesota Historical Society Press, 1992), 64–67.

5. Neil B. Thompson, *Minnesota's State Capitol: The Art and Politics of a Public Building* (St. Paul: Minnesota Historical Society Press, 1974), 5, 8–9.

6. For the competition and Seabury, see Thompson, *Minnesota's State Capitol,* 10–15, 8, respectively. A spirited account of the capitol and its architect can be found in Henry-Russell Hitchcock and William Seale, *Temples of Democracy: The State Capitols of the USA* (New York: Harcourt Brace Jovanovich, 1976), 215–26.

7. Alan K. Lathrop, "Architecture in Minnesota at the Turn of the Century," in Michael Conforti, ed., *Art and Life on the Upper Mississippi: Minnesota 1900* (Newark, Del.: University of Delaware Press, 1994), 51.

8. Quoted in Thompson, *Minnesota's State Capitol,* 15.

9. The finalists' drawings are reproduced in Thompson, *Minnesota's State Capitol,* 13–15.

10. *St. Paul Pioneer Press,* October 31, 1895, p. 4.

11. Thompson, *Minnesota's State Capitol,* 11; for illustrations of the various state capitol buildings, see also Willis J. Ehlert, *America's Heritage: Capitols of the United States* (Madison, WI: State House Publishing, 1993).

12. Graves, "Introductory Address," 14.

13. Irish, "West Hails East," 205.

14. Kenyon Cox, "The New State Capitol of Minnesota," Architectural Record, vol. 18 (August 1905): 97.

15. Quoted in Thompson, *Minnesota's State Capitol,* 15.

16. The stone controversy is treated in detail in Thompson, *Minnesota's State Capitol,* 24–31, and summarized in Irish, "West Hails East," 206.

17. Daniel C. French to CG, May 26, 1903, CGP, MHS. The quadriga is described in detail in Thomas O'Sullivan, *North Star Statehouse: An Armchair Guide to the Minnesota State Capitol* (St. Paul: Pogo Press, 1994), 57–62.

18. Julie C. Gauthier, *The Minnesota Capitol: Official Guide and History* (St. Paul: Pioneer Press Manufacturing Depts., 1907), 11.

19. Graves, "Introductory Address," 14.

20. *Fourth Biennial Report of the Board of State Capitol Commissioners* (St. Paul: Pioneer Press Co., state printers, 1901), 12–15.

21. Gauthier, *The Minnesota Capitol,* 14–15.

22. Edwin H. Blashfield, *Mural Painting in America* (New York: Charles Scribner's Sons, 1913), 111.

23. Elmer E. Garnsey, "The Color Decoration of the Minnesota State Capitol," *Western Architect,* vol. 4 (October 1905): 19.

24. "Story of Building of Minnesota's New Capitol," *St. Paul Globe,* September 18, 1904, p. 38.

25. "Pupils Study Capitol Murals," *Minneapolis Journal,* January 21, 1905, p. 7.

26. Garnsey, "The Color Decoration," 25; Elmer E. Garnsey to CG, January 23, 1905, CGP, MHS.

27. CG to Channing Seabury, January 12, 1904, BSCCP, MHS.

28. *Fifth Biennial Report of the Board of State Capitol Commissioners* (St. Paul: Pioneer Press Co., state printers, 1903), 17.

29. Thompson, *Minnesota's State Capitol,* 48–55.

30. Cox, "The New State Capitol," 105.

31. CG to Channing Seabury, May 5, 1903, BSCCP, MHS.

32. Channing Seabury to CG, August 20, 1903, BSCCP, MHS.

33. Gauthier, *The Minnesota Capitol,* 13.

34. Ibid.

35. For Gilbert's early Colonial revival work, see Irish, *Cass Gilbert, Architect,* 21–22, and chapter 12 of this volume.

36. Edwin A. Jaggard to CG, January 28, 1905, CGP, MHS

37. CG to Board of State Capitol Commissioners, May 5, 1903, BSCCP, MHS; *St. Paul Pioneer Press,* February 4, 1904, p. 2, and January 8, 1905, pp. 1–3.

38. Gauthier, *The Minnesota Capitol,* 26.

39. *St. Paul Pioneer Press,* June 24, 1903, p. 3.

40. Cox, "The New State Capitol," 111.

41. CG to Channing Seabury, December 27, 1904, BSCCP, MHS.

42. Douglas Volk to CG, August 15, 1904, CGP, MHS.

43. CG to Channing Seabury, December 27, 1904, BSCCP, MHS.

44. CG to George H. Carsley, November 7, 1908, CGP, MHS

45. Gary Phelps, *History of the Minnesota State Capitol Area* (St. Paul: Capitol Area Architectural and Planning Board, 1985; reprint 1993), 7–16.

46. David T. Mayernik and Thomas N. Rajkovich, *Project for the Completion of the Capitol Mall, St. Paul, Minnesota* (St. Paul: Capitol Area Architectural and Planning Board, 1988).

47. CG to Channing Seabury, June 6, 1904, BSCCP, MHS.

48. *St. Paul Pioneer Press,* August 5, 1910, p. 4.

49. Donald R. Torbert, "A Century of Art and Architecture in Minnesota" in William Van O'Connor, ed., *A History of the Arts in Minnesota* (Minneapolis: University of Minnesota Press, 1958), 53.

50. David Gebhard and Tom Martinson, *A Guide to the Architecture of Minnesota* (Minneapolis: University of Minnesota Press, 1977), 88.

51. Robert A. M. Stern, "Editor's Foreword," in Irish, Cass Gilbert, Architect, 7.

52. Michael Conforti, "Introduction," in Conforti, ed. *Art and Life on the Upper Mississippi,* 17.

53. Ehlert, *America's Heritage,* 126–27. Gilbert's role in these later projects is recounted in Hitchcock and Seale, *Temples of Democracy,* 243, 262 (for Arkansas); 271–72 (for West Virginia).

54. Cass Gilbert, An Address by Cass Gilbert on the Presentation of the President's Medal of the National Academy of Design to Edwin Howland Blashfield (New York, privately printed, 1934), 11–12.

CHAPTER 6

The author wishes to thank the staff of the Minnesota Historical Society and Professors William H. Gerdts and Kevin Murphy of the Graduate Center, City University of New York for their assistance and advice.

1. Kenyon Cox, "The New State Capitol of Minnesota," *Architectural Record* 18: 95.

2. Michael Conforti, ed., *Minnesota 1900, Art and Life on the Upper Mississippi, 1890–1915* (Newark, DE: University of Delaware Press, 1994).

3. Henry Van Brunt, "Architecture in the West," *Atlantic Monthly* (December 1889): 772; reprinted in *Architecture and Society, Selected Essays of Henry Van Brunt* (Cambridge: Harvard University Press, 1969).

4. "The Mural Painters and Sculptural Decorations of the St. Paul Capitol," *International Studio,* supplement (October 26, 1905): lxxiv.

5. Lillian Miller, *Patrons and Patriotism, The Encouragement of the Fine Arts in the United States, 1790–1860* (Chicago: University of Chicago Press, 1966).

6. Sally Webster, "Writing History/Painting History: Early Chronicles of the United States and Pictures for the Capitol Rotunda," in Harriet Senie and Sally Webster, eds., *Critical Issues in Public Art: Content, Context, and*

Controversy (Washington, D.C.: Smithsonian Institution Press, 1998), 33–43.

7. Henry-Russell Hitchcock and William Seale, *Temples of Democracy, The State Capitols of the U.S.A.* (New York: Harcourt Brace Jovanovich, 1976).

8. James Philip Noffsinger, *The Influence of the Ecole des Beaux-Arts on the Architects of the United States* (Washington, D.C.: Catholic University of America Press, 1955).

9. David Van Zanten, "Architectural Composition at the Ecole des Beaux-Arts from Charles Percier to Charles Garnier," in Arthur Drexler, ed., *The Architecture of the Ecole des Beaux-Arts* (New York: Museum of Modern Art, 1977), 112.

10. Henry Van Brunt, "The New Dispensation of Monumental Art," *Atlantic Monthly* 43 (May 1879): 633–41; reprinted in *Architecture and Society, Selected Essays of Henry Van Brunt,* 135–44. This article was the second of two by Van Brunt about the Albany statehouse. The other one, "The New Architecture at Albany," appeared in *AABN* (January 8, 1879): 19–21 and (January 25, 1879): 128–29; reprinted in *Architecture and Society,* 126–134. Also see Sally Webster, "The Albany Murals of William Morris Hunt" (Ph.D. dissertation, City University of New York Graduate Center, 1985).

11. Hitchcock and Searle, *Temples of Democracy,* 215.

12. Herbert Small, *The Library of Congress, Its Architecture and Decoration* (Washington, D.C.: Library of Congress, 1901; reprint New York: Norton, 1982).

13. Ibid., 25.

14. Ibid., 102, 105.

15. An announcement of the formation of the Mural Painters society, and a clipping from *The Evening Post New York* (April 1895) describing its establishment, are in the CGP, MHS.

16. C. R. Lamb to CG, February 5, 1896, CGP, MHS.

17. Michele H. Bogart, *Public Sculpture and the Civic Ideal in New York City,* 1890–1930 (Chicago: University of Chicago Press, 1989), and Gregory G. Gilmartin, *Shaping the City, New York and the Municipal Art Society* (New York: Clarkson Potter, 1995).

18. William H. Wilson, *The City Beautiful Movement* (Baltimore, MD: Johns Hopkins University Press, 1989).

19. Channing Seabury to Charles R. Lamb, March 17, 1896, BSCCP, MHS.

20. CG, transcript, December 26, 1902, PC, Box: Minnesota State Capitol, Fldr.: 1, CGC, NYHS.

21. Frank E. Hanson, minutes, March 15, 1902, State Capitol Commissioners Board SB, MHS.

22. Quoted in "Story of the Capitol Paintings Bared," *Minneapolis Journal* (April 6, 1931): 14.

23. CG to Channing Seabury, September 26, 1902, CGP, MHS.

24. CG, transcript, December 26, 1902, PC, Box: Minnesota State Capitol, Fldr.: 108, CGC, NYHS.

25. CG, "Minnesota Capitol Report," January 15, 1903, PC, Minnesota State Capitol, Fldr.: 8, NYHS.

26. Edwin Blashfield, "Description of the Two Lunettes . . . for the Senate Chamber of the State Capitol of Minnesota," April 20, 1903, PC, Box: Minnesota State Capitol, Fldr.: 10, CGC, NYHS.

27. Ibid.

28. Ibid.

29. Ibid.

30. John La Farge to CG, September 7, 1903, CGP, MHS.

31. Sally Webster, "The Architecture and Sculptural Decoration of the Appellate Division Courthouse," in *Temple of Justice, The Appellate Division Courthouse* (New York: Architectural League of New York, 1977), 23–28.

32. CG to the Board of State Capitol Commissioners, January 3, 1904, CGP, MHS.

33. Ibid.

34. Julia C. Gauthier, *The Minnesota Capitol: Official Guide and History* (St. Paul: Pioneer Press, 1907), 16.

35. Ibid.

36. Warren Upham to Channing Seabury, June 24, 1903, and Gen. James H. Baker to Channing Seabury, June 23, 1903, both in CGP, MHS.

37. CG to Channing Seabury, April 21, 1904, CGP, MHS.

38. John Ireland to CG, February 24, 1904, CGP, MHS.

39. *St. Paul Dispatch,* February 27(?), 1904, n. p. CGP, MHS.

CHAPTER 7

1. The most recent studies of the movement are William H. Wilson, *The City Beautiful Movement* (Baltimore, MD: Johns Hopkins Press, 1989), and Jon Peterson, "City Planning: 1911–1917: Elusive Quest," in *The Birth of American City Planning,* publication forthcoming.

2. CG to Channing Seabury, April 3, 1903, BCSSP, MHS.

3. "Cass Gilbert Believed Minnesota Capitol Was Best Work He Ever Did," *St. Paul Pioneer Press,* May 24, 1934, Channing Seabury and Family Papers, MHS.

4. Charles Lamb to CG, March 4, 1896, CGP, MHS.

5. CG to the Board of State Capitol Commissioners, December 31, 1902, BSCCP, MHS.

6. Edwin H. Blashfield, "Mural Painting in America," *Scribner's* 54 (September 1913): 353; Edwin H. Blashfield, *Mural Painting in America* (New York: Scribners, 1913): 98; E. H. Blashfield, "A Word for Municipal Art," *Municipal Affairs* 3 (December 1899): 582.

7. George B. Post to CG, February 16, 1903, CGP, MHS.

8. Samuel Isham, *The History of American Painting* (1905; revised edition New York: Macmillan Company, 1936), 556.

9. CG to BSCC, May 5, 1903, BSCCP, MHS.

10. CG to Channing Seabury, April 3, 1903, BSCCP, MHS.

11. CG to Channing Seabury, August 27, 1903, BSCCP, MHS.

12. CG to Channing Seabury, November 16, 1904, BSCCP, MHS.

13. CG to Channing Seabury, January 12, 1904, BSCCP, MHS.

14. CG to Channing Seabury, May 5, 1903, and August 27, 1903, BSCCP, MHS.

15. CG to W. K. Bixby, July 2, 1923, W. K. Bixby Papers, Missouri Historical Society.

16. Copy of letter of agreement between the Association of Interior Decorators & Cabinet Makers of the City of New York and the New York District Council of the Brotherhood of Painters, Decorator and Paper Hangers of America, December 20, 1903, attached to a letter from George Schaettler, secretary of the Association of Interior Decorators & Cabinet Makers of the City of New York to "Labor Editor" [no newspaper specified], January 12, 1903, CGP, MHS. At the top of the letter is typed "Copy of letter mailed to the Press."

17. Neil B. Thompson, *Minnesota's State Capitol: The Art and Politics of a Public Building* (St. Paul: Minnesota Historical Society, 1974), 59.

18. See H. Barbara Weinberg, "John La Farge: Pioneer of the American Mural Movement," in *John La Farge* (New York: Abbeville Press, 1987), 161–93, for a discussion of the artist's mural style.

19. H. Wayne Morgan, *Kenyon Cox, 1856–1919* (Kent, OH: Kent State University Press, 1994), 154.

20. CG to Channing Seabury, January 18, 1904, BSCCP, MHS.

21. Channing Seabury to CG, May 19, 1904, CGC, NYHS. Gilbert's annotation is dated May 31, 1904. CG to Channing Seabury, June 14, 1904, BSCCP, MHS.

22. CG to Edward Simmons, June 7, 1904, BSCCP, MHS; CG to Edward Simmons, July 23, 1904, BSCCP, MHS. The carbon copy has a cover note attached, in which Gilbert writes to Seabury: "this is plain talk—Do you think it is too plain?"

23. Miss E. N. Cardizo, January 31, 1905, to Channing Seabury, BSCCP,

MHS; John Ireland to CG, February 24, 1904, CGP, MHS.

24. CG to Channing Seabury, December 27, 1904, BSCCP, MHS.

25. CG to Charles F. Owsley, January 18, 1908, Blashfield Papers, NYHS.

26. Mural contracts, PC, Essex County Courthouse files, CGC, NYHS.

27. W. Hawkins Ferry, *The Buildings of Detroit: A History* (1968; revised edition Detroit: Wayne State University Press, 1980), 220.

28. Joseph G. Dreiss, *Gari Melchers: His Works in the Belmont Collection* (Charlottesville, VA: University Press of Virginia, 1984), 54.

29. Dreiss, Gari Melchers, 54–56;

30. Leonard Amico, *The Mural Decorations of Edwin Howland Blashfield* (1848–1936) (Williamstown: Sterling and Francine Clark Art Institute, 1978), 49.

31. "Mural Paintings in Public Buildings in the United States," *American Art Annual* 19 (1922): 407–38.

CHAPTER 8

1. *Legislative Manual of the State of Minnesota,* (St. Paul: Secretary of State, 1905), 134, 229.

2. William B. Dean, "A History of the Capitol Buildings of Minnesota, with Some Account of the Struggles for the Location," *Collections of the Minnnesota Historical Society* (St. Paul, 1908), 33.

3. CG to J. H. Schoonmaker, February 23, 1926, PC, Box: Minnesota State Capitol/#12, Fldr.: 10, CGC, NYHS.

4. Miller Dunwiddie Architects, *Minnesota State Capitol: A Comprehensive Preservation Plan* (St. Paul: Capitol Area Architectural and Planning Board, 1988), 7.

5. Sherri Gebert Fuller, "Oral History Interview with Edward A. Burdick, Chief Clerk, House of Representatives," *Alterations Study,* Book 5, Capitol Historic Site, MSC, 1987, 5.

6. Governor Rudy Perpich to Commissioner of Administration, Sandra Hale, September 12, 1984, State Capitol Subject notebook 8b, vol. 2, 1881, Legislative Reference Library.

7. *Minnesota Statutes,* Chapter 138.67, 138.68, and 138.69 (St. Paul: Revisor of Statutes, 1998), 750–51.

8. "Specifications for the Cabinet Work, Furniture, and Furnishings of the State Capitol Building," 1903, BSCCP, MHS.

9. Carolyn Kompelien, Kendra Dillard, and Sherri Gebert Fuller, *Attention to Detail: 1905 Furniture of the Minnesota State Capitol* (St. Paul: Minnesota Historical Society, 1989), 3.

10. Gebert Fuller, *Alterations Study,* Book 2; *St. Paul Pioneer Press,* July 22, 1970, p. 29.

11. Honorable E. A. Jaggard to CG, January 28, 1905, CGP, MHS.

12. Ethel L. Phelps to G. H. Spaeth, January 27, 1939, Capitol Historic Site, MSC.

13. Museum Collections, MHS.

14. Private collection of J. Thomas family.

15. Joan Ulrich, *Minnesota State Capitol Furnishings Plan Report,* Phases 1 and 2 (St. Paul: Capitol Historic Site, 1993–95).

16. Ibid.

17. "Specifications for the Cabinet Work, . . . ," 1903, MHS.

18. Julie C. Gauthier, *The Minnesota Capitol: Official Guide and History* (St. Paul: Pioneer Press Manufacturing Depts., 1907), 43.

19. Ulrich, *Furnishings Plan Report,* Phase 1, 44.

20. Ibid., Phase 2, 218.

21. Cass Welsh to Sy Vang, Lao Vachong, Sao Vang, Drew Xiong, and Khang Vang, February 12, 1987, Capitol Historic Site, MSC.

22. Stanley Applebaum, *The Chicago World's Fair of 1893* (New York: Dover, 1980), 27.

23. Daniel Chester French to CG, May 26, 1903, CGP, MHS.

24. Linda Merk-Gould, *Technical Study Report,* Fine Objects Conservation (Westport, CT: Department of Administration Division of State Building Construction, 1993), 6.

25. Linda Merk-Gould, *Conservation Treatment Report,* Conservation Technical Associates LLC (Westport, CT: Department of Administration Division of State Building Construction, 1995), 11.

26. Conservation treatment met standards of the American Institute of Conservation.

27. Bazille & Partridge to Board of Capitol Commissioners, December

28. 1906, BSCCP, MHS. D. C. French to CG, September 27, 1906, D. C. French Papers, LC/MS.

29. CG to Channing Seabury, June 14, 1904, CGP, MHS.

30. Monthly Reports, 1995, Capitol Historic Site, MSC.

31. Governor Theodore Christianson to J. H. Schoonmaker, January 3, 1931, Governor F. B. Olson Papers, MHS.

32. The original glass plate negatives are in the MHS collections.

33. Dan Tarnoveanu, *Recovery of Designs Report,* Renaissance Art, Restoration & Architecture (West St. Paul: Miller Dunwiddie Architects, 1999), 3–4.

34. Architectural drawings were made of all design motifs for MHS Archives.

35. Dan Tarnoveanu to Carolyn Kompelein, November 3, 1999, Capitol Historic Site, MSC.

36. During the 18-month restoration, it was learned that Minnesota's Capitol rathskeller is one of three known Cass Gilbert buildings in which he incorporated a rathskeller. The other two locations are the Montana Club rathskeller (extant) in Helena, Montana (identified by Patty Dean, Curator, MHS Museum Collections), and the Woolworth Building restaurant rathskeller (not extant) (identified by Gail Fenske, professor at the School of Architecture, Roger Williams University, Bristol, R.I.).

37. The collection of Cass Gilbert correspondence at both the MHS and NYHS gives some details about his continuing involvement in the Minnesota capitol.

38. CG, "Report of Meeting of Colvill Capitol Commission," September 14, 1907, PC, Box: Minnesota State Capitol, Fldr.: 1, CGC, NYHS.

39. G. A. Carsley to CG, June 20, 1907, PC, Box: Minnesota State Capitol/#5, Fldr.: 1, CGC, NYHS.

40. Ulrich, *Furnishings Plan,* Phase 2; CG to Thomas Holyoke, December 7, 1914, Capitol Custodian Correspondence, CGP, MHS.

41. CG to J. H. Schoonmaker, February 23, 1926, PC, Box: Minnesota State Capitol/#12, Fldr.: 10, CGC, NYHS.

42. CG to Governor F. B. Olson, April 18, 1933, PC, Box: Minnesota State Capitol/#5, Fldr.: 9, CGC, NYHS.

43. Ibid.

CHAPTER 9

1. Regarding the earlier profile views, see Spiro Kostof, *The City Shaped: Urban Patterns and Meanings Through History* (London: Thames and Hudson, 1991), 283–309. For the New York skyline, see William Taylor, "New York and the Origin of the Skyline: The Commercial City as Visual Text," in William R. Taylor, ed., *In Pursuit of Gotham: Culture and Commerce in New York* (New York: Oxford University Press, 1992), 23–33.

2. John C. Van Dyke, *The New New York: A Commentary on the Place and the People* (New York: The Macmillan Company, 1909), 8. See also Gail Fenske, "Cass Gilbert's Skyscrapers in New York: The Twentieth-Century City and The Urban Picturesque," in Margaret Heilbrun, ed., *Inventing the Skyline: The Architecture of Cass Gilbert* (New York: Columbia University Press, 2000), 229–88, which touches upon skyline views of New York in the context of analyzing Gilbert's skyscraper designs.

3. Cass Gilbert, "Introduction," in Vernon Howe Bailey, *Skyscrapers of New York* (New York: William Edwin Rudge, 1928), n.p.

4. Frank Woolworth, "Executive Office" [General Letter to Store Managers], September 25, 1914, PC, Woolworth Building, CCG, NYHS.

5. Earle Shultz and Walter Simmons, *Offices in the Sky* (New York: Bobbs-

Merrill Company, 1959), 56.

6. Taylor, "New York and the Origin of the Skyline," 23. The terms *picture* and *picturing* were frequently used after the century's turn. See for instance Charles Mulford Robinson, "The Picture of the City," *Independent* 54 (September 1902): 2207, and "New York's Big Buildings," *Architectural Record* 20 (September 1906): 249.

7. "High Buildings," in "The Field of Art," *Scribner's* 19 (January 1896): 127.

8. Montgomery Schuyler, "The Sky-Line of New York, 1881–1897," *Harper's Weekly* 41 (March 20, 1897): 295. Although no evidence exists to indicate that Gilbert read this particular essay, he was personally acquainted with Schuyler and read his criticism.

9. A. D. F. Hamlin, "The Tall Building from an American Point of View," *Engineering Magazine* 14 (December 1897): 441. See also Sarah Bradford Landau and Carl Condit, *Rise of the New York Skyscraper, 1865–1913* (New Haven: Yale University Press, 1996), 275.

10. John De Witt Warner, "Matters That Suggest Themselves," *Municipal Affairs* 2 (March 1898): 123.

11. Charles Mulford Robinson, *Modern Civic Art or the City Made Beautiful* (New York: G. P. Putnam's Sons, 1903), 39–41, 49–50, 57.

12. About Gilbert and the City Beautiful, see Gail Fenske, "The 'Skyscraper Problem' and the City Beautiful: The Woolworth Building" (Ph.D. dissertation, MIT, 1988), 111–37, and Barbara Snowden Christen, "Cass Gilbert and the Ideal of the City Beautiful: City and Campus Plans, 1900–1916" (Ph.D. dissertation, City University of New York Graduate Center, 1997).

13. Cass Gilbert, "Grouping of Public Buildings and Development of Washington," in Glenn Brown, compiler, *Papers Relating to the City of Washington* (Washington, D.C.: Government Printing Office, 1901), 78–82.

14. Cass Gilbert, untitled lecture on American cities, the City Beautiful Movement, and the grouping of public buildings [Art School, Yale University], 1907, Box: 17, CGP, LC/MS.

15. Regarding General Howard Carroll and the West Street Building, see Sharon Irish, "A 'Machine That Makes the Land Pay': The West Street Building in New York," *Technology and Culture,* vol. 30 (April 1989): 380, 396.

16. See for instance Gilbert's travel diary of November 7, 1897, to March 9, 1898, Box: 1, CGP, LC/MS. The diary describes visits to Antwerp, Malines, Brussels, Ghent, and Bruges. Gilbert described the Cathedral of St. Rombout, Malines, in an unpublished essay of December 2, 1897, Box: 6, CGP, LC/MS.

17. Cass Gilbert, "Tenth Birthday of a Notable Structure," *Real Estate Magazine of New York* 11 (May 1923): 345.

18. "Architecture of the Low Countries—II," *AABN* 39 (March 18, 1893): 163–67, and H. W. Brewer, " 'Commercial Art': A Composition," *American Architect* 80 (June 27, 1903), pl. 1435. Julien Guadet, *Eléments et théories de l'architecture,* livre 8 (Paris: Librairie de la construction moderne, 1901–1904), 455–60.

19. [Montgomery Schuyler], "The West Street Building, New York," *Architectural Record* 22 (August 1907): 108–09.

20. Regarding New York as the nation's major tourist center, see Neil Harris, "Urban Tourism and the Commercial City," in William R. Taylor, ed., *Inventing Times Square* (1991; reprint Baltimore: Johns Hopkins University Press, 1996), 66–67, 75–76.

21. Sylvester Baxter, "The New New York," *Outlook* 73 (June 23, 1906): 415.

22. Henry James, as quoted in Leon Edel, "Introduction," in Henry James, *The American Scene* (1907; reprint Bloomington: Indiana University Press, 1969), vii.

23. Montgomery Schuyler, "Some Recent Skyscrapers," *Architectural Record* 22 (September 1907): 161.

24. "The Skyscraper and the Silhouette," *AABN* 92 (September 21, 1907): 89.

25. Giles Edgerton [Mary Fanton Roberts], "How New York Has Redeemed Herself from Ugliness—An Artist's Revelation of the Beauty of the Skyscraper," *Craftsman* 11 (January 1907): 458, 471.

26. For the Broadway Chambers Building, see Cass Gilbert to Elizabeth Gilbert, February 26, 1899, Box: 6, CGP, LC/MS. The fantasy sketch inspired by the West Street Building is housed in LC/PP.

27. Charles Rollinson Lamb's municipal building of 650 feet is described in "From Battery to Harlem: Suggestions of the National Sculpture Society," *Municipal Affairs* 3 (December 1899): 641–45, as are R. H. Robertson's descriptions of 100-story and 1000-foot skyscrapers. For Starrett's skyscraper, see *New York Herald,* May 13, 1906, sec. 3, 8, as cited in Rem Koolhaas, *Delirious New York: A Retroactive Manifesto for Manhattan,* 2nd ed. (New York: Monacelli Press, 1994), 90, 314 n. 7. "Tower 1,000 Feet High," *New York Times,* July 19, 1908, pt. 2, 1:2, describes Flagg's tower.

28. "New York, the Unrivalled Business Centre," *Harper's Weekly* 46 (November 15, 1902): 1673.

29. Montgomery Schuyler, " 'The Towers of Manhattan' and Notes on the Woolworth Building," *Architectural Record* 33 (February 1913): 104.

30. O. F. [Otto Francis] Semsch, ed., *A History of the Singer Building Construction: Its Progress from Foundation to Flagpole* (New York: Trow Press, 1908), 9. Regarding Flagg and skyscraper reform, see Mardges Bacon, *Ernest Flagg: Beaux-Arts Architect and Urban Reformer* (New York and Cambridge, Mass.: Architectural History Foundation and MIT Press, 1986), 220–23.

31. Ernest Flagg, "The Limitation of Height and Area of Buildings in New York," *AABN* 93 (April 15, 1908): 126.

32. Regarding the relation between the Singer Company's building program and internal organizational changes, see Gail Fenske and Deryck Holdsworth, "Corporate Identity and the New York Office Building, 1895–1915," in David Ward and Olivier Zunz, eds., *The Landscape of Modernity: New York City, 1900–1940* (1992; reprint Baltimore: Johns Hopkins University Press, 1997), 135–37.

33. Concerning the relation of Singer's architectural publicity to the criticism of big business, see Kenneth Turney Gibbs, *Business Architectural Imagery in America, 1870–1930* (Ann Arbor, Mich.: UMI Research Press, 1984), 148.

34. Van Dyke, *The New New York,* 148.

35. "Skyscraping up to Date," *Architectural Record,* vol. 22 (January 1908): 74.

36. Harrison Rhodes, "New York—City of Romance," *Harper's Monthly Magazine* 99 (November 1909): 914.

37. Joseph B. Gilder, "The City of Dreadful Height," *Putnam's Monthly Magazine* 5 (November 1908): 136, 141, 143.

38. Van Dyke, *The New New York,* 4–5.

39. "Towered Cities," *Living Age* 42 (January 2, 1909): 47.

40. Harris, "Urban Tourism," 82, analyzes the city's "abnormal taste" and "dizzy heights" as a form of "commercial extravagance."

41. Cass Gilbert, "The Woolworth Building," in *Masterpieces of Architecture in the United States* (New York: Charles Scribner's Sons, 1930), 215.

42. John K. Winkler, *Five and Ten: The Fabulous Life of Frank Woolworth* (New York: Robert M. McBride and Company, 1940), 151–52, 160, 173.

43. Cass Gilbert, "Tenth Birthday," 344.

44. Julia Gilbert, "An Experience" [1911], Box: 17, CGP, LC/MS.

45. Winkler, *Five and Ten,* 172–76; William R. Taylor, "The Evolution of Public Space: The Commercial City as Showcase," in William R. Taylor, ed., *In Pursuit of Gotham,* 46.

46. Schuyler, " 'The Towers of Manhattan,' " 104.

47. Montgomery Schuyler, "The Woolworth Building" [1913], in William H. Jordy and Ralph Coe, eds., *American Architecture and Other Writings by Montgomery Schuyler,* vol. 2 (Cambridge: Harvard University Press, 1961), 606, 608.

48. John Marin, as quoted in Ruth E. Fine, *John Marin* (Washington, D.C. and New York: National Gallery of Art and Abbeville Press, 1990), 126.

49. Henry Adams, "Nunc Age (1905)," in *The Education of Henry Adams* (1907; reprint New York: Library of America, 1983), 1176.

50. Regarding the urban condition to which Adams was responding, see Alan Trachtenberg, "Image and Ideology: New York in the Photographer's Eye," *Journal of Urban History* 10 (August 1984): 453–65. See also Landau and Condit, *Rise of the New York Skyscraper,* 281–82.

51. "Proposed Brooklyn Bridge Terminal and City Offices," *Architect's and Builder's Magazine* 4 (August 1903): 483–89; Gregory F. Gilmartin, *Shaping the City: New York and the Municipal Art Society* (New York: Clarkson Potter Publishers, 1995): 78–80.

52. "The Proposed Brooklyn Bridge Terminal Improvements," *AABN* 81 (August 15, 1903): 50.

53. Gilmartin, *Shaping the City,* 79, 121–22.

54. "The City Majestic," *Independent* 69 (September 15, 1910): 604.

55. Regarding Gilbert and the so-called City Practical, see "A Protest That Is Timely," *Architectural Record* 27 (February 1910): 202.

56. CG to Emily Gilbert, October 8, 1912, Box: 8, CGP, LC/MS.

57. Ibid.

58. Cass Gilbert, "Introduction," in Vernon Howe Bailey, *Skyscrapers of New York* (New York: William Edwin Rudge, 1928), n.p.

59. Ibid.

CHAPTER 10

1. Dorothy Norman, *Alfred Stieglitz: An American Seer* (1960; reprint New York: Random House, 1973), 99.

2. William T. Morgan, "The Politics of Business in the Career of an American Architect: Cass Gilbert 1878–1905" (Ph.D. dissertation, University of Minnesota 1972; Ann Arbor, Mich.: University Microfilms, 1982), 13; Gail Fenske, "'The Skyscraper Problem' and the City Beautiful: The Woolworth Building" (Ph.D. dissertation, MIT, 1988), xiii, 132–36; and Sharon Irish, "Cass Gilbert's Career in New York, 1899–1905" (Ph.D. dissertation, Northwestern University, 1985; Ann Arbor, Mich.: University Microfilms, 1987), 388–89.

3. Steichen, "291," *Camera Work* 47 (July 1914): 63, quoted in Geraldine Wojno Kiefer, "Alfred Stieglitz, Camera Work, and Cultural Radicalism," *Art Criticism* 7 (1992): 3.

4. Merrill Schleier, *The Skyscraper in American Art 1890–1931* (New York: Da Capo, 1986), 41–68; Kiefer, "Alfred Stieglitz, *Camera Work,*" 4; and John Szarkowski, "Alfred Stieglitz," in *Looking at Photographs* (New York: Museum of Modern Art, 1973), 74.

5. Irish, "Cass Gilbert's Career," 388. For a reevaluation of Stieglitz's professed radicalism, see Abigail Solomon-Godeau, "The Return of Alfred Stieglitz," *Afterimage* 12 (Summer 1984): 22.

6. Schleier stated that the skyscraper photographs of Stieglitz, Steichen, and Coburn probably piqued Marin's interest in the new building type. Schleier, *The Skyscraper in American Art,* 55. Marin's first images of the Woolworth Building, watercolors, date from 1912. See Sheldon Reich, *John Marin: Catalogue Raisonné,* vol. 2 (Tucson: University of Arizona Press, 1970), 373.

7. Schleier, *The Skyscraper in American Art,* 63–68, and "French Artists Spur on American Art," *New York Tribune,* October 24, 1915, sec. IV, p. 2. For Duchamp's remark on the Woolworth Building as ready-made, see Marcel Duchamp, "L'Infinitif," in *Salt Seller: The Writings of Marcel Duchamp,* eds. Michel Sanouillet and Elmer Peterson (New York: Oxford University Press, 1973), 75.

8. C. A. Leidy to CG, letter of November 14, 1910, and 1911 United States Copyright Notice, CGC, NYHS. Mentioned in the Leidy letter, postcard rights were an important issue for Gilbert, as reproduction rights are a contested issue today. See David W. Dunlap, "What's Next? A Fee

for Looking?" *New York Times,* August 27, 1998, sec. F, pp. 1, 8. I am grateful to Michael Radow for this reference.

9. Invoices from the Wurts Brothers indicate Gilbert commissioned them, but the Atlantic Terra Cotta Company, which won the lucrative contract for the Woolworth cladding, commissioned Underhill and Underhill photography for articles and their own advertising. The company also gratefully presented Gilbert with a portfolio of platinum prints, the Rolls Royce of photographic processes. Tebbs-Hymans' details of the terra cotta cladding appear in *Architectural Record,* vol. 33 (February 1913): 109–23. See Wurts Brothers to CG, February 2, 1913 invoice; and Edward Putnam to CG, Letters of February 13, 1913, and February 5, 1914, CGC, NYHS. Norman and Lionel Wurts established their business for architectural, legal, and general photography in 1894. See December 31, 1913(?), Invoice, CGC, NYHS. Irving Underhill opened his business in 1896 and provided artistic portraits, city views and panoramas, group photographs, marine, legal, and machinery photography. See Irving Underhill to CG, Letter of May 5, 1913, CGC, NYHS.

10. CG to J. B. Millet, January 21, 1913; Edward Putnam to CG, April 23, 1913; and CG to J. J. Jusserand, January 1, 1914; CGC, NYHS.

11. Bonnie Yochelson, "Karl Struss's New York," in *New York to Hollywood: The Photography of Karl Struss,* Barbara McCandless et al., eds. (Fort Worth, Texas: Amon Carter Museum, 1995) 100–101, and Cervin Robinson, "Architectural Photography: Complaints about the Standard Product," *Journal of Architectural Education* 29 (November 1975): 10–15.

12. Jan-Christopher Horak, "Paul Strand: Romantic Modernist," in *Making Images Move: Photographers and Avant-Garde Cinema* (Washington, D.C.: Smithsonian Press, 1997) 88.

13. Stieglitz to Marsden Hartley, letter of May 12, 1914, quoted in Schleier, *The Skyscraper in American Art,* 44.

14. See Hugh McAtamney to CG, February 15, 1913, CG, NYHS.

15. Dickrun Tashjian, "An American Dada," *William Carlos Williams and the American Scene 1920–1940* (New York: Whitney Museum of American Art, 1978) 58–59; Horak, "Paul Strand: Romantic Modernist," 98; and Ellen Handy, "The Idea and the Fact: Painting, Photography, Film, Precisionists, and the Real World," in *Precisionism in America 1915–1941: Reordering Reality,* Gail Stavitsky, ed. (New York: Harry A. Abrams, 1995) 45–46. See Charles Downing Lay, "New Architecture in New York," *Arts* 4 (August 1923): 67–85, for Sheeler's commercial architectural photography.

16. Dell Upton, "Architectural History or Landscape History?" *Journal of Architectural Education* 44 (August 1991): 195–99. Neil Harris's *Building Lives: Constructing Rites and Passages* (New Haven: Yale University Press, 1999) is the first study of the life cycles of buildings.

17. Sue Davidson Lowe, *Stieglitz: A Memoir/Biography* (New York: Farrar, Straus, Giroux, 1983), 276, 387.

18. Norman, *Stieglitz,* 45

19. In fact, Stieglitz may have been one of the first artists to depict the Flatiron in any medium. The first painting Merrill Schleier cites is Birge Harrison's *The "Flatiron" after Rain,* c. 1907. See Schleier, *The Skyscraper in American Art,* 15, 23, 33, and figure 20. While Steichen photographed the Flatiron Building in 1905, Coburn made his views in 1904. In 1910 Coburn published one of his Flatiron photographs as a photogravure in a portfolio entitled *New York,* to which H. G. Wells contributed an introductory essay. See Schleier, figure 23, for a reproduction of Steichen's Flatiron photograph, and Nancy Romero and George Hendricks, eds., *Alvin Langdon Coburn and H. G. Wells: The Photographer and the Novelist* (Champaign-Urbana, Ill.: University of Illinois Press, 1997), figures 8 and 18, for the Coburn images.

20. Norman, *Stieglitz,* 45.

21. Schleier, *The Skyscraper in American Art,* 6–11, and McKim to Lawrence Grant White, April 21 and May 18, 1909, Charles Follen McKim Papers, LC/MS.

22. Wanda Corn, "The New New York," *Art in America* 61 (July–August

1976): 60–61.

23. Pierre Apraxine, "Turn of the Century: Chrysalis of the Modern," in Maria Morris Hambourg et al., eds., *The Waking Dream: Photography's First Century* (New York: Metropolitan Museum of Art, 1993), 172–75.

24. Ian Jeffreys, "Morality, Darkness and Light: The Metropolis in Pictures," in Martin Caiger-Smith, ed., *Site Work: Architecture and Photography* (London: Photographers' Gallery, 1991), 57.

25. Alvin Langdon Coburn, *An Autobiography,* Helmut and Alison Gernsheim, eds. (1966; reprint New York: Dover Books, 1978), 14, 18, 86.

26. Ibid., 84.

27. Ibid., and Schleier, *The Skyscraper in American Art,* 49–50.

28. Bonnie Yochelson wrote that Coburn photographed the Liberty Tower from atop the Woolworth Building. See her "Karl Struss's New York," in *New York to Hollywood,* 108. But she is wrong; Coburn could not see the finished elevation shown in his photograph from atop the Woolworth Building. Only an angled view or the unfinished party wall of Liberty Tower is visible from the Woolworth Building. Positioning himself on the Singer Tower and looking from Broadway eastward allowed Coburn to look down on the west facade of the Liberty Tower shown in the photograph. The other buildings visible in the photograph, like the party wall of the Lorsch Building, also accord with the view Coburn would have had from the Singer Tower looking from west to east in 1912.

29. Sarah Bradford Landau and Carl Condit, *Rise of the New York Skyscraper 1865–1913* (New Haven: Yale University Press, 1996), 337–38.

30. Coburn, *Autobiography,* 46.

31. Schleier, *The Skyscraper in American Art,* 55. Hugh McAtamney, the public relations agent for the Woolworth Building, was the publisher of *Above the Clouds and Old New York.* The relationship, if any, between the Coburn photograph and the brochure cover illustration is unknown. Coburn's 1913 exhibition *New York from Its Pinnacles* was in London, but there was a catalog. As publicity agent for the Woolworth Building, McAtamney might have seen this catalog. But I have found no references to Coburn or any of the art photographers in the CGC, NYHS.

32. Nancy Romero and George Hendrick, "A Door in Their Wall: The Coburn-Wells Connection," in *Alvin Langdon Coburn and H. G. Wells,* 12.

33. Gilbert's remark quoted in Fenske, "'The Skyscraper Problem' and the City Beautiful," 137. The cathedral metaphor appears in Edwin Cochrane's *The Cathedral of Commerce* (New York: Broadway Park Place Company, c. 1916).

34. In reality, the Woolworth Building did not reconcile the cathedral with commerce. Carol Willis observes it "was widely known in real estate circles as a poor performer, earning only about two and half to three percent return." See Carol Willis, *Form Follows Finance: Skyscrapers and Skylines in New York and Chicago* (New York: Princeton Architectural Press, 1995), 45.

35. Mike Weaver, *Alvin L. Coburn: Symbolist Photographer 1882–1966* (New York: Aperture/Eastman House, 1986), 79.

36. Romeo and Hendrick, "A Door in Their Wall," 61. Whistler painted *The Symphony in White No. 2: The Little White Girl* in 1864. It was part of a series of canvases entitled "harmonies" or "symphonies" to emphasize his exploration of purely formal and perceptual issues. See John Wilmerding, *American Art* (Harmondworth, Middlesex, England: Penguin Books, 1976), 146–47 and plate 177.

37. Barbara McCandless, "A Commitment to Beauty," and Bonnie Yochelson, "Karl Struss's New York," *From New York to Hollywood: The Photography of Karl Struss,* 18–19, 24–25, and 103–104.

38. Schleier, *The Skyscraper in American Art,* 50. Struss made over 400 negatives and well over 100 exhibition prints of New York between 1909 and 1916. See Yochelson, "Struss's New York," 98.

39. Charles Mulford Robinson, *Modern Civic Art,* (New York: Putnam, c. 1918), quoted in Fenske, "'The Skyscraper Problem' and the City Beautiful," 17; and Coburn, "The Relation of Time to Art," *Camera Work* 36 (October 1911): 72.

40. Janet Parks, "Hughson Hawley," in *New York on the Rise: Architectural Renderings by Hughson Hawley* eds. Kathy Benson, Jeanne Sullivan, and Nancy Ten Broeck (New York: Museum of the City of New York, 1998), 9–10 and plate 26.

41. Roland Rood, "The Origins of Poetical Feeling: Landscape," *Camera Work* 11 (July 1905): 24.

42. Fenske, "'The Skyscraper Problem' and the City Beautiful," xiii–xv, 66–67, and Norman, *Stieglitz,* 45.

43. Coburn, "The Relation of Time to Art," 72.

44. Sadakichi Hartmann, "A Plea for the Picturesqueness of New York," *Camera Notes* 4 (October 1900): 91–92.

45. Fenske, "'The Skyscraper Problem' and the City Beautiful," 188–190, 196–99. Daniel Bluestone also explores the skyscraper in late-nineteenth-century Chicago. See "A City under One Roof: Skyscrapers, 1880–1895," in his *Constructing Chicago* (New Haven: Yale University Press, 1991), 104–51.

46. Robert H. Wiebe, *The Search for Order,* 1877–1920 (New York: Hill and Wang, 1967), and M. Christine Boyer, *Dreaming the Rational City: The Myth of American Planning* (Cambridge: MIT Press, 1990).

47. Fenske, "'The Skyscraper Problem' and the City Beautiful," 121.

48. Ibid., 121–22, and Boyer, *Dreaming the Rational City,* 27.

49. Fenske, "'The Skyscraper Problem' and the City Beautiful," 1, 130–32, 136.

50. Ibid., 224–25. Designed by McKim, Mead & White, the Municipal Building provided office space for the burgeoning city government. The commission was won in competition. McKim, whose dislike of the skyscraper has already been noted, was not happy, but William Kendall, a second-generation partner and chief designer for the Municipal Building, prevailed. See Landau and Condit, *Rise of the New York Skyscraper,* 366–68, and Leland Roth, *McKim, Mead and White, Architects,* (New York: Harper and Row, 1983), 337.

51. Fenske, "'The Skyscraper Problem' and the City Beautiful," 112–15.

52. McCandless, "A Commitment to Beauty," 20.

53. Yochelson, "Karl Struss's New York," 101, 108, 111–12. See Schleier, *The Skyscraper in American Art,* 49–50.

54. Paul Strand criticized pictorialism in the 1920s, as did subsequent art historians. See his "Photography and the New God," *Broom* 3 (1922): 252–58, and Corn, "The New New York," 61.

55. Strand, "Photography and the New God," 252–58; Alfred Stieglitz, "Paul Strand," *Camera Work* 48 (October 1916): 11; and Yochelson, "Struss's New York," 123.

56. Jan-Christopher Horak, "Paul Strand: Romantic Modernist," 83, 92.

57. Ibid., 85, 88.

58. Jan-Christopher Horak, "Modernist Perspectives and Romantic Desires: Manhatta," *Afterimage* 15 (November 1987), 9–10.

59. While Whitman used *Mannahatta* for his poem, the original title Strand and Sheeler chose for their film is something of a mystery. Neither refers to a film title in their correspondence from the 1920s. Only in later years did Strand refer to the film by title, but he spoke of both Manhatta, now commonly used, and Mannahatta. See Horak, ibid., 9.

60. Lewis Mumford, "Metropolitan Milieu," in Waldo Frank et al., eds., *America and Alfred Stieglitz: A Collective Portrait* (Garden City, N.Y.: Doubleday, Doran, and Company, 1934), 48, 49; Handy, "The Idea and the Fact: Painting, Photography, Film, Precisionists, and the Real World," in *Precisionism in America 1915–1941*: 40–45; and Horak, "Paul Strand: Romantic Modernist," 80.

61. W. H. Crocker to CG, February 27, 1913, CGC, NYHS.

62. CG to H. T. Parson, president of Woolworth Company, January 26, 1924, CGC, NYHS.

63. "Who Was the Architect?" *Architecture,* vol. 48 (December 1933): 407. I am grateful to Professor Gail Fenske for this reference.

The author wishes to thank the following people for their assistance in the researching and writing of this chapter: Tom Blanck, Barbara Christen, Carolyn Dry, Steven Flanders, Carmine Giordano, Christopher Gray, Pamela Hepburn, James W. Phillips, Amy Slaton, and Francis Young.

1. Sarah Bradford Landau and Carl W. Condit, *Rise of the New York Skyscraper, 1865–1913* (New Haven: Yale University Press, 1996), 8.

2. The Gotzian store in St. Paul is located at 352 Wacouta Street; the U.S. Realty Warehouse is at First Avenue North and North First Street, also near the river on the Minneapolis side.

3. Russell Sturgis, "The Warehouse and the Factory in Architecture," *Architectural Record* 15 (January and February 1904): 1–17, 122–33. Russell Sturgis (1836–1909) had trained in Munich at the Academy of Fine Arts and Sciences where practical construction methods as well as medieval styles were emphasized.

4. Russell Sturgis, "Factories and Warehouses," *Architectural Record* 19 (May 1906): 369.

5. CG, draft of "Brooklyn, New York," n.d., p. 2, CGC, NYHS.

6. Charles H. Patton, "Warehouses: Their Planning and Construction," *Architectural Record* 27 (1910): 339. See also "The Literature of Reinforced Concrete," *AABN* 9 (1906): 159.

7. Arthur S. McEntee, "Recent Developments in the Architectural Treatment of Concrete Industrial Buildings," *Architecture* 43 (1921): 20.

8. "$40,000,000 Supply Base for Brooklyn," *New York Times,* May 17, 1918; "Goethals Explains Plans," *New York Times,* May 17, 1918; *A Record of War Activities* (New York: Turner Construction Company, 1918), 75–104.

9. For general information about all the terminal facilities, see Roy S. MacElwee, *Ports and Terminal Facilities* (New York: McGraw-Hill [1918], 1926): 278ff. Also see Cass Gilbert, "United States Army Supply Base, Brooklyn, NY," *AABN* 116 (November 26, 1919): 651–58.

10. "Brooklyn, New York," n.d., pp. 1–2, CGC, NYHS.

11. For background about the acute shortage of space and rail traffic congestion, see Carl W. Condit, *The Port of New York,* vol. 1 (Chicago: University of Chicago Press, 1980), 111–21.

12. "The Brooklyn Army Supply Base," file memo, December 30, 1919, p. 7, CGC, NYHS.

13. Diary, March 21, 1918. George Washington Goethals Papers, LC/MS.

14. The cost of the land was $8,796,600. Officer in Charge of Construction Division to CG, May 4, 1918, and daily memo, June 8, 1918, CGC, NYHS.

15. Herbert S. Crocker, *The U. S. Army Supply Base Construction Completion Report* (hereafter cited as CCR), Record Group 77, p. 80, NARA. See also "Freight Handling at the Brooklyn Army Base," *Engineering News-Record* 88 (September 18, 1919): 555. See also Peter Slatin, "Renovating the Brooklyn Army Terminal," *Metropolis* 8 (March 1989): 23–24.

16. Reyner Banham, *A Concrete Atlantis: U.S. Industrial Building and European Modern Architecture* (Cambridge: MIT Press, 1986): 56.

17. *Fifty Years of Buildings by Turner* (New York: Turner Construction Company, 1952). Subcontractors on the job included Otis Elevators, Post and McCord (structural steel), Raymond Concrete Pile Co. CCR, p. 195, NARA.

18. Daily memo, June 14, 1918, CGC, NYHS, and CCR, pp. 126, 129–31, 135, and Appendix H, NARA.

19. CCR, p. 83, NARA. Toxement had also been used on the Woolworth Building foundations. Toxement was made by Toch Bros., Long Island City, New York. CG to Henry Turner, August 31, 1918, CGC, NYHS; *Sweets Architectural Catalogue,* 13th ed. (New York: Sweet's Catalogue Service, 1918), 50–51.

20. For more on concrete, see John Sedgwick, "Strong but Sensitive,"

Atlantic Monthly 267 (April 1991): 70–82, and Cecil D. Elliott, *Technics and Architecture: The Development of Materials and Systems for Buildings* (Cambridge: MIT Press, 1992).

21. CCR, p. 87, NARA.

22. CCR, pp. 84–85, 89, and Appendix F, NARA.

23. *A Record of War Activities,* 91.

24. CCR, p. 85, NARA.

25. CCR, pp.118–19, 121–23, NARA.

26. Amy Elisabeth Slaton, "Origins of a Modern Form: The Reinforced Concrete Factory Building in America, 1900–1930" (Ph.D. dissertation, University of Pennsylvania, 1995), 48.

27. James W. Phillips, ed., *Arthur Newell Talbot: Proceedings of a Conference to Honor TAM's First Department Head and His Family* (Champaign, Ill.: Theoretical and Applied Mechanics, Report 762, 1994).

28. Slaton, "Origins of a Modern Form," 86.

29. Henry Turner to A. N. Talbot, October 10, 1911, Arthur Newell Talbot Papers, University of Illinois Archives, Urbana, Illinois.

30. CCR, pp. 17–18, NARA.

31. CCR, p. 106, NARA.

32. CCR, p. 107, NARA.

33. Terry Smith, *Making the Modern: Industry, Art and Design in America* (Chicago: University of Chicago Press, 1993).

34. "Points to Be Considered in Preparation of a Proposed Agreement with Mr. Cass Gilbert as Architect," April 20, 1918, p. 1, CGC, NYHS, noted that the "Constructing Quartermaster will have full personal charge and supervision of entire project." See also Appendix C, NARA/CCR.

35. "Experts Take Over All Army Building," *New York Times,* March 17, 1918.

36. Scrapbook, George Washington Goethals Papers, LC/MS, and Phyllis A. Zimmerman, *The Neck of the Bottle: George W. Goethals and the Reorganization of the U.S. Army Supply System, 1917–18* (College Station: Texas A&M University Press, 1992).

37. George C. Nimmons, "Modern Industrial Plants," *Architectural Record,* vol. 45 (March 1919): 266.

38. "Army Supply Base, Brooklyn, NY," February 17, 1918, CGC, NYHS.

39. Diary, p. 1, February 18, 1918, George Washington Goethals Papers, LC/MS.

40. "Preliminary Plan for War Department Supply Base, So. Brooklyn," February 21, 1918, CGC, NYHS.

41. One can track developments in daily memos dictated by Gilbert, beginning in March 1918, CGC, NYHS.

42. CCR, pp. 62, 79, NARA; telegram from R. C. Marshall to CG, May 23, 1918, CGC, NYHS.

43. Constructing Quartermaster to Turner Construction Company, with copy to CG, May 24, 1918, CGC, NYHS.

44. Walker Evans, "The American Warehouse," *Architectural Forum* 116 (April 1962): 94.

45. "Freight Handling at the Brooklyn Army Base," 555.

46. "Brooklyn Army Supply Base," December 30, 1919, p. 5, CGC, NYHS.

47. CCR, p. 101, NARA; Daily memo, April 27, 1918, CGC, NYHS.

48. "Terminal Warehouse Group, South Brooklyn," January 23, 1918, CGC, NYHS.

49. "Principles of Design for Operation," n.d., CGC, NYHS. See also "Freight Terminal Design a Traffic Problem," *Engineering News-Record* 83 (September 18, 1919): 540–41.

50. CCR, p. 80, NARA

51. "Principles of Design for Operation," p. 4, CGC, NYHS; also the letter from William Bassett, Otis Elevator Company, to CG, April 4, 1919, CGC, NYHS, outlined the analysis of freight elevator capacity recommended.

52. Sturgis, "Warehouse and Factory in Architecture," 16.

53. Francis S. Onderdonk Jr., *The Ferro-Concrete Style: Reinforced Concrete in Modern Architecture* (New York: Architecture Book Publishing Co., 1928), 248–50.

54. Cass Gilbert, "Industrial Architecture in Concrete," *Architectural Forum* 39 (September 1923): 83.

55. CCR, p. 74, NARA.

56. MacElwee, *Port and Terminal Facilities,* 300.

57. McEntee, "Recent Developments," 20.

58. MacElwee, Ports and Terminal Facilities, 268.

59. Hugh Ferriss to CG, November 6, 1918, CGC, NYHS. These renderings are in the CGC, NYHS.

60. Sturgis, "Warehouse and Factory in Architecture," 133.

61. Diary, August 15 and 29, 1918, George Washington Goethals Papers, LC/MS.

62. R. C. Marshall Jr. (by Col. Lincoln Bush) to B. F. Cresson, September 24, 1918, CGC, NYHS.

63. CCR, p. 14, NARA.

64. "Brooklyn Army Supply Base," December 30, 1919, p. 7, CGC, NYHS.

65. Albert Kahn, "Reinforced-Concrete Architecture These Past Twenty Years," *American Concrete Institute Proceedings* 20 (1924): 113.

66. Gilbert, "Industrial Architecture," 83.

67. Banham, *A Concrete Atlantis,* 53.

68. Le Corbusier, *Towards a New Architecture,* transl. by Frederick Etchells (New York: Praeger, 1946), 42.

CHAPTER 12

1. "Cass Gilbert Visits England," *American Architect* 118 (August 18, 1920): 213.

2. For more about each of these projects and the local citizens whose input was crucial to the designs' development, see Barbara Snowden Christen, "Cass Gilbert and the Ideal of the City Beautiful: City and Campus Plans, 1900–1916" (Ph.D. dissertation, City University of New York Graduate Center, 1997).

3. William H. Truettner and Thomas Andrew Denenberg, "The Discreet Charm of the Colonial," in William H. Truettner and Roger B. Stein, eds., *Picturing New England: Image and Memory* (New Haven: Yale University Press and National Museum of American Art/Smithsonian Institution, 1999), 78–109. Also see Joseph S. Wood, *The New England Village* (Baltimore: Johns Hopkins University Press, 1971), 1–8.

4. For a general discussion of the Federal style, see Leland M. Roth, *American Architecture: A Concise History* (New York: Harper and Row, 1979), 58–66; Ralph W. Hammett, *Architecture of the United States* (New York: John Wiley and Sons, 1976), 3–7; and William H. Jordy Jr., *American Buildings and Their Architects: The Colonial and Neoclassical Styles* (Garden City, N.Y.: Doubleday and Company, 1970), 210–39.

5. "An Example of the Work of a Connecticut Architect," *Bulletin of the Metropolitan Museum of Art* 22 (October 1927): n.p. The portico, with fluted columns of solid oak and capitals of clear pine, was exhibited at the museum before it was sold at auction. See donation correspondence November 1914–February 1915, Chron., Box: 1915/#2, Fldr.: Misc., and George Dudley Seymour to CG, May 3, 1918, Misc., Box: 1917, Fldr.: #103 R-T 1918, CGC, NYHS. Gilbert's donation to the Metropolitan Museum of Art likely came about because a descendent of the Bristols, a member of the Dana family, was closely allied with the museum.

For photographs of the house before it was demolished, see "The Judge William Bristol House," in Bertha Chadwick Trowbridge, ed., *Old Houses of Connecticut* (New Haven: Yale University Press, 1923), 488–96, of which a copy can be found in the Bristol House file at the Keeler Tavern Museum, Ridgefield, Connecticut. Also see Sharon Irish, *Cass Gilbert, Architect: Modern Traditionalist* (New York: Monacelli Press, 1999), e.n. 33; G. D. Seymour to CG, September 27 and October 18, 1907, Misc., Box: 1907–12, Fldr.: New Haven [6]; and CG's sketch of portico attached to F. W. Seagrist to CG, October 5, 1907 and N. Ehrlich

to G. H. Wells, October 8, 1907, CGP, Box: 1909–10, Fldr.: 1907 [*sic*], CGC, NYHS. For Gilbert's original intentions to reuse the Bristol House portico in an entrance to his home in Ridgefield, see CG to Eugene S. Bristol, October 29, 1907, CGPer.-LB February–December 1907, CGC, NYHS. For the campaign to restore Monticello, see ca. June 1914, CGPers., Box: January 1911–June 30, 1915, CGC, NYHS.

6. Everett G. Hill, *A Modern History of New Haven and Eastern New Haven County,* vol. 2 (New York: S. J. Clarke, 1918), 884–85, and "G. Seymour, Expert on Hale's Life Dies," *New York Times,* January 22, 1945, p. 17. George Dudley Seymour's publications include *New Haven* (New Haven: privately printed, 1942); "An Open Letter to the Honorable Board of Alderman of the City of New Haven," pamphlet (New Haven, 1914); and "Our City and its Big Needs," a series of four articles reprinted by the New Haven Chamber of Commerce from the *New Haven Journal-Courier,* December 16–19, 1912. Further archival materials about Seymour can be found at Yale University Library/Manuscripts and Archives, and the Connecticut State Archives/Connecticut State Library in Hartford.

7. [Montgomery Schuyler], "Along the Harlem River Branch," *Architectural Record* 24 (December 1908): 417–29.

8. For information about the role the railroad was to have played in New Haven, see Barbara S. Christen, "The Architect as Planner: Cass Gilbert's Responses to Historic Open Space," in Margaret Heilbrun, ed., *Inventing the Skyline: The Architecture of Cass Gilbert* exhibition catalog (New York: Columbia University Press, 2000), 177–228.

9. See *Report of the Capitol Approaches Commission to the Common Council of the City of St. Paul* (St. Paul: Pioneer Press, 1906).

10. CG to Frederick Law Olmsted Jr., August 5, 1907, CGPer.-LB February–December 1907, and G. D. Seymour to CG, October 1, 1907, Misc. corr., Box: 1907–12, Fldr.: New Haven [6], CGC, NYHS.

11. "Library Plans Are Accepted," [newspaper not named], clipping in SB (1907–10), n.p., CGC, NYHS; G. D. Seymour to Glenn Brown, April 10, 1911, George Dudley Seymour Papers, RG 801, SR5, Box: 4, Fldr.: 8 (AIA).

12. George Dudley Seymour, "Would Restore Center Church," *New Haven Journal-Courier,* December 9, 1909, SB (1907), n.p., CGC, NYHS. See articles in Misc. Box: 1911-18, Fldr.: #103 S-T 1916, CGC, NYHS.

13. CG to George W. Watrous, November 19, 1907, CGPer.-LB February–December 1907, CGC, NYHS.

14. "Cass Gilbert Will Submit Final Sketches of the Ives Library: Style to be Colonial," [newspaper unnamed], clipping from ca. late 1907, SB (1907–10), CGC, NYHS.

15. CG to G. D. Seymour, May 21, 1910, CGPer.-LB, April 1910–January 1911, CGC, NYHS.

16. See "Statement by Commission on New Courthouse," *New Haven Evening Register,* April 6, 1909, SB (1907–10), CGC, NYHS, and CG to John K. Beach, two letters dated February 26, 1909, Misc.-LB September 1908–July 1909, CGC, NYHS. For a general discussion of the competition system in the decades preceding Cass Gilbert's presidency of the AIA, see Mary N. Woods, *From Craft to Profession: The Practice of Architecture in 19th-Century America* (Berkeley: University of California Press, 1999), 36–38, and 42–44.

17. "Dispute Over Architect," *New Britain [Conn.] Herald,* March 27, 1909; "The Courthouse Plan," *New Haven Evening Register,* April 1, 1909; "Many Score Commissioners," *New Haven Journal-Courier,* April 3, 1909; and "Beach Off the Commission on Court Building," New Haven Evening Register, April 4, 1909; clippings in SB (1907-10), CGC, NYHS.

18. *Register Manual of the State of Connecticut* (Hartford: Case, Lockwood and Brainard, 1895–1923), and "Candidacy of Jacob D. Walter," Saturday Chronicle, October 27, 1906, p. 11.

19. "Beach off the Commission on Court Buildings," *New Haven*

Evening Register, April 4, 1909; "Can Get along without Beach," *New Haven Journal-Courier,* April 5, 1909; and "Beach Explains His Resignation," *New Haven Evening Register,* April 5, 1909; clippings in SB (1907-10), CGC, NYHS.

20. Frank S. Bishop to CG, March 14, 1912, PP, Box: G-S, Fldr.: New Haven 1912. For background about White, see "Thomas Gilbert White" entries in Glenn B. Opitz, ed., *Mantle Fielding's Dictionary of American Painters, Sculptors and Engravers,* (Poughkeepsie: Apollo, 1986), 1022, and in Peter Falk Hastings, ed., *Who Was Who in American Art,* (Guilford, Conn.: Soundview Press, 1985), 675.

21. R. A. Farrelly to CG, March 16, 1912, PP, Box: G-S, Fldr.: New Haven 1912, CGC, NYHS.

22. CG to George W. Watrous and Harry D. Day, March 17, 1912 and CG to his office staff, March 13, 1912, both in PP, Box: G-S, Fldr.: New Haven 1912; and CG to G. D. Seymour, June 19, 1909, CGPer.-LB, February 1909–May 1910, all in CGC, NYHS.

23. "Beach off the Commission on Court Building," *New Haven Evening Register*, April 4, 1909; "County Bar Will Protest: Special Meeting to Show Lawyers' Disapproval of Court House Commissioners' Acts to Be Called Soon," *New Haven Journal-Courier,* April 12, 1909; and "The County Courthouse," *New Haven Journal-Courier,* April 5, 1909; all clippings in SB (1907–10), CGC, NYHS.

24. "Beach off the Commission on Court Building," *New Haven Evening Register,* April 4, 1909, SB (1907–10), CGC, NYHS.

25. G. D. Seymour to CG, June 25, 1910, Misc., Box: 1907–12, Fldr.: New Haven #164 [4], CGC, NYHS; also see G. D. Seymour to CG, December 18, 1916, Misc., Box: 1911–18, Fldr.: #103 S-T 1916, CGC, NYHS.

26. For further details about street reconstruction elsewhere in town, see William J. Pape, *History of Waterbury and the Naugatuck Valley, Connecticut,* vol. 1 (Chicago: S. J. Clarke, 1918), 31.

27. Tony P. Wrenn, "Waterbury Municipal Center Complex," National Register of Historic Places report, U. S. Department of the Interior, National Park Service, 1978, item 8, p. 2.

28. "Henry Sabin Chase" in *Who Was Who in America, 1897–1942,* vol. 1 (Chicago: Marquis, 1966), 213; obituary, *New York Times,* March 5, 1918, p. 11.

29. "Frederick Starkweather Chase" in *Who Was Who in America,* vol. 2 (Chicago: A. N. Marquis Co., 1950), 111; *National Cyclopaedia of American Biography,* current vol. G (1943–46) (New York: James T. White and Company, 1946), 433–34; "F. S. Chase, 85, Dies: A Brass Executive," *New York Times,* December 7, 1947, p. 76.

30. Wrenn, "Waterbury Municipal Center Complex," item 8, p. 3.

31. Daily report by CG, September 17, 1919, PC, Box: Waterbury Club, Fldr.: Office reports, CGC, NYHS.

32. Wrenn, "Waterbury Municipal Center Complex," item 8, p. 4.

33. Pape, *History of Waterbury,* vol. 1, 44. Gilbert's winning competition design was published as "Accepted Competition Plans, City Hall, Waterbury," Connecticut," *Architecture* 28 (October 15, 1913): 230.

34. Pape, *History of Waterbury,* vol. 1, 45. For period views of these spaces, see "Municipal Building, Waterbury, Conn.," *American Architect* 108 (December 15, 1915): n.p., 14 plates.

35. CG to G. D. Seymour, July 8, 1914, CGPer.-LB December 1913–December 1914, CGC, NYHS.

36. Henry Sabin Chase to CG, July 26, 1913, PC, Box: Waterbury Municipal Building, Fldr.: Misc. A-Z 1913, CGC, NYHS.

37. The author thanks Mary Beth Betts for her reference to CG to G. D. Seymour, December 1, 1913, CGPer.-LB December 1913–December 1914, CGC, NYHS.

38. G. D. Seymour to CG, December 10, 1913, Chron., Box: 1913/#1, Fldr.: Misc., CGC, NYHS.

39. CG to G. D. Seymour, December 1, 1913, CGPer.-LB December 1913–December 1914, CGC, NYHS. For Seymour's response, see G. D.

Seymour to CG, December 13, 1913, Box: Waterbury Municipal Building 1913-1917, Fldr.: Misc. A-Z 1913, CGC, NYHS.

40. CG to John P. Elton, March 4, 1916, Waterbury Municipal Building-LB, December 1915–March 1921, CGC, NYHS.

41. See Pape, *History of Waterbury,* vol. 1, 46; CG to R. D. Read [ca. September 25, 1916], Charles A. Colley to CG, October 7, 1916, and Henry Sabin Chase to CG, October 20, 1916, in Box: Waterbury Municipal Building, Fldr.: A–C 1916, and CG to John P. Elton, October 9 and 13, 1916, in Waterbury Municipal Building-LB, December 1915–March 1921, CGC, NYHS.

42. G. D. Seymour to CG, December 13, 1913, Box: Waterbury Municipal Building 1913–17, Fldr.: Misc. A-Z 1913, CGC, NYHS.

43. Ibid.

44. G. D. Seymour, November 20, 1913, Chron., Box: 1913/#2, Fldr.: Q-R, CGC, NYHS.

45. CG to G. D. Seymour, July 8, 1914, CGPer.-LB December 1913–December 1914, CGC, NYHS.

46. Ibid. For an overview of the interior details of the Wynn House, see Doreen Yarwood, *Robert Adam* (New York: Charles Scribner's Sons, 1970), 196–97, and Joseph and Anne Rykwert, *Robert and James Adam: The Men and the Style (*New York: Electa/Rizzoli, 1985), 156–58.

47. CG to G. D. Seymour, July 8, 1914.

48. Ibid.

49. See Wood G. Dunlap to CG, July 14, 1922, and April–May 1922 correspondence, in PC, Box: Waterbury/New Business 1917–1924, Fldr.: 1922, CGC, NYHS. See Paul W. Barlett to G. D. Seymour, November 25, 1915 (copy forwarded to CG), Chron., Box: 1915/#2, Fldr.: [Misc.], CGC, NYHS.

50. Daily report, August 29 and 30, 1916, PC, Box: Chase Companies 1917–25, Fldr.: Daily reports, CGC, NYHS.

51. Henry Sabin Chase to CG, April 19, 1917, PC, Box: Chase Companies 1917–25, Fldr.: "C", CGC, NYHS.

52. Daily report, April 24, 1917, PC, Box: Chase Companies 1917–25, Fldr.: Daily reports, CGC, NYHS.

53. Daily report, May 18, 1918, PC, Box: Chase Companies 1917–25, Fldr.: Daily reports, CGC, NYHS.

54. Henry Sabin Chase to CG, July 12, 1917, PC, Box: Chase Companies 1917–25, Fldr.: "C", CGC, NYHS.

55. Ibid.

56. Wrenn, "Waterbury Municipal Center Complex," item 7, p. 13.

57. Daily report, August 29–30, 1916, PC, Box: Chase Companies, 1917–25, Fldr.: Daily reports, CGC, NYHS.

58. CG to Oscar Hagen, March 28 and April 1 and 8, 1896, General office book October 1895–September 1898; CG to Paul Wenzel, February 3, 1900, CGPer.-LB October 1899–November 1900; CG to A. DeNeef & Co., March 18, 1908, Misc.-LB January 1908–August 1908; and CG to Tice and Lynch, March 30, 1911, CGPer.-LB February 1911–June 1912, CGC, NYHS.

59. Daily report, September 26 and October 12, 1917, Box: New Business 1917–24, Fldr.: YMCA, CGC, NYHS.

60. CG to Henry Sabin Chase, December 4, 1917, Box: New Business 1917–24, Fldr.: YMCA, CGC, NYHS.

61. Henry Sabin Chase to CG, December 7, 1917, Box: New Business 1917–24, Fldr.: YMCA, CGC, NYHS.

62. Daily report, August 2, 1918, PC, Box: Waterbury National Bank 1920-22, Fldr.: Conference reports 1920 [*sic*], CGC, NYHS, *History of Waterbury,* and also see Pape, vol. 2, 545–46.

63. G. D. Seymour to CG, September 3, 1909, Misc. Box: II. 1909–10, Fldr.: Misc. 1909–10, CGC, NYHS.

CHAPTER 13

1. For a description of the development of buildings on the University of

Texas at Austin campus, see Roxanne Kuter Williamson, "A History of the Campus and Buildings of the University of Texas with Emphasis on Sources for the Architectural Styles," 1965, bound manuscript, Architecture and Planning Library, General Libraries, University of Texas at Austin. For a more general discussion of the role of the campus in the development of Austin, see Roxanne Kuter Williamson, *Austin, Texas: An American Architectural History* (San Antonio: Trinity University Press, 1973). For a thorough discussion of Paul Cret's work at the University of Texas and its relationship to the work of previous architects, see Carol McMichael, *Paul Cret at Texas: Architectural Drawings and the Image of the University in the 1930s,* exhibition catalog (Austin: Archer M. Huntington Gallery, 1983). For an examination of Gilbert's interaction with representatives of the University of Texas, see Barbara Snowden Christen, "Cass Gilbert and the Ideal of the City Beautiful: City and Campus Plans, 1900–1916" (Ph.D. dissertation, City University of New York Graduate Center, 1997), 359–435. For a reference on the general context of American campus planning and design of which this work was a part, see Paul Venable Turner, *Campus: An American Planning Tradition* (Cambridge: MIT Press, 1984).

2. Williamson, "A History of the Campus and Buildings of the University of Texas," 2–8.

3. Ruffini's drawings are in the Ruffini Manuscript Collection, Texas State Archives, Austin.

4. The first two buildings were completed under the firm Coughlin and Ayers and the third under Atlee B. Ayers. Drawings of various Ayers-related practices are located in the Alexander Architectural Archives, Architecture and Planning Library, General Libraries, University of Texas at Austin.

5. The "Bird's Eye View of University Grounds," which best describes the Coughlin and Ayres master plan, is in the Barker Texas History Center, University of Texas at Austin.

6. Mann's papers are in the University Archives, University Libraries, University of Minnesota, Twin Cities, Minneapolis. Information on his drawings may be obtained from the Northwest Architectural Archives, St. Paul, Minnesota.

7. The "Bird's Eye View: Group Plan for the University of Texas," which best describes Mann's master plan, is in the Barker Texas History Collection, University of Texas at Austin.

8. Letters between Gilbert and Colonel House and between Gilbert and various University of Texas officials can be found in University of Texas President's Office Records, file VF15D, "University Building Program," Barker Texas History Collection, University of Texas at Austin.

9. McMichael, *Paul Cret at Texas,* 18.

10. For a discussion of Gilbert's career in this period, see Sharon Irish, *Cass Gilbert Architect: Modern Traditionalist* (New York: Monacelli Press, 1999), 74–113.

11. Ibid., 100.

12. For a brief appreciation of Battle Hall's use over time, see Lawrence W. Speck, "Timeliness and Timelessness," *Center* 2 (1986): 118–19.

13. For a description of the Sutton Hall renovation, see Jeffrey Karl Ochsner, "The Renewal of Sutton Hall: Architecture Complex Taking Shape at UT-Austin," *Texas Architect* 33 (March/April 1983): 60–63.

14. Both of the latter two drawings can be found at the New-York Historical Society, New York, New York.

15. Irish, *Cass Gilbert Architect,* 136.

16. Most of Herbert M. Greene's work and the work of Greene, La Roche & Dahl at the University of Texas is documented in drawings located in the Alexander Architectural Archives, Architecture and Planning Library, General Libraries, University of Texas at Austin. Greene's work at University of Texas is discussed in McMichael, *Paul Cret at Texas,* 115–18.

17. Ibid.

CHAPTER 14

1. Olmsted Brothers to H. C. King, June 20, 1903, HCKP, OCA.

2. F. N. Finney to H. C. King, October 13 and December 31, 1903, HCKP, OCA.

3. F. N. Finney to CG, September 12, 1905, Letter Received, CGC, NYHS; CG to H. C. King, January 18, 1905, HCKP, OCA.

4. CG to Miller & Patten, March 22, 1905 (copy), Letters Received, CGC, NYHS.

5. CG to C. W. Williams, February 27, 1908, LB, CGC, NYHS.

6. Paul Baker, *Stanny: The Gilded Life of Stanford White* (New York: Free Press, 1989), 359–60.

7. CG to F. N. Finney, March 22, 1905 (copy), HCKP, OCA.

8. CG to F. N. Finney, April 8, 1905, LB, CGC, NYHS; CG to H. C. King, March 31, 1906, HCKP, OCA; H. C. King to CG, May 23, 1907, Letters Received, CGC, NYHS.

9. CG to George Feick, January 25, 1908, CG-LB, CGC, NYHS.

10. CG to G. H. Wells, December 30, 1907, CG to Stephen Gladwin, January 7, 1908, CG-LB, CGC, NYHS.

11. CG to C. H. Williams, January 9, 1908, CG-LB, CGC, NYHS; Robert Venturi "Plain and Fancy Architecture by Cass Gilbert at Oberlin," *Apollo* 103 (February 1976): 7–8.

12. CG to F. N. Finney, October 15 and October 26, 1908, CG-LB, CGC, NYHS; Finney to H. C. King, October 29, 1908, HCKP, OCA; Finney to CG, February 5, 1909, Letters Received, CGC, NYHS.

13. Samuel Yellin to CG Jr., May 21, 1934, Letters Received, CGC, NYHS.

14. H. Wayne Morgan, *Kenyon Cox, 1856–1919: A Life in American Art* (Kent, Ohio: Kent State University Press, 1994), 174–77.

15. Dudley P. Allen to CG, July 3, 1908, Letters Received, CG to H. C. King, August 7, 1914, CG-LB, CGC, NYHS; *Oberlin News,* June 16, 1915.

16. Julia Gilbert to Mrs. Storer, May 8, 1914, CGP, LC/MS.

17. I. T. Frary, "The Dudley Peter Allen Memorial Art Building, Oberlin, Ohio," *Architectural Record* 44 (August 1918): 105–109; CG to Mrs. Dudley P. Allen, November 5, 1915 (copy), HCKP, OCA.

18. CG to Samuel Yellin, August 25, 1915, CG to H. C. King, September 17, 1915, CG-LB,CGC, NYHS.

19. CG to H. C. King, June 9, 1916, HCKP, OCA; Geoffrey Blodgett, "Peters at Risk," *Oberlin Alumni Magazine* 88 (Winter 1993): 17–19, and "The Meaning of Peters Hall," *Oberlin Alumni Magazine* 93 (Fall 1997): 11–21.

20. CG, entries of January 13, February 20, and June 30, 1920, and June 27, 1924, Diaries, CGP, LC/MS.

21. CG to Julia Gilbert, June 21, 1924, CGP, LC/MS; D. E. Lyon to E. H. Wilkins, November 30, 1927, Wilkins Papers, OCA.

22. K. W. Haskell to E. H. Wilkins, April 25, 1928, Wilkins Papers, OCA.

23. Cass Gilbert Jr., Memoranda dated March 13, 1930, and April 17, 1931, CG Letters Received, CGC, NYHS; Cass Gilbert Jr. to CG, July 8, 1929, and August 1, 1930, CGP, LC/MS.

24. For the controversy about the ALCOA stock, see George David Smith, *From Monopoly to Competition: The Transformation of ALCOA, 1888–1986* (Cambridge: Cambridge University Press, 1988), 153–58, and Donald Love, "Conversations with H. H. Johnson," October 25, 1936, Love Papers, OCA. For Johnson's subsequent policies toward Hall Auditorium, see [Ernest Hatch Wilkins], "*Annals* of the *Auditorium:* A Confidential Memorandum Prepared in July 1942 for the Information of the Trustees of Oberlin College," (Oberlin, 1942), 1–70, Wilkins Papers, OCA.

25. "*Annals* of the *Auditorium,*" 21, 21a.

26. CG to G. B. Rose, October 4, 1933, CGP, LC/MS.

27. William Stevenson, "Hall Auditorium: Memorandum of Conference with Homer H. Johnson, Oberlin, Ohio, December 5, 1949," Stevenson Papers, OCA; Board of Trustees Executive Committee Minutes, March 1, 1950, OCA.

28. Geoffrey Blodgett, Oral history interview with William E. Stevenson, Aspen, Colorado, July 18–20, 1979, 38–39, OCA.

29. S. Frederick Starr, Oberlin president from 1983 to 1994, initiated many of the preservation projects noted here.

CHAPTER 15

1. The Works of Herman Melville, *Redburn, His First Voyage, Being the Sailor-boy Confessions and Reminiscences of the Son of a Gentleman in the Merchant Service,* standard ed., vol. 5 (1849; reprint London: Constable and Company, 1922), ch. 27, 162.

2. Francis S. Swales, "The Work of Cass Gilbert," *Architectural Review* 31 (January 1912): 16.

3. For Reilly and the Liverpool School of Architecture, see C. H. Reilly, *Scaffolding in the Sky—A Semi-architectural Autobiography* (London: George Routledge and Sons, 1938); Lionel B. Budden, ed., *The Book of the Liverpool School of Architecture* (Liverpool: University Press of Liverpool and Hodder and Stoughton, 1932); and Joseph Sharples, Alan Powers, and Michael Shippobottom, *Charles Reilly & the Liverpool School of Architecture, 1904–1933,* catalog of an exhibition held at the Walker Art Gallery, Liverpool, October 25, 1996–February 2, 1997 (Liverpool: Liverpool University Press and National Museums and Galleries on Merseyside, 1996).

4. C. H. Reilly, *Some Liverpool Streets and Buildings in 1921* (Liverpool: Liverpool Daily Post and Mercury, 1921), 13–15.

5. Reilly, *Some Liverpool Streets,* 8–9.

6. May 3, 1909, Reilly LB, S 3205, Liverpool University Archives.

7. Three were published by the proprietors of the *Architectural Review* under the title *The Liverpool Architectural Sketchbook* in 1910, 1911, and 1913; the fourth appeared in 1920, renamed *The Liverpool University Architectural Sketchbook.*

8. *The Architects' & Builders' Journal* 36 (July 10, 1912): 37–38.

9. December 7, 1910, Reilly LB, D 207/2/3, Liverpool University Archives.

10. January 4, 1911, Reilly LB, D 207/2/3, Liverpool University Archives.

11. C. H. Reilly, *McKim, Mead & White* (London: Ernest Benn, 1924), 7–8.

12. *Proceedings of the 57th Annual Convention of the American Institute of Architects,* 1924. Corbett made his remarks in a discussion of the Beaux-Arts Institute of Design, on May 23, 1924.

13. This information comes from an unidentified press cutting of October or November 1920, in press cuttings book, S 3216, pp. 88–89, Liverpool University Archives.

14. C. H. Reilly to Paul Cret, March 24, 1931, Collection of John Sheppard Fidler.

15. H. S. Goodhart-Rendell, *English Architecture since the Regency—An Interpretation* (London: Constable and Company, 1953), 236.

16. C. H. Reilly, *Some Architectural Problems of To-day* (Liverpool: University Press of Liverpool and Hodder and Stoughton, 1924), 19–24.

17. September 12, 1910, Reilly LB, D 207/2/3, Liverpool University Archives.

18. Reilly, *Some Liverpool Streets,* 63.

19. For Reilly's involvement with the New Arts Building, and other university buildings, see A. R. Allan, "Si Monumentum Requiris Circumspice: A note on the Older Plans in the Custody of the Chief Engineer," *University of Liverpool Recorder,* no. 81 (October 1979): 162–67.

20. *Town Planning Review* 3 (1912): 80 ff.

21. Reilly, *McKim, Mead & White,* 17.

22. Reilly, *Scaffolding in the Sky,* 73.

23. Unidentified press cutting of ca.1933 in a scrapbook owned by Liverpool graduate Anthony Minoprio.

24. For Emley & Williamson, see Clive M. Chipkin, *Johannesburg Style—Architecture and Society 1880s–1960s* (Cape Town: David Philip, 1993), 77–80.

25. For Holford, see G. E. Cherry and L. Penny, *Holford—A Study in Architecture, Planning and Civic Design* (London: Mansell Publishing, 1986).

26. Reilly, *Scaffolding in the Sky,* 227–31.

27. These unpublished letters, known collectively as *The Chronacle* [*sic*], are in the ownership of the University of Glasgow. It is not permitted to publish direct quotations from them.

28. Maxwell Fry, *Autobiographical Sketches* (London: Elek Books, 1975), 136.

29. C. H. Reilly, "The First Great Modern Bank Building," *Banker* 37 (February 1936): 186–202.

CHAPTER 16

My thanks to Barbara Christen and Steven Flanders, organizers of the Cass Gilbert symposium, for their encouragement and hard work; to Sally Buchanan Kinsey, editor of *Nineteenth Century,* for permitting me to use portions of an essay published previously in her journal; to the extremely helpful staff members at the Missouri Historical Society, the St. Louis Art Museum, and the St. Louis Public Library; and most of all, to my husband, Jeff Bruce, and my daughter, Emma, for their love and forbearance while this project was under way.

1. Robert R. Archibald, president of the Missouri Historical Society, introduction to Timothy J. Fox and Duane R. Sneddeker, *From the Palaces to the Pike: Visions of the 1904 World's Fair* (St. Louis: Missouri Historical Society Press, 1997), ix.

2. On the architecture of the Washington University campus as a whole, see Buford Pickens and Margaretta J. Darnall, *Washington University in St. Louis: Its Design and Architecture* (St. Louis: Washington University, 1978); for Gilbert's other campus designs, see Barbara Snowden Christen, "Cass Gilbert and the Ideal of the City Beautiful: City and Campus Plans, 1900–1916" (Ph.D. dissertation, Graduate Center of the City University of New York, 1997).

3. For further information on the relationship of Olmsted's firm to the campus plan, as well as more specifics on the competition, see Margaretta J. Darnall, "Campus Planning in the 1880s–1890s, the Olmsted Contribution, and the Competition," in Pickens and Darnall, *Washington University in St. Louis,* 27–49.

4. For an invaluable general source on university planning in the United States, see Paul Venable Turner, *Campus: An American Planning Tradition* (Cambridge: MIT Press, 1984). Two articles addressing the designs for the Stanford University campus are David Newman, Alan Plattus, and Jon Hlafter, "Campus Architects as Clients—Stanford, Princeton, Yale," *Oculus* 61 (March 1999): 7–9, and Diane Kostial McGuire, "Early Site Planning on the West Coast: Frederick Law Olmsted's Plan for Stanford University," *Landscape Architecture* 57 (January 1957): 344–49. About Charles McKim's involvement at Columbia, a particularly good source is Francesco Passanti, "The Design of Columbia in the 1890s: McKim and His Client," *Journal of the Society of Architectural Historians* 36 (May 1977): 69–84.

5. For a complete listing, with bibliographies, of important world's fairs held internationally for the past century and a half, see John E. Findling, ed., and Kimberly D. Pelle, assist. ed., *Historical Dictionary of World's Fairs and Expositions, 1851–1988* (New York: Greenwood Press, 1990).

6. The two best sources on the Philadelphia Centennial Exposition are Robert C. Post, ed., *1876: A Centennial Exhibition* (Washington, D.C.: National Museum of History and Technology, Smithsonian Institution,

1976), and John Maass, *The Glorious Enterprise: The Centennial Exhibition of 1876 and H. J. Schwarzmann, Architect-in-Chief* (Watkins Glen, N.Y.: American Life Foundation, 1973).

7. A great deal has been published on the World's Columbian Exposition. Two of the most complete histories are David F. Burg, *Chicago's White City of 1893* (Lexington: University Press of Kentucky, 1976), and Reid Badger, *The Great American Fair: The World's Columbian Exposition and American Culture* (Chicago: Nelson Hall, 1979).

8. Daniel H. Burnham, "Charles Bowler Atwood," *Inland Architect and News Record* 26 (January 1896): 56–57.

9. A recent history of the Art Institute of Chicago may be found in Linda S. Phipps, "The 1893 Art Institute Building and the 'Paris of America': Aspirations of Patrons and Architects in Late Nineteenth-Century Chicago," *Art Institute of Chicago Museum Studies* 14, (1988).

10. A useful contemporary source on the Pan-American Exposition is the *Pan-American Art Hand-Book: Sculpture, Architecture, Painting* (Buffalo, N.Y.: David Gray, 1901).

11. Walter H. Page, "The Pan-American Exposition," *World's Work*, vol. 2 (August 1901), 1026.

12. *Illustrated Buffalo Express,* December 16, 1900.

13. Sources on the Louisiana Purchase Exposition include the director's report, Charles M. Kurtz, *Universal Exposition Commemorating the Acquisition of the Louisiana Territory, St. Louis, USA, 1904: An Illustrated Handbook* (St. Louis: Gottschalk Printing Company, 1904); Sharon Lee Irish, "Cass Gilbert's Career in New York, 1899–1905" (Ph.D. dissertation, Northwestern University, 1985); and for a wealth of beautifully reproduced illustrations, Timothy J. Fox and Duane R. Sneddeker, *From the Palaces to the Pike: Visions of the 1904 World's Fair* (St. Louis: Missouri Historical Society Press, 1997). For a recent architectural history and analysis of the St. Louis Art Museum, see Osmund Overby, "The Saint Louis Art Museum: An Architectural History," *Saint Louis Art Museum Bulletin*, n.s. 18 (Fall 1987): 2–36. For the most recent assessment of Gilbert's career, see Sharon Irish, *Cass Gilbert, Architect: Modern Traditionalist* (New York: Monacelli Press, 1999).

14. Theodore Roosevelt, *Address of President Roosevelt upon the Occasion of the Opening of the Louisiana Purchase Exposition, St. Louis, April 30th, 1903* [*sic*] (reprint; no publishing information), 5–6.

15. Frederick M. Mann, "Architecture at the Exposition," *American Architect* 85 (July 2, 1904): 5.

16. Kurtz, *Universal Exposition . . . 1904,* 30.

17. Louis LaBeaume, "Looking Backward at St. Louis Architecture," *Missouri Historical Society Bulletin* 14 (Jan 1958): 186.

18. Kurtz, *Universal Exposition . . . 1904,* 27–30.

19. James H. Lambert, *The Story of Pennsylvania at the World's Fair, St. Louis, 1904,* vol. 2 (Philadelphia: Pennsylvania Commission, 1905), 98.

20. Halsey Ricardo, "Architecture at the St. Louis World's Fair," *Architectural Review* 16 (October 1904): 165.

21. Mann, "Architecture at the Exposition," 5.

22. Montgomery Schuyler, "The Architecture of the St. Louis Fair," *Scribner's Magazine* 35 (April 1904): 387.

23. Mann, "Architecture at the Exposition," 5.

24. Schuyler, "Architecture of the St. Louis Fair," 390.

25. Ibid., 387.

26. Mann, "Architecture at the Exposition," 5.

27. "Plans Prepared to Make Forest Park the Nation's Municipal Beauty Spot," *St. Louis Post-Dispatch,* Sunday Magazine, January 7, 1917.

28. See William H. Wilson, *The City Beautiful Movement* (Baltimore: Johns Hopkins University Press, 1989), for information and background on this subject.

29. For these and other grand manner museum plans, see Ingrid Steffensen-Bruce, *Marble Palaces, Temples of Art: Art Museums, Architecture, and American Culture, 1890–1930* (Lewisburg, Penn.: Bucknell University Press, 1998).

30. Guy Study, "The St. Louis Public Library," *American Architect* 101 (March 1912): 125.

31. See Abigail Van Slyck, *Free to All: Carnegie Libraries and American Culture, 1890–1920* (Chicago: University of Chicago Press, 1995).

32. St. Louis Public Library, *Program of Conditions and Instructions to Govern a Competition for the Selection of an Architect for a New Central Building for the Saint Louis Public Library* (St. Louis: St. Louis Public Library, 1907), unpaginated [p. 8].

33. Quoted in Ray Harder, "Carnegie Libraries: Reflections on the American Dream," *Classic America* 4 (Summer 1989): 23.

34. Tom P. Barnett, "A Plea for the Ideal," *Western Architect* 19 (July 1913): 59.

35. Philip Sawyer (of York & Sawyer, New York architects) to Paul Blackwelder (assistant librarian, St. Louis Public Library), June 11, 1907, Central Library Competition, 1906–7, Box 3, St. Louis Public Library Archives.

36. Study, "The St. Louis Public Library," 126.

37. Ibid. 127.

38. "New Library Building," *The Realty Record and Builder* [St. Louis] 14 (July 1907): unpaginated.

39. CG to Paul Blackwelder, July 22, 1907, Box: 1, Central Library Construction, St. Louis Public Library Archives.

40. Barnett, "A Plea for the Ideal," 59.

41. *A City Plan for St. Louis* (St. Louis: Civic League of Saint Louis, 1907), 33.

42. Ibid. 8.

43. *The Central Library Building of the Public Library of the City of St. Louis* (St. Louis: Shelly Print, n.d.), 48.

CHAPTER 17

1. See Mary N. Woods, "Professional Organizations and Agendas," in *From Craft to Profession: The Practice of Architecture in Nineteenth-Century America* (Berkeley: University of California Press, 1999).

2. For information on Burnham's work at the World's Columbian Exposition, see Thomas S. Hines, *Burnham of Chicago: Architect and Planner* (Chicago: University of Chicago Press, 1979).

3. For more information on Ives's work in Chicago, see Carolyn Kinder Carr and George Gurney, *Revisiting the White City: American Art at the 1893 World's Fair* (Washington, D.C.: National Museum of American Art, National Portrait Gallery, 1993).

4. Halsey C. Ives to CG, November 16, 1901, PC, Box: Louisiana Purchase Exposition/#1, CGC, NYHS.

5. Halsey C. Ives to CG, November 29, 1901, Box: 2, Fldr.: 2, HIP, SLAM.

6. Office memorandum dated December 16, 1901, CGC, NYHS.

7. Report of the Department of Art, Box: 5, Series III, Subseries II, Fldr.: 1, HIP, SLAM.

8. Report to Frederick Skiff for the month ending October 31, 1901, Box: 9, Fldr.: 1, HIP, SLAM.

9. Minutes of the Committee on Fine Arts, April 11, 1902, Box: 5, Series III, Subseries II, Fldr.: 5, HIP, SLAM.

10. Report to Frederick Skiff for the month ending October 31, 1901, Box: 9, Fldr.: 1, HIP, SLAM.

11. Report to Frederick Skiff for the month ending November 30, 1901, Box: 9, Fldr.: 1, HIP, SLAM.

12. Halsey C. Ives to Isaac W. Morton, March 7, 1902, Box: 8, Fldr.: 5, HIP, SLAM.

13. Halsey C. Ives to Isaac W. Morton, March 24, 1902, Box: 8, Fldr.: 5, HIP, SLAM.

14. Report to Frederick Skiff covering the period from March 6 to March 31 [1902] inclusive, Box: 9, Fldr.: 1, HIP, SLAM.

15. CG to Halsey C. Ives, October 24, 1901, Box: 2, Fldr.: 2, HIP,

SLAM.

16. CG to Isaac S. Taylor, November 13, 1901, Box: 2, Fldr.: 2, HIP, SLAM.

17. CG to Emanuel Masqueray, April 2, 1902, PC, Box: Louisiana Purchase Exposition/#1, CGC, NYHS.

18. CG to Isaac W. Morton, March 29, 1902, Box: 2, Fldr.: 10, HIP, SLAM.

19. CG to Isaac W. Morton, April 7, 1902, PC, Box: Louisiana Purchase Exposition/#1, CGC, NYHS.

20. CG to Emanuel Masqueray, April 2, 1902, PC, Box: Louisiana Purchase Exposition/#1, CGC, NYHS.

21. Halsey C. Ives to Isaac W. Morton, April 15, 1902, Box: 8, Fldr.: 5, HIP, SLAM.

22. Emanuel Masqueray to CG, September 15, 1901, PC, Box: Louisiana Purchase Exposition/#1, CGC, NYHS.

23. John Rachac to CG, November 27, 1901, PC, Box: Louisiana Purchase Exposition/#1, CGC, NYHS.

24. Isaac S. Taylor to the Architect's Commission, January 2, 1902, PC, Box: Louisiana Purchase Exposition/#1, CGC, NYHS.

25. Isaac S. Taylor to CG, January 2, 1902, PC, Box: Louisiana Purchase Exposition/#1, CGC, NYHS.

26. Isaac S. Taylor to CG, January 8, 1903, PC, Box: Louisiana Purchase Exposition/#1, CGC, NYHS.

27. CG to David Rowland Francis, January 12, 1904, PC, Box: Louisiana Purchase Exposition/#1, CGC, NYHS.

28. Frederick Ruckstuhl to David Rowland Francis, December 11, 1902. Box: 2, Series II, Subseries I, Fldr.: 2, Louisiana Purchase Exposition Collection, Missouri Historical Society, St. Louis, Missouri. Ruckstuhl, a sculptor who was active in the founding of the National Sculpture Society, would later change the spelling of his last name to Ruckstull.

29. "The Resignation of Fred. W. Ruckstuhl," *New York Times,* December 28, 1902, p. 2.

30. Ibid.

31. CG to David Rowland Francis, April 5, 1904, PC, Box: Louisiana Purchase Exposition/#1, CGC, NYHS.

32. Transcript of lawsuit. Box: 11-56, Fldr.: 3-17-1905–3-31-1905, David R. Francis Papers, Missouri Historical Society, St. Louis, Missouri.

CHAPTER 18

1. See "Slogans to Fit the Occasion," McGurn, 104 United States Supreme Court Yearbook, 1982, Public Information Office, United States Supreme Court.

2. G. K. Chesterton, *Tremendous Trifles* (New York: Dodd, Mead & Co., 1913): 117.

CHAPTER 19

This chapter is adapted from a lecture delivered to justices of the Supreme Court and members and guests of the Supreme Court Historical Society in the chamber of the United States Supreme Court on March 24, 1999. The exhibition "'As Pure in Style as I Can Make It': Cass Gilbert's Supreme Court Building," prepared by Supreme Court photographer Franz Jantzen, is an important part of the reappreciation of Gilbert's work. I am grateful to Mr. Jantzen and that exhibition for the plans and elevations used here and in the lecture and for the careful and sometimes startling chronology of the evolution of Cass Gilbert's design for the Supreme Court that forms the focus of this discussion.

1. Geoffrey Blodgett, "Cass Gilbert, Architect: Conservative at Bay," *Journal of American History* 72 December 1985): 634.

2. Ibid.

3. See Paul Spencer Byard, *The Architecture of Additions: Design and Regulation* (New York: W. W. Norton and Company, 1998), 39–43.

POSTSCRIPT

1. "Cass Gilbert," walking tour booklet prepared for Downtown Open House, October 11, 1998, by Alliance for Downtown New York. Published a few months after the symposium is the only monograph that exists about Gilbert and his work—Sharon Irish, *Cass Gilbert, Architect: Modern Traditionalist* (New York: Monacelli Press, 1999).

2. Robert A. M. Stern, Gregory Gilmartin, and Thomas Mellins, *New York 1930: Architecture and Urbanism between Two World Wars* (New York: Rizzoli, 1987), 92.

3. See chapter 9 and Gail Fenske's dissertation, "The 'Skyscraper Problem' and the City Beautiful: The Woolworth Building" (Ph.D. dissertation, MIT, 1988), which is being revised for publication.

4. Mullet's career and its impact are addressed at several points in L. Craig, et al., *The Federal Presence: Architecture, Politics and Symbols in United States Government Building* (Cambridge: MIT Press, 1978).

5. John J. Kenney and Elliot B. Nixon, "The Federal Courthouse at Foley Square," 1. This exhibition booklet, published by the second circuit and the Federal Bar Council on April 17, 1985, for an exhibition and celebration of the courthouse in that year, is also the source for the account herein of the origins and construction history of the courthouse.

6. Lewis Mumford, "Concerning Foley Square," *New Yorker* (October 13, 1934): 59. Curiously—but fortunately for Gilbert's reputation—this "Skyline" article does not appear in the standard microfilm held by many libraries, which reproduces only the version of the magazine intended for distribution outside New York.

CONTRIBUTORS

MARY BETH BETTS is the director of research of the New York City Landmarks Preservation Commission. She was previously curator of architectural collections, including the Cass Gilbert Collection, at the New-York Historical Society (1990-99) and holds a Ph.D. from the Graduate Center, City University of New York. Dr. Betts has written about twentieth-century architecture and design, New York City Hall, and the New York waterfront.

THOMAS BLANCK, practicing architect, and **CHARLES LOCKS,** professional writer, consult on historic preservation. Collaborative projects include guidelines for historic preservation of New Richmond, Wisconsin; a comprehensive catalog of Cass Gilbert's early work (1878-1911) for the University of Minnesota; and, for the Cass Gilbert Society Inc., three walking tours of historic St. Paul, Minnesota neighborhoods that feature churches and residences designed by Cass Gilbert

GEOFFREY BLODGETT graduated from Oberlin College and received the Ph.D. from Harvard University. He is Danforth Professor of History Emeritus at Oberlin College. He has published essays on Frederick Law Olmsted, Philip Johnson, and Cass Gilbert, and is currently at work on a biography stressing the personal and political aspects of Gilbert's career as well as his architecture.

PAUL SPENCER BYARD, ESQ., FAIA, is a principal of Platt Byard Dovell Architects, New York. The director of the Historic Preservation Program at Columbia University School of Architecture, Planning and Preservation, he is author of *The Architecture of Additions: Design and Regulation* (New York: W. W. Norton, 1998). Mr. Byard is a member of the Supreme Court bar.

BARBARA S. CHRISTEN is a research associate at the Center for Advanced Study in the Visual Arts, National Gallery of Art, Washington, D.C. As executive director of the Committee on Cass Gilbert Projects (1998-99), her work included curating an exhibition surveying Gilbert's career and organizing the symposium that became the impetus for this volume. She received her Ph.D. from the Graduate Center, City University of New York .

GAIL FENSKE received her Ph.D. from MIT and is professor of Architecture in the School of Architecture, Art, and Historic Preservation at Roger Williams University. She has held visiting appointments at Cornell University and MIT. Her publications include articles about Cass Gilbert and the New York skyscraper, and she has recently completed a book about the Woolworth Building.

STEVEN FLANDERS is a consultant in New York. Author of numerous studies concerning judicial administration in the United States and abroad, he was circuit executive for the Second Judicial Circuit of the United States and a senior researcher at the Federal Judicial Center. He previously taught political science at the University of Vermont.

JUDGE JEFFRY H. GALLET was appointed in 1993 to the United States Bankruptcy Court for the Southern District of New York. He was a judge of New York State's family court and New York city's civil and criminal courts, and at the time of his death in 2001, adjunct professor of law at Brooklyn Law School and St. John's University, and of political science at Wilkes University.

SHARON IRISH has taught at the School of Architecture at the University of Illinois, Urbana-Champaign. Her monograph about Cass Gilbert (Monacelli Press, 1999) has won the David Gebnard Award (2000) from the Minnesota Chapter of the Society of Architectural Historians and the Publication Award (2000) of the Metropolitan Chapter of the Victorian Society of America. She has also written four other articles about Gilbert and published a book-length bibliography with Edward Kaufman about medievalism in art and architecture.

JUDGE DENNIS JACOBS was appointed in 1992 to the United States Court of Appeals for the Second Circuit. A lifelong New Yorker, he practiced law with the firm of Simpson Thacher & Bartlett from 1973 until his appointment to the bench (partner since 1980).

CAROLYN KOMPELIEN, historic site manager since 1988, collaborates with other state agencies to restore the Minnesota State Capitol to its appearance in 1905, the date of the building's completion. She also directs programs that interpret Cass Gilbert's art and architecture and Minnesota's political history and government to 135,000 capitol visitors annually.

SUSAN LUFTSCHEIN received her doctorate in art history from the Graduate Center, City University of New York. She has published works on American medallic art and on various American social realist and early modernist artists. She teaches at the Parsons School of Design, New School University.

PATRICIA ANNE MURPHY is the executive director of the Oberlin Historical and Improvement Organization/Oberlin Heritage Center in Ohio. Her M.A. thesis from the University of Virginia was entitled "The Early Career of Cass Gilbert." She was guest curator of a University of Minnesota touring exhibition about Gilbert and wrote an essay about him for *Master Builders: A Guide to Famous American Architects* (Washington, DC: National Trust for Historic Preservation/ Preservation Press, 1985).

THOMAS O'SULLIVAN is the author of *North Star Statehouse: An Armchair Guide to the Minnesota State Capitol* (St. Paul, Minn.: Pogo Press, 1994). As curator at the Minnesota Historical Society (1980-99), he worked on capitol preservation and interpretation issues.

JOSEPH SHARPLES has been assistant curator of fine art at the National Museums & Galleries on Merseyside (England) since 1990. In 1996 he organized the exhibition *Charles Reilly and the Liverpool School of Architecture 1904-1933* at the Walker Art Gallery, Liverpool.

LAWRENCE W. SPECK, FAIA, has been an educator and practicing architect since 1975. He has taught at MIT and the University of Texas, where he has been dean of the School of Architecture since 1993. He is the author of more than forty articles on architectural topics, and his award-winning designs have been published in more than fifty instances in journals in the United States and abroad.

INGRID A. STEFFENSEN received her Ph.D. from the University of Delaware and presently teaches art history at Rutgers University. She is the author of *Marble Palaces, Temples of Art: Art Museums, Architecture, and American Culture, 1890- 1930* (Lewisburg, Penn.: Bucknell University Press, 1998).

ROBERT A. M. STERN is principal of Robert A. M. Stern Architects in New York, dean of the Yale School of Architecture, and author of *New York 1880, New York 1900, New York 1930, New York 1960,* and *Pride of Place.*

BAILEY VAN HOOK is associate professor of art history at Virginia Tech. She is the author of *Angels of Art: Women and Art in American Society, 1876-1914* (University Park, PA: Penn State Press, 1997). She is currently working on a book of essays on American Beaux-Arts mural painting.

SALLY WEBSTER is professor of art history at Lehman College and the Graduate Center, City University of New York. A specialist in American art of the late nineteenth century, she is the author of *William Morris Hunt* (Cambridge University Press, 1991). Her anthology, *Critical Issues in Public Art,* was reissued recently by Smithsonian Institution Press.

MARY N. WOODS is professor of urban and architectural history in the Department of Architecture at Cornell University. Her most recent publication is *From Craft to Profession* (Berkeley: University of California Press, 1999), a history of American architectural practice. She is currently working on a study of New York City skyscrapers in film and photography.

INDEX